高等学校本科英语教改新教材 | 总主编 史宝辉
Textbooks for Undergraduate English Courses

英语国家概况

（第二版）

主　编　訾　缨
副主编　李　芝　祖国霞　高月琴
编　者（按姓氏拼音排序）
　　　　白雪莲　郭　陶　李　宇
　　　　卢晓敏　吕丽塔　朱红梅

北京大学出版社
PEKING UNIVERSITY PRESS

图书在版编目(CIP)数据

英语国家概况 / 訾缨主编. — 2版. — 北京：北京大学出版社，2021.10
高等学校本科英语教改新教材
ISBN 978-7-301-32461-5

Ⅰ.①英… Ⅱ.①訾… Ⅲ.①英语–阅读教学–高等学校–教材 Ⅳ.①H319.4

中国版本图书馆CIP数据核字(2021)第178769号

书　　名	英语国家概况（第二版） YINGYU GUOJIA GAIKUANG (DI-ER BAN)
著作责任者	訾　缨　主编
责任编辑	李　颖
标准书号	ISBN 978-7-301-32461-5
出版发行	北京大学出版社
地　　址	北京市海淀区成府路205号　100871
网　　址	http://www.pup.cn　　新浪微博：@北京大学出版社
编辑部邮箱	pupwaiwen@pup.cn
总编室邮箱	zpup@pup.cn
电　　话	邮购部 010-62752015　发行部 010-62750672　编辑部 010-62754382
印刷者	大厂回族自治县彩虹印刷有限公司
经销者	新华书店
	787毫米×1092毫米　16开本　16印张　572千字 2010年8月第1版 2021年10月第2版　2025年5月第5次印刷
定　　价	59.00元

未经许可，不得以任何方式复制或抄袭本书之部分或全部内容。
版权所有，侵权必究
举报电话：010-62752024　电子信箱：fd@pup.pku.edu.cn
图书如有印装质量问题，请与出版部联系，电话：010-62756370

第二版前言

《英语国家概况》第一版出版于2010年，是北京市高等教育精品教材立项项目，高等院校本科阶段英语通识课教材，采用纸质版教材与电子教程光盘相结合的编写模式。纸质版教材供课堂教学使用，内容包括美国、加拿大、英国、爱尔兰、澳大利亚和新西兰等六国概况。电子教程光盘供学生拓展学习使用，为课堂教学内容的拓展与延伸，除上述六国概况外，还介绍了新加坡、南非和印度三国概况，共计九国概况。附有配套习题七百余道。自出版以来，被全国多所学校采用，受到普遍认可。由于近年来一些国家的政治经济情况发生了变化，许多高校在使用中也希望增加覆盖面，有必要对教材内容进行更新和补充，因此本教材纸质版第二版进行了较大幅度的修订，对全书所有数据和内容进行了更新，删除了陈旧内容，增加了英国脱欧和目前美国所面临的社会问题等新章节，例如新冠疫情、种族主义、非洲裔美国人所遭受暴力伤害等。内容更加丰富，与时俱进；选篇内容既有时效性，也保持了一定的前瞻性。结构更为清晰合理，便于学习。

一、整体框架

1. 纸质版教材

纸质版教材供课堂教学使用。全书内容分为十五章进行讲授；内容包括美国、加拿大、英国、爱尔兰、澳大利亚和新西兰等六个国家的概况，任课教师可根据教学要求和学生情况对上述国家的内容进行选择性教学。

2. 电子教程光盘与教学课件

本教材第二版在原有学生版拓展学习光盘的基础上，新增了教师版电子课件供教师备课和课堂教学使用。教师版课堂教学电子课件与纸质版教材框架结构相同，采用PPT呈现形式，包含大量精美插图、背景知识介绍和音视频教学资料，能够极大减轻教师的备课负担，增加课堂教学的趣味性。学生拓展学习光盘中涵盖六大部分内容，第一部分至第五部分为美国、加拿大、英国和爱尔兰、澳大利亚和新西兰以及新加坡、南非和印度等九国的国家概况，为课堂教学内容的拓展与延伸；第六部分为课程习题集和答案。

二、主要内容

每一国家的概况介绍编写体例基本相同，均涵盖以下四方面的内容：

1. 国家概况综述 (A General Survey)

包括国名、国土面积、人口、官方语言、国旗、国歌、国徽、国花、国鸟、货币等项内容。

2. 地理与历史 (Geography and History)

包括地理特点、气候、山脉河流、区划、主要地区、城市简介；历史进程及重要历史事件介绍。

3. 政治与经济 (Political System and National Economy)

政治概况包括政府、政体、政党、宪法；经济概况包括工农业、旅游、商业、金融等情况的介绍。

4. 社会与文化 (Culture and Society)

包括文化的概念、文化群体、价值观、中小学教育和高等教育、文学艺术、体育运动、社会习俗、衣食住行、重要节日的介绍。

三、教程特色

1. 编写形式新颖

本教程采用纸质教材与学生版电子教程光盘、教师版课堂教学电子课件相结合的编写模式，集知识性和趣味性于一体，在实现通识课教材多元化方面进行了有益的尝试，对激发学生学习兴趣、提高通识课大班教学效果具有良好的促进作用。

2. 电子资源丰富

本教程图文并茂，充分利用电子教程的资源优势，根据所授内容插入相应人物、景物、事件等的图片、录像片断、演说录音、歌曲等等，使课程内容生动、直观，符合当代大学生的认知心理。电子教程丰富的图文与音视频教学资源可满足本科阶段对英语国家文化背景知识的要求。

四、读者对象

本教程读者群宽泛，适用范围广阔，主要对象为高等院校本科生，也可用于英语爱好者自学。既可用于本科英语课堂教学，亦可用于学生课外拓展学习，同时它还是教师备课的优质资源库。

五、编写队伍

本教程主要编写人员均有国外留学、访学经历，主讲过英美概况、美国历史与文化、英国历史与文化、西方文化等本科生和研究生课程，教学经验丰富，所编教材针对性、实用性强。

本教材是高等学校本科英语教改新教材系列之一，得到了教育部"双万计划"一流本科专业建设项目、北京市与在京高校共建项目、中央高校基本科研业务费专项资金（项目编号：2015ZCQ-WY-01）和北京林业大学教务处的支持和资助。

由于在本次修订过程中更新和增加了大量内容，任务量大，难免出现这样或那样的问题和疏漏，欢迎广大教师、学生和使用者提出宝贵意见，以便我们及时做出修改。

编者
2021.7

第一版前言

《英语国家概况》是大学英语提高阶段的公共选修课教材。本书采用电子教程光盘与纸质版教材相结合的编写模式，配套使用。

一、整体框架

1. 电子教程光盘

电子教程光盘供拓展学习使用。光盘与纸质版教材基本框架结构相同，但内容更加丰富，为课堂教学内容的拓展与延伸，包含大量精美插图和音、视频教学资料；涵盖六大部分内容，第一至第五部分为美国、加拿大、英国和爱尔兰、澳大利亚和新西兰以及新加坡、南非和印度等九国的国家概况，分为十八单元进行介绍；第六部分为课程习题集和答案。具体框架如下：

1) 美国部分　　　　　　　　　　（第1—4章　共4章）
2) 加拿大部分　　　　　　　　　（第5—8章　共4章）
3) 英国/爱尔兰部分　　　　　　（第9—13章　共5章）
4) 澳大利亚/新西兰部分　　　　（第14—17章　共4章）
5) 其他英语国家部分(新加坡，南非，印度)(第18章，共1章)
6) 课程习题集与答案

2. 纸质版教材

纸质版教材供课堂教学使用。全书内容分为15章进行讲授，推荐学时为30—40学时；内容包括美国、加拿大、英国、爱尔兰、澳大利亚和新西兰等六个国家的概况，任课教师可根据教学要求和学生情况对上述国家进行选择性教学。

二、主要内容

每一国家的概况介绍编写体例基本相同，均涵盖以下四方面的内容：

1. 国家综述 (General Survey)

包括国名、国土面积、人口、官方语言、国旗、国歌、国徽、国花、宗教和货币等。

2. 地理与历史 (Geography and History)

包括地理特点、气候、山脉河流、区划、主要地区、城市简介；历史进程及重要历史事件介绍。

3. 政治与经济 (Political System and National Economy)

政治概况包括政府、政体、政党、国家元首和政府首脑介绍；经济概况包括工业、农业、旅游业、商业、金融业等情况的介绍。

4. 社会与文化 (Society and Culture)

包括文化群体、价值观、中小学教育和高等教育、文学艺术、体育运动、社会习俗、衣食住行、重要节日等的介绍。

三、教程特色

1. 本教程编写形式新颖。目前国内英语国家概况教材大多为纸质版教材，供大学英语使用的此类教材尚未见电子教程出版。本教程突破了传统模式，采用纸质教材与电子教程光盘相结合的编写模式，集知识性和趣味性于一体，在实现公共选修课教材立体化、网络化方面进行了有益的尝试，对激发学生学习兴趣、提高选修课大班教学效果具有良好的促进作用。

2. 本教程图文并茂，采用了插图式的讲授方法。在讲授过程中，充分利用电子教程的资源优势，根据所授内容插入相应人物、景物、事件等的图片、录像片段、演说录音、歌曲等等，使课程内容生动、直观，符合当代大学生的认知心理。电子教程丰富的图文与音视频教学资源可满足大学英语基础与提高阶段对文化背景知识的要求。

3. 本教程使用便捷。电子教程光盘字号大小、版式设计均已按照上课需要进行了设定，教师上课时可直接使用，不必自行调试，省时省力。学生课下可结合课堂教学内容，利用拓展内容进行复习，深化所学知识，完成所学章节的练习内容，并根据电子教程上所提供的听力原文和答案进行自检。

四、习题形式

本教程附有配套习题集，含各类练习题七百余道。每节配有练习题10题 (Section Exercises)，习题形式包括正误判断、多项选择和连线等客观题型；每章配有综合练习题15—20题 (Chapter Exercises)，主要形式为填空、短语解释和简答等主观题型。练习题部分的设计可为学生通过四、六级考试和研究生英语入学考试提供帮助。

五、读者对象

本教程读者群宽泛，适用范围广阔。既可用于课堂教学，亦可用于学生课外拓展学习，同时它还是教师备课的优质资源库。

教程难度对应《大学英语课程教学要求》所规定的较高要求。对于英语专业本科生及研究生，教师可通过拓展内容提高教学难度。

六、编写队伍

本教程主要编写人员均有国外留学、访学经历，主讲过英美概况、美国历史、西方文化等本科和研究生课程，教学经验丰富，所编教材针对性、实用性强。

由于编写这样一部教材是一个新的尝试，时间紧、任务重，缺点错误在所难免，欢迎广大教师、学生和使用者提出宝贵意见，以便我们及时做出修改。

编　者

Contents

Understanding the United States

A General Survey of the United States 1
Chapter 1   Geography 5
Chapter 2   History 22
Chapter 3   Political System.. 51
Chapter 4   National Economy 59
Chapter 5   Society and Culture 65

Understanding Canada

A General Survey of Canada 96
Chapter 6   Geography and History... 100
Chapter 7   Political System and National Economy 114
Chapter 8   Society and Culture 121

Understanding the UK & Ireland

A General Survey of the UK 129
Chapter 9   Geography and History of the UK 136
Chapter 10   Political System and Economy of the UK 153
Chapter 11   Society and Culture of the UK.. 166
Chapter 12   Understanding the Republic of Ireland 186

Understanding Australia and New Zealand

A General Survey of Australia 206
Chapter 13   History, Politics and Economy of Australia 215
Chapter 14   Culture and Society of Australia 225
Chapter 15   Understanding New Zealand 235

Understanding the United States

A General Survey of the United States

> **章节导读**
> 本章为全书的开端篇，旨在通过对美国国家基本概况的介绍，使读者对美国有一全面了解，为后续章节的学习奠定基础。

Covering the central part of North America, the United States is a vast country to explore. It is a federal republic consisting of 50 states with dazzling (耀眼的) landscape and variable geography, also an exciting mixture of cultural diversity and diplomatic controversy. Before we scrutinize this young but powerful nation, let's have a glimpse of some basic facts about it.

Country Name

The conventional official name is the United States of America, shortened as the United States, US, or USA. On July 4, 1776, *The Declaration of Independence* announced that the thirteen North American colonies would be the United States of America, free and independent of Great Britain. It has a nickname, "Uncle Sam." The image came from a meat provider named Samuel Wilson (commonly called "Uncle Sam") during the war of 1812. The American Congress officially recognized Uncle Sam as a national symbol in 1961.

Capital

Located on the Potomac River, Washington D. C. is the capital and political center of the United States. It is named after both George Washington and Christopher Columbus, who discovered the New World in 1492. There are a number of important institutions in this city, such as the White House (residence of the President) and the Capitol Hill (home to the American Congress).

Language

English is the de facto (事实上的) national language of the United States, with 82% of the population claiming it as a mother tongue. The variety of English spoken in the United States is known as American English; together with Canadian English it makes up the group of dialects known as North American English, in contrast with the British English.

Population

As of April 1, 2010, the United States has a total resident population of 308,745,538 according to the 2010 Census, and the country entered 2016 with an estimated population of 322,762,018 according to an end-of-year estimate from the U.S. Census Bureau. That makes the United States the world's third most populated country, after China and India, and the most populous of today's developed countries with a very urbanized population: 81% residing in cities and suburbs (the worldwide urban rate was 49%).Most Americans are descended from immigrants. Immigration now contributes roughly a third of the annual U.S. population increase.

Religion

Religion in the United States is characterized by both a wide diversity of religious beliefs and practices and by a high adherence level. According to the American Religious Identification Survey (ARIS), The majority of Americans (76% to 80%) identify themselves as Christians. Those who identify themselves as Catholics make up about 25% of the adult population, while "other Christians" account for another 51%. Other religions (including, for example, Judaism, Buddhism, Islam, and Hindu) collectively make up about 4% of the adult population, another 15% of the adult population claim no religious affiliation, and 5.2% said they did not know, or they refused to reply.

Currency

The United States dollar (sign: $) is the official currency of the United States. It is divided into 100 smaller cent (¢) units. Today, the circulating paper money consists of Federal Reserve Notes, also the United States banknotes. The present denominations of U.S. currency in production are $1, $2, $5, $10, $20, $50 and $100. Notes above the $100 denomination stopped being printed in 1946 and were officially withdrawn from circulation in 1969. Circulating coins exist in denominations of 1¢, 5¢, 10¢, 25¢, 50¢, and $1.00. Now the U.S. dollar is one of the most circulated currencies of the world.

1 Dollar Note	George Washington	1st U.S. President
2 Dollar Note	Thomas Jefferson	3rd U.S. President
5 Dollar Note	Abraham Lincoln	16th U.S. President
10 Dollar Note	Alexander Hamilton	1st Secretary of the Treasury
20 Dollar Note	Andrew Jackson	7th U.S. President
50 Dollar Note	Ulysses Grant	18th U.S. President
100 Dollar Note	Benjamin Franklin	Statesman

National Flag

On June 14, 1777, at Philadelphia, the Marine Committee of the Second Continental Congress offered the resolution which resulted in the adoption of the flag of the United States.

The flag of the U.S. goes by many names: Stars and Stripes, Old Glory, Star-Spangled (星光灿烂的) Banner, or the Red, White, and Blue. The fifty stars represent the fifty states. The thirteen red and white stripes represent the first thirteen colonies. The flag is red, white, and blue. According to the Department of State, red stands for hardiness and courage, white is the symbol of purity and innocence, and blue is the color of vigilance, perseverance, and justice.

National Anthem

"The Star-Spangled Banner" is the national anthem of the United States. It was composed by Francis Scott Key in 1814. The United States Congress made the "Star-Spangled Banner" the national anthem of the United States in 1931.

Oh, say can you see, by the dawn's early light, What so proudly we hailed at the twilight's last gleaming? Whose broad stripes and bright stars, through the perilous fight, O'er the ramparts we watched, were so gallantly streaming? And the rockets' red glare, the bombs bursting in air, Gave proof through the night that our flag was still there. O say, does that star-spangled banner yet wave O'er the land of the free and the home of the brave? (The first stanza)	哦你可看见，透过一线曙光， 我们对着什么，发出欢呼的声浪？ 谁的阔条明星，冒着一夜炮火， 依然迎风招展，在我军碉堡上？ 火炮闪闪发光，炸弹轰轰作响， 它们都是见证，国旗安然无恙。 你看星条旗不是还高高飘扬 在这自由国家，勇士的家乡？

National Flower

In the fall of 1986, President Reagan and Congress signed legislation that proclaimed the rose the National Floral Emblem. This is a fitting title for a flower that has been growing in the country for many years and is undoubtedly the most recognizable flower in the world. The American people hold the rose dear as the symbol of life, love and devotion, of beauty and eternity.

National Bird

The bald eagle is a large eagle with white-feathered head and neck. It was chosen in 1782 as the emblem of the U.S., because of its long life, great strength and majestic looks, and also because it was then believed to exist only on the continent.

National Tree

The oak was designated as the official national tree in 2004. More than 60 species of oak grow in the United States and they are native to 49 of the 50 U.S. states. Oaks are strong, useful and embedded in the U.S. history. Since Colonial days they've been sawed into ships, homes, and furniture, and cherished for their beauty, abundant shade, and top-quality lumber.

National Gemstone

Sapphire is the national gemstone of the United States, and thirty-five of the fifty states have designated an official gem or gemstone. It is typically blue in color, but natural "fancy" sapphires also occur in yellow, purple, orange, and green colors; The only color which sapphire cannot be is red — as red colored corundum (刚玉) is called ruby. Sapphire is the birthstone for September and the gem of the 45th anniversary.

The Great Seal (国玺)

The Seal of the United States depicts a bald eagle with a shield of 13 alternating red and white stripes representing the 13 original States on its breast. Across the top of the shield is a blue field that unites all the stripes into one. The blue chief represents the United States Congress. In his talons (爪) the eagle grasps an olive branch representing peace, and 13 arrows representing war. Above the eagle are 13 stars inside a circular design, representing a "New Constellation." In his beak the eagle grasps a flowing ribbon bearing the first MOTTO of the United States: E Pluribus Unum. These Latin words are translated "Out of many, One."

Social Issues in the New Age

No doubt United States is a powerful country in the world today. It has made its mark in the history by building a strong economy. However, America also has some serious social issues that need to be dealt with, such as unequal distribution of wealth, alarming rate of poverty, unequal educational funding, increasing crime rate, health issues, increasing cost of living, etc.[①]

A Collection of Fast Facts of the United States

Official name	United States of America
Capital	Washington, D.C.
Population	308,745,538 people
Rank among countries in population	3rd
Major cities	New York, Los Angeles, Chicago, Houston, Philadelphia
Total area	9,372,615 km^2
Rank in area worldwide	4th
Highest point	Mt. McKinley 6,194 meters
Lowest point	Death Valley 6 meters
Currency	United States dollar
Principal Language	English
Major Religion	Christianity
Largest state:	Alaska, 1,720,000 km^2
Smallest state:	Rhode Island, 4,000 km^2
Most populous state:	California, 39,250,017 People (Population Estimate as of July 1, 2010 Census)
Least populous state:	Wyoming, 585,501 people (Population Estimate as of July 1, 2010 Census)
Independence Day	July the 4th

---

① 美国社会所面临的具体问题详见本书第2章第11节。

Chapter 1　Geography

> **章节导读**
> 本章内容为美国地理概况简述，分为五节，分别介绍了美国的地理特征、主要河流湖泊、山脉、自然资源和气候状况、区域划分及主要城市。

I Geographical Features

The United States is located in the central part of North America, bordering the North Atlantic Ocean in the east and the North Pacific Ocean in the west. With a total area of 9,372,615 square kilometers, it ranks the fourth largest country in area in the world, after Russia, Canada and China.

The landscape is one of the most varied among those of the world's nations. As far as geographical features are concerned, the country can be separated into three major divisions: the highlands in the east, the mountains (Rocky Mountains, Sierra Nevada) in the west, and a vast plain region in between. In order to explain more clearly, we can begin by dividing the continent of North America into 7 regions. These regions are large areas where the landforms (地貌) are similar. The 7 regions are:

- the Atlantic and Gulf coastal plain
- the Appalachian Mountains
- the Central Lowlands and the Great Plains
- the Rocky Mountains
- the Great Basin (山间高原盆地)
- the Pacific Coastal Ranges and Lowlands
- the Canadian Shield [also called the Laurentian Shield (加拿大地盾，劳伦地盾)]

The Coastal Plain

The coastal plain extends all along the Atlantic and Gulf coasts of the United States. This narrow plain begins far up the coast and becomes wider as you travel south. It is low and flat. In some places, there are large areas where the land is covered with shallow water. These areas are called swamps or wet lands. The swamps are thick with plants, and there are many wild animals.

The Appalachian Mountains

West of the coastal plain are the Appalachian Mountains. The Appalachians are a chain of thickly wooded mountains that stretch from Maine all the way to Georgia and Alabama. The topography (地形学) of these mountains is different, and not many of them are nearly as tall as west-coast ranges. Much cultivation and urbanization has occurred in the Appalachians, but there are still many remote areas. The Appalachian Mountains are different from other ranges because most of their trees are deciduous (每年落叶的).

The Appalachians are old mountains. This means that they were formed millions of years ago. Since then, they have been worn down by the wind and the weather. Today, most of these mountains have rounded tops. The highest peak of the Appalachians is only a little over 2000 meters. The valleys between them do not have steep sides. In parts of the Appalachians, the land is not good for farming and farmers here barely grow enough for themselves to eat. Much coal is found in these mountains.

The Great Plains

West of the Appalachians, the land drops to the mighty Mississippi River. Still west is a vast open area called the Great Plains. The Great Plains is a vast expanse of flat land, much of it covered in prairie, steppe (没有树木的大草原) and grassland, stretching from the Rocky Mountains to the Missouri River and from the Rio Grande (美国和墨西哥之间的格兰德河) to northern Canada — an area more than 3,200 km from north to south and more than 800 km from east to west, approximately 1,300,000 km^2. The Great Plains region includes all or parts of Colorado, Kansas, Montana, Nebraska, New Mexico, North Dakota, Oklahoma, South Dakota, Texas, Wyoming, Minnesota, Iowa and the Canadian provinces of Alberta (阿尔伯塔省), Manitoba (曼尼托巴省) and Saskatchewan (萨斯喀彻温省). The region is known for supporting extensive cattle ranching and dry farming (非灌溉农业).

The Canadian portion of the Plains is known as the Prairies.

It is usually divided by Missouri River into two regions: 1) the Central Lowland in the east, and 2) the Great Plains in the west.

➢ *The Central Lowland*

The plains in the east of the Missouri River are called the Central Lowland. It stretches from the five Great Lakes to central Texas. Here is some of the most fertile land in the world. On these plains, the farmers grow corn, soybeans, and wheat. The Central Lowland is also rich in oil and natural gas. Many of the large cities in the U.S. are located in the Central Lowland.

➢ *The Great Plains*

To the west of the Missouri River is the Great Plains. Most of the area is treeless grassland. Great herds of cattle and sheep feed on its grasses. Places such as South Dakota's Ordway Prairie Preserve ensure that some of the natural prairie land survives.

Rocky Mountains

West of the Great Plains are the Rocky Mountains, spanning the country from Alaska to Mexico. High with rugged peaks and steep valleys, the Rocky Mountains rise over 4,260 meters

above sea levels and form the continental divide (分水岭) of the United States. On one side of this great divide, all rivers flow west to the Pacific Ocean. On the other side, the rivers flow east. Rocky Mountains are younger than the Appalachians. Some of the people living in the Rocky Mountains earn their living by mining and logging. Rocky Mountains also attract visitors who come for sports and vacations. The breathtaking sunsets, glaciated valleys (冰川谷), pristine (原始的) forests, and snow-crested peaks — this is nature of drama (刺激).

Plateaus and the Great Basin

West of the Rockies are the two great plateaus: the *Columbia Plateau* in the north and the *Colorado Plateau* in the south, with the Great Basin in between. The Columbia Plateau is largely underlain (位于……的下面) by ancient lava (熔岩) flows, while Colorado Plateau includes spectacular canyons, high plateaus, and mountains.

A number of ancient salty lakes are found in the basin, including the famous Great Salt Lake of Utah. The rivers here do not flow toward the sea and most of them are shallow and salty. Many flow into the Great Salt Lake. This land receives little rainfall. Much of it is desert. Death Valley is on the western edge of this region. This valley, 200 kilometers long and 86 meters below the sea level, is the lowest point and hottest place in the U.S. There are few big cities in this part.

The Pacific Coastal Ranges

Farther west, along the coast, stands another great system of mountains, the Pacific Coastal ranges, including the Sierra Nevada (内华达山脉) and Cascade ranges (喀斯喀特山脉). It is truly a unique landscape consisting of various physiographic (地形学的) regions. With dynamic landforms such as California's white sand beaches in the south and the rugged and rocky coasts of Washington in the north, the Pacific Coast is very different from other coastal regions in the U.S. Another unique feature running along the Pacific Ocean is the Coast Ranges, which have peak elevations of about 1,200 meters in the state of Oregon.

Canadian Shield

The last main region of North America is a plateau region called the Canadian Shield, also known as the Laurentian Plateau, which covers an area of 4,790,000 km^2 and has the shape of a giant shield. It stands mainly in Canada, extending from Newfoundland in the east, to the Beaufort Sea (波弗特海：加拿大和美国阿拉斯加州北部的北冰洋边缘海) in the northwest, and south through Wisconsin and Minnesota in the U.S. This is a large area of rocky hills covered with forests, and forms the central land mass of North America. Few people live in the northern region along the Arctic Circle which is comprised of rocky frozen tundra. But the land is rich in minerals such as nickel, copper, and silver. There are many streams and lakes in the Canadian Shield. These waters attract many Canadians and Americans from farther south for vacations.

II Major Rivers, Lakes, and Mountains

Rivers

The United States of America has over 250,000 rivers. The longest river is the Missouri River, which is a tributary of the Mississippi River and is 4,087 km long, but the biggest in terms of water volume is the deeper Mississippi River. The longest undammed (无水坝的，无障碍的) river in the contiguous USA is the Yellowstone River (1,114 km).

Rivers provide drinking water, irrigation water, transportation, electrical power, drainage, food, and recreation. Rivers also erode (侵蚀) land and carry it downstream to the sea. This kind of erosion can even form canyons, like the Grand Canyon, and waterfalls, like Niagara Falls.

Mississippi River

Flowing entirely in the United States, the Mississippi River rises in northern Minnesota and meanders (蜿蜒而行) slowly southwards for 3,734 km to the Mississippi River Delta at the Gulf of Mexico. But if it is measured from the source of its chief headstream (the main branch), the Missouri River, it is over 6,000 kilometers with more than 40 tributaries. The two major tributaries are the Missouri River and Ohio River. With its many tributaries, the Mississippi's watershed (流域) drains all or parts of 31 U.S. states and 2 Canadian provinces between the Rocky and the Appalachian mountains. It ranks the fourth longest and fifteenth largest river in the world by discharge (流量) and is known as the Father of Waters.

Missouri River

The Missouri River is the longest river in North America. It flows about 4,087 kilometers from western Montana among the Rocky Mountains to just north of St. Louis, Missouri, where it joins the Mississippi River. When combined with the lower Mississippi River, it forms the world's fourth longest river system.

For many years, people have depended on the Missouri River and its tributaries as a source of sustenance and transportation; during the 19th century it was one of the main routes for the westward expansion of the United States. The river is nicknamed "The Big Muddy" as it has a great deal of mud in it. The three largest cities along the Missouri are Omaha in Nebraska, and Kansas City and St. Louis in Missouri.

Ohio River

The largest tributary, by volume, of the Mississippi is the Ohio River (1,579 kilometers), which rises from the rainy east at Pittsburgh, Pennsylvania and joins the Mississippi at Cairo, Illinois. It served as the gateway to the West at the beginning of the 1800s for the early settlers moving west from the Appalachians. By the 1820s, steamboats had arrived on the Ohio River and traffic on the Ohio rapidly increased. Three cities became important centers of trade because of their locations on the busy waterway: Pittsburgh, Cincinnati (in Ohio), and Louisville (in Kentucky). Traffic on the river lessened in the late 1800s, after the railroads were built. The Ohio River is a naturally shallow river that was artificially deepened by a series of dams.

By the mid-1900s, the Ohio River had become severely polluted with sewage and industrial wastes dumped in it and it is ranked as the most polluted river in the U.S. based on 2009 and 2010 data.

St. Laurence River

Another important river is the St. Laurence, which forms part of the boundary between Canada and the United States. The St. Lawrence River is the chief outlet of the Great Lakes and serves as a major water route to the interior of the United States and Canada, linking the Great Lakes with the Atlantic Ocean.

Colorado River and Columbia River

On the Pacific side there are two great rivers: the Colorado River and the Columbia River. The Colorado River ("colored", with an implication of reddish) begins in the Rocky Mountains and flows southwest for some 2,300 kilometers and empties into the Gulf of California. For 342 of these kilometers the Colorado flows through the magnificent Grand Canyon in Arizona, which is one of the most beautiful places in the United States. The Colorado drains an enormous area. All the farms and cities of the southwestern corner of the country depend on its water. Many dams have been built in the Colorado River system. Hoover Dam, built in 1936 by the federal government, is the largest of the dams located on the Colorado River.

The Columbia River is the largest river in the Pacific Northwest region and the fourth largest river, by volume, in the United States. It rises in the Rocky Mountains of western Canada, continues in the U.S. for about 1,900 kilometers and flows into the Pacific Ocean. Its drainage basin is roughly the size of France and extends into seven U.S. states and a Canadian province. The river's heavy flow and relatively steep gradient (坡度) gives it tremendous potential for the generation of electricity.

➢ *Rio Grande River*

Another important river in the southwest America is the Rio Grande River (3,051 km long). It begins in south-central Colorado in the United States and flows to the Gulf of Mexico. Along the way, it forms part of the Mexico-United States border.

➢ *Rivers east of the Appalachians*

The rivers east of the Appalachians are usually short. All of them run to the Atlantic Ocean. The Potomac River is famous not only because Washington D.C. is located on its bank but also because it is the dividing line between the South and the North. The Hudson River is famous because New York City stands at the river mouth. It is there (at New York City) that the Hudson River meets the Atlantic Ocean. Linked by canals with the five Great lakes, the Hudson River serves as an important route for inland waterway traffic.

Lakes and Niagara Falls

➢ *Great Lakes*

Along the U.S.-Canada border lies the world's largest group of freshwater lakes — the five interconnected Great Lakes, including (from largest to smallest) Lake Superior (the second largest lake in the world by area), Lake Huron, Lake Michigan, Lake Erie, and Lake Ontario. They are connected to the Atlantic Ocean by the St. Lawrence River. The lakes are a part of both countries and are shared by both. Only Lake Michigan lies entirely within the United States. Four of North America's largest cities are located on the edge of the Great Lakes. They are Chicago, Detroit, Toronto (Canada), and Cleveland.

The Great Lakes cover an area of 244,106 square kilometers and hold about 21% of all the fresh water on the Earth's surface. They were formed by glaciers, and are fed by rainwater and snow-melt runoffs (融雪径流), so they are freshwater. Due to their sea-like characteristics (rolling waves, sustained winds, strong currents, great depths, and distant horizons), the five Great Lakes have also long been referred to as inland seas.

➢ *Great Salt Lake*

Located in the northern part of the U.S. state of Utah, the Great Salt Lake is the largest salt water lake in the Western Hemisphere, and the eighth-largest terminal lake (终端湖，尾闾湖) in the world. Its maximum depth is 8 meters. As a terminal lake, the Great Salt Lake is far saltier than seawater, making it easy to float in. It contains about 4.4 billion tons of minerals. About three fourths of this total is common table salt. Surrounded by stretches of sand, salt land and marsh, the lake remains isolated, though in recent years it has become important as a source of minerals, as a beach and water-sports attraction, and as a wildlife preserve. The Great Salt Lake lends its name to Salt Lake City, the capital and largest city of Utah.

➢ *Niagara Falls* (尼亚加拉瀑布)

Niagara Falls is the collective name for three waterfalls that straddle (跨越) the international border between Canada and the United States. From largest to smallest, the three waterfalls are the Horseshoe Falls (also called the Canadian Falls), the American Falls and the Bridal Veil Falls. The Horseshoe Falls, so called because of its horseshoe shape, lie entirely on the Canadian side; the American Falls and the smaller Bridal Veil Falls are entirely on the American side.

The Niagara Falls in the USA and Canada from Skylon Tower on May 28, 2002 by Robert F. Tobler

Located on the Niagara River, the combined falls form the highest flow rate of any waterfall in the world that has a vertical drop of more than 50 meters. The larger Horseshoe Falls are about 790 meters wide while the American Falls are 320 meters wide. The Niagara Falls is famed both for its beauty and as a valuable source of hydroelectric power.

Mountains

Beside the Appalachian Mountains and the Rocky Mountains, there are still a few more worth mentioning here. Mount McKinley (also known as Denali) in Alaska is the tallest mountain in the United States. It rises 6,194 meters above sea level. In the Sierra Nevada of eastern California, Mount Whitney, at 4,418 meters, is the highest peak in the United States outside of Alaska. The Sawatch Mountains (沙瓦奇山脉,科罗拉多州中部山脉，落基山脉的一支) form part of the Continental Divide, which runs through western Colorado. It marks the point at which all rivers to the east flow toward the Atlantic Ocean and all rivers to the west flow toward the Pacific Ocean. The Cascade Range is a major mountain range extending from northern California through Oregon and Washington into British Columbia, Canada.

III Natural Resources and Climate

Natural Resources

➢ *Minerals and Metals*

The United States is a land rich in natural resources. Many minerals, such as water, iron ore, coal, oil, silver, and gold, are especially plentiful in the country. It ranks first in the world in coal deposits, most of coal reserves are found in the Appalachians, the Central Plain, and the Rockies. The country also possesses rich oil and natural gas deposits.

Other basic metals and minerals mined on a large scale include lead, zinc (锌), copper, sulfur (硫磺), silver, and phosphate (磷酸盐) rock, but the country is short for tin, manganese (锰) and nickel (镍).

> *Forests*

The forest resources are among the world's largest. Today about one-third of the nation is forested (33%). Properly managed forests prevent flooding and soil erosion, and stabilize climatic conditions. About 91 million hectares (公顷)① of the U.S. forest land is reserved by law as "National Forest" for the use of all the people. These 155 protected forests provide Americans with large recreation areas and they also serve as essential watershed and safe habitats for wildlife.

Forests are chiefly found in the eastern and western highlands of the country. Along the Pacific coast there are more thick forests. The heavy rainfall there helps the trees to grow very large. This is the home of giant trees like the redwoods of California. Redwood trees often grow to be 61 — 91 meters tall. But in the Southwest, there are deserts where only small shrubs and cacti (仙人掌，仙人球) can grow.

> *Water*

Another natural resource that contributes to the welfare of the country is water. The nation is blessed with large supplies of fresh water except in the desert regions of the West. Such mighty rivers as the Mississippi, the Ohio, the Hudson and the Colorado irrigate the croplands. The early development of a prosperous agricultural system and the later development of an industrial base were made possible largely by vast water resources.

> *Soil*

The country's fertile soil is one of the most important natural resources. Farmland in the United States make up 13.5% of the arable (适于耕种的) lands in the world, and they are among the richest and most productive. Fertile farmland gave the nation the foundation to grow and prosper over centuries and will continue to supply the nation generously.

Climate

Climates throughout the United States are as varied as its geographical features. It is mostly temperate, but tropical in Hawaii and Florida, arctic in Alaska, semiarid (半干旱的) in the great plains west of the Mississippi River, and arid in the Great Basin of the southwest. Most of the nation experiences all four seasons, with cold and snow winters and warm summers. The southwest and southeast experience fewer variations in climate and rarely receive snow in the winter.

The United States are exposed to various natural hazards: tsunamis (海啸), volcanoes, and earthquake activities around Pacific Basin; hurricanes along the Atlantic and Gulf of Mexico coasts; tornadoes (龙卷风) in the Midwest and southeast; mud slides in California; forest fires in the west; flooding; permafrost in northern Alaska.

IV State Regions

According to their climate, geography, traditions and history, the 50 states of the United States are divided into six regions as shown in the following table.

---

① 1公顷=10,000平方米=15亩

New England	Connecticut, Maine, Massachusetts, New Hampshire, Rhode Island, Vermont
Middle Atlantic	Delaware, Maryland, New Jersey, New York, Pennsylvania
South	Alabama, Arkansas, Florida, Georgia, Kentucky, Louisiana, Mississippi, North Carolina, Oklahoma, South Carolina, Tennessee, Virginia, West Virginia
Midwest	Illinois, Indiana, Iowa, Kansas, Michigan, Minnesota, Missouri, Nebraska, North Dakota, Ohio, South Dakota, Wisconsin
Southwest	Arizona, New Mexico, Texas
West	Alaska, California, Colorado, Hawaii, Idaho, Montana, Nevada, Oregon, Utah, Washington, Wyoming

New England

New England is the smallest of all six regions comprising six states of the northeast United States: Connecticut, Maine, Massachusetts, New Hampshire, Rhode Island, and Vermont. It played a dominant role in American development. From the 17th century until well into the 19th century, New England was the country's cultural and economic center.

Puritan Separatist Pilgrims from England first settled in the region in 1620, forming the Plymouth Colony, the second successful English settlement in the Americas, following the Jamestown Settlement in Virginia founded in 1607. Ten years later, more Puritans settled north of Plymouth Colony in Boston, thus forming Massachusetts Bay Colony. The earliest European settlers of New England found it difficult to farm the land in large lots, by 1750, many settlers had turned to other pursuits. The mainstays (支柱) of the region became shipbuilding, fishing, and trade.

New Englanders gained a reputation for hard work, shrewdness, thrift, and ingenuity. These traits came in handy as the Industrial Revolution reached America in the first half of the 19th century and new factories sprang up in this region. Boston had become the financial heart of the nation.

New England also supported a vibrant (充满活力的) cultural life. Education is the region's strongest legacies. There are such top-ranking universities and colleges as Harvard, Yale, Brown, Dartmouth, Wellesley (widely acknowledged as the nation's top college for women founded in 1870. Notable alumnae include Hillary Clinton, Madeleine Albright, the first woman Secretary of State, the three Soong sisters, etc.) and Williams (a highly selective private liberal arts college established in 1793. Currently ranked 1st place in the U.S. News & World Report's liberal arts), unequaled by any other regions.

By the 21st century the region had become famous for its leadership roles in the fields of education, medicine and medical research, high-technology, finance, and tourism.

The Middle Atlantic States

If New England provided the brains and dollars for 19th-century American expansion, the Middle Atlantic States provided the muscle. It has been called "the typically American" region and has played an important role in the development of American culture, commerce, trade, and industry. It is a relatively affluent region of the nation.

This region was settled by a wider range of people than New England, and it served as a bridge between North and South. The region's largest states, New York and Pennsylvania, became centers of heavy industry (iron, glass, and steel). Religious pluralism and ethnic diversity have been important elements of Mid-Atlantic society from its early settlement to the current day.

After the American Revolution, the Mid-Atlantic region hosted each of the historic capitals of the United States, including the current federal capital, Washington, D.C. Philadelphia was home to the Continental Congress that organized the American Revolution and the birthplace of the Declaration of Independence in 1776 and the U.S. Constitution in 1787. New York City, with its skyscrapers, subways, and headquarters of the United Nations, emerged in the 20th century as an icon of modernity and American economic and cultural power. By the 21st century, the coastal areas of the Mid-Atlantic were thoroughly urbanized.

The South

The South is perhaps the most distinctive and colorful American region. The American Civil War (1861 — 1865) devastated the South socially and economically. Nevertheless, it retained its unmistakable identity.

Southern settlers grew wealthy by raising and selling cotton and tobacco on plantations, which required the work of many laborers. To supply this need, plantation owners relied on slaves brought from Africa, and slavery spread throughout the South. As slavery was disapproved by the Northerners, in 1860, 11 southern states left the Union intending to form a separate nation, the Confederate States of America. This rupture (决裂) led to the Civil War, the Confederacy's defeat, and the end of slavery.

The scars left by the war took decades to heal. However, a new regional pride expressed itself under the banner of "the New South." Today the South has evolved into a manufacturing region, and high-rise buildings crowd the skylines of such cities as Atlanta and Little Rock.

Most of the South has long, hot summers and short and cool winters. There is abundant rainfall. This combination gives the South a long growing season. Owing to its mild weather, the South has become very popular with retirees from other U.S. regions and from Canada.

The Midwest

The Midwest United States (or Middle West) is an informal name for a group of north-central states of the United States of America, usually including Illinois, Indiana, Iowa, Kansas, Michigan, Minnesota, Missouri, Nebraska, North Dakota, Ohio, South Dakota and Wisconsin. Chicago is the most populated and the largest city in the region and the third most populous in the entire country, followed by Detroit and Indianapolis. Economically the region is balanced between heavy industry and agriculture. Large sections of the region's fertile land make up the United States' Corn Belt and made it possible for farmers to produce abundant harvests of cereal crops such as wheat, oats, and corn. Thus the region is known as the nation's "breadbasket." Its central location makes it a transportation crossroads.

The Mississippi River has acted as a regional lifeline. The river inspired two classic American books, both written by a native Missourian, Mark Twain: *Life on the Mississippi* and *The Adventures of Huckleberry Finn*. Midwesterners are praised as being open, friendly, and straightforward. The Midwest gave birth to one of America's two major political parties, the Republican Party, which was formed in the 1850s to oppose the spread of slavery into new states.

The Southwest

The United States Geological Survey (USGS) does not define regions, so regional definitions vary from source to source. The Southwest always includes New Mexico and Arizona, but often takes in western Texas. Parts of the Southwest once belonged to Mexico. The United States obtained this land following the Mexican-American War of 1846 — 1848. Its Mexican heritage continues to exert a strong influence on the region.

The population density of the region is less than three people per square mile. The Southwest is also more ethnically varied than neighboring regions, with significant European American, Mexican American, and American Indian populations.

The Southwest contains many large cities and metropolitan areas of the country, despite the low population density of the region as a whole. Phoenix, Dallas, San Antonio, and Houston all rank among the top ten most populous cities in the country. Outside the cities, the region is a land of open spaces, much of which is desert. The magnificent Grand Canyon is located in this region, as is Monument Valley. Compared with the adjoining Midwest, the Southwest is drier in weather, less densely populated, and has strong Spanish-American and Native-American components.

The West

The West is the largest and the most geographically diverse region of the country, covering more than half the land area of the United States. It is a region of scenic beauty on a grand scale and is known for arid to semi-arid plateaus and plains, forested mountains, the massive coastal shoreline of the American Pacific Coast and the rainforests of the Pacific Northwest. All of its states are partly mountainous, and the ranges are the sources of startling contrasts. To the west of the peaks, winds from the Pacific Ocean carry enough moisture to keep the land well-watered. To the east, however, the land is very dry.

The "West" had played an important part in American history; the Old West is embedded in America's folklore. The Western region contains the largest number of minorities in the U.S. and also contains much of the Native American population, particularly in the large reservations in the mountain and desert States.

In much of the West the population is sparse, and the federal government owns and manages millions of hectares of undeveloped land. Americans use these areas for recreational and commercial activities, such as fishing, camping, hiking, boating, grazing, lumbering, and mining. The largest city in the region is Los Angeles, located on the West Coast.

Alaska, the northernmost state in the Union, is a vast land of few people and great stretches of wilderness, protected in national parks and wildlife refuges. Hawaii is the only state in the union in which Asian-Americans outnumber residents of European stock.

V Major Cities

List of United States Major Cities by Population (last changed on 2 January 2017)

Rank	City	State	Population (2014)
1	New York	New York	8,491,079
2	Los Angeles	California	3,928,864
3	Chicago	Illinois	2,722,389
4	Houston	Texas	2,239,558
5	Philadelphia	Pennsylvania	1,560,297
6	Phoenix	Arizona	1,537,058
7	San Antonio	Texas	1,436,697
8	San Diego	California	1,381,069
9	Dallas	Texas	1,281,047
10	San Jose	California	1,015,785

Washington, D.C.

The north (top) and south (bottom) sides of the White House

Washington, D.C. is the capital of the United States. D.C. stands for the federal District of Columbia, the name of the capital territory. Columbia was a poetic name for the United States commonly in use at that time. Washington is the name of the city that fills the entire District of Columbia. Formed from land donated by the states of Maryland and Virginia and named in honor of President George Washington, the City of Washington was founded in 1791 to serve as the new national capital. Congress held its first session in Washington on November 17, 1800. The U.S. Census Bureau estimates that the District's population was 681,170 on July 1, 2016 with a significant African American population (48.3%). Hispanics of any race made up 10.6% of the District's population. Washington, D.C. has fourteen official sister city agreements. Beijing, China is one of them.

➢ *The White House*

The White House is a grand mansion with 132 rooms at 1600 Pennsylvania Avenue in the middle of Washington, D.C. It is the America's oldest federal building, where the president of the United States works and lives. George Washington, the first U.S. president, helped lay the building's first stone in 1792. John Adams, the second president, was the first president to live in the White House.

➢ *Capitol Hill*

The United States Capitol is located in Washington, D.C. It has been the seat of the U.S. Senate and House of Representatives since 1800. William Thornton, a man with no formal training in architecture won the competition for design of a new United States Capitol in the early 1790s. George Washington laid the cornerstone for the new Capitol on 18 September 1793, and it was completed over a period of decades under the supervision of many architects. The building is situated on Capitol Hill, overlooking the Potomac River.

➢ *The Smithsonian Institution*

The Smithsonian Institution is the largest museum complex (建筑群) in the world. Built in 1846, it was a bequest (遗赠) from British scientist James Smithson. The Smithsonian owns dinosaur bones, historic airplanes, a zoo full of wild animals, famous paintings, and so on. At the Air and Space Museum you can see the first airplane, which the Wright brothers flew in 1903, and the command module (太空船驾驶舱) from

Apollo 11, which was the first human mission to land on the Moon.

➢ *Washington Monument*

Washington, D.C. is well known for its monuments. No building in the District of Columbia is taller than the 169-meter-high Washington Monument, which was built between 1848 and 1884 to honor George Washington, first President of the United States.

➢ *Thomas Jefferson Memorial*

Thomas Jefferson Memorial, completed in 1943, honors the man who was principal author of the Declaration of Independence, the nation's third president, and the first U.S. Secretary of State. The memorial's walls are inscribed with some of Jefferson's most famous quotations. Inside the round building stands a bronze statue of Thomas Jefferson.

➢ *Lincoln Memorial*

Lincoln Memorial, a monument dedicated to President Abraham Lincoln (1861 — 1865), stands in Potomac Park in Washington, D.C. The structure was inspired by classical Greek architecture, and it houses a grand, marble statue of Lincoln. His short Gettysburg Address is inscribed on a marble wall. He delivered this speech in 1863 during the Civil War. The Lincoln Memorial is where 200,000 people in 1963 heard Martin Luther King, Jr., give his famous "I Have a Dream" speech, which expressed the hopes of the civil rights movement in moving words.

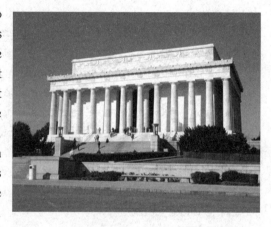

➢ *Roosevelt Memorial*

Franklin Delano Roosevelt Memorial consists of four outdoor rooms with waterfalls, pools, and gardens. A quotation from Roosevelt is engraved on the wall. There is only one statue of Roosevelt in the memorial, sitting in a chair with his faithful dog, Fala. Roosevelt was the 32nd president of the United States. He led the nation through the difficult years of the Great Depression (1930s) and World War II (1939 — 1945).

There is a statue of First Lady Eleanor Roosevelt, the first wife of a president to be honored in a national memorial. She is shown before the seal of the United Nations (UN) to which she was the first U.S. delegate in 1948.

New York City

A financial, commercial, and cultural center, New York City is the most populous and largest city in the United States and the fourth largest in the world (after Tokyo in Japan, Mexico City in

Mexico, and São Paulo in Brazil) with an estimated 2015 population of 8,550,405. New York served as the capital of the United States from 1785 until 1790.

In 1626, Peter Minuit, Director of the Dutch colony of New Netherland acquired Manhattan from the Indians in exchange for trade goods worth 60 guilders, often said to be worth US$24. At first, it was called New Amsterdam by the Dutch settlers and later, following its capture by the English in 1664, the former Dutch territory of New Netherland and its principal port, New Amsterdam, were named the Province and City of New York in honor of the then Duke of York (later James II of England). The city grew rapidly from a deserted island into now a great metropolis. The fast expansion is largely due to its location. It is situated on the best American harbor on the Atlantic Ocean and it also lies on the Hudson River, which allows water transportation into the middle of the United States.

The city is composed of five boroughs; they are Manhattan, Queens, the Bronx, Brooklyn, and Staten Island. As a city of islands, the Bronx is the only borough on the mainland. The other boroughs are on islands.

New York is the world's most ethnically diverse city. About one-third of New York's residents were born in other countries. It is famous for its Chinatown and also has the largest Jewish population of any city outside Israel. After the blacks were released from slavery, a large number of them moved into cities like New York, Philadelphia, and Washington.

New York City is a constellation of famous buildings. The most outstanding ones include the Empire State Building, United Nations headquarters, Rockefeller Center, and the rebuilt complex World Trade Center.

> *Empire State Building*

The Empire State Building is a 102-story skyscraper in Manhattan. Its name is derived from the nickname for the state of New York, the Empire State. The Empire State Building is an American cultural icon. It was designated as a National Historic Landmark and has been named as one of the Seven Wonders of the Modern World by the American Society of Civil Engineers.

> *United Nations Headquarters*

The landmark buildings of the United Nations (UN) stand in Manhattan, alongside the East River. Although it is situated in New York City, the land occupied by the United Nations Headquarters and the spaces of buildings that it rents are under the sole administration of the United Nations and not the U.S. government. Established in 1945, the UN moved into its New York headquarters in the fall of 1952, and the majority of the world's nations are now members. Each country displays its flag near the entryway.

> *Rockefeller Center*

Rockefeller Center is a vast complex of 19 commercial buildings covering 89,000 m^2 in the center of Midtown Manhattan. It is entertainment and shopping center, and home to NBC-TV and radio and other media. Built by the Rockefeller family, it was declared a National Historic Landmark in 1987. It is famous for its annual Christmas tree lighting, which is a world-wide symbol of the holidays. More than a half million people pass by the tree each day while it is on display, making Rockefeller Center the epicenter of New York City's holiday celebrations.

> *The Statue of Liberty*

Standing on Liberty Island in New York Harbor, the Statue of Liberty was a gift of friendship from the people of France to the people of the United States and is a universal symbol of freedom and democracy. The Statue of Liberty was dedicated on October 28, 1886, designated as a National Monument in 1924 and a UNESCO World Heritage Site in1984. It was restored (修复) for her centennial on July 4, 1986. As an American icon, the Statue of Liberty has been depicted on the country's coinage and stamps and it is a frequent subject in popular culture.

➢ *World Trade Center*

The World Trade Center is a partially completed complex of buildings under construction in the heart of New York City's downtown financial district, replacing an original complex of seven buildings (1973 — 2001) with the same name on the same site that were damaged or destroyed in the terrorist attacks of September 11, 2001. The site is being rebuilt with six new skyscrapers, a National September 11 Memorial & Museum, and a transportation hub. The main building of the rebuilt complex is One World Trade Center (also known as Freedom Tower). It is the tallest building in the Western Hemisphere, reaching more than 100 stories upon its completion in November 2014.

One World Trade Center

➢ *Central Park*

Central Park, which has been a National Historic Landmark since 1962, is one of the most famous sightseeing spots and the most visited urban park in the United States, with approximately 35 million visitors annually. Although planting and land form in much of the park seem natural, it is in fact almost entirely landscaped. The park contains several natural-looking lakes and ponds, extensive walking tracks, two ice-skating rinks, playgrounds, the Central Park Zoo, the Central Park Conservatory Garden, a wildlife sanctuary, a large area of natural woods, a reservoir, an outdoor amphitheater (圆形露天剧场), etc. Central Park's size and cultural position, similar to London's Hyde Park, has served as a model for many urban parks.

➢ *Wall Street*

Wall Street is an eight-block-long street running through the historical center of the financial district in New York City. Over time, the term has become a metonym for the financial markets of the United States as a whole. It is the first permanent home of the New York Stock Exchange. You can find many banks, stock markets, stockbrokers, and other financial institutions there.

➢ *Broadway Theater District*

Broadway is an entire area on and adjacent to Broadway Street in midtown Manhattan, in and around Times Square, and includes several theaters of varying sizes and popularity. Broadway theatres are widely considered to represent the highest level of commercial theatre in the English-speaking world. The great majority of Broadway shows are musicals which became enormously influential forms of American popular culture.

➢ *Times Square*

Times Square is a busy intersection of art and commerce in New York City and has achieved the status of an iconic world landmark which is principally defined by its spectacular, animated (栩栩如生的) digital advertisements. It is the site of the annual New Year's Eve ball drop, which began on December 31, 1907, and continues today, attracting over a million visitors to Times Square every New Year's Eve.

Formerly known as Longacre Square, it was renamed in 1904 after *The New York Times* moved its headquarters to the newly erected Times Building, the site of the annual ball drop.

> *Fifth Avenue*

Fifth Avenue is a major thoroughfare in the center of the borough of Manhattan. It serves as a symbol of wealthy New York and is consistently ranked as one of the most expensive and best shopping streets in the world.

Los Angeles

Located along the Pacific Ocean, Los Angeles is the largest city in the state of California and the second largest in the United States. Often abbreviated as L.A. and nicknamed The City of Angels, Los Angeles has an estimated population of 3.8 million and the Los Angeles Metropolitan Area is home to nearly 12.9 million residents. Its inhabitants are known as "Angelinos." The city is known for its Mediterranean climate, ethnic diversity, sprawling (不断扩张的) metropolis, extensive network of freeways and highways, and as a major center of the American entertainment industry, and a leading producer of aircraft and military equipment. It is also an important banking center. The city's seaport is one of the busiest in the United States. According to Forbes, Los Angeles, together with San Francisco Bay Area and Toronto, is the tenth most influential city in the world, with London and New York at the top of the list.

> *History and People*

Los Angeles was founded in 1781 by Spanish governor. It became a part of Mexico in 1821, following its independence from Spain. In 1848, at the end of the Mexican-American War, Los Angeles and California were purchased as part of the peace treaty between the United States and Mexico, thereby becoming part of the United States. It grew rapidly after railroads linked it to the Midwest and Eastern United States, in 1982 it surpassed Chicago to become the second largest U.S. city and it is still growing.

Los Angeles is home to a large number of people from China, Japan, Vietnam, and other places around the globe. Nearly half of the city's people are Hispanic. Most of the Hispanics are of Mexican ancestry. More Mexicans live in Los Angeles than in any other city except Mexico City. The city is also renowned for its great population of Chinese immigrants and displays of Chinese tradition and culture. It has one of the largest Chinatowns in the United States.

> *Capital of Movies*

Los Angeles is called the capital of movies. Most of the movie studios are located in a part of Los Angeles, which is called Hollywood. In 1923, a real estate agency put up a huge sign on a hilltop to advertise the area. The letters of the sign, which spell Hollywood, stand 14 meters tall and serve as the city's landmark.

Chicago

Chicago's iconic Willis Tower

Located on the southwestern shores of Lake Michigan, Chicago is the largest city in the U.S. state of Illinois, the 3rd largest city in the United States with more than 2.7 million residents. Chicago's downtown business district is called the Loop. An elevated railway (高架铁道) travels in a loop around the area, giving the center of the city its name. The city has many nicknames, the best-known being the Windy City and the "Hog Butcher to the World" for its once prosperous slaughter houses.

> ### History and People

Chicago was founded in 1833 and grew rapidly in the mid-nineteenth. By 1850, the city had become a busy Great Lakes port and a major transportation and telecommunications hub. Today, the city retains its status as a major hub, both for industry and infrastructure, with its O'Hare International Airport as the second busiest airport in the world. The region also has the largest number of U.S. highways and rail road freight. In modern times, the city has taken on additional dimension as a center for business and finance.

Chicago is a stronghold of the Democratic Party, and has been home to influential politicians, including the former President, Barack Obama. There are many colleges and universities in the Chicago area; among these, Northwestern University, the University of Chicago, and the University of Illinois at Chicago are classified as "highest research" doctoral universities.

People from all over the world live in Chicago. The most common languages in the city, after English, are Spanish and Polish. Immigrants have left their mark on the city. Each group settled in its own part of the city, and many of these neighborhoods hold on to customs and traditions.

> ### Chicago Firsts

Throughout the city's history, Chicagoans have demonstrated their ingenuity in matters large and small. Chicago was the birthplace of:

- The nation's first skyscraper, the 10-story, steel-framed Home Insurance Building, was built in 1885.
- When residents were threatened by waterborne illnesses from sewage flowing into Lake Michigan, they reversed the Chicago River in 1900 to make it flow toward the Mississippi.
- Start of the "Historic Route 66".
- The refrigerated rail car (Swift).
- Mail-order retailing (Sears and Montgomery Ward).
- The car radio (Motorola).
- The TV remote control (Zenith).
- The first self-sustaining nuclear chain reaction, ushering in the Atomic Age, took place at the University of Chicago in 1942.
- The 442-meter Willis Tower (formerly Sears Tower), completed in 1974, is Chicago's tallest building and the second tallest building in the Western Hemisphere after One World Trade Center in New York City.

Boston

Boston is the capital and largest city of Massachusetts, with an estimated population of 667,137 in 2015. It is considered the economic and cultural center of the region and is sometimes regarded as the unofficial "Capital of New England."

Being one of the oldest cities in the United States, Boston was founded by Puritan colonists from England in 1630. During the late 18th century, it was the scene of several major events during the American Revolution, including the Boston Massacre, the Boston Tea Party, Paul

Revere's midnight ride etc. Several early battles of the American Revolution, such as the Siege of Boston, the battles of Lexington and Concord, and Bunker Hill, occurred within the city and surrounding areas. It is sometimes called the "cradle of American independence."

After American independence was attained, Boston became a major shipping port and manufacturing center, and its rich history now helps attract 16.3 million visitors annually. The city was the site of several firsts, including the United States' first public school, Boston Latin School (1635), first subway system, the Tremont Street Subway (1897), and first public park, Boston Common (1634).

As a global city, Boston is placed among the top 30 most economically powerful cities in the world. The area's many colleges and universities make Boston an international center of higher education, attracting more than 350,000 college students from around the world, who contribute more than $4.8 billion annually to the regional economy. Some of the universities, such as Harvard and the Massachusetts Institute of Technology (MIT), are world famous, winning the city such reputation as "the intellectual capital of the United States" and "Athens of America." The city's economy is also based on research, electronics, engineering, finance, and technology — principally biotechnology. Now Boston has one of the highest costs of living in the United States.

Philadelphia

Philadelphia is the largest city in Pennsylvania and the fifth-most populous city in the United States, with an estimated population of 1,567,442 as of 2015. The deep Delaware River connects the city with the Atlantic Ocean 100 miles to the east, helping make Philadelphia a major port.

Philadelphia was founded as a Quaker (基督教友会教徒) colony by Englishman William Penn in 1681 on the site of an earlier Swedish settlement. The name he chose comes from Greek words meaning "city of brotherly love."

A commercial, educational, and cultural center, the city was once the second-largest in the British Empire (after London), and the social and geographical center of the original 13 American colonies. Philadelphia's importance and central location in the colonies made it a natural center for America's revolutionaries. The city hosted the First Continental Congress before the war; the Second Continental Congress, which signed the United States Declaration of Independence, during the war; and the Constitutional Convention after the war. Several battles were fought in and near Philadelphia as well. After the war, Philadelphia served as the new United States' capital in the 1790s.

The Liberty Bell, an important symbol of American Independence

Philadelphia is home to many national historical sites that relate to the founding of the United States. Independence National Historical Park is the center of these historical landmarks. Independence Hall, where the *Declaration of Independence* was signed, and the Liberty Bell are the city's most famous attractions. Philadelphia is home to the United States' first zoo and hospital.

Chapter 2 History

章节导读

　　学习美国历史文化的过程是理解、分享和阐释美国人民历史经验和文化建树的过程。本章旨在通过对美国历史文化的介绍，使读者了解美利坚合众国的形成及其历史发展进程、重大历史事件及其对美国政治、经济、文化和社会生活的影响。

　　本章内容分为十一节：第一节解答了北美洲最早的定居者是哪些人，他们在何时、从何地、如何来到北美洲等基本问题；第二节主要介绍了北美殖民地的形成和发展；第三节主要内容为美国独立战争；第四节为西进运动，包括路易斯安那置地、血泪之路、领土扩张、第一条横贯铁路的修筑、淘金热等项内容；第五节为美国内战与战后重建；第六节内容是第一次世界大战中的美国；第七节主要介绍了经济大萧条和罗斯福新政；第八节和第九节分别介绍了美国在第二次世界大战和冷战期间的情况。第十节主要介绍了美国黑人民权运动、妇女解放运动和反主流文化运动。第十一节简述了美国当前所面临的种种社会问题。

　　United States History is the story of how the republic developed from colonial beginnings in the 16th century when the first European explorers arrived, until modern times. From its beginnings as a remote English colony, the country has developed the largest economy in the world. Throughout its history, the United States has faced struggles, both within the country — between various ethnic, religious, political, and economic groups — and with other nations. The efforts to deal with and resolve these struggles have shaped the United States of America into the 21st century.

I the First Inhabitants

　　No people lived in the Americas before the Indians arrived. For a great many years, anthropologists have debated the origins of the first Americans. Today most agree that America's first settlers came from northeast Asia and entered the New World in the general area of Bering Strait [白令海峡，为丹麦航海家Vitus Bering (1681 — 1741) 所发现], during the last Ice Age. During that period, which began about 70,000 B.C. and ended about 10,000 B.C., the weather in the northern half of the earth changed greatly. It grew colder. Much of the land was covered with huge glaciers. Sea water froze, and the water level in the sea dropped. The Bering Strait, which today is a narrow area of water that separates Asia and North America, probably became very shallow during the Ice Age. In some places it dried up completely and formed a land bridge. The earliest Americans must have crossed the bridge from Siberia into Alaska as bands of hunters followed big animals such as giant buffalos and mammoths (猛犸象,已绝种).

Group after group moved across the bridge to the unexplored continent of North America. They passed through what is now Alaska and western Canada. This crossing took place over hundreds of years. Because the people migrated in separate waves over such a long period of time, they were very different from one another in physical characteristics, skills, and talents. By the time the first Europeans came to shores of America, the early immigrants had already spread throughout the New World and developed cultures in keeping with the different terrains (地形) and climates in which they had settled. Those first people to live in the Americas are now known as Indians or Native Americans.

II Colonial Period

Colonial History of America was formed by European nations and the colonial period started from the beginning of European settlement to the time of the independence of thirteen colonies from Britain in 1776.

Christopher Columbus' Discovery

Between 1492 and 1504, Columbus made a total of four voyages for Spain. In the island Hispaniola[①], he founded the first European settlement in the New World.

Two years after he returned from his fourth voyage, Columbus died, still firmly convinced that he had found a western route to Asia and never knew that he had found a New World.

However, the land Columbus discovered never bore his name. It was named for Amerigo Vespucci, another Italian who explored for Portugal shortly after Columbus sailed for Spain. Vespucci realized his party had arrived at a new continent. His claim led a German mapmaker to suggest in 1507 that the newly discovered world be called the "land of Americus, for Americus its discoverer."

For more than a century after Columbus no European power other than Spain had more than a brief foothold in the New World. Then starting in the late 16th century, the Spanish, the English, the French, Swedes and the Dutch began to colonize eastern North America. Many early attempts ended in failure, but successful colonies were soon established.

European Colonial Ventures

European countries developed colonies for many reasons and in a different way, but primarily to generate income. They used colonies to provide raw materials for trade and to serve as markets for finished products. Spain made a great mining and agricultural empire in Mexico, South America, and the Caribbean. Portugal created a slave-based agricultural colony in Brazil. The French, who had the largest empire in North America, made profitable business of fishing and fur trading. The Dutch and the Swedes established successful colonies in the northeastern part of North America. Among the European invaders of North America, only the English established colonies of agricultural settlers, whose interests in Native Americans was less about trade than about the acquisition of land. That fact would have huge implications in the long struggle for control of North America. English colonies eventually became dominant in North America because

---

① 伊斯帕尼奥拉岛(即海地岛)：拉丁美洲西印度群岛中部一岛屿，为今海地和多米尼加共和国所在地。哥伦布1492年发现了该岛。岛的西部(现在的海地)于1697年被西班牙割让给法国。

many settlers were drawn to their political systems. These systems encouraged representative government, religious toleration, economic growth, and cultural diversity.

The First European Settlements in North America

Country	Name of Settlement	Present-Day Location	Year of First Settlement
Spain	St. Augustine	Florida	1565
France	Quebec	Canada	1603
England	Jamestown	Virginia	1607
Holland	New Amsterdam	New York	1624
Sweden	New Sweden	New Jersey	1638

Development of the Thirteen English Colonies

The first colonies in North America were along the eastern coast. Settlers from Spain, France, Sweden, Holland, and England claimed land beginning in the 17th century. But it was the English who eventually dominated the continent.

The British Empire settled its first permanent colony in the Americas at Jamestown, Virginia in 1607. This was but the first of 13 colonies in North America. By 1733, there were 13 colonies along the eastern seaboard under English control. They were Massachusetts, New Hampshire, Connecticut, Rhode Island, New York, New Jersey, Pennsylvania, Maryland, Delaware, Virginia, North Carolina, South Carolina, and Georgia. These colonies had been founded in a variety of ways and for a variety of reasons. Regional differences had developed in their cultures and economies. All, however, had their English heritage in common.

The historians usually lump these colonies into three groups in geographical order, from the north to the south: New England Colonies, the Middle Colonies, and the Southern colonies (which included the Chesapeake Bay Colonies, also called the Upper South, and the Lower South).

➤ *New England Colonies*

A group of people called Puritans came to America to seek freedom of religion and founded the New England colonies of Massachusetts, New Hampshire, Rhode Island, and Connecticut. By and large, the people who settled in the New England Colonies wanted to keep their family unit together and practice their own religion. They were used to doing many things themselves and not depending on other people for much. Some of these people came to New England to make money, but they were not the majority. The people living in the colonies made a living by fishing and building ships. They also carried on much of the slave trade.

New England Colonies	Mid-Atlantic Colonies	Southern Colonies
Massachusetts	Delaware	Maryland
New Hampshire	New York	North Carolina
Rhode Island	New Jersey	South Carolina
Connecticut	Pennsylvania	Georgia

Quick Facts of the New England Colonies

Fact 1 — Geography	The geography of New England consisted of mountains thick with trees, rivers and poor rocky soil that was difficult to farm and unsuitable for agriculture
Fact 2 — Natural Resources	Fish, whales, forests. Imported agricultural products from other colonies
Fact 3 — Religion	Puritans — No religious freedom
Fact 4 — Climate	Coldest of the three regions, leading to difficult winters but less disease

➤ *Mid-Atlantic Colonies*

The Mid-Atlantic Colonies, composed of Pennsylvania (1682), Delaware (1638), New York (1624), and New Jersey (1623), were a mix of both northern and southern features, creating a unique environment of early settlement by non-English Europeans, mostly Dutch and German. A combination of both urban and rural lifestyles made it more cosmopolitan, religiously pluralistic, and socially tolerant within a commercial atmosphere. From early colonial times, the Mid-Atlantic region was settled by a wider range of European people than in New England or the South. The people who founded the Mid-Atlantic Colonies were looking to practice their own religion (Pennsylvania mainly) or to make money. Many of these people didn't bring their families with them from England and were the perfect workers for the hard work required in ironworks and shipyards.

In contrast to the South where the cash crop plantation system dominated, and New England whose rocky soil made large-scale agriculture difficult, the Mid-Atlantic had rich farmland and a moderate climate which made farming much easier. Due to the ease of farming these colonies were able to provide food for their own people and to send to the other colonies; the Mid-Atlantic colonies became known as the breadbasket colonies.

Market towns were extremely important in the colonies because people needed to go to town to trade the products they grew or made. Cities grew along major shipping routes and waterways. Such flourishing cities included New York City on the Hudson River, Philadelphia on the Delaware River. These cities gave rise to brilliant thinkers such as Benjamin Franklin, who earned respect on both sides of the Atlantic.

Quick Facts of the Mid-Atlantic Colonies

Fact 1 — Geography and Climate	The geography and climate of the Middle Colonies was a mix of the New England and Southern features.
Fact 2 — Natural Resources	Good farmland, timber, furs and coal. Iron ore was a particularly important natural resource.
Fact 3 — Religion	Not dominated by a specific religion which gave way to religious freedom for Quakers, Catholics, Lutherans, Jews and others.

➤ *Southern Colonies*

The hope of gold, resources, and virgin lands drew English colonists to the Southern Colonies, which consist of the Upper South (Chesapeake region: Virginia and Maryland) and the Lower South (Carolina, which eventually split into North and South Carolina, and Georgia). The first permanent English settlement in the New World was Jamestown, Virginia, founded by the London Company. The five southern English colonies displayed many similar characteristics.

They all relied on a plantation economy, grew their own food focusing most of their efforts on cash crops including tobacco, cotton and indigo. They provided some religious toleration, allowing different religious groups to flourish.

Slavery was permitted and accepted in all the southern colonies. A rich and powerful aristocracy was dominant in the southern colonies.

Quick Facts of the Southern Colonies

Fact 1 — Geography	The geography of the Southern Colonies was hilly coastal plains with plenty of forests.
Fact 2 — Natural Resources	The Southern colonies concentrated on developing plantations that eventually grew cotton, tobacco, rice, sugar cane and indigo (a purple dye).
Fact 3 — Religion	Not dominated by a specific religion which gave way to religious freedom for Baptists, Anglicans and others.
Fact 4 — Climate	Warmest of the three regions, not difficult to survivine winters, warmer climate gave rise to the spread of disease.
Fact 5 — Trade and Industry	Trade and Industry was dominated by the Slave Plantations.

➤ *Three Types of Colonization*

As for the approach to colonization, the British Empire used three main types as it sought to expand its territory to distant parts of the earth. These three types were Charter Colonies (特许殖民地), Proprietary Colonies (业主殖民地) and Royal Colonies.

A charter colony was established by an individual trading company which had a Royal Charter with the British crown establishing the rules under which the colony was to be governed. Charter colonies had more control over their own affairs than did the other types of colonies, which were ruled more directly by the British. Colonies of this type for the most part either disappeared or changed their status early and became royal colonies. By 1776 only two charter colonies, Connecticut and Rhode Island, remained.

Proprietary colony was the predominating form to colonization during the period 1660 — 1690. By this method the British crown awarded huge tracts of land in the New World to a person or a group called proprietors (英王特许独占某块殖民地的业主), who were often friends of the king or people to whom the Crown owed a debt. Proprietors owned the land they received and usually made any laws they wished, as long as they were consistent with English law. The land was titled in the proprietors' name, not the king's. A good example is the Province of Pennsylvania, granted to William Penn (the state of Pennsylvania still bears the name meaning "woodlands of Penn") by King Charles II of England.

The major flaw with the proprietary colony model was that it invested (赋予) people with tremendous amounts of power. By 1690 concern about the colonies' growing independence from control by British officials led to the end of proprietary grants.

Royal colony, also called "Crown colony," became the standard form of colonial government by the 18th century. Such colony is under direct control of the king of the sovereign nation, who named a governor and a council to assist him, and who was also responsible for appointing colonial judges. The Crown controlled all unsold public lands, and the royal governor retained the power to disperse those lands. The first of what would later become known as royal colonies was the Colony of Virginia, after the Crown took control from the Virginia Company in 1624.

➢ *Characteristics of the English Colonization*

From the very beginning the pattern of English colonization differed significantly from the Spanish and the French.

First, New Spain and New France were developed by their kings, while the English colonies were developed by their people. There was no official attempt by the English government to create a colonial empire at the start of the 17th century. Charter companies and joint-stock companies played a crucial role in exploration.

Second, the Spanish, French, and Dutch wanted to find precious metals in the Americas, to trade with the indigenous peoples, and to convert them to Christianity, so relatively few Europeans settled permanently in the colonies. In contrast, England sent more people to the Americas than other European nations — about 400,000 in the 17th century — and established more permanent agricultural colonies.

Third, the England had a different model in their experience. Spain's experience during the Reconquista (8 — 15世纪西班牙和葡萄牙驱逐阿拉伯人收复失地的斗争) gave their American colonization efforts qualities of centralized governmental control, military conquest, and religious missionary efforts. In contrast, English colonization of America had qualities of merchant-based investment and much less government control. There was no Aztec or Inca Empire to conquer and rule. The colonists thus had to establish their own communities within a largely wilderness setting.

➢ *Colonial Government*

Both the structure and philosophy of American government evolved out of English political thought and tradition, and Colonial government was modeled on English government. In the colonies, representative government was put into practice with the colonial assemblies (议会), which had a variety of names, such as House of Delegates, House of Burgesses, or Assembly of Freemen. In both England and America, government was representative only to the extent that people had the right to vote. In both cases, only free adult white males had the privilege. Sometimes there were religious requirements, as with the Puritans of Massachusetts. Almost always there were property requirements. The organization of government was also modeled after the familiar English system. Each colony had an executive branch, a legislative branch, and a judicial branch. The governor (总督) was the chief executive in the colonies, as the king was in England,

➢ *Education in Colonial Period*

Education was most emphasized in New England. They passed laws to establish necessary schools for their children. As early as 1647, Massachusetts established a public school system. The public schools were financed partly by tuition and partly by taxes. In the South, where there were few towns and people lived far apart, young children were usually educated by their parents or by tutors. In the middle colonies, schools were started by various churches.

The first college, Harvard, was set up in Massachusetts in 1636. By the mid-eighteenth century several well-known colleges were founded, including Yale in Connecticut, Columbia in New York and Princeton in New Jersey. Colonial schools laid the foundation of the American educational system in which all the American schools were left to the care of communities or the local authority. Education was closely related to religion. The first colleges — Harvard, William and Mary, and Yale — were established mainly to train ministers. In all the colonies, schools were mostly for boys. Colleges were for sons of the upper class. Lower and middle class boys could receive training by becoming apprentices or indentured servants.

At first, the course of study generally imitated that of English colleges. Greek, Latin, Hebrew, logic, ethics, and rhetoric were taught. Later, other subjects such as history, science, French, and German were offered.

Dame School

The first schools were called "dame schools," which were in the homes and housewives were the teachers. Neighborhood children would meet at one house and sit around the fireplace and be taught to read, write, and spell while the housewife did her chores around the house. Everywhere, the reality embodied in the proverb — as the twig is bent, so the tree inclined — was that early education was female centered in early America. In 1647 public schools were started. The school was made of logs. There was usually only one room. School began at seven or eight in the morning and didn't end until four or five in the afternoon. Saturday was also a school day, so the children went for six days of the week.

> ➤ *End of the Colonial Period*

The colonies began in the early 1600s. As decades passed, people from other countries brought new ideas and different religions to the colonies. By the time America declared its independence from Britain in 1776, the differences had become one of the most notable characteristics of the new people. They were no longer British colonists, but American citizens.

III The Struggle for Independence

By the beginning of the eighteenth century, European powers had been alternately exploring the New World and sparring (争论) over what they found. It was time for the main event: a showdown (决战) for control of the American continent.

French and Indian War

In the 17th and 18th centuries, England and France emerged as the world's most powerful countries. Between 1689 and 1763 the two countries fought four major European and inter-colonial wars for the domination of Europe and the control of an overseas empire. The first three of these wars were focused primarily on battles in Europe and only secondarily on conflicts in the colonies. However, in the fourth and the last of these wars, the fighting actually began in the colonies and then spread to Europe. This war, known in Europe as the Seven Years' War (1756 — 1763) and in North America as the French and Indian War (1754 — 1760), was regarded by some historians as the first truly world war and resulted in British domination of that continent.

> ➤ *Treaty of Paris, 1763*

The War lasted nearly nine years, and ended in 1763 with the signing of the *Treaty of Paris*. Under the terms of this treaty, Britain received from France Canada and all French territory east of the Mississippi River except New Orleans. From Spain, Britain received Florida. In return, Spain, which had entered the war on the side of France in 1762, received French lands west of the Mississippi River as well as the port of New Orleans. Thus the British controlled all of North America from the Atlantic Ocean to the Mississippi River.

> *Effects of the War*

The French and Indian War had profound effects for both the British Empire and the American colonists. It is often seen as the source of much of the resentment between the English government and the colonists that eventually led to the American Revolution of 1775.

Change in British Policy

With the end of the French and Indian War, England turned its attention to America. Victory had brought Great Britain vast new territories but also a number of new problems. One of these was the disposal of western lands. The British government faced the problem of Indian resistance to westward expansion. In the spring of 1763, Pontiac, an Ottawa chief, led a rebellion against the British. Pontiac's rebellion forced the British government to act. The attempted solution was the *Proclamation of 1763*, which established the crest (顶部) of the Appalachians as a boundary line between white and Indian lands. Although this was a temporary measure, the colonists resented both the line and the presence of British troops sent to enforce the new law.

In addition, the British government's attempts to raise revenue through direct taxation to pay for the huge debt left by the war aroused even greater resentment in the colonies. Colonial protests and British determination to force the colonies to submit to parliamentary authority led to open warfare that eventually split the two apart.

The Declaration of Independence

On June 7, Richard Henry Lee of Virginia introduced a resolution in the Second Continental Congress declaring "That these United Colonies are, and of right ought to be, free and independent states…" Immediately, a committee of five was appointed to prepare a formal declaration of Independence. This committee included Benjamin Franklin, John Adams, Robert Livingston, Roger Sherman and Thomas Jefferson. Jefferson was chosen to do the writing of the Declaration, which he divided into three sections.

The first part established the natural rights of all people. "All men are created equal." People had the basic right to "life, liberty, and the pursuit of happiness." Governments ruled only with the consent of the people. The second section listed the reasons why the colonies felt they had to declare independence. Jefferson described the ways that King George had treated the colonies unfairly. The last part formally stated that the colonies wanted to cut all political ties with Great Britain. Jefferson declared the colonies to be "free and independent states."

On July 4, 1776, the Second Continental Congress adopted the Declaration of Independence, in which the 13 Colonies officially broke away from Britain and formally declared their independence as the United States of America.

The pronouncement of independence had far-reaching effects. It transformed the rebellion into a revolution and committed the mass of Patriots to separation. It also led to increased foreign aid and prepared the way for French intervention on the American side. In order to achieve and maintain independence, however, the new nation had to face full-scale war with Britain.

Four Phases of the War

In total, the war lasted for eight years and had four phases, each with a distinct strategy and character.

Phase One	the Opening Campaigns	April 1775 — July 1776
Phase Two	the British Northern Offensive	July 1776 — Oct. 1777
Phase Three	the War in the South	early 1778 — Oct. 1781
Phase Four	Peace Negotiations	Oct. 1781 — Sept. 1783

During the first phase, the Patriots' goal was to turn the revolt into an organized rebellion, while British governors and armed Loyalists tried to suppress the uprising.

The second phase of the war began with a major British invasion of New York in July 1776 and ended with the American victory at Saratoga in October 1777.

During the third phase of the war Britain tried to subdue the South. Beginning in early 1778 it used regular troops to take territory and local Loyalists to hold it. Patriots used guerrilla warfare to weaken British forces, and then used French assistance to achieved ultimate victory over the British at Yorktown, Virginia, in October, 1781.

The final phase of the war came when astute Patriot diplomacy won a treaty recognizing the independence of the United States in September 1783.

Treaty of Paris, 1783

By the terms of the *Treaty of Paris, 1783*, Britain recognized the independence of the United States and gave up all its territories between the Atlantic coast and the Mississippi River, extending from Florida to the Great Lakes. The British agreed to withdraw their forces and granted the United States fishing rights off Newfoundland. Spain, which had joined in the war against Great Britain in 1779, received Florida.

IV The Westward Movement

American development involved moving toward the west. The Westward Movement referred to the movement of people from the settled regions of the United States to lands farther west. It began soon after the first English colonists reached North America in the early 1600's. In a little over 200 years, American settlers moved west across what was called the frontier. By 1848 the United States stretched unchallenged from sea to sea, a distance of nearly 5,000 kilometers. This westward movement was one of the most influential forces to shape North American history and had an important impact on American institutions and American characters.

Extending the Land — Louisiana Purchase of 1803

The Louisiana Territory was a vast area of in the middle of the present United States, extending from the Mississippi River westward to the Rocky Mountains. France had claimed the land in 1682 and named it to honor Louis XIV. It became a formal French colony in 1731 and remained so until it was ceded (割让) to Spain in 1762 as a result of the French and Indian War. However, in 1800, the French dictator Napoleon Bonaparte[①] signed a treaty with Spain that gave Louisiana Territory back to France.

By this time, the United States had won its independence from Great Britain. The Mississippi River formed the western boundary of the United States. Only Florida in the east belonged to Spain. President Thomas Jefferson viewed French control of Louisiana as a danger to the United States. Spain was not powerful enough to interfere seriously with the American dream of expanding westward to the pacific, but the ownership of Louisiana by France was a much greater threat. America's main concern was the port city of New Orleans. Whoever controlled New Orleans controlled trade on the river.

President Thomas Jefferson determined to gain control of New Orleans. In 1803, he sent diplomat James Monroe to France to negotiate the purchase of the port city. At that time, France faced a series of troubles, including the threat of war with Great Britain. The French leader, Napoleon Bonaparte, worried that Britain might seize Louisiana if war broke out, so he decided to sell it to the Americans. Besides, he needed money badly and lacked troops to defend the large Louisiana Territory. In April 1803, the French made an astonishing offer to the American officials in Paris. France would sell to the United States not just New Orleans but all of the Louisiana Territory which was about 2,100,000 square kilometers of land. France's price for the Louisiana Territory was $15 million dollars. In December 1803, the United States took control of Louisiana and raised the American flag in New Orleans.

The Louisiana Purchase was the most important accomplishment of Jefferson's presidency and was the biggest land deal in American history. It doubled the size of the United States and opened the door for America's westward expansion. Later, all or parts of 15 states were carved from this vast region.

Exploring the Land — Lewis and Clark Expedition (1804 — 1806)

The Louisiana Purchase in 1803 sparked interest in expansion to the west coast. Just a few weeks after the purchase, President Thomas Jefferson, had U.S. Congress appropriate (拨出款项) $2,500 to send a small U.S. Army unit led by Army Captain Meriwether Lewis, and his former Army comrade William Clark to explore the west all the way to the Pacific Ocean. The purpose of the expedition was to claim control of the western part of North America and to explore the area's natural resources. Jefferson also placed special importance on declaring U.S. sovereignty over the native tribes along the Missouri River. In addition, one of Jefferson's main objectives was for the unit to find a waterway that would connect the east to the west.

Lewis and Clark

Lewis and Clark set out in May 1804 near St. Louis, Missouri. Their team, known as the "Corps of Discovery," consisted of approximately 40 men. During the journey, they were braving grizzly bears (大灰熊), gray wolves, steep mountain passes, and harsh winter weather to explore a vast wilderness. Along the way they met many native peoples and made important discoveries.

---

① 拿破仑，1769 — 1821，法国皇帝，1804 — 1815年在位。

In November 1805, after about a year and a half of tough travel, they finally reached the Pacific Ocean, near present-day Astoria, Oregon, and returned safely to St. Louis on September 23, 1806 with enormous amounts of information about the new territory of the United States as well as the people living there.

The Lewis and Clark Expedition was the first expedition of an overland nature that was taken in the United States to the Pacific Coast and then back, and the third recorded transcontinental crossing of the land of North America. It made the first scientific study of a vast territory and strengthened U.S. claims to western lands.

One of the most important contributions of the Lewis and Clark Expedition was that they were able to provide a better perception of the geography of the Northwest and produced the first accurate maps of the area.

Another achievement was getting a better understanding of the natural resources of the Northwest. The expedition recorded more than 200 types of plants and animals that had been previously unknown to Euro-Americans, and revealed the astonishing richness and beauty of the American West and paved the way for the settlement of the West.

A third major achievement of the expedition was that it noted at least seventy-two different Indian tribes and was able to establish relations of a friendly nature with many of the Native Americans.

However, try as they might, they found no trace of a Northwest Passage. There was no way to cross North America by water.

The Lewis and Clark Expedition was not simply a scientific journey, it was "An extension of American power" and laid a part of the groundwork for the westward movement of the United States of America. Expansion by American settlers would begin over the next few years.

Indian Removal — The Trail of Tears

During the 1820's and 1830's as economic growth reinforced the institution of slavery and accelerated westward expansion, policy makers struggled to preserve white hegemony (统治权). President Andrew Jackson's attitude toward Indians was the typically western one that they were barbarians and better off out of the way.

In 1830 with the encouragement of President Andrew Jackson, Congress passed a law called the *Indian Removal Act*, which required that the Indians living east of the Mississippi River should move to Indian Territory west of the Mississippi. This territory later became part of the state of Oklahoma. Most Indian tribes did not want to leave their land. But the government sent in the army to force tribes to move.

This was an incredibly sad time in American history. During the winter of 1838 — 1839, the Cherokees, along with some other Indian groups of the region, were forced to leave their homelands in Tennessee, Alabama, North Carolina and Georgia and marched more than 1,600 kilometers to their new home in the Indian Territory that is today known as Oklahoma. The impact was devastating — an estimated 4,000 of the 15,000 Cherokees died during this forced migration. This tragic chapter in American and Cherokee history became known as the "Trail of Tears." This process of uprooting had been going on for a long time. By 1840, most Indians had been removed from their traditional lands east of the Mississippi River and relocated farther west.

Moving West — Addition of Territory

Between 1845 and 1848 the United States rapidly pushed the national border to the Pacific Ocean, increasing its territory by more than 3.1 million square kilometers, more land than was added by the Louisiana Purchase. It acquired these lands in three great chunks, through annexation (合并), diplomacy, and a war. This acquisition of land was probably the most important step taken by the U.S. government in encouraging westward expansion.

Many Americans believed it was the destiny (fate) of the United States to control all the land from the Atlantic to the Pacific. In 1845 the United States annexed Texas, which had been an independent republic since winning its independence from Mexico in1836. In 1846 Britain handed over the Oregon Territory in a treaty. Also in that year, the United States went to war with Mexico. The war aims of the United States were to gain the Mexican provinces of New Mexico and California and to keep the war as short as possible.

After almost two years of fighting, the Mexican Government agreed to sign the **American-Mexican Treaty of Guadalupe-Hidalgo** on February 2, 1848. Out of this important treaty came the newly created territory, which later became the States of California, Nevada, and Utah, and parts of Colorado, Arizona, New Mexico, and Wyoming. Mexico also relinquished its claims to Texas. With the addition of California and New Mexico, the United States stretched from ocean to ocean.

On December 30, 1853 the treaty of **Gadsden Purchase** was signed in Mexico City, which settled the dispute over the exact location of the Mexican border west of El Paso, Texas, giving the U.S. claim to approximately 76,800 sq km of land, which is almost as large as Pennsylvania, in what is now southern Arizona and southwestern New Mexico, for the price of $10 million, about thirty-three cents an acre. With the acquisition of this territory, the United States had reached its present continental boundaries. The nation had fulfilled its manifest destiny.

The Gold Rush of 1849

Victory in war with Mexico, along with purchases and treaty agreements, expanded the United States from the Atlantic Ocean to the Pacific Ocean. Once the United States gained control over large areas of the West, Americans began moving into these lands in ever increasing numbers.

One event which drew people to the West was the discovery of gold in California. This discovery was made in January 1848 by James Marshall, a worker at John Sutter's sawmill in California's Sacramento Valley. News of Marshall's find quickly spread throughout the nation. Gold fever brought a huge wave of people into the West. In 1849 over 80,000 people, known as "Forty-Niners," traveled west to the California gold fields. New Western settlements sprang up almost overnight. Although many of the newcomers returned home after the uproar died down, enough stayed to establish California as a state just two years after the gold rush began. More than $1 billion in gold was mined in California. This money helped build railroads and factories, establishing America as a nation of industry.

The Transcontinental Railroads

With explosive growth in population on the Pacific Coast, there was a need to connect these distant communities with the eastern states. The answer seemed to be a railroad linking the two parts of the continent.

In 1862 Congress agreed to loan hundreds of millions of dollars to two companies to construct the railroad. These companies were also given millions of acres of western land to sell in order to pay back the loan. With the help of thousands of Irish immigrant laborers, the Union Pacific Railroad was built westward from Omaha, Nebraska. At the same time, the Central Pacific was built eastward from northern California, edging (逐渐推进) over the Sierra Nevada through the efforts of Chinese workers imported for the job. In 1869 the two railroads joined at Promontory Summit, Utah. Over the next 20 years, other transcontinental railroads were built. By the 1890s a web of steel rails covered much of the West. The growth of railroads encouraged westward expansion more than any other single development.

The Significance of the Westward Movement

The westward movement is of great significance in the American history. It added more than three million square miles to the nation's territory. For many Americans, the West represented freedom, hope, and a fresh start. It has produced great wealth and has supplied enormous resources to others in the nation and the world. The westward movement helped turn the United States into a large, powerful and wealthy nation. Today the West is the most rapidly growing part of the United States. It is also one of the most ethnically diverse as people from other cultures continue to be drawn to the West. The West has become part of American folklore. Movies, television shows, books, and art have celebrated the American West.

V Civil War and Reconstruction

Brief Introduction

The American Civil War (1861 — 1865), also known as the War Between the States, was a civil war in the United States of America. Eleven Southern slave states declared their secession (脱离) from the U.S. and formed the Confederate States of America (the Confederacy,美国南部邦联). Led by Jefferson Davis, they fought against the U.S. federal government (the Union), which was supported by all the free states and the five border slave states (Delaware, Kentucky, Maryland, Missouri, and West Virginia) in the north. The Union won a decisive victory. The American Civil War was the deadliest war in American history, producing more than 970,000 casualties (3% of the population), including 620,000 soldier deaths. The war ended slavery in the United States, restored the Union, and strengthened the role of the federal government. The social, political, economic and racial issues of the war brought changes that helped make the country a united superpower.

Causes of the Civil War

➤ *Economic Factors*

In the days of the American Revolution and of the adoption of the Constitution, differences between the North and the South were small under their common interest in establishing a new nation. But in the 19th century the South and the North developed in different directions. Before the Civil War began in 1861, the South remained almost completely agricultural and was dominated by a settled plantation system based on slavery. There was very little urbanization or industrialization. Slave owners controlled politics and economics, and all of the Southern states had slave codes which defined slaves as property.

On the other hand, the North was by then firmly established as an industrial society with a large and rapidly growing urban areas and population and no slavery outside the Border States. It had a rapidly growing economy based on family farms, industry, mining, commerce and transportation. The manufacturing economy of the North demanded high tariffs to protect its own products from cheap foreign competition.

➢ *Political Factors*

As Northern and Southern patterns of living differed, their political ideas also developed marked differences. The North needed a central government to build an infrastructure of roads and railways, protect its complex trading and financial interests, and control the national currency. The South depended much less on the federal government than did other regions, and Southerners therefore felt no need to strengthen it. In addition, Southern patriots feared that a strong central government might interfere with slavery.

➢ *The Issue of Slavery*

The chief and immediate cause of the war was slavery. After the Mexican War, the dominant political issue was the spread of slavery into the western territories. The South wanted to expand slavery into the new territories. But the North opposed to this because slavery was regarded as violation of human rights as a free person. The government balanced the disagreement with the passage of *Compromise of 1850* and the *Kansas-Nebraska Act* in 1854. The *Compromise of 1850* provided a temporary respite (缓解) from sectional conflict, but the passage of *Kansas-Nebraska Act* had an extremely divisive effect on the nation and spurred the creation of the Republican Party, formed largely to keep slavery out of the western territories. Soon the Republican Party emerged as the dominant force throughout the North.

Secession

The election of Lincoln as a Republican President in 1860 resulted in the secession of seven southern states in February 1861. As an outspoken opponent of the expansion of slavery in the United States, Abraham Lincoln had long regarded slavery as an evil; therefore, the election of Lincoln as president was viewed by the South as a threat to slavery without which the South felt that they could not survive. During the campaign many Southerners had threatened that their states would secede from the Union if Lincoln was elected.

South Carolina led the way in secession in December, 1860. This was even before Lincoln took office in March 1861. Within six weeks South Carolina was followed by six other cotton-growing states: Mississippi, Florida, Georgia, Alabama, Louisiana, and Texas. The seven seceding states met in Montgomery, Alabama and formed the Confederate States of America in February 9, 1861. They chose Jefferson Davis as president and picked Richmond, Virginia, as their capital. The constitution of the Confederate States was similar to that of the United States, except the power of the central government was much more limited. Slavery was explicitly protected.

Lincoln's Position

Lincoln took the oath of office on March 4, 1861. In his inaugural address Lincoln eloquently called for the preservation of the Union. To the south he was both conciliatory and firm. He promised that he would not interfere with slavery where it already existed. But he also said that the

Union was perpetual and that secession was illegal. Lincoln hoped that the seceded states would return to the Union with time, and without force.

Fort Sumter

After Lincoln's inauguration, attention was drawn to the federal forts in the South, especially Fort Sumter in Charleston harbor. Fort Sumter was lightly garrisoned (守卫) and had provisions for only six weeks. As supplies dwindled, Lincoln informed the Confederate authorities that he was sending a ship with supplies to the fort. He promised he would not send troops without notice.

The Confederates had thousands of troops encamped around Charleston and cannons placed so that they could bomb Fort Sumter. When Lincoln's message arrived, Jefferson Davis ordered Confederate General Pierre G. T. Beauregard to demand the fort's surrender. When the commander of the fort refused, Confederate shore cannons began firing at the fort on April 12. The American Civil War had begun. In the spring of 1861, each side expected a brief war and an early victory. Few people foresaw that four years of bloody struggle lay ahead. The Union would survive, and slavery issue would be settled, but at great cost.

Civil War

The attack on Fort Sumter outraged people in the North. President Lincoln issues a Proclamation calling for 75,000 militiamen, and summoning a special session of Congress for July 4. On April 19, 1861, he ordered a blockade against Southern ports.

Left: Union general holding US flag
Right: Confederate general holding Confederate battle flag

The South, regarding this as declaration of war, also called for volunteers to fight. At this point, four more slave states — Virginia, Arkansas, Tennessee, and North Carolina — seceded from the Union, thus forming an eleven state Confederacy with a population of 9 million, including nearly 4 million slaves. The Union will soon have 21 states and a population of over 20 million.

➢ *North versus South*

The war aims of both sides were simple. The goal of the South was to defend independence. The goal of the North was to restore the Union by force. Although neither side was prepared for war, each was confident of its military superiority.

The confidence of the North lied in the knowledge of its advantages in human and material resources. The North, with its larger population, better transportation system, and more productive economy, had advantages that outweighed the South's superior military leadership during the war.

The South had a stronger military tradition, and many of the nation's outstanding military leaders were southerners. In addition, the South had the popular support of the southern people in their quest for independence. More importantly, they had the advantage of being able to fight a defensive war on familiar home ground, and, therefore, their lines of communication and supply would be shorter. Another advantage of the South was that it had the sympathy of many Europeans.

Comparison of Union and CSA*		
	Union	**CSA**
Total population	22,100,000 (71%)	9,100,000 (29%)
Free population	21,700,000	5,600,000
Soldiers	2,100,000 (67%)	1,064,000 (33%)
Railroad miles	21,788 (71%)	8,838 (29%)
Manufactured items	90%	10%
Firearm production	97%	3%
Bales (大包) of cotton in 1860	Negligible (微不足道的)	4,500,000
Pre-war U.S. exports	30%	70%

* The table shows the relative advantage of the Union over the Confederate States of America (CSA) at the start of the war.

➢ *The war*

The South's strategy was to fight a defensive war, whereas the North, on the other hand, had to invade Confederate territory and subdued the South completely. At the outset of the Civil War, neither side possessed the material nor manpower required for what would prove to be the first modern industrialized war. The North at least had a navy and the Union's naval superiority was a significant factor contributing to the defeat of confederate forces.

In the early stage of the war, the Union forces were successful in the west, but the Confederate forces held out (坚决顶住) against Union attacks in the East. Confederate General Robert E. Lee's first invasion of the North was repulsed (击退) at the strategic battle of Antietam[①] in September 1862.

➢ *The Emancipation Proclamation*

The Union victory at Antietam gave Lincoln an opportunity to expand the meaning of the war and to make the announcement of freeing the slaves. He issued *the Emancipation Proclamation* on January 1, 1863. The proclamation declared that "all persons held as slaves" within the rebellious states "are, and henceforward shall be free." It also authorized the enlistment of blacks "into the Union army."

The Proclamation had two effects that were beneficial to the Union's war effort. First, it weakened the South and encouraged 190,000 African Americans to join the Union Army. Second, it had positive effect on diplomacy and caused a swing of European public opinion towards the Union cause, and the possibility of European aid to the South became more remote.

The Emancipation Proclamation also had a great long-range effect. It reflected a shift in the war objectives of the North — reuniting the nation was no longer the only goal, and represented a major step toward the ultimate abolition of slavery in the United States and a "new birth of freedom." It gave a high moral purpose to the struggle and strengthened the Union both militarily and politically. As a milestone along the road to slavery's final destruction, *the Emancipation Proclamation* has taken a place among the great documents of human freedom and it led to 13th amendment to the Constitution, which abolished slavery throughout the nation.

---

① 安提坦：美国马里兰州中北部的一条小河，注入波托马克河。1862年9月17日在其沿岸进了残酷而未分胜败的安提坦战役，南方人称之为夏普斯堡战役（Battle of Sharpsburg）。这是整个南北战争中最为血腥的"一日战役"，是一次决定性战役。在这场鏖战中，南军伤亡9,000至1万人，北军伤亡约1.2万人。该战役之后，诞生了林肯的废奴宣言。

Gettysburg

The Battle of Gettysburg was one of the most critical battles of the Civil War and the Union victory in July of 1863 ended the South's last chance for military victory. The cost of the battle was high — the North had 23,000 casualties and the South, 28,000. No more men fought and died in any other battle before or since on the land of North America. The battle ended Confederate hopes of formal recognition by foreign governments. The tide of war began to turn against the South.

President Lincoln dedicated a portion of the Gettysburg battlefield as a national cemetery, and delivered "Gettysburg Address" on November 19, 1863 to the throng of fifteen thousand for two minutes. The short speech has come to be regarded as the best remembered speech of the Civil War and one of the best speeches in American history.

Final Victory

In March 1864 Lincoln made Ulysses S. Grant commander of all the Union armies. The President had finally found military genius to match Lee. Under Ulysses S. Grant, the Union armies used tactics of attrition (消耗) and total war to deplete Confederate forces. Lee's army surrendered to Grant at Appomattox, Virginia on April 9, 1865 and within a few weeks, the remaining southern armies also laid down their arms. Jefferson Davis was captured. The war was over.

Reconstruction

The Civil War left the South physically and economically devastated. The nation faced the huge task of "reconstructing" and reuniting a war-ravaged South. During the Reconstruction era, from 1865 to 1877, there was a sharp disagreement among northerners on how to handle the problem of southern reconstruction. Some northerners wanted the former Confederate states returned to the Union with little or no changes in their social, political, and economic life. Others called for former Confederate political and military leaders to be imprisoned or executed and the South rebuilt in the image of the rest of the nation.

Lincoln developed a plan that was designed to restore the old relationship between North and South. Congress opposed Lincoln's plan as too lenient (宽容的) and developed its own plan for reconstruction.

After Lincoln's assassination, the task of presidential reconstruction then fell to Lincoln's Vice President Andrew Johnson, who put into effect a reconstruction program that was intended to help the common people of the South and exclude the planter aristocracy from government. For Johnson, the common people were the white small farmers who cultivated their own lands, not the freedmen. Under Johnson's plan, ex-Confederates quickly regained control of the south and passed laws known as the Black Codes that severely limited the rights of blacks.

Alarmed by conditions in the South, Radical Republicans in Congress passed their own reconstruction acts. The Radicals' reconstruction program led to the control of southern states by a coalition of southern Unionists (美内战时期的合众国拥护者), blacks, and northerners who had moved south.

Johnson's opposition to the Radicals' program resulted in his impeachment.

Southern whites were bitterly opposed to Radical regimes (政权), and they sometimes resorted to violence in an effort to overthrow the Republicans. By 1877 the southern states were back under the control of the southern whites. With the Southern Democrats again in power, blacks suffered a loss of their political rights.

VI America in the First World War

In 1914 the United States found itself in the midst of a European crisis. World War I broke out in Europe with the Allied Powers of Great Britain, France, and Russia facing the central powers of Germany and Austria-Hungary. Over the next few years the war involved 28 countries including the United States. Although the principal campaigns were fought in Europe, armies also fought in the Middle East, Africa, and China, and navies clashed on all the oceans. The direct cause of the World War I was the assassination of Archduke Francis Ferdinand, heir to the throne of Austria-Hungary, on June 28, 1914.

expeditionary force (远征军) nicknamed the dough boys because of the white belts they wore which they cleaned with pipe clay (白黏土) or dough

When the war broke out, most Americans wanted no part of a European war and the U.S. government adopted neutral policy. American neutral policy was aimed at making a profit, for it enabled America to continue its trade with the warring countries.

Many factors contributed to America's final entry into the War. In May 1915, a German submarine sank the British luxury liner *Lusitania* and killed 128 American passengers. Then German submarines sank five American merchant ships bound for or leaving Allied seaports. The Germany foreign minister promised to help Mexico to recover the territory it lost during the war with America in 1848. In addition, American business men feared that German winning of the war would make them suffer a big loss because they sold their products to Britain and France and provided large loans to the English government to finance the War. All these factors made America to support Britain and helped to draw the United States into the First World War. In April 1917, President Wilson asked Congress for a declaration of war against the Central Powers. He explained America's entry into war as a right to preserve democracy and freedom and hoped by going to war America could influence the peace and reshape international relations in conformity with his idealistic, progressive principles.

The first U.S. troops, designated as the Allied Expeditionary Force (AEF), reached France in October 1917. Eventually, the total number of US combatants (作战者) in WWI reached more than 2 million. America's economic might and fresh troops soon turned the tide of battle. The successful Meuse-Argonne offensive (默兹-阿尔贡战役)[①] ended the war. On November 11, 1918, Germany surrendered and an armistice based on allied demands was signed by both sides.

The war had caused terrible destruction and death. More than 125,000 American lives were lost during the brief period the United States was engaged militarily in the war.

---

① 默兹-阿尔贡战役：1918年9月26日至11月11日由美国发起的一场进攻。是美军在第一次世界大战中参加的最大一次战役。100多万美军由英军和法军在两翼配合，进行了7个星期的战斗，共打败德军47个师，俘获德军2.6万人，缴获大炮和机枪共4,000件。美军伤亡11.7万人。11月11日达成停战协议时，美军已推进到色当，切断了德军与外界的一切联系。

At a peace conference in Paris, 27 countries took part in drawing up the *Treaty of Versailles*, which imposed harsh measures against Germany and included an agreement to form a League of Nations. The U.S. Senate never ratified this treaty and the U.S. did not join the League, despite President Woodrow Wilson's active campaigning in support of the League. The United States negotiated a separate peace with Germany, finalized in August 1921.

Yanks (美国兵) & Tommies (英国兵) waving American, British & French flags during Armistice celebration, at end of WWI.
Date taken: November 1918

In the aftermath of the war, the political, cultural, and social order of the world was drastically changed in many places. Four empires disappeared: the German, Austro-Hungarian, Ottoman, and Russian. The map of Europe was redrawn, with several independent nations restored or created, and Germany's colonies were parceled out among the victors.

VII Great Depression and New Deal

The Great Depression

Although Americans enjoyed prosperity during the 1920's, the nation's economy was slowing down as a result of overproduction, reduced purchasing power, and government policies on taxes and tariffs (政府向进出口商品所征收的关税). The weakened economy could not sustain the stock market boom. In the fall of 1929 the market crashed, wiping out the fortunes of many Americans. The crash ushered in the Great Depression of the 1930's — the worst and longest economic decline in the history of the United States, lasting from the end of 1929 until the early 1940's.

Unemployment, low wages, and the collapse of farm prices resulted hard times for millions of Americans. Countless factories got bankrupt and closed down. Many farmers lost their farms. A large number of unemployed workers wandered all over the country looking for jobs. Families not able to pay their rent or mortgage were driven out of their homes. Desperate for shelter, homeless citizens built shantytowns in and around cities across the nation. These camps came to be called Hoovervilles, after the country's 31st president, Herbert Hoover, who believed that self-reliance and self-help, not government intervention, were the best means to meet citizens' needs.

President Roosevelt and His "New Deal"

President Hoover, following his personal and political beliefs concerning the role of government, took limited steps to improve the nation's economy. In 1932 the American people elected a new President, Democrat Franklin D. Roosevelt (1882 — 1945), who promised action to help victims of the Great Depression. President Roosevelt set to work immediately after taking office. Declaring in his inaugural speech that "the only thing we have to fear is fear itself," Roosevelt quickly lifted the nation's spirits. He attacked the Great Depression and presented an unprecedented number of new government programs known as the New Deal, which aimed to restore the nation's economy and the faith of the American people by reducing unemployment, assisting businesses and agriculture, regulating banking and the stock market, and providing security for the needy, elderly, and disabled. Under the New Deal, the federal government became involved in direct public relief for the first time.

The Lasting Impact of the New Deal

The New Deal had a strong influence on American life and culture. It was based on the concept that the government was responsible for the healthy development of national economy and social security, and that the growth of production could be maintained only if the great body of the consumers could continue to purchase its output. During the years of the New Deal, the size of the federal government grew at a rapid rate and government interference in the nation's economic life increased dramatically. The economy became fixed to government regulation and control. As a result of Roosevelt's New Deal, the responsibilities of the federal government for economic and social welfare increased to new level. Today, America would not be what it is without the efforts and legacy of the New Deal.

VIII America in the Second World War

Introduction

World War II, which lasted from 1939 to 1945, was a global military conflict which involved more than 100 million people from over 30 countries. The great powers were organized into two opposing military alliances: the Allies (同盟国) and the Axis (轴心国). The war fought in the Soviet Union, North Africa and the Mediterranean, Western Europe and the Far East. Marked by mass deaths of civilians and the strategic bombing of industrial and population centers, it resulted in an estimated 50 million to 85 million fatalities. These made World War II the most widespread and devastating war in human history.

Causes of the War

➢ *The Failure of Peace Efforts*

During the 1920's, attempts were made to achieve a stable peace. The establishment of the League of Nations in 1920 was the first action intended for this goal. But it turned out to be a failure. During the 1930's, Britain and France followed the Appeasement policy (绥靖政策).They were not ready to help the League take decisive measures to prevent the expansion of Germany and Italy, and the League failed to foster a sense of co-operation among the member states, so Germany and Italy became more aggressive. They defied (蔑视) the League.

➢ The Rise of Fascism

During the first twenty years of the twentieth century, there were frequent riots and strikes in Italy. The state of affairs gave Benito Mussolini the opportunity to rise to power. In 1919, Mussolini founded the fascist Party in Milan, Italy. After the Fascists had marched on Rome in October 1922, King Victor Emmanuel III named Mussolini prime minister. In the following four years, Mussolini established the first Fascist dictatorship by destroying civil liberties, outlawing all other political parties, and imposing a totalitarian (极权主义的) regime on the country by means of terror.

➢ Hitler as a Dictator

Throughout the early 1920's, Germany was trapped in a series of troubles, such as high unemployment, inflation, and political turmoil. Extremist groups and political parties often used violent actions to compete for the control of the country. One of these groups was Adolf Hitler's National Socialist German Workers' Party (国家社会主义德意志劳工党), or Nazi party founded in 1918. Hitler joined the party in 1919 and soon became prominent by his eloquent emotion-arousing oration (演讲). He designed the Nazi program, which held that only true Germans were a "master race."

In 1933 Hitler was appointed chancellor and soon demanded and received absolute power from the legislature. He withdrew Germany from the League of Nations immediately after he gained the power. He also undertook large-scale rearmament (重整军备) and began to demand more territory. He annexed Austria in March 1938 with the support of Mussolini and benefited from the Appeasement policy of Britain and France. The United States at that time took the neutral position, refusing to provide any material assistance to all parties in foreign conflicts.

➢ Formation of the Axis Coalition

In October, 1935, Mussolini invaded Ethiopia (埃塞俄比亚) with German's full support. Totalitarianism also emerged in Japan which proclaimed the puppet (傀儡) state of Manchukuo in northeast China in 1932 and occupied the main Chinese ports in 1937 — 1938.

Treaties between Germany, Italy, and Japan from 1936 to 1940 brought about the formation of Rome-Berlin-Tokyo Axis. The Axis thereafter became the collective term for those countries and their allies.

On September 1, 1939, Hitler invaded Poland. Britain and France declared war on Germany two days later. World War II broke out.

The United States at War

At the beginning of World War II, the United States was determined not to be involved in the war. However, with the fall of France and the air war against Britain in 1940, public sentiment increasingly favored the Allied powers that opposed German expansion.

On the morning of December 7, Japanese carrier-based (从航空母舰上起飞的) planes launched a devastating, surprise attack to the U.S. Pacific fleet at Pearl Harbor, Hawaii. Nineteen ships, including five

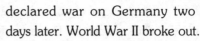

The Big Three: Franklin D. Roosevelt, Stalin, and Churchill in Teheran, Iran (November 29, 1943).

battleships, and about 150 U.S. planes were destroyed; more than 2,300 soldiers, sailors and civilians were killed. On December 8, U.S. Congress declared a state of war with Japan; three days later Germany and Italy declared war on the United States.

Countries and organizations that opposed to the Axis powers formed the Allies of World War II. The leaders of the United Kingdom, Soviet Union and the United States were known as "The Big Three." On November 28 at Tehran (德黑兰，伊朗首都和最大城市), Roosevelt, Churchill and Joseph Stalin agreed to establish a new international organization, the United Nations.

➢ *The Normandy Landing*

Under the command of General Eisenhower, the first contingents (队伍) of Allied Expeditionary Force (AEF), including U.S., British and Canadian troops, landed on the beaches of Normandy (诺曼底) in northern France on June 6, 1944. The day was named D-Day[①], the term used for the day of actual landing.

The landing，which took place along a 80-kilometer stretch of the Normandy coast, was the largest amphibious (两栖作战的) operation in history, involving 175,000 troops landing on D-Day, 195,700 Allied naval and merchant navy personnel in over 5,000 ships. The subsequent battle of Normandy involved over a million men from America, Canada, Britain, France, Poland, and Germany. The Allied armies continued to move across France toward Germany and helped seal (决定) the fate of Hitler's. On August 25 Paris was liberated.

➢ *Japan Surrender*

In the central Pacific Ocean, the Battle of Midway[②] became the turning point for the Allies, resulting in the first major defeat of the Japanese navy, ending the Japanese advance across the central Pacific.

➢ *The Yalta Conference*

In February 1945, the leaders of the three Great Powers — the Soviet Union, the United States of America and Great Britain — met at Yalta[③] in the southern Soviet Union, Out of this meeting came *the Yalta Agreement*, in which they have agreed that in two or three months after Germany has surrendered and the war in Europe has terminated, the Soviet Union shall enter into the war against Japan on the side of the Allies.

The postwar status of Germany was also settled at Yalta. Germany was to be divided into four zones of occupation by the three countries and France, as was the city of Berlin.

It was decided to ask China and France to join in sponsoring a conference to found the United Nations.

➢ *The Atomic bomb*

From July 17, to August 2, 1945, the Allied leaders (Stalin, Truman, and Churchill) met at Potsdam, a suburb outside Berlin, to discuss operations against Japan, the peace settlement in

---

① D-DAY为预定进攻发起日，是美军常用军事术语。此处指第二次世界大战中盟军在法国北部诺曼底海滩对德发起进攻日(1944年6月6日)。

② 中途岛：面积4.7平方千米，距美国旧金山和日本横滨均为2,800海里，处于亚洲和北美之间的太平洋航线的中途，故名中途岛。中途岛海战是第二次世界大战的一场重要战役。这是一次航母战斗群对航母战斗群的战争，也是美国海军以少胜多的一个著名战例。战役于1942年6月4日展开，美国海军不仅成功地击退了日本海军对中途岛环礁的攻击，还得到了太平洋战区的主动权，因此成为第二次世界大战太平洋战区的转折点。

③ 雅尔塔：苏联西南欧部分一城市，位于黑海沿岸，是1945年2月同盟国会议的会址。

Europe, and a policy for the future of Germany. They issued *the Potsdam Declaration*① on July 26, in which Japan was urged to surrender immediately. Still, Japan refused to heed (听从) the warning. As a result, on August 6, U.S. dropped an atomic bomb on the city of Hiroshima (广岛,日本本州岛西南部一城市), a center of the Japanese munitions industry. The bomb destroyed three-quarters of the city and killed or injured more than 160,000 persons. The Japanese, however, still did not surrender. Therefore, a second atomic bomb was dropped on August 9 — this time on the city and naval base of Nagasaki (长崎,日本九州岛西部一城市).

Meanwhile, on August 8, the Soviet Union declared war on Japan.

On August 14, the Japanese government agreed to unconditional surrender. On September 2, 1945 the Japanese premier and military leaders signed the formal surrender on board the U.S. battleship Missouri, in Tokyo Bay.

Mushroom Cloud from Atomic Bomb

Japanese Foreign Minister Mamoru Shigemitsu signs the final documents for the surrender of Japan on September 2, 1945 aboard the USS Missouri.

The United Nations

One of the most far-reaching decisions concerning the shape of the postwar world took place on April 25, 1945. As planned at Yalta, the Representatives of 50 nations met in San Francisco, California, to discuss the framework of the United Nations. The constitution which they drafted outlined a world organization in which international differences could be discussed peacefully. In contrast to its rejection of U.S. membership in the League of Nations after World War I, the U.S. Senate promptly ratified the U.N. This marked a turn away from the traditional isolationism and toward more international involvement. It also signaled to the world that the United States intended to play a major role in international affairs.

United Nations formally came into being on October 24, 1945, a date celebrated every year as United Nations Day.

Effect of World War II

Lasting six years, World War II involved a majority of countries all over the world and caused

---

① 1945年7月17日,苏、美、英三国首脑在柏林近郊波茨坦举行会议,会议期间发表对日最后通牒式公告,全称《中美英三国促令日本投降之波茨坦公告》。这篇公告的主要内容是声明三国在战胜纳粹德国后一起致力于战胜日本以及履行《开罗宣言》等对战后日本的处理方式的决定。

millions of people to suffer, costing 55 million lives and material damage of some 3 billion dollars. It was a war that was more cruel, bitter and extensive than any other wars in history.

After World War II the United States and the Soviet Union became the two leading world powers. They set the stage for the Cold War, which lasted for the next 46 years.

The economy of the United States benefits greatly from World War II. The depression was brought to an end, and new industrial complexes were built all over the United States. After 4 years of military buildup, the U.S. had also become the leading military power in the world.

IX Cold War

At the end of World War II, the United States emerged as the most powerful nation in the world. However, it soon faced a growing challenge from its wartime ally, the Soviet Union. Differences in ideology and policy pulled the two countries apart and eventually led to a struggle between them known as the Cold War (1945 — 1991), so called as there was no bloody "hot war" between the two sides. Each nation sought world influence by means short of total war, such as the threat of force, propaganda, espionage (间谍活动), nuclear arms race, extensive aid to weaker nations, and economic and technological competitions, such as the Space Race.

The Soviet Union created the Eastern Bloc (集团), the former Communist states of Eastern and Central Europe, including the member states of the Warsaw Pact (华沙条约组织, 1955 — 1991): Poland, East Germany, Czechoslovakia, Hungary, Romania, Bulgaria, along with Yugoslavia (南斯拉夫) and Albania, which were not aligned with the Soviet Union after 1948 and 1960 respectively.

The U.S. and some western European countries established containment (牵制政策) of communism as a defensive policy, establishing alliances (e.g. NATO, 1949) to that end. Several such countries also coordinated the rebuilding of Western Europe, especially western Germany, which the USSR opposed.

The Cold War featured periods of relative calm and of international high tension — the Berlin Blockade (1948 — 1949), the Korean War (1950 — 1953), the Berlin Crisis of 1961, the Vietnam War (1959 — 1975), the Cuban Missile Crisis (1962), the Soviet War in Afghanistan (1979 — 1989), and the Able Archer 83 NATO exercises[①] in November 1983. Both sides sought détente (国际关系的缓和) to relieve political tensions and deter (阻止) direct military attack.

The early 1980's witnessed a final period of friction between the United States and the USSR. In 1980, Ronald Reagan became the U.S. president and he set about strengthening American military capabilities.

---

① "神射手"1983演习是一期持续10天的北约模拟核战争演练，它被看作是北约核战争的预演，始于1983年11月2日，由北约设立在比利时卡斯提乌的欧洲盟军最高指挥中心直接指挥，其模拟的是北约与华约从常规冲突到有限核冲突最终发展为全面核战争的情况。当时苏联担心会遭受美国及其北约盟国的突然核打击，很多人主张对西欧美军和核导弹"潘兴2"的部署地点进行先发制人的打击。在冷战中，除了1962年的古巴危机，这是最危险的一次美苏核对峙。

In the mid-1980's Mikhail Gorbachev came to power in the USSR. He brought a revolution to Soviet foreign policy, seeking new and far-reaching agreements with the West. From 1985, Gorbachev and Reagan held a series of summit talks, and in 1987 the two leaders agreed to eliminate a whole class of their countries' nuclear missiles. The USSR agreed to reduce its forces in Eastern Europe, and in 1989 it pulled its troops out of Afghanistan. That year the Berlin wall that had divided East and West Germany since 1961 was torn down. In 1991 the USSR dissolved, and Russia and the other Soviet republics emerged as independent states. This led to the end of the Cold War period.

X American Society in Transition

American society from 1950's to 1970's witnessed rapid social change ranging from civil rights movements by women and minorities to countercultural movement by young generation. From 1970's the Middle Americans advocated a return to the traditional system and its norms.

Civil Rights Movement

Beginning in the mid-1950's, race relations and civil rights dominated domestic events. For the first time, black Americans in large numbers began to organize and struggle for their rights.

On December 3, 1955, the blacks of Montgomery, Alabama, began a boycott of the city's segregated bus system. A few days earlier, a 43-year-old seamstress (女裁缝) named Rosa Parks had refused to give up her bus seat to a white man. She was arrested and fined for breaking a law that required segregation on city buses. The black community was outraged at the arrest and planned the boycott. Martin Luther King, Jr., a young Baptist minister, was chosen to lead it. He asked the blacks of Montgomery to avoid violence and to practice civil disobedience. The black community supported King for an entire year by refusing to ride city buses. Finally, in December 1956, the Supreme Court ruled that the Montgomery bus segregation law was unconstitutional and Montgomery integrated (使取消种族隔离) its buses.

Because of the bus boycott, Martin Luther King, Jr. became a nationally-known figure. He soon formed the Southern Christian Leadership Conference (SCLC) to press for civil rights through peaceful means. During the winter of 1959 and 1960, civil rights groups held marches, demonstrations, and boycotts to end segregation in public places. They employed a tactic known as "sit-in" to integrate public places.

By 1960 the crusade for civil rights had become a national movement. In 1963, more than 200,000 people — both white and black — marched in Washington, D.C. to demonstrate their commitment to equality for all. The highlight of that event was a speech "I Have a Dream" by Martin Luther King Jr., who had emerged as the preeminent (杰出的) spokesman for civil rights.

The Women's Liberation Movement

American women were also involved in the struggle for equality in the 1960's. Their struggle became known as the women's liberation movement. One of the chief objectives of this movement was to eliminate discrimination in employment. Another goal publicly financed day-care centers for the children of working mothers.

The Civil Rights Act of 1964 is a landmark of civil rights and U.S. labor law in the United

States that prohibited discrimination on the bases of sex as well as race, color, religion and national origin. Some activists pressed for ratification of an Equal Rights Amendment (ERA) to the Constitution and it was passed by Congress in 1972. The courts also promoted sexual equality. In 1973 the Supreme Court sanctioned (准许) women's right to abortion (人工流产) during the early months of pregnancy — a significant victory for the women's movement.

Counterculture — the Youth Protest

Within the civil rights, feminist, and gay rights movements, young college-age adults were among the loudest and most militant calling for change. Many young people began to question the country's long-standing basic ethic of hard work, respectability, and competition for material success. Because there were so many youths, they and their opinions had an influence they had never had before.

Early in the 1960's, a generation gap developed between many older and younger Americans. The young condemned what they called the hypocrisy (虚伪) of the older generation, which meant anyone over the age of 30. They thought the older generation was too materialistic, too obsessed (迷恋) with power and wealth, and too addicted to violence. Many young people rebelled against authority and discipline of any kind. These youths formed their own culture.

By the late 1960's the generation gap had widened and spread, especially in the cities and on college campuses as the baby boomers were heading off to college in record numbers. Many students began to question the goals of education, the role of the university, and the rights of students. They complained that education seemed sterile (无生气的，缺乏创造力的) — an assembly line producing standardized products, not a crucible (熔炉) of ideas creating independent, thinking individuals. They wanted to play a greater part in running schools and demanded more concern for the individual, more freedom of expression, and a more flexible curriculum. Some activists urged that the campus should be a haven for free thought and a place for efforts to change society significantly. The term **youth culture**, which referred to the way adolescents lived, no longer seemed comprehensive enough. It was replaced with the term **counterculture**, which covered everything about the young from their clothes and hair styles to their views on life, sex, and politics. The counterculture, basically a revolt against American affluence and technology, became a special feature of the 1960's. It put emphasis on the individual, and it made personal commitment and freedom to "do your own thing" its major goal.

➢ *Hippies*

Perhaps the most colorful and best-known advocates of the counterculture and its ideals were the hippies who are interested in the new and unconventional. They all professed to be anti-violence. Seeking a life of peace, love, and self-awareness, hippies tried to distance themselves from traditional society.

Like the beatniks[①], the hippies rejected conformity and were interested in self-exploration, mysticism (神秘主义), and drugs. In the 1960's, they took "Make love, not war" as their slogan; their style of dress and grooming (装束) greatly influenced young Americans. Hippie fashions and values had a major effect on culture, influencing popular music, television, film, literature, and the arts.

---

① "垮掉的一代"：20世纪50年代后期出现的一群摈弃传统生活、着装和行为方式的年轻人，后来叫做"披头族"。

➢ Drugs

Another aspect of the counterculture was drugs. Many young people saw drugs as the means to truth and road to pleasure. Using drugs offered another way to be free of the older generation's value and to express their new religion of love and freedom. At least half the college students in the late 1960's tried marijuana (大麻). A more dangerous drug also became popular with some members of the counterculture: LSD (摇头丸，非法的强致幻药物). Drugs proved to be destructive and deadly, contributing to the deaths of several counterculture figures.

➢ Philosophy of free love

Another realm of traditional American values the counterculture overturned was sex. Some young people shocked their parents and society by questioning the values that placed restrictions on sexual activities. New openness about sexuality and relaxation of the stigma on extramarital (婚外的) sex turned out to be significant legacies of the 1960's, but the philosophy of free love also had a negative side as increased sexual activity contributed to a rapid rise in cases of sexually transmitted diseases. The notion of free love also exposed women to increased sexual assault as some men assumed that all "liberated" women desired sexual relations.

➢ Lasting Effects

Despite its transience (短暂) and its excesses, the counterculture had some lasting effects on American society. It led many people of all generations to examine their beliefs and commitments. Some of the values of the counterculture, such as the emphasis on personal relationships and on spiritual rather than material progress, had a strong influence on the establishment culture. Some of the counterculture's goals, such as peace and saving the environment, became more acceptable to society in general. Unfortunately, some of the worst features of the counterculture — particularly the use of drugs — also spread to other parts of society.

XI Social Issues in the New Age

The major social issues include:

➢ Unequal Distribution of Wealth

Privatization (私有化) is increasing in America which provides opportunities only to those who can afford. The efforts of socialists to distribute wealth equally are opposed by the ruling government. Due to this, rich people are becoming richer and poor becoming poorer.

➢ Poverty

It is shocking but true. Around 13% — 17% American population lives below the federal poverty line[①]. And this number is increasing at an alarming rate.

---

① 美国贫困线标准是美国健康与人类服务部发表的衡量美国人贫困水平的标准，依据家庭人数和所在州所决定，主要供政府用来决定什么人符合某些政府福利项目。此贫困线标准每年年初由该部根据上一年的贫困水平得出新一年的贫困线标准并在联邦注册上发表。美国大陆相连接的48个州和首都华盛顿为一个标准，阿拉斯加和夏威夷分别有自己的标准。

2017 POVERTY GUIDELINES FOR THE 48 CONTIGUOUS STATES AND THE DISTRICT OF COLUMBIA	
PERSONS IN FAMILY/HOUSEHOLD	POVERTY GUIDELINE
For families/households with more than 8 persons, add $4,180 for each additional person.	
1	$12,060
2	$16,240
3	$20,420
4	$24,600
5	$28,780
6	$32,960
7	$37,140
8	$41,320

➢ *Unequal Educational Funding*

The U.S. government provides compulsory education for first 12 years. This education system is controlled by state government and a very little portion of control is held by local government, which determines the funding and school system of each municipality. Large numbers of childbearing families from affluent communities seem to be funded heavily compared to less affluent and fewer childbearing families. The problem of "school dropouts" is also increasing due to poor school condition and services.

➢ *Crime and Incarceration (监禁)*

Due to increased unequal opportunities, the crime rate is also increasing. Prison population is growing every day. Most of the prisoners are drug offenders who use or sell recreational drugs. Incarceration of criminals for long sentences has led to incarceration for life after three felonies (重罪).

➢ *Health Issues*

Moreover, the United States does not provide health care to all. It does not have a socialized medicine or public health care system. Only employed people get health insurance as employee benefit but unemployed, part-time, and self-employed workers have to pay for their own insurance which is very expensive. Some studies have shown that medical bills are one of the major causes of declaring bankruptcy in the United States.

➢ *Police Brutality Against the Colored People*

On 25 May 2020, George Floyd, an unarmed black man, died after being arrested by the police. A video of his arrest shocked the world — he was killed horrifically by an officer kneeling on his neck for nine minutes as he pleaded for breath. This terrible case sickened the world, and triggered mass protests to stop racism and police brutality against the African Americans.

A campaign called Black Lives Matter got the support of more people in the aftermath of the death of George Floyd. The movement was born in 2013, after the man who shot and killed an unarmed black teenager, Trayvon Martin, was cleared of his murder. Some studies have found that in the United States, black residents of low-income neighborhoods are more likely to be stopped and searched by police officers, even if statistically white residents are more likely to be caught carrying guns and drugs. Racism and police brutality are still systematic problems in the U.S.

➢ *Failure on Pandemic Response*

Since December 2019, many countries in the world began to experience the outbreak of

COVID-19 pandemic, caused by a new strain of coronavirus that has not been previously identified in humans. The U.S. detected its first known COVID-19 patient on Jan. 20, 2020. Instead of taking effective measures, Donald Trump administration first downplayed the pandemic and then sent mixed messages to the public, resulting in by far the highest case and death count globally. As of July 2, 2021, there were 33,679,482 confirmed cases and 605,019 deaths of covid-19 in the U.S.

It can be found that the U.S. policy to counter the pandemic was nothing but a patchwork of responses by state and local governments, divided sharply along partisan lines. COVID-19 has weakened the U.S. and exposed the systemic fractures in the country, as well as the gulf between what this nation promises its citizens and what it actually delivers.

➤ *Increasing Cost of Living*

With growing inflation, the cost of living in the United States is also increasing significantly. But the minimum wage is not increasing in the same fashion and so, many people find it difficult to fulfill their daily basic requirements. The working population makes more money and again spends more on living which hardly leaves anything behind for savings. America has the lowest saving rate compared with any other developed countries.

Apart from these, there are many other social issues in the United States that need immediate attention, such as alcohol abuse, divorce and child support, domestic violence, dating disorders, food safety and drug safety, public health care reform, illegal immigration, juvenile crime justice, copyright and intellectual property rights, child abuse, HIV/AIDS and so on.

Chapter 3 Political System

章节导读

本章分为五节，分别介绍了美国的政治体制，包括美国宪法、三权分立与权力制衡、代议制、联邦制、两党制、总统制等项内容。

The United States was created after the bloody War of Independence against the British rule on the basis of 13 colonies, each having its own powers and traditions. So the founding fathers of this new nation tried to design a political system which was different from the British monarchical system and achieved a "Great Compromise" of the interests of the individual states. The United States is now an indirect democracy — that is, the people rule through the representatives they elect. In the beginning, only white men with property could vote. Over time, the vote has been given to more and more people. Today any citizen who is over 18 years old can vote. It is a federal republic in which the president, Congress, and courts share powers of the federal government and the federal government shares sovereignty with the state governments.

I The Constitution

The Constitution of the United States has been the fundamental law of the United States for more than 200 years. Of all the written national constitutions in the world, the United States Constitution is the oldest that is still in operation.

Birth of the Constitution

The peace treaty of 1783 recognized the Independence of the United States and the former 13 British colonies along the east coast of the Atlantic became 13 states of the new nation. Although the Declaration of Independence proclaimed that the 13 united colonies were free and independent states, they were not very clear about the future political system of the U.S. and the relationships between the states and the government of the new nation. A constitution was badly needed.

Then in 1787, four years after America won its independence from Great Britain, the United States Constitution was written. As drafted by its framers at the Constitutional Convention in Philadelphia, the Constitution establishes the framework for the Federal Government and guarantees rights, freedom and justice to all. It was sent to the Congress of Confederation for approval and then sent to the states for ratification (批准). In 1788, after nine states ratified it, the Constitution became the law of the land. By May 29, 1790 all 13 states had ratified the Constitution.

Before the ratification of the Constitution, the states were governed under the **Articles** of Confederation (邦联条例), which served as a constitution. Under the articles, the central government was much weaker than the state governments. The men who drafted the Constitution favored a stronger central government and recognized the United States as a government of the people, not of the states.

Contents of the 1787 Constitution

The Constitution drafted in 1787 consists of seven articles. The first three define the powers of the U.S. Congress, President, and federal courts and Article Four deals with the relations between states and the federal government. Under the Constitution, each state has its own government. There is also a federal government for the whole country. The Constitution states what powers each one has. Article Five lays out the process for amending the constitution. Article Six establishes the Constitution to be the supreme law of the land. Article Seven describes the process for setting up the new government.

A system called "**separation of powers**" was established by the Constitution, which is meant to prevent any of the three branches from having too much power. Under this system, power is spread between three branches of the state: the executive (President & Cabinet), the legislature (House of Representatives & Senate) and the judiciary (Supreme Court & federal circuits). No one branch has too much power. An individual can only be a member of one branch.

This system is also called **checks and balances** (制衡). Each branch has authority of its own and certain controls over the other branches. For example, Congress makes the laws, but the President can veto (否决) a law, and the Supreme Court can decide that the law is unconstitutional, while the Congress can remove the President from office in exceptional circumstances.

Federalism (联邦制) is also the key content of the Constitution. It means that there are individual states, each with its own government, and there is a federal, or national, government. The U.S. Constitution gives certain powers to the federal government, other powers to the state governments, and yet other powers to both. For example, only the national government can print money; the states establish their own school systems; and both the national and the state governments can collect taxes.

The ultimate strength of the U.S. Constitution is that it not only establishes a government, but it establishes a government which, to use Thomas Jefferson's words, can "govern itself." The Constitution plays a role in virtually every aspect of life in the United States.

Changes to the Constitution

In the 200 years of its history, the United States has greatly grown and changed. Yet the Constitution works as well today as when it was written. One reason is that the Constitution can be changed. Each change is called an amendment (修正案). It involves a complicated process. The Congress generally suggests amendments, though states can suggest them, too. Two-thirds of The Congress must approve an amendment. After that, three-fourths of the states must say yes to it. Only then is an amendment added to the Constitution. The Constitution now has 27 amendments, of which only 25 are active and new ones may still be added. For example, the Thirteenth Amendment abolished slavery, the Fourteenth Amendment defined citizenship, the Fifteenth Amendment gave black Americans the right to vote and the Nineteenth Amendment gave women the right to vote.

Another reason is that the Constitution is flexible: its basic principles can be applied and interpreted differently at different times. The Supreme Court determines what the Constitution means. It tends to interpret the Constitution in a dynamic way and take into account the need of contemporary society. That is why people sometimes call the Constitution a "living document."

Bill of Rights

To limit of the power of the central government and protect the individual rights of the citizens, the first U.S. Congress drafted 12 amendments, from which the states ratified 10 in 1791. Those 10 amendments became known as the *Bill of Rights*. In the *Bill of Rights*, Americans are guaranteed freedom of religion, of speech, of the press and freedom to protest against government policies. They have the right to assemble in public places, to protest government actions and to demand change. They have the right to own weapons if they wish. The *Bill of Rights* guarantees Americans the right to a fair and speedy trial if accused of a crime.

II Three Branches of Government

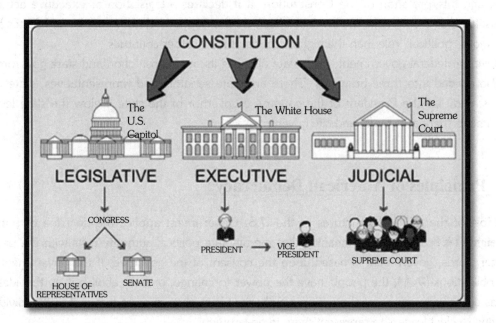

Within the national government, power is divided among three branches: the legislative (立法的) branch, the executive (行政的) branch, and the judicial (司法的) branch.

The Legislative Branch

The Constitution gives the legislative power to the Congress, which consists of two parts — the House of Representatives (众议院) and the Senate (参议院). The Congress's main function is to make laws. There are 100 senators (two from each state) and 435 representatives (the number from each state depends on the size of the state's population). A Senate term is six years and a Representative serves a two-year term. There is no limit to the number of terms an individual can serve as either of them.

The head of the House of Representatives is called the Speaker (美国众议院议长). He or she is chosen by the majority party and has considerable power, such as setting the agenda. The Speaker is second in line to succeed the President, after the Vice President. The leader of the Senate is the Vice President of the United States, but he is not a member of the Senate.

The Executive Branch

The Constitution gives the executive power to the President alone, who is also head of the country. The executive branch administers (执行) the laws. In addition to the President and the Vice-President, the executive branch consists of departments and agencies. The President appoints the department heads, or advisers, who together make up the President's Cabinet (内阁). There are 15 major departments in the executive branch. They employ about 1.6 million civilian employees. All the executive departments and independent agencies are responsible to the President.

The Judicial Branch

The federal court has the judicial power. The judicial branch is represented by three levels of federal courts. The Supreme Court is the most important body. It has nine members, who are appointed for life. Below the Supreme Court, there are Courts of Appeal, and, below these courts, there are District Courts. They represent the federal judicial system together.

The Supreme Court deals with matters related to the federal government, disputes between states, and interpretation of the Constitution. If it declares a legislation or executive action as unconstitutional, it can make the law lose effect. So the Supreme Court in the United States has a much more "political" role than the highest courts of many other countries.

Like the federal government, each state also has its own constitution and state governments are also divided into three branches. There are state senators and representatives, state court systems, and, like the President of the country, a governor of the state. Below the state level of government, there are county and city governments.

III Principles of American Democracy

Most of the political structures of the U.S. Government applies the doctrine of **popular sovereignty** (人民权利至上论), meaning that the ultimate political authority rests with the people. In other words, government is based upon the consent of the governed. If the government fails in its obligations (职责), the people have the power to change, or even abolish it. In this idea the citizens collectively represent the nation's authority. They then express that authority individually by voting to elect leaders to represent them in government.

The second principle of U.S. democracy is **representative government**. In a representative government, the people delegate [授(权)] their powers to elected officials. In the United States, candidates compete for the presidency, the Senate, and the House of Representatives, as well as for many state and local positions. In turn these elected officials represent the will of the people and ensure that the government is accountable (负有责任的) to its citizens. This accountability is an important feature of the American system of representative government.

The third principle of American democracy is the **system of checks and balances**. The three branches of government restrain and stabilize (使稳定平衡) one another through their separated functions. The legislative branch, represented by Congress, must pass bills before they can become law. The executive branch — namely, the president — can veto (否决) bills passed by Congress, thus preventing them from becoming law. In turn, by a two-thirds vote, Congress can override the president's veto. The Supreme Court may invalidate (使无效) acts of Congress by declaring them contrary to the Constitution of the United States, but Congress can change the Constitution through the amendment process.

The fourth principle of democracy in the United States is **federalism**. In a federal system, power is shared between a central government and smaller government units. There is a federal, or central, government for the entire country. In addition, each of the 50 states has its own government. The federalist system granted certain powers to the national government, reserved others to the states, and allowed some to exist on both level. This arrangement is an embodiment (体现) of the American political principle of division of powers.

Division of Powers

Exclusive Powers of the National Government	Concurrent Powers (并存权力)	Reserved Powers of the State Governments
declare war and conduct foreign affairs	levy taxes	maintain a system of public education
coin money	borrow money	create local governments
manage a postal system	define and punish crimes	provide public education
establish lower courts	charter banks	direct traffic laws
raise and support armed forces		

Powers Denied to the National Governments	Powers Denied to the National & State Governments	Powers Denied to the State Government
tax exports	deny due process of law	coin money
suspend writ (正式文件) of habeas corpus (人身保护权)	pass ex post facto laws (有追溯效力的法令)	enter into treaties
grant titles of nobility	pass bills of attainder (剥夺财产和公民权的法案)	void (使无效) contracts

IV Two-Party System

American citizens choose their government by voting. American elections seem rather democratic, but the American people have only a small area of choice in elections. There are only two major parties in the country and they are almost the same in nature. American voters have no alternative but to give their votes to one party or the other.

The two main political parties are the Democratic Party and the Republican Party. There are also several smaller political parties known as "third parties" which play little, if any, role. There are no clear differences between the Republican and Democratic parties. In general, the Republicans tend to be more conservative and to have more support among the upper classes, while the Democrats tend to be more liberal and to have more support among the working class and the poor.

The Democratic Party

The Democratic Party is almost as old as the United States and traces its origins to the Democratic-Republican Party, founded by Thomas Jefferson, James Madison, and other influential opponents of the Federalists[①] in 1792.

Its history started with a feud between Alexander Hamilton and Thomas Jefferson, America's third president. In the 1790s, Hamilton was appointed Secretary of the Treasury. He advocated that the federal government should have the power to direct the economy, and a society built on industrial interests. Thomas Jefferson, who was at that time the first Secretary of the State, disagreed with Hamilton. He felt the national government should have limited powers and a society with independent farming. Thomas Jefferson, with the help of James Madison, formed what was then called the Democratic-Republican Party, fighting strongly against the Federalist Party which Hamilton helped form. Thus, Thomas Jefferson was known as the Founding Father of the Democratic-Republican Party, which became the dominant political party in the United States from 1800 until the 1820s. When it split into competing factions (派系), one of the factions became the modern-day Democratic Party. The party advocated westward expansion, Manifest Destiny, greater equality among all white men, and opposition to the national banks.

The Republican Party

The Republican Party is often referred to as the Grand Old Party or the GOP (大老党). When the Republican Party was created, the two major parties in the United States were the Democratic Party and the Whig Party.

The party is named after republicanism, the dominant value during the American Revolution. Founded in 1854 by people who wanted to keep slavery from spreading to other parts of the country, the Republican Party rose to prominence with the election of Abraham Lincoln, the first Republican president. The party presided over the American Civil War and Reconstruction. There have been a total of 19 Republican presidents, the most from any one party. The first was the 16th president Abraham Lincoln, and the most recent being the 45th president Donald Trump, who took office on January 20, 2017.

The Republican Party's current ideology is American conservatism, which contrasts with the Democrats' more progressive platform (also called modern liberalism).

The Democratic Donkey and the Republican Elephant

Did you ever wonder what the story was behind these two famous party animals? The now-famous Democratic donkey was first associated with Democrat Andrew Jackson's 1828 presidential campaign. His opponents called him a jackass (a donkey), and Jackson decided to use the image of the strong-willed animal on his campaign posters. Later, cartoonist Thomas Nast used the Democratic donkey in newspaper cartoons and made the symbol famous.

Nast invented another famous symbol —

---

① 联邦党人：1787年5月，各州代表会议在费城召开了美国历史上著名的制宪会议。新宪法通过后，提交各州批准。大陆会议决定，十三个州中如果有九个州同意，新宪法即可生效。但是各州在批准过程中，对新宪法表现出两种截然相反的态度，由此发生了美国历史上一场最激烈的政治思想论战。时任华盛顿政府财政部部长的汉密尔顿及其支持者拥护联邦宪法，史称"联邦党人"。联邦党人主张提倡一个强大的中央政府、放宽对于宪法的解释，以及一个由精英统治的政府。他们代表了东部新英格兰地区富人、土地投机者、南部种植园奴隶主的利益。1812年至1814年美英战争期间，联邦党人由于采取亲英立场，不得民心，1815年瓦解。第二任美国总统约翰·亚当斯是美国历史上唯一的联邦党人总统。

the Republican elephant. In a cartoon that appeared in *Harper's Weekly* in 1874, Nast drew a donkey clothed in lion's skin, scaring away all the animals at the zoo. One of those animals, the elephant, was labeled "The Republican Vote." The elephant characterized the Republican vote which had been scared by the possibility of the Democratic Party seeking a third term for President Ulysses S. Grant. In time, other cartoonists used the elephant, which came to define the party. Democrats today say the donkey is smart and brave, while Republicans say the elephant is strong and dignified.

V Presidency of the United States

The U.S. President is the head of its Administration. Chosen through a general or presidential election, the president is the most prominent figure in the United States. He is known as the First Citizen and his wife, the First Lady. Of all the federal officials he is the only one to have an official residence, the White House.

The Job of the President

The president heads up the executive branch of the U.S. government. The executive branch is in charge of running the country and defending it from enemies. The president takes an oath to uphold the Constitution and can issue rules, regulations and instructions which, known as executive orders, have the binding (有约束力的) force of laws upon federal agencies.

Presidents suggest new laws. They appoint most of the country's judges, including the judges of the Supreme Court, and appoint ambassadors. The president also serves as commander-in-chief of the country's military forces, and has the power to raise, train, supervise, and deploy American armed forces, provided Congress shows no disagreement. Presidents cannot declare war — only Congress can do that. Once a war has started, however, the president gives the orders.

Every president has a group of advisers called the Cabinet. Each Cabinet member, except the attorney general (司法部部长), is called a secretary (部长) and heads a different department. There are 15 Cabinet posts in all.

How Long Do Presidents Serve?

A president is elected to serve for four years. He/she may then run for one more term. When the nation was born, no law limited how many times a president could serve. By custom, however, no president ran more than twice. Then, in the 20th century, Franklin Delano Roosevelt ran and won four times. After Roosevelt died, a new law was added to the Constitution. It said presidents could serve no more than two terms.

Presidential Impeachment

If the president is accused of a serious crime, Congress can bring charges against the president. This is called impeachment (弹劾). The House of Representatives draws up the charges. Representatives can impeach the president if a majority in the House votes to do so. The Senate then sits as a court to hear the charges. Afterward, the Senate may vote to remove the president from office. Congress has never removed a president from office. It did impeach President Andrew Johnson in 1868. Johnson kept his job by one vote in the Senate. Congress investigated President Richard Nixon for possible crimes in 1974. Nixon resigned before he could be impeached. In 1998, President Clinton was impeached in the House. But he won his trial in the Senate and kept his job.

Presidential Election

Every four years, the United States holds a general election for its president. The election occurs on Tuesday after the first Monday in November. To become president it's best to become the candidate of a big political party. No law says presidents must belong to a party. It's just that it's hard to win such a job without help. Every president since 1853 has belonged to one of its two major parties, the Democratic or the Republican. Now, most states hold primary elections (初选)before the presidential election. Citizens decide who should run for their party by voting in the primary.

The general election in the United States is an indirect one, in which the popular vote does not determine the winner. Instead, Presidential elections use the **Electoral College**[①], which consists of 538 presidential electors from the fifty states and Washington, D.C. The number of electors each state gets is determined by how many members of Congress (House and Senate) the state has. A candidate must receive an absolute majority of electoral votes (currently 270) to win the presidency or the vice presidency. If no candidate receives a majority, the House chooses the president, while the Senate chooses the vice president.

Inauguration Day occurs every four years on January 20 (or January 21 if January 20 falls on a Sunday) at the U.S. Capitol building in Washington D.C. On this federal holiday, the President-elect and Vice-President-elect are sworn in and take office.

---

① 总统选举团，由各州选民投票推选组成，代表本州参加总统、副总统选举投票。

Chapter 4 National Economy

> **章节导读**
>
> 本章通过翔实的数据，介绍了美国经济的总体情况、企业的主要类型，以及农业、采矿业、制造业、金融保险业等国民经济主要产业的历史及发展状况。

I An Overview

For the most part, the United States has a market economy in which individual producers and consumers determine the kinds of goods and services produced and the prices of those products. A guiding principle of the U.S. economy, dating back to the colonial period, has been that individuals own the goods and services they make for themselves or purchase to consume.

The United States emerges as a world leader in producing various goods and services and generates more than 22% of worldwide gross domestic product (GDP, 国内生产总值). The economy is marked by steady growth, low unemployment and inflation, and rapid advances in technology.

Major Economic Sectors

From colonization till the beginning of the 20th century the United States was largely an agricultural nation with the majority of Americans working on farms.

The Industrial Revolution that started in England in the 18th century contributed to the rapid growth of American industry. In 1890, for the first time, the output of American factories exceeded that of American farms. By 1913 more than 1/3 of the world's industrial production came from the United States.

New technologies and computerization enabled many of the newly rising industries to be highly automated. Fewer workers were needed in traditional industries and entirely new kinds of jobs and businesses are created. Since the mid-20th century, services (such as health care, entertainment, and finance) have grown faster than any other sector of the economy. A large proportion of the workforce entered service industry in recent years.

Free Enterprise & Government Role

U.S. economy is mainly a free enterprise system, in which the person whose money is at risk is the person who gets to decide. Wrong or right, foolish or wise, whoever has the gold makes the rules. Government plays a limited role in economic decision making in the open, market economy; the initiative (主动权) for production and consumption decisions lies in individuals or companies.

However, business in this free enterprise system is not purely free. The consolidation of small businesses into increasingly powerful corporations in the 20th century spurred government intervention to protect small industries and consumers. Every year, the government produces thousands of pages of new laws and regulations, often spelling out in painstaking detail what businesses can do and cannot.

The federal government provides services and goods that the market cannot provide effectively, such as national defense, assistance programs for low-income families, and interstate highways and airports. It regulates private industry in two ways — economic regulation and social regulation. Economic regulation seeks primarily to control prices. Social regulation, on the other hand, promotes objectives that are not economic — such as workplace safety or environmental protection.

Business Forms

Most businesses in the United States operate under one of three different legal forms: sole proprietorships (独资企业), partnerships (合营企业), or corporations.

In a sole proprietorship, the proprietor owns and operates the business and collects all profits. Most small businesses in the United States are individual proprietorships. They are flexible and respond quickly to changing economic conditions. Small retail stores, restaurants and farms tend to be organized in this way.

Another kind of business is the partnership. According to the Census Bureau, there are more than one million American partnerships. Two or more people operate a partnership. They generally reach a legal agreement to specify each member's rights and duties. Partnerships can end at any time and exist only as long as the owners are alive. They enable entrepreneurs to pool their talents, but serious disagreements constantly arise. Law firms are always established as partnerships.

In the United States, most large businesses are organized as corporations. A corporation has legal standing itself. Ownership in a corporation is divided into shares. The owner can trade his shares or keep them as long as the company is in business. A corporation may have a few major shareholders. Or ownership may be spread among the general public. As a result, corporations may survive the death of any particular owners and, thus, have an unlimited lifetime. Shareholders (股东)are paid in the form of dividends (股息) in return for their investments. A board of directors makes major corporate decisions and appoints top company executives. The directors might or might not hold shares in the corporation.

	Facts
1	New York City is the center of American financial, publishing, broadcasting, and advertising industries.
2	Los Angeles is the most important center for film and television production.
3	Detroit, known as the Motor City, serves as the historic center of the American automotive industry.
4	Chicago is the world's most celebrated center of architecture innovation and a significant transportation hub.
5	The San Francisco Bay Area and the Pacific Northwest are major centers for technology.
6	The Midwest is a major area for manufacturing and heavy industry.
7	The Southeast is known for its reliance on agriculture, tourism and lumber industry.

II Agriculture

American agriculture benefits greatly from its fertile soils and rich climate variation. It represents about 1% of annual GDP and feeds nearly 60% of the world's production. It assumes a vastness and diversity unmatched in most other parts of the world. In 2014, 17.3 million full- and part-time jobs were related to agriculture, accounting for 9.3 percent of total U.S. employment. American farmers have generally been successful at producing crops cheaply and in quantity. They produce as much as half of the world's soybeans and corn for grain, and from 10 to 25 percent of its cotton, wheat, tobacco and vegetable oil.

Agricultural Regions

Cultivated farmland accounts for 19 percent of the land area. The Central Plain of the Mississippi River system is the chief agricultural region, the "Barn of America". Each year this region produces large quantity of corn, wheat, soybean, and to the south, rice and cotton.

On the Atlantic Coast and in the Great Lake region, many of the farms, known as truck farms (商品蔬菜农场), are devoted to dairy farming, poultry and the growing of vegetables. Dairy farmers grow hay and corn as fodder (饲料) crops. Fruit farming in this region is also very popular.

The states to the west of Rockies now grow some wheat, barley, and sugar beets (甜菜). California is well-known for its large variety and huge quantity of fruits. The Great Central Valley of California is one of the most beautiful and productive agricultural regions of the world. It produces a full quarter of the nation's food supplies. Another important industry in the west is cattle ranching and sheep-raising.

Crops & Livestock

The United States is the world's largest producer of corn, soybeans, and sorghum (高粱). Corn (also called maize) is the most important of all American crops. "You cannot buy anything at all in a North American supermarket which has been untouched by corn...," wrote a canadian anthropologist. Its annual product constitutes more than half the total grain output, and approximately 13% of its annual yield is exported. It is mainly used for fodder and exportation, and only a small fraction is used for food.

Soybean, the nation's second most valuable crop after corn, was discovered in China about 13,000 years ago. Not until the 18th century did the first American plant a soybean from China in American soil. During the 19th century, American farmers began cultivating the soybean, and now the U.S. is the world's number one producer of the plant, taking up 32% of world total in 2016. Much of the soybean production goes to exports.

The United States ranks second in the production of wheat, oats, citrus (柑橘属水果) fruits, and tobacco. It is also a major producer of sugar cane, potatoes, peanuts, cotton and beet sugar. Vegetables are grown widely in the United States. California is the leading vegetable producing state. Nuts grow on irrigated land in the Central Valley of California and in parts of southern California.

Cattle production is one of the most important industries in the United States. It ranks fourth in the world after India, Brazil and China. Texas has the most cattle followed by Nebraska and Kansas. The U.S. is the largest producer of beef in the world, producing nearly 19% of the world's beef. The total U.S. beef consumed was 24.807 billion pounds.

Forestry

Forests represent a crucial resource for U.S. industry. About 1/3 of the land area of the United States is covered with forests. There are mainly three forest areas: the Pacific Northwest; the South Atlantic and Gulf states; the Appalachian Highland and parts of the Great Lakes.

The United States leads the world in lumber production and is second in the production of wood for pulp and paper manufacture. These high production levels, however, do not satisfy all of the U.S. demand for forest products. It is the world's largest importer of lumber, most of which comes from Canada.

According to the American Forest and Paper Association, the U.S. forest products industry employs about one million workers and accounts for approximately six percent of the total U.S. manufacturing GDP.

Fishing

Fisheries play an enormous role in the U.S. economy. In most years, the United States ranks fifth among the nations of the world in weight of total catch, behind China, Peru, Chile, and Japan. It is the World's second largest consumer of seafood after China according to data from the Food and Agriculture Organization of the United Nations.

Alaska leads all states in both volume and value of the catch. Other leading fishing states, ranked by value, are Maine, Massachusetts, Louisiana, and Washington. Much of the annual U.S. tonnage of commercial freshwater fish comes from aquatic farms.

III Mining & Manufacturing

Mining Industry and Major Mineral Products

The United States enjoys rich mineral deposits and abundant energy resources within its borders. Mining industry employs over 3 million people directly and indirectly and accounts for about 2 percent of annual GDP. The nation exports $27 billion worth of minerals and material produced from minerals each year. California is the largest producer of non-fuel minerals of any U.S. states.

The nation's three chief mineral products are natural gas, petroleum, and coal. American petroleum industry has been greatly influenced by Standard Oil founded by John D. Rockefeller in 1870.

Manufacturing

The United States has large manufacturing industries. There are 12.3 million manufacturing workers in the United States, accounting for 9 percent of the workforce. Manufacturing is the country's fourth largest employer (用工单位) after health care and social assistance, retail trade and accommodation (住宿) and food services.

The vast majority of manufacturing firms in the United States are quite small. Three-quarters of the firms have fewer than 20 employees.

Now nearly 6 in 10 U.S. export dollars come from manufacturers. A key theme in 2016 presidential race is the competitiveness of American industry. Donald Trump believed that the United States has lost its economic edge (优势) since China has displaced (取代) the U.S. as the largest manufacturing nation, so he was determined to drop some agreements which he believed has hindered the development of U.S. manufacturing and trade. He signed his first executive order on January 23, 2017, withdrawing the U.S. from TPP[①] (Trans-Pacific Partnership).

[①] TPP（跨太平洋伙伴关系），也被称作"经济北约"，是目前重要的国际多边经济谈判组织。《跨太平洋伙伴关系协定》（Trans-Pacific Partnership Agreement）是由亚太经济合作组织成员国中的新西兰、新加坡、智利和文莱等四国发起，从2002年开始酝酿的一组多边关系的自由贸易协定，旨在促进亚太地区的贸易自由化。2016年2月4日，美国、日本、澳大利亚、文莱、加拿大、智利、马来西亚、墨西哥、新西兰、秘鲁、新加坡和越南12个国家在奥克兰正式签署了《跨太平洋伙伴关系协定》。2017年1月23日，时任美国总统特朗普正式签署命令，开始启动美国撤出"跨太平洋伙伴关系"的进程。

High-Tech Industry

High-tech industry has been the fastest growing sector of American manufacturing. The largest component is electronics industry. The revenues generated by the overall U.S. electronics industry today exceed the combined revenues of all U.S. automobile, steel and chemical manufacturers. Most of these revenues were produced by less than ten companies. Silicon Valley has become a metaphor for all high-tech businesses in the area. It is the southern part of the San Francisco Bay Area in Northern California. Silicon refers to the high concentration of semiconductor and computer-related industries in the area; Valley refers to the Santa Clara Valley.

IV Finance & Insurance

Federal Reserve System

The Federal Reserve System[①], established by Congress in 1913, functions as a central bank for other banks and for the federal government. All nationally chartered commercial banks are required by law to be members of the Federal Reserve System; membership is optional (非强制的) for state-chartered banks. The Federal Reserve System performs several important functions in the national economy. By far the most important function is controlling the nation's money supply and the overall availability of credit (信贷总量) in the economy.

Because the Federal Reserve System exercises great influence over the U.S. economy, the chairman of the Federal Reserve Board is often considered as one of the world's most powerful individuals.

Currency

More than 99 percent of the total dollar amount of paper money in circulation in the U.S. today is made up of Federal Reserve notes. The Federal Reserve System issues Federal Reserve notes through its 12 Federal Reserve Districts. The U.S. Mint, which makes all U.S. coins, was established by Congress in 1792 and became an operating (业务上的) bureau of the Treasury Department in 1873.

Banks

Banks safeguard money and the valuables and perform their primary role in the financial system — provide loans, credit, and payment services. With the passage of the Financial Modernization Act in 1999, banks also may offer investment and insurance products.

Commercial banks, which dominate this industry, offer a full range of services for individuals, businesses, and governments. These banks come in a wide range of sizes, from large global banks to regional and community banks. In recent years, online banks have entered the market, with some success. However, many traditional banks have also expanded to offer online banking.

---

① 美国联邦储备系统，简称美联储，为直属美国总统的独立行政机构之一，负责履行美国的中央银行的职责。这个系统是根据《联邦储备法》（Federal Reserve Act）于1913年成立的。美联储的核心管理机构是美国联邦储备委员会。联邦储备系统由位于华盛顿特区的联邦储备委员会和12家分布全国主要城市的地区性的联邦储备银行组成。美联储的7名成员全部由总统任命，任期为14年，不得连任；美联储主席和副主席任期为4年。作为美国的中央银行，美联储从美国国会获得权力，行使制定货币政策和对美国金融机构进行监管等职责。

Large banks in the U.S., in terms of assets, are J.P. Morgan Chase & Co., headquartered in New York City; Bank of America, headquartered in Charlotte, North Carolina; Citigroup, headquartered in Manhattan, New York City; Wells Fargo, headquartered in San Francisco, California, and Goldman Sachs, also headquartered in Manhattan.

Stock Exchanges

A stock exchange is a corporation providing facilities for stock brokers to trade company stocks (股票；证券) and other security (有价证券). It also provide facilities for the issue (发行) and redemption (赎回) of securities, as well as other financial instruments and capital events (资本活动) including the payment of income and dividends (股息). The American Stock Exchange (AMEX), located in Manhattan, is one of the major exchange houses in the U.S. The New York Stock Exchange (NYSE) is the largest in the world. NASDAQ is the largest electronic screen-based equity securities in the United States and the primary market for trading NASDAQ-listed stocks.

Insurance

Consisting of 5,926 insurance companies in 2015, the U.S. insurance industry is the world's largest insurance market, accounting for $1.2 trillion or 27 percent of worldwide premiums (保险费). Insurance is sold either directly by insurers (保险公司) or through the independent agency system, exclusive agencies (独家代理) and brokers. In the United States, private insurers pay for about 40 percent of all health care costs. Medicare (医疗保险) is federal health insurance (联邦医疗保险) for people above the retirement age of 65. Medicaid[1] is federal and state health insurance for the poor. Workers who are injured on the job can receive workers compensation. States require employers to pay into this form of insurance. And workers who lose their jobs may collect unemployment insurance, for up to twenty-six weeks.

On March 23, 2010, President Barack Obama enacted a federal statute called The Patient Protection and Affordable Care Act (PPACA)[2], nicknamed Obamacare. It expanded insurance coverage, lowered the uninsured rate, and reduced the costs of healthcare. The percentage of people without health insurance fell from 16.0% in 2010 to 8.9% during the January — June 2016 period.

---

[1] 由各级政府资助、以穷人和伤残者为对象的医疗补助（制度），即美国政府向贫困者提供的医疗保险。
[2] 《患者保护与平价医疗法案》，通常也被称作奥巴马医疗法案（Obamacare），是由美国总统奥巴马在2010年签署的一部联邦法。该法案的主要目的是由美国政府主导增加美国人民的医疗保险覆盖率以及降低美国的医疗费用。主要包括四方面内容：一是所有美国民众必须购买医疗保险，否则就会罚款，其中低收入者享受政府不同数目的补贴，此为奥巴马医改的"强制条款"；二是保险机构不能因投保者有既往病史而拒保，并且这些人的保费和其他健康同龄人相同，此为奥巴马医改的"保证条款"；三是26岁以下的年轻人可以纳入自己父母的家庭医保计划中；四是政府放开各类医保方案的定价权。美国第45任总统特朗普就职未满24小时，便签发首道行政命令，叫停"奥巴马医保"计划，践行了其竞选期间的承诺。

Chapter 5 Society and Culture

章节导读

本章分为七个部分，集中介绍美国的社会和文化，包括主要族群、核心价值观、生活方式、教育制度、文学、体育和重要节日。

I Cultural Groups

What Is a Cultural Group?

A cultural group is made up of people who share the same behavior, belief, and language (people who share the same culture). In the United States, there are many cultural groups. The dominant or major culture group is British American. It is the most powerful and influential group whose people make up about 45% of the American population and control most of the national wealth and political powering of the nation. The minor groups are called subcultures (亚文化群体). Among them are Hispanic Americans (Spanish-speaking Americans), Native Americans, African Americans, Italian Americans, Asian-Americans, etc.

People in the same cultural groups do things in ways that are alike or similar and also share a common language. Language shows what is important in a culture. It shows how the people of culture think. More than 300 languages are spoken in the United States. According to the American community survey in 2011, the languages spoken with over 100,000 speakers older than five in the United States are:

English	230 million
Spanish	37.58 million
Chinese	2.88 million (mainly Cantonese, Taishanese① and Standard Mandarin Chinese)
French	1.30 million
Tagalog②	1.59 million

Social Theories of Immigration

The U.S. is a country of immigrants. Different groups of immigrants integrate in different way. Sociologists have identified a few major theories on how newly arrived immigrants integrate themselves into American society. Over time all new immigrants adopt some aspects of American

---

① 台山话（四邑话）是以粤语为主体，并受到闽南语影响和融合的一种独特语言，与广州话差异明显。主要分布在中国广东省的新会、台山、开平、恩平四地，以及江门市区、鹤山的部分地区、中山小部分地区和珠海的斗门区，海外的华侨社区（尤其是北美）。
② 塔加洛语/他加禄语，菲律宾主要民族他加禄族的母语，菲律宾的官方语言之一（另一种为英语）。1962年被定为菲律宾的官方语言，并新命名为Filipino，最终形成了以他加禄语为基础的菲律宾语。

culture and add something new.

Melting Pot Theory	According to the Melting Pot Theory, peoples from various cultures come to America and contribute aspects of their culture to create a new, and unique American culture. The result is that contributions from many cultures are indistinguishable (不能区别的) from one another and are effectively "melted" together.
Salad Bowl Theory	According to the Salad Bowl Theory, there are times when newly arrived immigrants do not lose the unique aspects of their cultures like in the melting pot model. Instead they retain them. Much like the ingredients (成分) in a salad, the unique characteristics of each culture are still identifiable (可确认的) within the larger American society, yet contribute to the overall makeup of the salad bowl. This theory is also referred to as pluralism (多元化的社会形态).
Assimilation	Assimilation (同化) is the concept that eventually immigrants or their decedents adopt enough of the American culture, while they may retain aspects or traditions of their cultural heritage, and they are identifiable as uniquely "American."

Introduction of Some Cultural Groups

1. Hispanic and Latino Americans

Hispanic (西班牙裔的) Americans and Latino (拉美裔的) Americans are people in the United States who are descendants of the Spanish-speaking and Portuguese-speaking countries of Latin America and Spain. The term "Latino" was officially adopted in 1997 by the United States Government in "Hispanic or Latino," which replaced the single term "Hispanic," because regional usage of the terms differs — "Hispanic" is commonly used in the eastern portion of the United States, whereas "Latino" is commonly used in the western portion. According to the Smithsonian Institution, the term "Latino" includes peoples with Portuguese roots, such as Brazilians, as well as those of Spanish-language origin.

Census Bureau data estimate that the U.S. Hispanic population topped 54 million on July 1, 2013. They make up the largest (16%) and the fastest-growing minority group in the United States, as a result of a high birth rate and continuing immigration.

Hispanics can be white, black or Latin-American Indian, or a mixture or races. Experts who study communities point out that Hispanics from different countries often have different cultures. Most Hispanic Americans speak English but continue to use Spanish as well. In addition to their language, Hispanic Americans have preserved many other traditions of their homelands. The foods, music, clothing styles, and architecture of these countries have greatly influenced U.S. culture.

Like other minorities, Hispanic Americans have suffered from discrimination in jobs, housing, and education. Many Hispanics are in lower-paid jobs. The most important obstacle to Hispanic success in the labor market is their low education. Hispanics have the highest school dropout rate of any major racial and ethnic group. One of the reasons is that for many Hispanic American children, Spanish is the only language spoken at home. When children reach school age, they speak and understand only Spanish, but the language in their school is English.

Today, especially in the southwest, this is changing. More and more lessons are taught in both Spanish and English. This means that children can learn in their first language. In this way, they won't fall behind in their lessons. Then, little by little, they can learn English as their second language. When this happens, they will become bilingual.

Most Hispanic Americans are members of the Roman Catholic Church. Many of the cities in the American Southwest are named after Catholic Saints. San Francisco, Santa Barbara, and San Antonio are examples.

Hispanic families tend to have large numbers of children, who typically occupy the center of family life. They are taught to respect the elders, to appreciate family unit, and to assume family responsibilities. Imbued (被灌输) with strong family values, Hispanics generally have lower divorce rates compared with Anglos. Hispanics are also likely to marry outside their group, especially among those with a higher socioeconomic status. Generally, the longer their families have been in the United States, the higher their rates of interethnic (不同种族间的) marriage.

The three largest Hispanic groups in the United States are Mexican Americans, Puerto Ricans, and Cuban Americans. Mexican Americans (or Chicanos奇卡诺人) are the largest Hispanic group in the United States today. They live in the Southwest, such as New Mexico, California, and Texas. Puerto Rican Americans are the second largest Spanish-speaking group. They live in the Eastern states, such as New York (Puerto Rico is an island southwest of Florida. All Puerto Ricans have been United States citizens since 1917). Cuban Americans are in Florida. Cubans came to the United States in large numbers in the 1960s. Most of them have become United States citizens.

2. African Americans

According to 2015 U.S. Census Bureau's estimate, there were 46,282,080 African Americans in the United States, making up 14.3% of the total American population.

African Americans are people whose ancestors were from Africa. The first blacks arrived in Jamestown Virginia in 1619, a year before the Pilgrims arrived on the Mayflower, as indentured servants (契约佣工). But very soon after 1619 blacks were brought to colonies as slaves.

The African American population is represented throughout the country, with the greatest concentrations in the Southeast and mid-Atlantic regions, especially Louisiana, Mississippi, Alabama, Georgia, South Carolina, and Maryland. African Americans have a long history in the United States. Some African American families have been in the United States for many generations; others are recent immigrants from places such as Africa, the Caribbean, or the West Indies.

> *African Americans' Contribution to America and to the World*

From their earliest presence in North America, Africans and African Americans have contributed literature, art, agricultural skills, foods, clothing styles, music, language, social and technological innovation to American culture. The cultivation and use of many agricultural products in the U.S., such as yams, peanuts, rice, okra (秋葵), sorghum (高粱), grits (粗玉米粉), watermelon, indigo dyes (靛青), and cotton, can be traced to African and African American influences.

African American music is one of the most pervasive cultural influences in the United States today. Blues, jazz, gospel (黑人福音音乐), hip-hop (嘻哈音乐，包括说唱和电子乐器演奏), R&B (Rhythm and Blues, 节奏布鲁斯), funk (乡土爵士乐), rock-and-roll, soul (灵歌), techno (一种快节奏的现代电子音乐) and many other contemporary American musical forms originated in black communities and have been incorporated into the popular music of almost every culture in the world. African Americans have also had an important role in the world of dance.

African Americans made great contributions during the wars. In the Revolutionary War (1776 — 1783), 10,000 African Americans served in the continental armies. In the American Civil War (1861 — 1865) 186,000 soldiers of African descent served in 150 regiments of the Union army, making up about almost 13% of the Union army's combat manpower. Another 30,000 were in the Navy. During America's participation in World War I (1914 — 1918) and World War II, Black Americans served their country both at home and overseas.

More and more African Americans play important roles in American politics. In 2001, General Colin Powell became the first black Secretary of State, and his successor, Condoleezza Rice, became the first black woman Secretary of State in 2005. Obama was the first African-American nominated by a major American political party for president and was the first African American holding the office from 2008 to 2016.

3. Native Americans

Native American inhabitants were incorrectly called Indians by early European explorers who mistakenly believed that they had reached India. Today, many people still refer to all Native Americans as Indians. Even some Native Americans call themselves Indians, but most of them prefer using their legitimate tribal names. It was not until 1924 that the Native Americans became United States citizens, with the right to vote.

➢ *How many Native Americans are there in the USA?*

American Indians and Alaska Natives (AI / AN) made up about 2 percent of the total population in 2014. The greatest concentrations of AI / AN populations are in the West, Southwest, and Midwest, especially in Alaska, Arizona, Montana, New Mexico, Oklahoma, and South Dakota. There are 569 federally recognized AI / AN tribes, plus an unknown number of tribes that are not federally recognized. Each tribe has its own culture, beliefs, and practices.

➢ *Five Indian Groups*

The American Indians can be divided into five groups, according to where they lived.

♦ **Pacific Northwest Indians** lived near the forests along 2,000 miles of coastline from southern Alaska to northern California. Basically, the Indians of this region were maritime people. They sailed along the Pacific coast in very long boats (up to 18 meters) called canoes, hunting for sea animals and fishing the great rivers for salmon. As food was easy to find, the Indians of the Northwest had time to develop artistic skills. They carved wood into houses, chests, dishes, spoons, canoes, boats and totem poles. The Northwest Indians believed in private property to a greater extent than Indians in other areas. Status depended on wealth.

♦ **California / Great Basin Indians** settled between the Rocky Mountains and the California coast. For the most part, California Indians hunted small game and ate seeds, berries, roots and nuts. Sometimes they fished or farmed. The most important source of food for most natives was the acorn, which was full of nutrients, and plentiful. East of California is a dry, desert-like area called the Great

Basin where food was scarce. Great Basin Indians had to move in a wide area searching for food, and their organization rarely rose above the family level. Survival was difficult because the land was short of water, plants, and animal life.

♦ **The Plains Indians** came from other areas after being pushed out by other tribes. In their old lands, they had been farmers. In the plains they became buffalo hunters. Before the arrival of the horse, hunting the buffalo was a slow and very dangerous thing to do. The introduction of the horse led to a new way of life for the Plain Indians. Horses allowed the Indian hunters to move farther and could overrun any buffalo.

♦ **The Southwest Indians** live in a hot, dry region, partly desert and partly canyons and cliffs. Most of them were farmers and grew corn, beans and squash, which they called the "Three Sisters."

♦ **The Eastern Woodland Indians** inhabited a wide area in the eastern part of the United States. The inhabitants in this region were forest dwellers. They tended to live near water in the forested areas and use wood and wood products as the basic raw materials in their lives. Many of the Eastern Woodland tribes were not nomadic and relied on agriculture to provide food for the tribe. Being expert farmers, farming was the main focus of their lives. Their tribes were primarily farmers and gatherers, but hunting and fishing were also important for their survival. Deer was probably the most important animal which was used for clothing, moccasins, and food. They also fished the fresh waters of many rivers and streams throughout the region.

➢ *Indian Reservation*

In the United States there are about 310 reservations today, which were areas that the United States government set up for native tribes that had lost their lands to European settlers. Some reservations are larger than American states. The largest is the Navajo[①] Reservation of some 16 million acres of land in Arizona, New Mexico, and Utah. Many of the smaller reservations are less than 1,000 acres with the smallest less than 100 acres. On reservations, much of their way of life is like that of other people in the U.S. But their cultures are still alive. They are being passed on to new generations with pride.

Some tribes have managed to profit from the natural resources on their lands and the inhabitants have become rather wealthy. On other reservations, the residents exploit thriving tourist businesses. Unfortunately, many tribes own few resources and the inhabitants of their reservations live in poverty. Because of isolation, unemployment and lack of business development, third world living conditions are typical of many reservations. Sometimes the unemployment rate reaches 38% to 63%. The average life expectancy for Native Americans has improved yet still trails that of other Americans by almost 5 years.

There is also a wide gap between Native Americans and other Americans in the field of education. College attendance rates among the Indian population is half that of the general population. In 2014 only 67 percent of American Indian students graduated from high school,

---

① 纳瓦霍人是美国印第安居民中人数最多的一支，20世纪末期约有170,000人，散居于新墨西哥州西北部、亚利桑那州东北部及犹他州东南部。如今纳瓦霍人口仅剩55,000左右，全部生活在美国境内的纳瓦霍族原始部族里，以纳瓦霍语为主要交际工具。纳瓦霍语是一种没有文字而又极为复杂的语言，依靠其族人世代口耳相传而得以延续。第二次世界大战期间，数百名纳瓦霍人被征召入伍，被美军训练成了专门的译电员，人称"风语者"。"风语者"们编制出的敌人无法破译的"无敌密码"，为盟军的最终胜利立下了汗马功劳。2002年，华裔导演吴宇森在好莱坞拍摄了一部名为《风语者》（*Windtalkers*）的影片，讲述了这段历史，纳瓦霍人才为世界上更多的人所熟知。

much lower than the national average of 80 percent.

➤ Family and Traditional Native American Values

Various Native American families shared certain characteristics. For example, infants were born in special birth huts. During the years of breastfeeding, mothers refrained from sex. Physical punishment was rarely used to discipline children, who were taught instead by example. Children learned adult roles at an early age, so that most girls were married between ages 12 and 15, and boys between ages 15 and 20. Most tribes were monogamous (一夫一妻的). Extended family networks predominated, and kinship ties and obligations to relatives flourished.

Today this traditional family life has disappeared among many Native Americans. Between 1870 and 1930 the U.S. government embarked (发动) on a program of destroying the Native Americans to the white culture by, among other things, sending their children to white-run boarding schools. Today only a small minority of Native Americans have successfully resisted assimilation (同化) and kept alive their traditional values, particularly the importance of kinship ties and obligations. The rest have either adopted white values completely or adopted a mixture of white and Indian values. Compared with other ethnic groups, Native Americans suffer from higher rates of poverty, alcoholism, suicide, and other problems, all of which create severe difficulties for many Native Americans.

➤ Native Americans' Contributions

Native Americans have made many contributions to world cultures, from pineapples and pumpkins to a model of government and the zero in math.

Food	Edible plants domesticated by Indians have become major staples in the diets of peoples all around the world. Such foods include corn (maize), manioc (木薯), potatoes, sweet potatoes, peanuts, squashes and pumpkins, tomatoes, papayas (木瓜), avocados (鳄梨；牛油果), pineapples, guavas (番石榴), chili peppers, chocolate, tomatoes, sunflowers, and many species of beans.
Animals	Indians were the first to raise turkeys, llamas (美洲驼), guinea pigs (豚鼠), and honeybees for food.
Non-edible plants	Other plants of great importance developed by Indians include cotton, rubber, and tobacco.
Medicines	What we know today as aspirin is made from an ingredient the Native Americans got from willow bark. At least 59 drugs, including quinine (奎宁, 治疗疟疾) have come from wild plants that Native Americans used as medicines. They developed pain medicines, birth-control drugs, and treatment for scurvy (坏血病). Many Indian medicines became part of what we call "folk medicine" and almost 200 plants used by Indians are now listed in the official United States Pharmacopeias Dictionary of Drug Names (药典).
Sports	The rubber ball came from native South Americans. Native North Americans invented lacrosse (长曲棍球).
Outdoor Gear	parkas (毛皮风雪大衣), snow Goggles (防雪盲的墨镜) and moccasins (鹿皮鞋)
Other things	Canoe, hammock (吊床) and toboggan (平底雪橇) were also invented by Native Americans, so were rubber, pipes, and cigars.

Language	The English language is full of Native American words. Many animals are called by their native names. Chipmunks (花栗鼠), skunks (臭鼬), moose (麋鹿), and raccoons (浣熊) are just a few such animals. Many tree names, such as hickory, catalpa (梓树), and pecan (美洲山核桃树), are also Native American. Words as different as powwow (巫师), hurricane (飓风), and totem (图腾) have their roots in Native American languages. In fact, half of the names of the U.S. states (including Arizona, Connecticut, Kansas, Kentucky, Massachusetts, Missouri, Mississippi, Ohio, to name a few) are derived ultimately from Amerindian words.
Mathematics	The Maya of Mexico appear to have been the first to use the zero in mathematics. Scholars believe that Asians traveled across the Pacific Ocean and learned about the zero from the Maya.
Government	Indian governments in eastern North America, particularly the League of the Iroquois, served as models of federated representative democracy to the Europeans and the American colonists. The United States government is based on such a system, whereby power is distributed between a central authority (the federal government) and smaller political units (the states). The United States government has representatives from each state as the League had representatives from each tribe.
Constitution	The draft of the U.S. Constitution was heavily influenced by the Iroquois constitution, which maintained the three main principles of peace, equity and justice and the "power of good minds."
Economy	Indian contributions to the modern world's economy have been enormous. In the 1500's, Indian labor produced the gold and other valuable metals that helped bring the Spanish Empire to the height of its power. In the following centuries, Indian labor in North American fur trade contributed significantly to the wealth of England, France, the Netherlands, and Russia. In addition, for hundreds of years the agrarian (农业的) economies of the Latin American nations have been based on Indian labor on plantations.

4. Amish People[①]

Quick Facts About Amish people

Amish	largely share a German or Swiss-German ancestry
Total population	308,030 (2016 estimate)
Regions with significant populations	United States, especially Pennsylvania, Ohio, Indiana, Maryland, Kalona, Iowa, Ontario, Canada
Language	Pennsylvania Dutch, English, High German
Religion	Anabaptist[②] Christianity

---

① 阿米什人，指17世纪、18世纪移居美国宾夕法尼亚州的德国人和瑞士人的后裔，亦称德裔宾州人。以拒绝汽车及电力等现代设施，坚守简朴而传统的生活而闻名。多数阿米什人不缴纳社会保险费，不接受政府的社会福利，不服兵役，不接受8年级以上的教育，不与外族通婚，但各种遗传病也在困扰着他们。阿米什人热爱家庭，崇尚顺从和团队精神。专注于农业生产。其服装款式仍停留在19世纪风格，通用的美学标准是"朴素"：女性多穿单色棉布长裙加围巾，头戴白色无边小帽。男性多戴宽边草帽，穿吊带裤，外套都是黑色。上衣没有领子，没有口袋。婚前不留胡须，婚后留髯须，嘴唇上面不准留须。他们主要分布在美国的27个州，其中俄亥俄州霍姆斯县（Holmes）的阿米什人最多，其次是宾夕法尼亚州兰开斯特县（Lancaster）。除英语外，阿米什人主要使用"宾夕法尼亚德语"方言进行交流。

② 再洗礼派教徒：16世纪宗教改革激进运动的成员，相信《圣经》的权威性，洗礼是对教徒个人内心信仰承诺的外部证明，主张政教分离、信徒和非信徒分离。

The Amish are found primarily in the United States and Ontario, Canada that are known for restrictions on the use of modern devices such as automobiles and telephones. Most Amish today descend primarily from 18th century immigrants. They are united by a common Swiss-German ancestry, language, and culture, and marry within the Amish community. The Amish are one of the fastest-growing population groups in America. The population in 2016 is about 308,000. Ohio has the largest Amish population, followed by Pennsylvania and Indiana.

Most Amish are trilingual. They speak a dialect of German called Pennsylvania Dutch or Pennsylvania German[①] at home; they use High German[②] at their worship services; and they learn English at school. They speak English when they deal with anyone who is not Amish.

The Amish separate themselves from civil society for religious reasons: They do not join the military, draw Social Security, or accept any form of assistance from the government, and many avoid insurance.

➢ *History*

The Amish were a small religious group in Europe whose beliefs were often different from the teachings of the main churches in Europe. So the Amish came to the New World to practice their own religious beliefs. Over the years, Amish culture has changed very, very slowly. They have kept all the old ways and chosen to do so even though most of the world is changing around them.

➢ *Some Important Amish Values*

1) Amish people lead a simple farming life and are self-sufficient.

2) They waste very little and their way of living does not harm the environment nor foul the air and rivers.

3) They help one another often and believe in a close family and community life. They look out for one another in times of need.

➢ *Lifestyle*

The Amish keep pretty much to themselves. They don't want too many ideas from the outside to change their way of life.

♦ **Amish House**

The Amish are friendly people. But unless you are Amish, you probably won't get to see the inside of their houses. Amish homes are large with several rooms opening into one large room where they hold church services. The houses are furnished very simply with benches on which the families sit to eat their meals. The floors are bare and the windows are covered with plain colored cloth. You won't see pictures of the family, as the Amish don't like their pictures taken.

♦ **Appearance and Attire** (服饰)

Symbolic of their faith, Amish clothing styles encourage humility and separation from the

---

① 宾夕法尼亚德语，德裔宾州人使用的一种混有英语的德语方言。
② 高地德语：主要通用于德国、奥地利、列支敦士登、瑞士和卢森堡，也用于一些临近的地区，是现代德语的主体。高地指阿尔卑斯山和临近的德国南部山区；而低地德语则是代表德国北部沿岸地区。

world. The Amish choose to wear simple homemade clothes. For some groups buttons are prohibited, allowing only *hooks and eyes* to keep clothing closed. The restriction on buttons is attributed in part to their former association with military uniforms, and also to their potential for serving as opportunities for vain display. In all things, the aesthetic value is "plainness": clothing should not call attention to the wearer by cut, color or any other feature. Prints such as florals,  stripes, polka-dots (圆点花纹图案), etc. are not encouraged in Amish dress.

Amish women usually wear modest long dresses in a solid, plain color and often wear white or black aprons. A cape (披肩) which consists of a triangular shape of cloth is usually worn beginning around the teenage years and pinned into the apron. They wear black stockings and flat shoes. In the cold months, they wear black wool shawls.

They never cut their hair, and wear it in a braid (发辫) or bun (圆髻) on the back of the head concealed with a small white cap or black bonnet. Amish women are not permitted to wear make-up or jewelry.

Amish men in general wear straight-cut dark suits and coats without collars, lapels (翻领), or pockets. Trousers never have creases (裤线) or cuffs (裤脚的外翻边) and are worn with suspenders. Belts are forbidden, as are sweaters, neckties and gloves. The Amish call such things "modern" or sometimes "English." They wear solid-colored (纯色) shirts, black socks and shoes, and black or straw broad-brimmed (宽边的) hats in the warmer months and black felt (毛毡) hats in the colder months. Typically, single Amish men are clean-shaven and married men grow a beard; a long beard is the mark of an adult Amish man. Mustaches are generally not allowed, because they are seen as symbols of both pride and the military.

From left to right — 1) Amish Suspenders; 2) Amish Haircut; 3) Clean shaven; 4) When a man is married he grows a beard by tradition. Different ages are judged by the grayness of the beard.

> ➢ *The Amish & Modern Technology*

Many Amish are renowned for their avoidance of modern technologies. Electricity, for instance, is viewed as a connection to the "World," the "English," or "Yankees" (the outside world). They think electricity or machines run by electrical power would complicate the Amish tradition of a simple life, and introduce individualist competition for worldly goods that would be destructive of community. They know what television is. They shop in stores that are brightly lit and air-conditioned. But they don't want such things as electric lights, TV sets, radios, computers etc. for themselves. Nor do they want other Amish to buy TV sets. The telephone is despised (厌恶)

because it eliminates face-to-face communication. Many Amish families have non-electric versions of vital appliances, such as kerosene-powered refrigerators. It is not proper for an Amish person to own a car, truck, or tractor. They drive in horse-drawn buggies (小型轻便的一匹马拉的四轮马车), which are usually painted black. The Amish will hire drivers for visiting family, monthly grocery shopping, commuting to the workplace off the farm, but hiring a taxi is forbidden on Sundays.

> *Amish Family Life*

The family is the most important social unit in the Amish culture. The **immediate family** (直系亲属), the **extended family** (大家庭), and the **church district** form the building blocks of Amish society. Amish parents typically raise about seven children, but ten or more children are not uncommon. Members of the extended family often live nearby. Amish people have long emphasized mutual aid as a Christian duty in the face of disaster and special need.

Amish marry Amish — no intermarriage is allowed. Young people typically marry in their early twenties. When the young people are married they are often given a parcel of land by one of the fathers from which they are to make their living. Divorce is not permitted and separation is very rare. Weddings and funerals occur at home.

> *Amish Schools & Education*

The Amish do not value formal education. Although they pay school taxes, they have fought to keep their children out of public schools. Amish children generally attend school through the

eighth grade in their own church-funded schools. Usually there is one teacher and two teacher's helpers, who are often Amish. They take turns teaching the various age groups in the class. The schoolbooks they use are written especially for Amish children. Some states have let the Amish set up vocational schools to follow the eighth grade. In the vocational schools, they learn more about farming and caring for the home.

Higher education is considered unnecessary and something that can lead one away from a life of simplicity and humility as well as the community. However, the Amish know the importance of informal education. The Amish society is a trade-school of sorts. It trains their young people in the fine art of craftsmanship, in fine cabinetry (细木家具), furniture, carpentry, farming, and last but not least homemakers.

5. Asian Americans

Asian Americans are Americans of Asian descent. According to the 2013 U.S. Census, the Asian population grew to 19.4 million. The states with the greatest concentration of Asian Americans are Hawaii, California, Washington, New Jersey, and New York.

Many Asian Americans are successful partly because they already had good skills when they came to the U.S. Experts say three Asian traditions best explain the success of Asian Americans: education, hard work, and family. Education is considered the key to success. Asian American parents expect their children to be the best students and Asian American young people spend more time studying than other American students. They are supposed to show gratitude toward parents by achieving success in educational and occupational activities.

Compared with other U.S. families, Asian American families generally are more stable, having lower divorce rate, fewer female-headed households, fewer problems with child-rearing, greater family solidarity, and stronger kinship associations.

Traditionally, Asian Americans have taken little part in politics in the United States. Now, a movement for more political power has begun. The reason is mainly the desire for political representation; all Asian-Americans do not share the same political goals, but share a desire to end all forms of racism (种族歧视).

➢ *Chinese Americans*

The largest group of Asian-Americans is the Chinese-Americans. With a population numbered approximately 3.8 million, they constitute 1.2% of the total U.S. population as of 2010.

The first Chinese immigrants arrived in 1820 and most Chinese immigration to the U.S. took place between 1850 — 1880 during the California Gold Rush, but they were banned from emigrating between 1885 and 1965 when the ban on Asian immigrants was lifted by the Immigration Reform and Control Act.

Some noteworthy historical Chinese contributions include building the western half of the Transcontinental Railroad, and levees (防洪堤) in the Sacramento River Delta; the popularization of Chinese American food; and the introduction of Chinese and East Asian culture to America, such as Buddhism, Taoism, and Kungfu.

Chinese immigrants to the United States brought many of their ideas and values with them. Some of these have continued to influence later generations. Among them are Confucian respect for elders and a feeling of responsibility to the family. The high regard for education which is deeply imbedded (植根于) in Chinese culture, and willingness to work very hard to gain advancement, are other noteworthy characteristics of theirs. This explains why so many descendants of uneducated laborers have succeeded in becoming doctors, lawyers, and other professionals.

II Basic American Values

Historically, the United States has been viewed as "the land of opportunity," attracting immigrants from all over the world. The opportunities they believed they would find in America and the experiences they actually had when they arrived nurtured this set of values. Six basic values have become "traditional" American values.

Three represent traditional reasons why immigrants have been drawn to America: the chance for individual freedom, equality of opportunity, and material wealth. In order to achieve these benefits, however, there were prices to be paid: self-reliance, competition, and hard work. In time, these prices themselves became a part of the traditional values system.

Individual Freedom and Self-reliance
Individual Freedom

The earliest settlers came to the North American continent to establish colonies that were free from the controls that existed in European societies. In 1776, the British colonial settlers declared their independence from England and established a new nation. In so doing, they overthrew the king of England and declared that the power to govern would lie in hands of the people. In 1789, when they wrote the Constitution, they separated church and state so that there would never be a government-supported church. They also expressly (明白地) forbade titles of nobility to ensure that an aristocratic society would not develop.

The historic decisions made by those first settlers have had a profound effect on the shaping of the American character. By limiting the power of the government and the churches, and eliminating a formal aristocracy, they created a climate of freedom where the emphasis was on the individual. The United States came to be associated in their minds with the concept of individual freedom. This is probably the most basic of all the American values.

Self-reliance

There is, however, a price to be paid for the individual freedom: self-reliance (自力更生). Individuals must learn to rely on themselves or risk losing freedom. This means achieving both financial and emotional independence from their parents as early as possible, usually by age 18 or 21.

This strong belief in self-reliance continues today as a traditional basic American value. In order to be in the mainstream of American life — to have power and/or respect — individuals must be seen as self-reliant. Although receiving financial support from charity, family, or the government is allowed, it is never admired.

Equality of Opportunity and Competition
Equality of Opportunity

Because titles of nobility were forbidden in the Constitution, no formal class system developed in the United States. When the Americans say they believe in equality of opportunity, they mean that each individual should have an equal chance for success. For them, equality means that everyone should have an equal chance to enter the race for success and win. This American concept of "fair play" (公正) is an important aspect of the belief in equality of opportunity.

Competition

There is, however, a price to be paid for this equality of opportunity: competition. People who like to compete and are more successful than others are honored by being called winners. On the other hand, those who do not like to compete and are not successful when they try are often dishonored by being called losers.

The pressures of competition in the life of an American begin in childhood and continue until retirement from work. Learning to compete successfully is part of growing up in the United States. The pressure to compete causes Americans to be energetic, but it also places a constant emotional strain on them.

Material Wealth and Hard Work
Material Wealth

The third reason why immigrants have traditionally come to the United States is to have a better life. Because of its incredibly abundant natural resources, the United States appeared to be a "land of plenty" where millions could come to seek their fortunes. The phrase "going from rags to riches" (从赤贫一跃而成巨富) became a slogan for the great American Dream (the belief that everyone in the U.S. has the chance to be successful, rich and happy if they work hard). Material wealth became a value to the American people and acquiring and maintaining a large number of material possessions is of great importance to most Americans. Why is this so? Probably the main reason is that material wealth has traditionally been a widely accepted measure of social status in the United States. Because Americans rejected the European system of hereditary (世袭的) aristocracy and titles of nobility, they had to find a substitute for judging social status. The quality and quantity of an individual's material possessions became an accepted measure of success and social status. Moreover, the Puritan work ethic associated material success with godliness (信仰).

Hard Work

Americans have paid a price for their material wealth: hard work. Hard work has been both necessary and rewarding for most Americans throughout their history. Because of this, they came to see material possessions as the natural reward for their hard work.

Each one of these values has a rich and complex heritage. Despite the transformations (变化) in America's life-styles, these core values have endured. Virtually all Americans share them. They make American culture distinctive and hold Americans together as a single people and nation.

III Ways of Life

The Impact of Consumerism

Consumption drives the American economy. The American lifestyle is often associated with buying things as well as with leisure time. As advertising stimulates the desire for updated or improved products, people increasingly equate (等同) their well-being with owning certain things and acquiring the latest model.

Living Patterns

The desire for residential privacy has remained a significant feature of American culture. Americans are committed to living in private dwellings set apart from neighbors. Despite the rapid urbanization that began in the late 19th century, Americans insisted that each nuclear family be privately housed and that as many families as possible own their own homes.

Food and Cuisine

The United States has rich and productive land that has provided Americans with plentiful resources for a healthy diet. American food also grew more similar around the country as malls and fast-food outlets (经销店) tended to standardize eating patterns throughout the nation, especially among young people. Nevertheless, American food has become more complex as it draws from the diverse cuisines that immigrants have brought with them.

Food Originated in America

Traditional American cuisine has included conventional European foodstuffs such as wheat, dairy products, pork, beef, and poultry. It has also incorporated products that were either known only in the New World or that were grown there first and then introduced to Europe. Such foods include potatoes, corn, tomatoes, peppers, pumpkin and other squashes, codfish (鳕鱼), molasses (糖蜜), and peanuts. The first pumpkin pie was baked in New Haven with English techniques in 1796. Apple pie is considered such a typical American dessert that it inspired the saying, "as American as apple pie." Chili in the form of meat hash (大杂烩) or stew with peppers started in the southwest in the 1800s. In 1977 Chili was declared the state food of Texas. George Crum[①] invented potato chips in 1853 in Saratoga Springs, New York.

Food Introduced by Immigrants

By the late 19th century, immigrants from Europe and Asia were introducing more variations into the American diet. American cuisine began to reflect these foreign cuisines, not only in their original forms but in Americanized versions as well.

Immigrants from Japan and Italy introduced a range of fresh vegetables that added important nutrients as well as variety to the protein-heavy American diet. Germans and Italians contributed new skills and refinements to the production of alcoholic beverages, especially beer and wine. Some imports became distinctly American products, such as hot dogs, which are descended from German sausage. Spaghetti and pizza from Italy grew increasingly more American and developed many regional spin-offs. Americans even adapted chow mein from China into a simple American dish.

America's foods began to affect the rest of the world. American emphasis on convenience and rapid consumption is best represented in fast foods such as hamburgers, French fries, and soft drinks. By the 1960s and 1970s fast foods became one of America's strongest exports as franchises for McDonald's and Burger King spread through Europe and other parts of the world, including China. By the late 20th century, Americans had become more conscious of their diets, eating more poultry, fish, and fresh fruits and vegetables and fewer eggs and less beef.

Dress

Americans do not have distinctive folk attire (服装) with a long tradition. American dress is derived from the fabrics and fashions of the Europeans who began colonizing the country in the 17th century. Early settlers incorporated some of the forms worn by native peoples, such as moccasins (软皮平底鞋) and garments made from animal skins, but in general, fashion in the United States adapted and modified European styles.

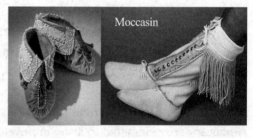

American style in the 20th and 21st centuries is eclectic (兼收并蓄的) and predominantly informal, more informal than in Europe. The informality in dress is such a strong part of American culture that many workplaces have adopted the idea of "casual Friday," a day when workers are encouraged to dress down from their usual professional attire. For many high-tech industries located along the West Coast, as well as among faculty at colleges and universities, this emphasis on casual attire is a daily occurrence, not just reserved for Fridays. In the 21st century there has been less and less clothing that is appropriate. Girls feel a need to show off their bodies to look attractive. They prefer

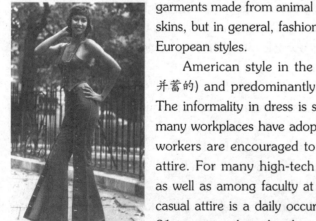

USA 1971 — Levi's jeans

---

① 尽管争议很大，但大多数人认为美国厨师乔治·克拉姆是薯片的发明者。1853年的一天，一位顾客抱怨他做的薯条太厚，于是他怀着报复心理将薯条切得很薄，并在油炸后撒上盐。没想到顾客很喜欢吃这种薯片，迅速成为最受世人欢迎的零食。

really short shorts and skirts, extremely low V necks and spaghetti strap shirts (细吊带上衣). Colors like pink and purple that show off femininity are extremely popular.

While Americans' diverse cultural roots are reflected in their clothing, cowboy hats, boots and leather motorcycle jackets are emblematic (代表性的) of specifically American styles.

American fashions more often come from popular sources. Blue jeans are probably the single most representative article of American clothing. They were originally invented by tailor Jacob Davis, who together with dry-goods (纺织品) salesman Levi Strauss patented the idea in 1873 as durable clothing for miners. By the late 1970s, almost everyone in the United States wore blue jeans, and youths around the world sought them.

IV Education

A Brief Introduction

Education has always been a great concern for Americans. When the Puritan settlers in Massachusetts came to the New World, they brought with them a belief that education was fundamental to religion and to service for the commonwealth (国民整体). Even before the American Revolution, several famous colleges were set up. The Boston Latin School was founded in 1635 and Harvard College in 1636.

Christopher Wren Building (1695 — 1699) of College of William & Mary, the oldest Academic building in use in America

Following the lead of the settlers in New England, the American colonies set up schools, academies, and colleges by the hundreds all through the colonial period. By the time of the American Revolution, public schools, charity schools, church schools, and academies were teaching children, and nine colleges scattered through the American wilderness. Among these colleges were College of William and Mary in Williamsburg, Virginia in 1639 and Yale in New Haven, Connecticut in 1701.

Since the U.S. Constitution mentions nothing on education, all educational matters are left to individual states. The Federal government has no power to make laws in the field of education; it can give financial help but not order. In America, there is not one but 50 educational systems. Each state has an educational administration, not subject (隶属于) to federal control, and the state authorities lay down general principles concerning the organization of schools and such matters as the ages of compulsory (义务的) education. Schools are managed by local community boards of education, whose members are elected. Most schools are run on taxes levied (征收) by local districts and states.

As early as 1853, the state of Massachusetts passed the first compulsory school attendance law. By 1918, all states had laws requiring children to receive at least primary education. Today, most states have passed laws extending compulsory education to the age of 16.

In America, education is carried out at various levels, which are mainly divided into elementary education, secondary education, and higher education.

Elementary and Secondary Education

Elementary and secondary education is compulsory. According to the U.S. Depart-ment of Education, in 2013 — 2014, there are nearly 67,034 public elementary schools and 24,053 public secondary schools, with a student body of 55.4 million. Public schools are free. An estimated 5.3 million students were enrolled in private schools at the elementary and secondary levels.

Elementary and secondary education covers 12 years from age 6 through 18. All the states have laws that require children to go to school, generally until the age of 16, unless they are seriously handicapped. In addition, the elementary school offers five-year-olds a year of kindergarten, usually half-day sessions (授课时间), before they have formal instruction in reading and writing in the first grade.

At elementary stage, nearly all the teachers are women, mostly married. The atmosphere is usually very friendly, and the teachers have accepted the idea that the important thing is to make the children happy and interested. Courses for children include reading, arithmetic, and language arts such as creative writing, spelling, and handwriting, and there are also social courses such as history, geography, and civics (公民学), science, art and music. They can also learn cooking and manual skills like carpentry and sewing. Children can do physical exercises on the playground or in gymnasiums.

A pupil goes to high school automatically after finishing his elementary school education. There is no entrance exam. High schools are made up of comprehensive, academic, vocational (职业的) and technical schools with somewhat different tasks. Comprehensive high schools provide both academic and vocational education; academic high schools only aim to prepare students for college; vocational and technical ones generally provide for a variety of occupations and vocations though some are specialized in a single vocational or technical area.

A typical high school curriculum includes almost all the subjects for elementary schools, but is more specialized. Many high schools offer dozens and sometimes hundreds of electives.

Higher Education

Higher education in the United States began with the founding of Harvard College in 1636. In the past years, it has developed into a big enterprise with a very complex system of undergraduate study and graduate study. According to a survey in 2013, there are all together 4,724 institutions of higher education in the U.S. Slightly more than half are privately supported, many of them by religious groups.

In fall 2016, some 20.5 million students attended American colleges and universities. Many of the top universities in the U.S. are private universities. The top 10 universities are all private ones. They are: Harvard University, Princeton University, Yale University, Massachusetts Institute of Technology (MIT), California Institute of Technology, Duke University, Stanford University, University of Pennsylvania, Dartmouth University, and Washington University in St. Louis.

There are different types of institutions. Two-year College was originally called "junior college," but now it is called "community college." Most community colleges are public institutions supported by both state and local taxes; so tuition for these schools is much lower than that at the state universities. It serves as a bridge which connects secondary schools and universities.

Four-year College is another type of institution, which is called a "liberal arts college" or "college of arts and science." Its curriculum is confined to humanities, social and behavioral sciences and the natural sciences.

An American university is an institution which is more comprehensive and complex than any other kind of U.S. higher educational establishment. An university may have several colleges within it and its curriculum is broader and deeper. Compared with four-year colleges, universities are generally larger in enrollment, with better libraries, more research work, and more teachers with doctorate degrees.

In the past ten years prices for undergraduate tuition, fees, room, and board at public institutions rose 33 percent ($16,188 for the 2014 — 2015 academic year), and prices at private nonprofit institutions rose 26 percent ($41,970). The price at private for-profit institutions decreased 18 percent ($23,372).

American colleges and universities offer three main categories of degrees: bachelor, master, and doctorate or Ph.D. After earning a bachelor's degree, students can go to graduate schools to study for a master's or doctor's degree. There are two ways for students to get the master's degree. One requires a thesis paper, which counts for a certain number of credits that usually constitute part of the degree program. Another one requires no thesis paper, but more credits in the process of study. And an oral or written examination may also be asked for the degree. A master's degree requires from one to three academic years of study beyond the bachelor's degree. A doctorate degree normally takes at least three years beyond the master's. To earn a Ph.D in almost every field, a student has to accumulate enough class credits: pass comprehensive written and oral examinations in his specialty, known as the preliminary or qualifying exams; produce a long research paper called thesis or dissertation that makes an original contribution to his or her field of study; and pass examinations in one or two foreign languages. Those who have a degree usually have better job chances.

Since the mid-20th century, many international students have come to study in the United States. International student enrollment in U.S. colleges and universities reached a record high of 975,000 in 2014 — 2015 school years.

V Literature

Americans started writing soon after the first European settlers arrived in the 1600s. After that, American literature had been greatly influenced by the European culture for a long period. It was not until America's independence, did Americans realize that they need national literature strongly, and American literature began to develop. The Civil War was a watershed in the history, after which American literature entered a period of full blooming. Like the flowers of spring, there were suddenly many different kinds of writing at the same time. Romantics, which emphasized individualism and intuition (直觉) and Transcendentalism (超验主义：一种文学和哲学运动) represented by Emerson came out into being. They have given depth and strength to American literature, and accelerated the forming of High Romantics. But due to the influence of Civil War, the American society was in a turbulent situation. The writings about local life, critical realism and unveiling the dark side of the society were increased. After the First World War, Americans were at a loss postwar, and the Modern American literature began.

The process of American literature can be briefly divided into the following five periods:

Colonial and early American literature;
American literature in the 18th century;
The flourishing of American literature in the 19th century;
American Literature during the Realistic Period;
Modern American Literature.

Colonial and Early American Literature

The American Continent had been inhabited by the Asian immigrants, later known as American Indians or Native Americans for more than two thousand years before Christopher Columbus discovered it in 1492. These inhabitants, though they did not have written literature, did develop a rich heritage of cultures and have colorful oral literature.

Then came the European settlers with different backgrounds and cultures. They were eager to tell people living in "the old world" what they saw and what they experienced in this "new world." So they wrote a lot of diaries, letters, and travel accounts to describe the new land. No wonder some critics say that the earliest American literature was the travel accounts written by European adventurers. Meanwhile, in order to prepare the new immigrants physically and spiritually for bearing the hardships of building up the new land into the Second Eden, they developed American Puritanism and spread it over the New England areas, which besides stressing predestination, original sin, hard work, thrift, piety and sobriety, advocated that earthly success was a sign of election, wealth and status being sought not only for themselves, but as welcome reassurances of spiritual health and promises of eternal life. So American writings of this period were dominated by the Puritan values. The most important figures of the period were John Smith, William Bradford and Anne Bradstreet.

American Literature in the 18th Century

With the development of colonial economy and society, colonial people in general began to seek their national identity politically and literarily. Some intellectuals considered Puritan values, of original sin in particular, had become obstacles to achieving these goals. So they energetically advocated to study "man" instead of "God," believing that the "evils" in human civilization stemmed from social injustice, not from "original sin," that man could "perfect himself" and decide his own destiny. They also put great stress on reason, education and scientific research. They called on people to pay attention to the social reality. This movement was referred to as American Enlightenment, which introduced ideas of justice, liberty and equality as the natural rights of man to American thoughts and, above all, prepared the colonial people ideologically for their independence and enhanced their determination to obtain their independence realistically.

Due to the particular situation in America, among all categories of the literary works, political essays occupied an outstanding position and most of the writers were active supporters or participants of the American Revolution. For all the Americans, the most important document from this period was a single sheet of paper called *The Declaration of Independence* (1776), mainly written by Thomas Jefferson and Benjamin Franklin. Benjamin Franklin, Thomas Paine and Philip Freneau were the most brilliant literary figures of the time.

The Flourishing of American Literature in the 19th Century

After Americans gained their independence politically, they immediately got down to seeking for their cultural identity internationally through developing national literature as they developed their economy and society. The country was prosperous and the people were optimistic about their own future and the future of their nation. In the tens of the 19th century, the territory of the country had been expanded as far as the Appalachians, and its population also doubled. Under such circumstances, when the Romantic Movement came to America, Americans tinted (给……着色) it with American color and came into being the American Transcendentalism (超验主义), which was, in essence, a romantic idealism on Puritan soil and an intellectual movement, exerting a tremendous impact on intellectual thinking in America. The transcendental movement was based on a fundamental belief in the unity of the world and God. The soul of each individual was thought to be identical with the world — a microcosm (缩影) of the world itself. The doctrine of self-reliance and individualism developed through the belief in the identification of the individual soul with God. It was the most significant development of American literature in the mid-19th century and regarded as the first Renaissance in the American literary history.

The Romantic Movement or Romanticism (浪漫主义) reached America around the year 1820. It placed emphasis on imagination, emotion, and individuality instead of formality, order and authority. The romantics showed a profound admiration and love for nature and for the wild and mysterious. Though influenced by their European counterparts, romantics in America expressed themselves in a distinctive American voice: they wrote about the exotic landscape, the frontier life, the westward expansion, the Puritan heritage and they tended to moralize, to edify rather than to entertain.

Early romanticism was best represented by Washington Irving, James Fenimore Cooper, and New England poets William Cullen Bryant and Henry Wadsworth Longfellow. Among the representatives of post-romanticism are novelists Nathaniel Hawthorne and Herman Melville; poets Edgar Allan Poe and Walt Whitman; essayists Ralph Waldo Emerson and Henry David Thoreau, etc.

Another thing worth mentioning is that during this period America produced its two great women writers for the first time: Harriet Beecher Stowe (1811 — 1896), the woman writer called by President Lincoln "the little lady who wrote the book that made this great war" with her anti-slavery novel *Uncle Tom's Cabin*, and Emily Dickinson (1830 — 1886), the poetess of about 1700 poems and one of the finest poets in the English language, who was a keen observer of nature and a wise interpreter of human passion and developed her own forms of poetry and pursued her own visions, not paying attention to the fashions of literature of her day.

American Literature during the Realistic Period (1875 — 1914)

After the Civil War (1861 — 1865), America was set on the ever-increasingly rapid path of all-round development. Westward expansion and the gold rush added freshness and new vision to the established eastern New Englanders' life and thus enlarged subject matter of literature. On the other hand, the American society was in a turbulent (动荡的) situation through several economical crises. Problems of urbanization and industrialization appeared. This was what Mark Twain called "The Gilded Age," an age of extremes: of decline and progress, of poverty and dazzling wealth, of gloom and buoyant (高涨的) hope. The writings of critical realism unveiling the dark side of the society were increased. They mainly focused on bankrupt in countries, difficult life or struggle of low-position people and so on. Thus Romanticism was on the wane (处于正在衰退的时期) with passing days, while Realism rose and became more and more popular. William Dean Howells (1837 — 1920), the most influential American literary realist in the last quarter of the 19th century, precisely defined it as "nothing more and nothing less than the truthful treatment of material and moral problems of society."

Local Color Fiction was one trend deserving our special attention. It first appeared in the early 19th century, and it had further developing after the Civil War. This kind of literature mainly describes the local life. Its keynote was optimistic, and the language was narrative and humorous. Mark Twain was also famous for his strong local colors.

Novels made unprecedented progress in this period in terms of technique and subject matter as well as the great amount. Sparkling novelists came one after another producing enduring works of their own. Besides Mark Twain, there were Henry James and Frank Norris, short story writer O. Henry (1862 — 1910) (penname for William Sidney Porter) with more than 300 short stories, all his characters being common people and always having an ironical and surprised ending, Jack London with his *The Call of the Wild*, an all-time best seller, and two towering pessimistic realists (also referred to as writers of naturalism) Stephen Crane and Theodore Dreiser.

Modern American Literature

The 20th century witnessed more historically and culturally influential events than previous ones. Catastrophic (悲惨的) and reform-oriented (导向的) events succeeded one after another. Firstly, the First World War not only brought misfortune on humanity and damaged the people's life, but also led to a turbulent situation of the American society. People of this time were named "The Lost Generation" (*The Lost Generation refers to a group of young disappointed American writers, such as Ernest Hemingway and F. Scott Fitzgerald, chose Paris as their place of exile and used their wartime experience as the basis for their works. Generally they rebelled against former ideals and values, unable to come to terms with the new era when civilization had gone mad, and showed a sense of loss and took up the despairing tone of The Waste Land*). On the other hand, it was an important factor in stimulating American economic expansion, which led America to the decade-long "thriving" stage, also frequently called "the Jazz Age." Then, the unexpected Great Depression shattered (严重破坏) the exciting acceleration in the tempo (发展速度) of American life, bringing all contradictions of the society to the front.

Even before Americans found solutions to this problem, the Second World War took place, in which, the United States was heavily involved and suffered great loss. After the war, Americans were brought to face a completely new world which old rules and guidelines turned out to be helpless.

The Cold War, the Korean War, the Vietnam War, etc. made disillusionment spread throughout the United States and anti-war movement grew in size. Meanwhile, social reforms aiming to better and perfect the American society were under way. The civil rights and women's rights movements accelerated the process of American democracy, resulting in "Renaissance of American blacks" and prosperity of American women literature.

In short, such complex social background posed great challenge as well as opportunity to American literalists. To mirror the reality or express their feelings about it, American poets and writers of the century resorted to a variety of unmodeled literary techniques and forms. Their bold and creative experiments endorsed American literature of the time a term "modernism," used to show the literary art possessing outstanding characteristics in conception, feeling, form and style after the First World War. American literature indisputably won a place in the world literature and American writing was translated into other languages. American writers began to influence writers in other countries.

Ezra Pound, T. S. Eliot and E. E. Cummings are three poets who opened the way to modern poetry. New England poet Robert Frost also deserves some space to mention. After World War II, there appeared a tendency that most of the poets are grouped under such poetical schools as Black Mountain, the Beat Generation, New York poets, Black poets, Confessional poets, and West Coast School. Robert Lowell (1917 — 1977) and Allen Ginsberg (1926 — 1997) are most brilliant poets after the war. Ginsberg identified as a representative of the Beat Generation, got his acclaim for the masterpiece "Howl" (1956), in which he shows his anger over the society and the government.

In terms of fiction, the 20th century was a stage on which all kinds of literary schools and movements competed interrelatedly to present themselves along with the traditional realism, such as the Lost Generation, the Beat Generation, psychological fiction, the Southern fiction, Jewish fiction, African-American fiction, science fiction, feminist fiction, etc., all of which produced brilliant novelists and displayed a prosperous panorama of literature. Among the greatest were Ernest Hemingway, William Faulkner, Saul Bellow and Toni Morrison.

The development of 20-century American drama owed a lot to Eugene O'Neill (1888 — 1953), who was the first American playwright awarded the Nobel Prize for Literature. His poetically autobiographical masterpiece *Long Day's Journey into Night* (1956) laid down a new criterion for American dramatists. Tennessee Williams (1911 — 1983) and Arthur Miller (1915 — 2005) are another two great figures of American theater, the former famous for his *A Streetcar Named Desire* (1949) while the latter produced a landmark work *Death of a Salesman* in 1949, a study of man's search for merit and worth in his life and the realization that failure invariably looms (逼近).

Epilogue (结语)

American literature is well on the way after about 300 years of development. The living American literature has been providing potent thinking headsprings (源泉) for the writers past and nowadays, and it will continue reanimating (激发) the talents to bequeath (把……传下去) and enrich the tradition of American literature, of which deserved to be proud. It has been not only a genuine reflection of American history, society and culture but also an indispensable part of world civilization.

VI Sports

Baseball

From Little League (美国少年棒球联合会) to the World Series[①], baseball is the game that most Americans know best. Most Americans have played some form of baseball and the game has been called America's national pastime. There are many phrases in English that are related to baseball. We say of a strange idea that it comes "out of left field." "Hitting a home run" signals success. "Throwing a curve ball" means giving somebody a surprise.

---

① 世界大赛：美国职业棒球大联盟（Major League Baseball, 简称MLB）每年10月举行的总冠军赛，是美国以及加拿大职业棒球最高等级的赛事。由美国联盟（American League）冠军和"国家联盟"（National League）冠军，进行7战4胜制的总冠军赛，获胜的一方获得世界大赛奖杯。"世界大赛"尽管称世界，事实上只有美国和加拿大的球队参加。

Basketball

Basketball is one of the world's most popular sports. It's played in more than 200 countries. In the United States, most high schools and colleges have basketball programs. At the end of the season, the best teams compete in local, state, or national tournaments. The highest level of play for men is in the National Basketball Association (NBA) and for women is in the Women's National Basketball Association (WNBA).

Football

What's the most watched single sports event on television most years? It's the Super Bowl! The Super Bowl is usually played on the last Sunday of January or the first Sunday of February and is sometimes referred to as an unofficial national holiday on which more than 100 million people worldwide typically watch the championship game of the National Football League (NFL). Large amounts of food and alcohol are consumed on Super Bowl Sunday. The event is the second-largest day of food consumption in the United States after Thanksgiving.

American football uses an oval-shaped ball. It is played at hundreds of colleges and universities across the United States and Canada. College football dates back to 1869. Each year, the top player in college football receives an award called the Heisman Trophy.

Ice Hockey

Toronto Maple Leafs (white) defend their goal against Washington Capitals (red) during the 2016 — 2017 NHL season.

It's been called the fastest game in the world and it is certainly one of the roughest. Players on ice skates collide (碰撞) at great speeds. Shots streak (飞奔) toward the goal at more than 161 kilometers per hour! The game is ice hockey, a sport invented in Canada and is played in many other countries, including the United States.

Today, Ice hockey is played by two teams of six players. It can be played indoors or outdoors. Teams from about 30 countries around the world compete in the Olympic Winter Games and other international hockey tournaments. Teams from Europe and Russia are among the best in the world, along with those from Canada and the United States. In 1980 inexperienced American team beat the heavily favored Soviet Union team in the Olympics and won its first gold medal in ice hockey.

The highest level of ice hockey competition occurs in the National Hockey League (NHL), which is considered the world's top professional league. The NHL season usually lasts from October to April. The top teams then compete in playoffs (决赛) for the Stanley Cup, the NHL championship trophy.

VII Holidays and Special Days

A holiday is a day that is set apart for religious observance or for the commemoration of some extraordinary event or significant person, or for some other public events. Originally, in ancient times, holidays were mainly religious. The word holiday is actually derived from "holy day." Afterwards, non-religious holidays commemorating historical occasions or distinguished people outnumbered holy days, despite the fact that many ancient religious rituals and customs have been carried over into modern times. Holidays and festivals connect the present with the past. They give new generations of people the chance to learn about people or events that shaped their culture. For religious and ethnic groups, holidays and festivals are a way to remember their roots.

Legal Holidays

U.S. Legal Holidays	
New Year's Day	January 1
Birthday of Martin Luther King, Jr.	Third Monday in January
Washington's Birthday (Presidents' Day)	Third Monday in February
Memorial Day	Last Monday in May
Independence Day	July 4
Labor Day	First Monday in September
Columbus Day	Second Monday in October
Veterans Day	November 11
Thanksgiving Day	Fourth Thursday in November
Christmas Day	December 25

In the following part, we will give a brief introduction to the major legal holidays observed in the United States.

1. New Year

New Year's Day is the first day of the year, January 1st. It is a celebration of the old year and the new one to come. New Year festivals are among the oldest and most universally observed.

Each year huge crowds of people celebrate New Year's Eve in Times Square in New York City. At midnight, confetti (五彩纸屑) is thrown from the tall buildings surrounding the square. This tradition started as early as 1904 when the New York Times inaugurated its new headquarters in Times Square and celebrate the renaming of Longacre Square to Times Square. The first Ball Lowering celebration was held on December 31, 1907 and is now a worldwide symbol of the turn of the New Year, seen via satellite by more than one billion people each year. At 11:59 p.m., the Ball begins its descent as millions of voices unite to count down the final seconds of the year, and celebrate the beginning of a new year full of hopes, challenges, changes and dreams. *Auld Lang Syne* is sung at the stroke (报时的钟声) of midnight in almost every English-speaking country in the world to bring in the new year. It wouldn't be New Year without it. Some of the New Year's traditions include: the making of New Year's resolution; the use of a baby to signify the New Year and the Tournament of Roses Parade.

Traditionally, it was thought that what one did or ate on the first day of the year would affect the luck they would have throughout the coming year. For that reason, it has become common for folks to celebrate the first few minutes of a brand new year in the company of family and friends. Parties often last into the middle of the night after the ringing in of a new year.

New Year foods are thought to bring luck. It is believed that anything in the shape of a ring is good luck, because it symbolizes "coming full circle," completing a year's cycle. For that reason, eating donuts or ring shaped cakes on New Year's Day is thought to bring good fortune. Many parts of the U.S. celebrate the New Year by consuming black-eyed peas, which are typically accompanied by either hog jowls (cured and smoked cheeks of pork) or ham to ensure health, prosperity and progress. There are a variety of explanations for the symbolism of black-eyed peas. One is that eating these simple legumes demonstrates humility and a lack of vanity. The humble nature of the black-eyed pea is echoed by the old expression: "Eat poor on New Year's, and eat fat the rest of the year." Another explanation is that dried beans loosely resemble coins. Yet another is that because dried beans greatly expand in volume, they symbolize expanding wealth. Hogs and pigs have long been a symbol of prosperity. It is believe that the bigger pig you eat on New Year's, the bigger your wallet will be in the coming year. Cabbage is a "good luck" vegetable whose leaves are considered a sign of prosperity, being representative of paper currency. In some regions, rice (which swelled in the cooking) and greens (like money) are also considered lucky foods to bring prosperity.

2. Birthday of Martin Luther King, Jr.

Each year on the third Monday of January, a day that falls on or near King's birthday of January 15, schools, federal offices, post office and banks across America close as people celebrate the newest American national holiday — Martin Luther King Jr. Day, the only federal holiday commemorating an African-American.

Dr. Martin Luther King, Jr. was the most important voice of the American civil rights movement. King spent his life protesting the unfair treatment of African Americans in the United States. He used peaceful marches and powerful speeches to make Americans realize that treating people differently because of their skin color was wrong. On August 28, 1963, Martin Luther King led the "March on Washington," one of the largest gatherings of black and white people that the nation's capital had ever seen and one of the first to have extensive television coverage (报导). On the steps of the Lincoln Memorial that day, Dr. King delivered a speech that was later entitled "I Have a Dream" to the 250,000 people presented.

The protests helped convince the U.S. Congress to pass *the Civil Rights Act of 1964*. This act made it illegal in America to treat blacks or other ethnic groups unfairly. That same year King's peaceful efforts to win civil rights earned him the Nobel Peace Prize. He was the youngest man to have received the Nobel Peace Prize.

On the evening of April 4, 1968, King was shot and died in hospital. He is remembered for the great changes he made to American society and for the peaceful means that he used to make them.

3. Presidents' Day

Presidents' Day, also known as Washington's Birthday, is a federal holiday held on the third Monday of February. The day honors presidents of the United States. In the weeks or days leading up to the holiday, schools often organize events and lessons for students about the presidents of the United States and George Washington in particular.

Two girls salute in front of the field of 37,000 US flags displayed on the Boston Common in Boston on Memorial Day.

4. Memorial Day

Memorial Day is observed every year on the last Monday in May, honoring people who died while serving in the U.S. military. Many Americans observe Memorial Day by visiting cemeteries or memorials, holding family gatherings and participating in parades. Unofficially, it marks the beginning of the summer season while Labor Day marks its end. It is also the traditional day for people to open up their swimming pools!

5. Independence Day

Independence Day, also known as the Fourth of July, is the birthday of the United States of America commemorating the formal adoption of the *Declaration of Independence* by the Continental Congress on July 4, 1776 in Philadelphia, Pennsylvania. This document declared that the American colonies no longer belonged to Great Britain. They were free and independent states. Although the signing of the Declaration was not completed until August, the Fourth of July has been accepted as the official anniversary of U.S. independence and is celebrated in all states and territories of the U.S.

Independence Day is the main patriotic holiday of the entire country. It is commonly associated with fireworks, parades, barbecues, carnivals, fairs, picnics, concerts, baseball games, family reunions, and political speeches and ceremonies. Shops display red, white, and blue decorations. Communities all over the country light up the night sky with fireworks to honor the nation's birthday. In 1941, the U.S. Congress proclaimed the Fourth of July a national holiday.

6. Labor Day

Labor Day is celebrated on the first Monday in September. It honors the American labor movement and the contributions that workers have made to the strength, prosperity, laws and well-being of the country. Labor Day is called the "unofficial end of summer." It is a signal to students across the country that school is ready to begin again!

The forms for the celebration of Labor Day include a street parade to exhibit to the public "the strength and esprit de corps (Fr. morale) of the trade and labor organizations," followed by a festival for the workers and their friends and families. This became the pattern for Labor Day celebrations. Speeches by prominent men and women were introduced later. More than 80 countries celebrate International Workers' Day on May 1 and several countries have chosen their own dates for Labor Day.

7. Columbus Day

Columbus Day, the second Monday in October, is celebrated in the United States to honor Christopher Columbus' first voyage to America in 1492. On that voyage Columbus encountered the islands that became known as the West Indies, in the Caribbean Sea.

Italian-Americans first began observing Columbus Day in New York City on Oct. 12, 1866, but the first official Columbus Day was declared in 1905. In April 1934, at the request of the Knights of Columbus[①], Congress and President Franklin D. Roosevelt set aside Columbus Day as a federal holiday.

8. Veterans Day

Veterans Day is celebrated annually on November 11 in honor of those who have served in the armed forces of the United States. Veterans Day is not to be confused with Memorial Day, which honors those who died while in military service. The observation was originally designated in 1919 by President Woodrow Wilson as Armistice Day (第一次世界大战停战纪念日). In 1938, Congress passed legislation which designated Armistice Day as a federal holiday. In 1954, President Eisenhower signed a law changing the name of the holiday to Veterans Day so that veterans of other wars could also be honored.

Veterans Day ceremonies involve gatherings of old soldiers with grateful citizens. In many cities and towns, there are parades and speeches to remind people of the sacrifices soldiers have made. Often, flowers are laid at the gravesides of dead soldiers. Special services take place at the Tomb of the Unknown Soldier in Arlington National Cemetery on Veterans Day. Today there are approximately 23.2 million military veterans in the United States.

9. Thanksgiving Day

Thanksgiving Day is a typical American holiday and not celebrated in continental Europe. It is a legal holiday marking the feast given in thanks for the harvest by the Pilgrim colonists in 1621. It is also celebrated in Canada.

People in the United States celebrate Thanksgiving Day on the fourth Thursday in November. In Canada, it occurs on the second Monday in October. People gather around a table with family and friends to share a holiday feast with a traditional turkey dinner, usually in the mid-afternoon. They give thanks for the blessings of the past year and also pay tribute (敬意) to the Pilgrims and Native Americans who shared the first Thanksgiving feast nearly 400 years ago. For Americans and Canadians alike, these activities are an important part of Thanksgiving Day celebrations.

Traditional Thanksgiving foods include turkey with bread stuffing, mashed potatoes, sweet potatoes, corn and cranberry sauce. Pumpkin pie is a classic dessert. A favorite side-dish of many families is cranberry sauce and cranberry relish. Most of these basic foods are native to North

---

① 哥伦布骑士会：世界上最大的天主教会兄弟会志愿者组织。1882年成立于美国，为纪念哥伦布而命名，致力于"慈善""团结""兄弟情谊""爱国主义"原则。会员资格限于18岁或以上的男性并要求是身体力行的天主教徒。

Traditional Thanksgiving Dinner

Tender, juicy roast turkey with old-fashioned gravy, cranberry sauce, smashed potatoes, baked green beans, sweet and sour cod (鳕鱼), steamed rice, pickled green papaya relish, leche flan (焦糖布丁), pig in a blanket (热狗面包), apple crisp, punch (潘趣酒：用酒，果汁，香料等调和的饮料)

America. They help Americans recall the simple way of life of the Pilgrims. But these traditional dishes are not the only foods of modern Thanksgiving celebrations. As people have immigrated to America from other lands, they have added their own traditions.

Every Thanksgiving Day since 1924, Macy's department store has hosted a parade in New York City. The parade is known for its huge balloons. The day after Thanksgiving Day is called Black Friday. It marks the unofficial beginning of the Christmas shopping season. Most major retailers open very early and offer promotional sales(促销).

10. Christmas

Christmas is a holiday celebrated every year on December 25. It commemorates the birth of Jesus Christ more than 2,000 years ago. In many countries of the world, the celebration of Christmas on December 25th is a high point of the year. Colored lights decorate many town centers and shops, along with shiny decorations, and artificial snow painted on shop windows. Christmas trees are decorated with lights and Christmas ornaments. Shopping centers become busier as December approaches and often stay open till late. Groups of people often sing carols on the streets to raise money for charity. Most places of work will hold a short Christmas party about a week before Christmas. People give gifts and post Christmas greeting cards to their friends and family, and Children wait excitedly for Santa Claus to arrive on Christmas Eve and leave presents under the Christmas tree. At midnight on Christmas Eve, most churches hold special candlelight services that feature decorations, candles, and singing. Christmas has become known as a time for family, friendship, giving, and cheer, a festival of goodwill, which many Americans wish could continue throughout the entire year.

➢ *How Long Is Christmas Season?*

The official Christmas season is popularly known as the Twelve Days of Christmas. It extends from the anniversary of Christ's birth on December 25 to January 5 (Epiphany[①] Eve), popularly known as the 12 Days of Christmas. The Epiphany honors Jesus' baptism and the arrival of the Three Wise Men in Bethlehem.

➢ *What Are the Christmas Traditions?*

There are many traditions associated with Christmas that individual families brought with them when they came to the United States.

♦ **Sending Christmas cards** started in Britain in 1840 when the first "Penny Post" public postal deliveries began. As printing methods improved, Christmas cards were produced in large numbers from about 1860. Traditionally, Christmas cards showed religious pictures — Mary, Joseph and baby Jesus, or other parts of the Christmas story. Today, pictures are often jokes, winter pictures, Father Christmas, or romantic scenes of life in past times.

♦ **Exchanging gifts** at Christmas came from the ancient Romans. The Biblical (圣经的) story of the Three Wise Men who presented gifts to baby Jesus also shaped this Christmas custom. Presents are usually opened on Christmas Eve or Christmas Day.

♦ **Christmas tree** began early in the 17th century, in Strasbourg, France, spreading from there through Germany and then into northern Europe. In 1841 Albert, prince consort of Queen Victoria (who was from Germany) introduced the Christmas tree custom to Great Britain; from there it accompanied immigrants to the United States in the 1800s and became very common in the United States in the early nineteenth century.

♦ **Decorating with mistletoe** (槲寄生) **and holly** at Christmas time dates to the Romans. They thought of mistletoe as a symbol of peace and enemies would resolve their differences when they met beneath it. The Christmas custom of kissing under the mistletoe is thought to come from this ancient belief. Holly is also a popular Christmas decoration. Its sharp, pointed leaves are considered a symbol of Christ's crown of thorns. Christ wore the crown when he was nailed to the cross.

♦ **Santa Claus** (or Father Christmas) is based on a real person, St. Nicholas, a Christian leader from Myra (in modern-day Turkey) in the 4th century A.D. It is said that Santa Claus lives near the North Pole, and arrives through the sky on a sledge pulled by reindeer. He comes into houses down the chimney at midnight and places presents in socks or bags in front of the family Christmas tree for every child who's tried to do their best.

♦ **The singing of christmas Carols**. Throughout the world, singing Christmas carols plays an important part in Christmas festivities, which symbolizes the Angels' Announcement of Christ's Birth.

♦ **Ornaments of stars and lights**. The Star of Bethlehem is one of the oldest symbols of Christmas. A star traditionally sits atop Christmas trees and is said to have guided the three Wise Men to Bethlehem on the holy night when Christ was born. Lighted candles have always been a part of Christmas celebrations. The candles represent Jesus Christ, who the Bible calls "the light

---

① 主显节，东正教为洗礼节，天主教及基督教的重要节日，纪念耶稣把自己显示给世人的三个核心事件：贤士来朝、耶稣受洗、变水为酒。

of the world."

♦ **Christmas cracker** makes a harmless exploding sound when two people pull it apart. It usually contains a small cheap toy, a joke and a paper hat, used at meals at Christmas.

♦ **Candy canes** are a traditional Christmas candy. They are curved on top to represent the walking sticks used by the shepherds who were the first visitors to the baby Jesus.

♦ **Sharing Christmas cookies** is also an American tradition.

Other Holidays

1. Valentine's Day

Valentie's Day, also called Saint Valentine's Day, is celebrated on February 14th. It is the traditional day on which lovers express their love for each other by sending Valentine's cards, presenting flowers, or offering candy, all in the name of St. Valentine. The day is most closely associated with the mutual exchange of love notes in the form of "valentines." Modern Valentine symbols include the heart-shaped outline, doves, and the figure of the winged Cupid.

There are varying opinions as to the origin of Valentine's Day. Some experts state that it originated from St. Valentine, a Roman who was martyred (殉难) for refusing to give up Christianity. He died on February 14, 269 A.D. Other aspects of the story say that Saint Valentine served as a priest during the reign of Emperor Claudius. Claudius then had Valentine jailed for performing weddings for soldiers who were forbidden to marry and for ministering to Christians, who were persecuted under the Roman Empire. Legend also says that St. Valentine left a farewell note for the jailer's daughter, who had become his friend, and signed it "From Your Valentine." In 496 A.D. Pope Gelasius set aside February 14 to honor St. Valentine. Gradually, February 14 became the date for exchanging love messages and St. Valentine became the patron saint of lovers.

2. Easter

Easter, also called Easter Sunday, is an annual Christian festival in commemoration of the resurrection of Jesus Christ, observed on the first Sunday after the first full moon after the Spring Equinox (春分), between 22 March and 25 April inclusive, For Christians, Jesus' resurrection offers hope for everlasting life in heaven after death. The Friday before Easter, called Good Friday, marks the day that Jesus was crucified (nailed to a cross), and the day after Easter Sunday is Easter Monday which is a holiday in some countries.

The Easter holiday is rooted in older festivals that celebrated the arrival of spring. Customs that have become associated with Easter include egg hunting, the Easter Bunny, and Easter parades. Many Americans follow the tradition of coloring hard-boiled eggs and giving baskets of candy. A modern custom is to substitute (用……代替) chocolate eggs, or plastic eggs filled with candy such as jellybeans. The egg is an ancient symbol of new life and rebirth, so they are symbolic of the resurrection of Jesus Christ. The bunny is a rabbit-spirit and was reportedly introduced to America by the German immigrants during the 1700s. The Hare and the Rabbit were the most fertile animals known and they served as symbols of the new life during the spring season. Today on Easter Sunday children wake up to find that the Easter Bunny has left them baskets of candy.

Rolling eggs on Easter Monday is a tradition observed by many Washington families, including those of the President. In 1878, the First Lady invited children to the White House for the Egg Roll and it has been held there ever since then, only canceled during times of war.

The tradition of the Easter parade began in the 1800s as people walked down 5th Avenue in New York City after Easter Sunday church services. The New York City Easter Parade features marchers in elaborate Easter

The Trumps hosted their first White House Easter Egg Roll

finery (华丽的服饰), including some of the fanciest Easter bonnets imaginable.

3. April Fool's Day

April Fool's Day is a day to play jokes on others. It is a "for-fun-only" observance. Nobody is expected to buy gifts or to take their "significant other" out to eat in a fancy restaurant. Nobody gets off work or school. It's simply a fun little holiday, but a holiday on which one must remain forever vigilant, for he may be the next April Fool!

Each country celebrates April Fool's Day differently. In England, people play jokes only in the morning. You are a "noodle" (笨人) if someone fools you. In the United States, pranks are played on just about everybody. Pranks range from the standard "Your shoe is untied," to some very creative and elaborate ideas. The only "rule" is that no one should be harmed. Corporations, newspapers, and television stations will also play practical jokes on April Fool's Day.

4. Halloween

Halloween is a celebration observed in most areas of North America and in some areas of Western Europe on 31 October, the eve of All Hallows' Day (also known as All Saints' Day). It is symbolically associated with death and the supernatural. Immigrants from Scotland and Ireland brought the holiday to the United States.

By tradition, Halloween begins after sunset. Long ago, people believed that witches gathered together and ghosts roamed (漫游) the world on Halloween. Today, most people no longer believe in ghosts and witches. But these supernatural beings are still a part of Halloween.

Halloween activities include trick-or-treating (so called because children used to play tricks on neighbors who didn't give treats), attending Halloween costume parties, carving pumpkins into jack-o'-lanterns (a hollowed-out pumpkin with a face carved on one side), lighting bonfires (篝火), apple bobbing①, playing pranks, visiting haunted attractions, telling scary stories and watching horror films. In many parts of the world, the Christian religious observances, including

---

① 叼苹果：万圣节的一个传统游戏。在游戏中，人们把盆子或桶盛满水，并把苹果放在水中，参加者设法只用嘴咬起漂浮在水上的苹果。。

attending church services and lighting candles on the graves of the dead, remain popular.

There are various symbols associated with Halloween. These include the spooks, ghosts and walking skeletons that represent the contact between the spiritual and physical world and between the living and the dead. Human figures represented on Halloween are witches and wizards (男巫), who are seen to have the power to contact the spirit world. Bats, black cats and spiders are often connected with this holiday. These animals are associated with the night and darkness.

5. Arbor Day

In the Unites States, Arbor Day is a nationally-celebrated observance that encourages tree planting and care to beautify towns or to forest empty areas of land. In Latin "arbor" means "tree." Founded by J. Sterling Morton in Nebraska in 1872, National Arbor Day is celebrated each year on the last Friday in April in the United States. Most public schools celebrate Arbor Day in order to teach about protecting the forests. In some states it is a legal holiday.

Understanding Canada

A General Survey of Canada

章节导读

本章为加拿大国家概览，简略介绍了加拿大的综合国情，包括人口、位置、国名、首都、语言、宗教、国旗、国歌、国徽等核心信息，建立加拿大概况的主体印象，以引入后续章节的详细描述。

With an area of 9,984,670 square kilometers, Canada is a huge country, second in size only to Russia and slightly larger than China. Yet it has only 35 million people (2016 Census), which is less than half the population of the United Kingdom.

Situated in northern half of the North America, it extends from the Great Lakes in the south to the majestic Rocky Mountains in the west, and the bleak Arctic Islands in the far north. With 10 provinces and 3 territories, Canada became a self-governing dominion (英联邦的自治领) in 1867 while retaining ties to the British crown. Economically and technologically the nation has developed in parallel with the U.S., its neighbor to the south across an unfortified (不设防的)border.

Country Name

The simple official country name of Canada has many explanations. The most popular one is as follows:

Jacques Cartier, the first European navigator who discovered what is now Canada, went ashore on July 24, 1534, at a spot later to be known as Québec City. There he asked some local Indians what that place was called. The Indians, thinking that he meant their little town, replied Kanada, which means "a settlement" in the Huron-Iroquois Indian language (休伦-易洛魁印第安语). On returning to Europe，Cartier announced that he had discovered a new land named Kanada. Thus in misunderstanding, the place later became known as Canada.

The name "Canada" later referred to a large area north of the St. Lawrence River. As more land was explored, "Canada" grew. The first time "Canada" was used as an official name was in 1791 for the colonies of Upper and Lower Canada. In 1867, at the time of Confederation, the new country became known as Canada.

Capital

The capital of Canada is the city of Ottawa, which is in the province of Ontario, located above the Great Lakes. Ever since it was named Canada's capital by Queen Victoria in 1857, Ottawa has grown into a city for all seasons, alive with vitality and rich in historic traditions.

Language

Parliament Hill on Ottawa River

Canada is a multilingual society with English and French as its official languages. In the 2011 Census, about 58% of Canadians reported English was their mother tongue while 22% reported their mother tongue was French. Most French speakers (francophone, 讲法语的) live in Québec where they form a majority. About 17.5 percent reported that they were bilingual in English and French.

As more Chinese immigrants settle in Canada, Chinese is reaffirmed as Canada's third most common mother tongue. Cree (克里语), as one of the Indian languages, has the largest language group in Canada.

Currency

The official currency of Canada is the Canadian dollar. It is normally abbreviated with the dollar sign $, or C$ to distinguish it from other dollar-denominated currencies. It is divided into 100 cents. As of 2016, the Canadian dollar was the 6th most traded currency in the world.

Canadian Dollars and Coins

Religion

Canada is religiously diverse, encompassing a wide range of beliefs and customs. Canada has no official church, and the government is officially committed to religious pluralism. According to the 2011 census, 67.3% of Canadians identify as Christian; of these, Roman Catholics make up the largest group, accounting for 38.7% of the population. Much of the remainder is made up of Protestants. The largest Protestant denomination is the United Church of Canada (accounting for 6.1% of Canadians), followed by Anglicans (5.0%), and Baptists (1.9%). 23.9% declared no religious affiliation. The remaining 8.8% are affiliated with non-Christian religions, the largest of which are Islam (3.2%) and Hinduism (1.5%).

National Flag

The National Flag of Canada, popularly known as the Maple Leaf and l'Unifolié (French for "the one-leaved"), is a base red flag with a white square in its center featuring a stylized, 11-pointed, red maple leaf. Adopted in 1964, the flag made its first appearance on February 15, 1965, which is now celebrated annually as Flag Day.

National Anthem

There have been a lot of patriotic songs written about Canada over the years, but until 1980 none held the lofty status of Canada's official national anthem. Initially, the country was just supposed to use "God Save the Queen," the royal anthem of Great Britain, for official purposes, but as the years went on there was growing interest in using a more uniquely Canadian song, with "The Maple Leaf Forever" (1867) and "O Canada" (1880) emerging as the two most popular tunes. "O Canada" eventually won out, and was given official anthem status when Parliament passed the *National Anthem Act* in 1980. "O Canada" was actually originally written in French and the Montreal judge and poet Robert Stanley Weir (1856 — 1926) wrote its English version. Like most national anthems, the Canadian anthem has several other verses as well, but these are never sung at public occasions since no one knows the words.

Prior to 2016, when *the Act to Amend the National Anthem Act* was passed, the line "in all of us command" was "in all thy sons command." It was changed to make the anthem "gender neutral."①

The lyrics to the anthem go like this:

O Canada!	啊！加拿大
O Canada! Our home and native land! True patriot love in all of us command. With glowing hearts we see thee rise, The True North strong and free! From far and wide, O Canada, we stand on guard for thee. God keep our land glorious and free! O Canada, we stand on guard for thee. O Canada, we stand on guard for thee.	啊，加拿大！我们的祖国，我们的家乡！ 您的儿女对您充满真爱！ 颗颗闪亮的心儿深情凝望， 那一片强大自由的北方！ 啊，加拿大！无论身处何地， 我们都保卫您。 上帝使我们的祖国自由辉煌！ 啊，加拿大！我们保卫您！ 啊，加拿大！我们保卫您！

National Emblems

Actually, there are two national emblems of Canada. The first one is the Canadian beaver, a clever and hardworking semi-aquatic (半水栖的) animal. It appears on the Canadian nickel and is often used by cartoonists to personify the country as a whole, much like "Uncle Sam" or a Chinese dragon. The original Canadian attraction to beavers was much less respectful: they had good fur for making hats. Prized for its smooth, waterproof texture, beaver fur was one of Canada's main exports to Europe during the 17th and 18th centuries. The animal was almost hunted to extinction by early Canadian fur traders. Saved by changing tastes in fashion, today they can be found lurking in riverbeds all across the country. Now it is officially regarded as the symbol of the sovereignty of Canada.

The second national emblem of Canada is the Canadian maple leaf. However, its use as the national symbol has shorter history, dating back only to the middle 19th century. With the proclamation of the national flag of Canada, it was confirmed as an official symbol. A maple leaf is always found on Canadian officials' business cards.

Coat of Arms

The Coat of Arms of Canada (also known as the national crest, 徽章) was officially adopted in 1921, and in its initial form it was virtually identical to Britain's Royal Coat of Arms. In 1994 it was modified slightly to include Canada's motto as well as some red and white maple leafs at the top. This combination of British, French and Canadian symbols reflects Canada's historic and

---

① 2016年6月15日加拿大众议院举行投票，以225票支持74票反对的压倒性优势通过了修改国歌的法案，从而使歌词性别中立，以响应新政府提出的性别包容的号召。加拿大国歌《啊！加拿大》(O Canada!) 有英文和法文两个版本。此次修改的部分是英文版中第二行歌词 "True patriot love in all thy sons' command (您的儿子，忠诚爱国)"，其中"all thy sons (儿子们)" 改为 "all of us (我们，意译为儿女们)"。

cultural traditions.

The Coat of Arms appears on things like passports, government publications and wax seals. Its symbolism is largely British: it depicts an English lion and a Scottish unicorn holding a shield displaying medieval icons of the English, Scottish, and Irish peoples of the British Isles, plus the fleur-de-lis (鸢尾，百合花，法国王室纹章花形) of the French and the maple leaves of Canada. At the creatures' feet sit a medley (混合物) of plants representing the Scottish, Irish, English, and Welsh. The animals stand below the flags of the United Kingdom and medieval France, symbolizing the "two founding nations" of modern Canada.

Canada has two national mottoes, both of which are inscribed in Latin on the crest. The first (on the red belt around the shield) is Desiderantes Meliorem Patriam, meaning "They Desire a Better Country," which acknowledges the immigrants who have built Canada. The other (on the blue ribbon at the bottom) is A Mari Usque Ad Mare, meaning "From Sea to Sea," which celebrates the country's vast geography.

A Collection of Fast Facts of Canada

Official Name	Canada
Capital	Ottawa
Population	35,151,728 people (2016 Census)
Rank among countries in population	38th
Major cities	Toronto, Montréal, Vancouver
Area	9,984,670 km²
Rank in area worldwide	2nd
Highest point	Mt. Logan, 5,959 meters
Currency	Canadian dollar
Principal Languages	English and French
Major Religion	Christianity
Literacy Rate	99%
Administrative divisions	10 provinces, 3 territories
National Day	Canada Day, 1 July (1867)

Chapter 6 Geography and History

> **章节导读**
>
> 本章介绍加拿大的地理历史基本知识。地理部分介绍了该国地质特征、山川河流、气候物产，行政区划、主要城市，并分地区描述各省的基本状况和特征。历史部分以时间为序，梳理加拿大从殖民时期到走向独立的历史进程。

A. Geography

I Geographic Features

"From Sea to Sea"

Occupying most of the northern portion of the continent of North America, Canada spans an immense territory between the Pacific Ocean to the west and the Atlantic Ocean to the east, with the United States to the south and northwest (Alaska), and the Arctic Ocean to the north; Greenland is to the northeast. It has the world's longest coastline of 202,080 kilometers.

Canada's Physical Regions

Canada has clearly defined political and physical regions. It is divided into 13 political regions: ten provinces and three territories. There are 6 physical regions, each with a very different landscape and climate. They are the Atlantic Region, the Great Lakes & St. Lawrence Region, the Canadian Shield, the Great Plains, the Cordillera and the North.

1. **Atlantic Region** is the most eastern region of Canada located between the Atlantic Ocean and the heavily forested Appalachian Mountain. It was the first physical region that was rediscovered and inhabited by the early European settlers. This region of low hills, plains, islands, and peninsulas includes the Atlantic Provinces of Newfoundland, Nova Scotia, Prince Edward Island and New Brunswick. The sea has long shaped the life of the Appalachian region.

2. **Great Lakes-St. Lawrence Region** is an area of fertile lowlands that stretches along the St. Lawrence River and the Great Lakes. The St. Lawrence Seaway, a system of locks (水闸) and highways connect the Canadian interior to the Atlantic Ocean. Good transportation, fertile soil and a mild climate have helped to make this region the agricultural and industrial center of Canada, containing Canada's two largest cities, Montreal and Toronto. In this small region, 50 percent of Canadians live and 70 percent of Canada's manufactured goods are produced.

3. **The Canadian Shield** covers almost half of Canada, stretching west and north from the Atlantic Ocean to the Arctic Ocean (北冰洋). It consists of low hills, swamps, lakes and streams. Because the soil is poor and the climate is cold, few people live in this region. Canadian Shield cuts the country in half and contributes to divisions between the easterners and westerners. The shield is rich in mineral resources. Its forest once supported huge numbers of fur bearing animals.

4. **Great Plains** lie farther west. It is a physiographic (地形学的) region in central Canada and the United States. The region has a vast, generally high plateau, called the plains, which feature productive grain and livestock farms (畜牧场) and extensive petroleum and coal deposits.

5. **The Cordillera** (Western Mountain Group) is a mountainous strip of land about 805 km wide, stretching from the towering Rocky Mountains to the Coastal Ranges along the Pacific. Between the mountains lie rugged plateaus. The word Cordillera is a Spanish word meaning mountain ranges. The natural resources of the Cordillera are forestry (this is the biggest industry in the region), agriculture, mining and fisheries.

6. **The North Region** includes Yukon, Northwest Territories, Nunavut, Northern Québec and the most extreme tip of Labrador and Newfoundland. This area is very unique compared to the rest of Canada: the Northern Landscape, a combination of the Cordillera, Plains and Canadian Shield, is the only landscape where the ground is frozen all year. The unique tilt of our Earth's axis gives this region 6 months of constant sunlight and then 6 months of continual darkness. In summer the sun would still be shinning at midnight. Because of the unique landscape and climate conditions (extremely cold in the winter months) this area has the lowest human population in Canada.

II Mountains, Rivers and Lakes

Mountains

Canada's vast area means it has many varying types of terrain (地形), much of which is mountainous. The principal mountainous region is the Cordillera, or Cordilleran. This region comprises a series of mountain belts some 800 kilometers wide along Canada's Pacific coast.

A second major mountain system in Canada is located along the north-eastern seaboard (沿海地方) from Ellesmere Island in Nunavut down through to the Torngat Mountains of Québec and Newfoundland and Labrador.

A third system of significance is the Appalachians which cross much of eastern Canada.

The highest peak in Canada is Mount Logan (5951 meters) in the Yukon Territory of northwest Canada.

Rivers and Lakes

The two principal river systems in Canada are the Mackenzie[①] and St. Lawrence. The St. Lawrence, with its tributaries, is navigable for over 3,058 km and empties into the Gulf of St. Lawrence. It is the largest river in Canada in volume of water discharged (流出) at its mouth. Flowing between the Canadian Shield and the Rocky Mountains in west Canada, the Mackenzie (4,241 km) is the longest river in Canada and the second largest river system of North America. It empties into the Arctic Ocean and drains a large part of northwestern Canada.

Canada contains more lakes and inland waters than any other country in the world. In addition to the Great Lakes on the American border (all partly within Canada except Lake

---

① 马更些河：北美洲仅次于密西西比河的第二长河，加拿大最长的河流，也是全球流经北极苔原地区的最大河流。发源于加拿大不列颠哥伦比亚省北部，从其上游支流芬利（Finlay）河源头算起，河流全长4241千米，流域面积180.5万平方千米。

Michigan), the country has 31 lakes or reservoirs of about 1,300 sq km in area.

Canada's two largest lakes are Superior and Huron, at 82,100 sq km and 59,600 sq km respectively. About one-third of Lake Superior and about three-fifths of Lake Huron are in Canada. The Great Lakes and the St. Lawrence Seaway, which is a deep waterway extending 3,700 km from the Atlantic Ocean to the head of the Great Lakes, form an important transportation network for eastern Canada, and have been important for the industrial development of the Great lakes-St. Lawrence Region.

Falls

People often say if you haven't been to Niagara Falls (尼亚加拉大瀑布), you cannot be said to have been to Canada. Is Niagara Falls the highest waterfall in the world? No. It is by no means the world's highest waterfall. Actually, it is not even the highest waterfall in Canada. Della Falls is the highest waterfall in Canada and tenth highest in the world.

The greatest waterfall by volume is Niagara Falls. It is present in the Canada-America border and consists of a set of waterfalls namely the American Falls, Bridal Veil Falls, both of which are on the American side, and the Horseshoe Falls, which is on the Canadian side and is considered to be the most impressive of the three falls. Approximately 90% of the water of the Niagara River flows over Horseshoe Falls, while the other 10% flows over the American Falls.

III Administrative Areas and Major Cities

Just as the United States is a federation of states, Canada is a federation of provinces. It is now made up of ten provinces and three territories. Each area has its own provincial flag.

Canada's capital is Ottawa and its largest city is Toronto. Other important cities include Vancouver (温哥华), Montreal (蒙特利尔), Québec (魁北克), Edmonton (埃德蒙顿), Calgary (卡尔加里), Winnipeg (温尼伯), Victoria, etc.

A Western Province: British Columbia (不列颠哥伦比亚省)

Popularly known by its initials, BC, British Columbia, the westernmost province of Canada is bounded on the west by the Pacific Ocean. Along its deeply indented (犬牙交错的) Pacific coast lie many islands, notably Vancouver Island (450 km long) and the sparsely inhabited Queen Charlotte Islands.

Victoria, a Garden City

The province is almost wholly mountainous, with three major mountain ranges: the Rocky mountains. in the southeast, the Coast mountains. along the Pacific, and the Stikine mountains. in the northwest. *Lake Louise* (路易斯湖), located in the Rockies, is the most famous image of the Canadian landscape. British Columbia attracts millions of visitors annually.

Victoria is the capital. In addition to its importance as the seat of provincial government, Victoria is noted as a garden city, a residential city because of its mild climate, beautiful scenery, many parks and drives. It is also a popular center for American and Canadian tourists.

The largest city and chief port is **Vancouver**. Situated on a peninsula opposite Vancouver Island, Vancouver is the third largest city in Canada (after Toronto and Montréal) and the most livable city in the world. Vancouver's Chinatown is the traditional center of one of the largest Chinese communities in North America. Mandarin Chinese and Cantonese are the mother tongues in so many Vancouver homes that Chinese has become the dominant "minority" ethnic group.

Three Prairie Provinces: Alberta, Saskatchewan, Manitoba

1. Alberta (阿尔伯塔省) — A Province Rich in Petrol and Natural Gases

Alberta is the westernmost of Canada's three Prairie Provinces, covering an area of some 661,185 square kilometers. It is a land of contrasts. Rolling plains cover much of the province, but in the southwest, the rugged Rocky Mountains and its foothills (丘陵地带) form part of Alberta's boundary with British Columbia. In the north the land is covered with forests and dotted with lakes and streams. On the vast Alberta plains, oil rigs (钻塔) rise above great wheat fields. Alberta possesses Canada's largest deposits of oil and natural gas, and the province has prospered with the rapid expansion of the petroleum industry after World War II.

Industrial cities such as Edmonton, the capital of Alberta, and Calgary, the largest city, thrive in the midst of rich agricultural lands. Edmonton, which describes itself as "The Gateway to the North," is the transportation and distribution center for an area reaching to the Arctic Ocean. Calgary has the most striking setting of all of Canada's prairie cities. It lies at the very edge of the high plains, where they rise into the foothills of the Rocky Mountains, on a site deeply carved by the Bow and Elbow rivers. Calgary is known as the Energy Capital of Canada as a number of oil companies have headquarters in the city. It is one of the country's most important business centers.

2. Saskatchewan (萨斯喀彻温省) — A Prairie Province Rich in Wheat and Oil

Saskatchewan borders Manitoba province on the east, Alberta province on the west. Its name is derived from the Cree term for "swiftly flowing," which was first applied to the Saskatchewan River. Saskatchewan became a province of Canada on September 1, 1905. It is one of the only two Canadian provinces with no saltwater coast (the other one being Alberta). This province was once famous for its "wheat economy," with wheat farming as its main industry. Now this area is also rich in farming, fur producing, mining, etc.

Regina (里贾纳) is the capital and the second largest city of Saskatchewan next to Saskatoon (萨斯卡通). The Latin word Regina means "queen" and the city is sometimes called the Queen City of the Plains because of its location in the heart of Canada's prairie region. Regina's main claim to fame is Royal Canadian Mounted Police (RCMP,加拿大皇家骑警) training center. The RCMP have called Regina home since the late 1800's. One evening each week during July to mid August, this prestige police force performs a special "Sunset Ceremony" — renowned as one of Canada's top 20 attractions.

RCMP Sunset Ceremonies

3. Manitoba (曼尼托巴省) — Keystone Province of Canada

As the easternmost of Canada's three Prairie provinces, Manitoba has been known as the keystone (拱顶石) of the continent from the Atlantic to the Pacific. Comparatively level, Manitoba generally ranges from 150 meters to 300 meters above sea level. Baldy Mountain is Manitoba's highest point, at 2831 meters. In northernmost Manitoba lies tundra (苔原) and permafrost (永久冻结带). All waters in Manitoba flow to Hudson Bay.

Winnipeg is the oldest city in the Prairie Provinces. In addition to being the capital of Manitoba, Winnipeg is also a leading trading center for the grain originating in all three Prairie Provinces and the site of one of the world's leading commodity exchanges, the Winnipeg Commodity Exchange. It is also a major railway junction, and railways and rivers together played a major role in the city's early development, making it "the gateway to the west."

Two Central Canada Provinces: Ontario and Québec

1. Ontario (安大略省) — the Heartland Province

Southernmost Province of Canada, Ontario is the second largest of Canada's ten provinces in area and the largest in terms of population. Commonly called the Heartland Province, Ontario is the center of Canada's industry, population, and agriculture.

There are over 250,000 lakes in Ontario — they make up about one-third of the world's fresh water. In summer, temperatures can soar above 30°C, while in winter they can drop to below -40°C.

Ontario's industries range from cultivating crops, to mining minerals, manufacturing automobiles, to designing software and leading-edge technology.

Toronto Skyline

Ottawa, the capital city of Canada, and **Toronto**, the province's capital and Canada's most populous city, are both situated in Ontario. Ottawa is situated in the southeastern part of the province of Ontario. The city and surrounding municipalities form Canada's National Capital Region, which includes government agencies, parks, and tourist sites. Ottawa is one of the coldest national capitals in the world and is a city of great natural beauty. Toronto has the largest metropolitan area in Canada and is the financial center of the country as well as the provincial capital of Ontario. The city is part of the Golden Horseshoe, a highly urbanized and industrialized region extending around the west end of Lake Ontario. Residents of Toronto are called **Torontonians**.

2. Québec (魁北克省) — the Largest Province of Canada

Québec is located in the eastern part of Canada and extends north from the United States border to Hudson Strait and east from the shores of Hudson Bay to the region of Labrador. Québec is nicknamed La Belle Province (the Beautiful Province) because of the splendor and diversity of its landscape and architecture. The site of the first permanent French settlement in North America, Québec is unique among the Canadian provinces in that the vast majority of its population is of French descent and speaks French as a first language. To many French Canadians, Québec is far more than a province; it is a cultural homeland. Settled by the French in the 1600s, it is the oldest province in Canada and one of the four original provinces that united in 1867 to form the Dominion of Canada.

Québec's most important river is the St. Lawrence River, which is 1,300 km long and traverses the entire province, connecting the Atlantic Ocean with the Great Lakes.

Québec City is the capital of the province of Québec. It is the second most populous city in the province — after Montreal, about 233 kilometers to the southwest. As of the 2016 Canadian Census, the city has a population of 545,485. Québec City is internationally known for its Summer Festival, Winter Carnival and the Château Frontenac (芬堤娜城堡饭店), a historic hotel built in 1892, which overlooks the St. Lawrence River, 100 meters below and dominates the Québec City skyline. It has a historic elegance possibly unmatched in North America. The ramparts (城墙) surrounding Old Québec are the only remaining fortified city walls that still exist in the Americas north of Mexico, and were declared a World Heritage Site by UNESCO in 1985 as the "Historic District of Old Québec."

Château Frontenac

Montreal is the second-largest city in Canada and the largest city in the province of Québec. It is the second-largest French-speaking city in the Western world after Paris. As of the 2016 Canadian Census, 1,704,694 people resided in the city of Montreal proper.

Four Atlantic Provinces — New Brunswick, Nova Scotia, Prince Edward Island, Newfoundland & Labrador

The three Atlantic Provinces (the Maritime provinces) of New Brunswick, Nova Scotia, and Prince Edward Island (PEI) are on the far east coast of the country. Rugged and sparsely populated, the provinces have traditionally made much of their income from the area's large fisheries. This is changing in the region, as oil production, information technology, biomedical research, post-secondary education and tourism become more important for local economies.

1. New Brunswick (新不伦瑞克省)

New Brunswick is the largest of Canada's three Maritime Provinces. It is bordered by the Canadian provinces of Québec and Nova Scotia, and the American state of Maine. It is blessed with two distinct shorelines; one with rocky cliffs, and the other fringed with long stretches of sand and dunes (海边被风吹积成的沙丘). Forests cover about 85 percent of the land and the manufacture of lumber, paper, and other forest products is important to the province's economy.

Fredericton (弗雷德里克顿) is the provincial capital, and Saint John is the largest city.

2. Nova Scotia (新斯科舍省)

Nova Scotia (Latin for New Scotland) is located on Canada's southeastern coast. It is the most populous province in the Maritimes, and its capital, Halifax, is a major economic center of the region. Nova Scotia is the second smallest province in Canada, with an area of 55,284 km² and yet it is the second most-densely populated with 17.4 inhabitants per square kilometer. As of 2016, the population was 923,598. Nova Scotia's economy is traditionally largely resource-based, but has in recent decades become more diverse. Industries such as fishing, mining, forestry and agriculture remain very important, and have been joined by tourism, technology, film production, music and the financial service industries.

The Bay of Fundy New Brunswick/Nova Scotia has the highest tides (16.2 meters) in the world and is renowned for its coastal rock formations.

Located in the south-central part of the province on the Atlantic Ocean, Halifax is the capital city of Nova Scotia and the largest city in the Atlantic Provinces of Canada. Founded in 1749, it served as an important naval base in the American Revolution, the War of 1812, and both World Wars. In the 19th and early 20th century, Halifax was the entry point for European immigration to Canada. Today, Halifax is a busy Atlantic seaport and the economic and cultural hub of Eastern Canada.

3. Prince Edward Island (爱德华王子岛省)

Prince Edward Island (PEI) is located in the southern Gulf of St. Lawrence. This maritime province is the smallest in the nation in both land area and population (excluding the territories). The island was discovered by Jacques Cartier in 1534 and named Île St. Jean by Samuel de Champlain in 1603. It was renamed in 1798 after Prince Edward, Duke of Kent and Strathearn (1767 — 1820), the fourth son of King George III and the father of Queen Victoria. It joined the confederacy in 1873.

Prince Edward Island has 142,907 residents (2016 Census). It is the 104th largest island in the world, and Canada's 23rd largest island. The 12.9-kilometre long Confederation Bridge links Prince Edward Island with mainland New Brunswick, Canada.

4. Newfoundland and Labrador (纽芬兰与拉布拉多省)

Newfoundland and Labrador is a province on the country's Atlantic coast in northeastern North America. This easternmost Canadian province comprises two main parts: the island of Newfoundland off the country's eastern coast, and Labrador on the mainland to the northwest of the island. St. John's is the capital and the largest city.

A former colony and dominion of the United Kingdom, it became the tenth province to enter the Canadian Confederation on 31 March 1949, named simply as Newfoundland. On 6 December 2001, an amendment was made to the Constitution of Canada to change the province's official name to Newfoundland and Labrador. In day-to-day conversation, however, Canadians generally still refer to the province itself as Newfoundland and to the region on the Canadian mainland as Labrador.

As of 2016, the province's population was 530,376. Approximately 90% of the province's population resides on the Island of Newfoundland (including its associated smaller islands).

St. John's is the provincial capital. It is the most easterly city in North America, as well as the second largest city in Atlantic Provinces after Halifax, Nova Scotia and 20th largest metropolitan area in Canada with a metro population of 205,955 (2016 Census).

Northern Canada (北部区)

Canada extends up north into the Arctic Circle to the North Pole. The north is a scarcely populated area of ice and oceans, which is sometimes called "the Land of the Midnight Sun." This region is currently divided into three administrative territories — the Yukon (育空地区), the Northwest Territories and Nunavat (努纳武特地区), a territory carved from eastern part of the original Northwest Territories in 1999.

As of 2016, only about 113,604 people were living in this vast area larger than the size of Western Europe. About half of the population of the three territories is Aboriginal, and the Inuit are the largest group of Aboriginal peoples in Northern Canada.

1. Yukon (育空)

Yukon is the westernmost and smallest of Canada's three federal territories. It was named after the Yukon River (3,700 km), which means "Great River" and empties into the Bering Sea. Created in 1898 as the Yukon Territory, the federal government's most recent update of the *Yukon Act* in 2003 confirmed "Yukon," rather than "Yukon Territory," as the current usage standard.

Yukon is a sparsely populated territory with a population of about 35,874(2016). Most of the territory is in the watershed (流域) of the Yukon River. Yukon abounds with snow-melt lakes and perennial snow-capped mountains. Mount Logan (5,959 m), in the territory's southwest, is the highest mountain in Canada and the second highest of North America (after Mount McKinley in the U.S. state of Alaska). Although the climate is Arctic and sub-arctic (亚北极的) and very dry, with long, cold winters, the long sunshine hours in short summer allow hardy (耐寒的) crops and vegetables, along with a profusion of flowers and fruit to blossom.

The Yukon's historical major industry has been mining. The territory's historical sites as well as the scenic wonders and outdoor recreation make tourism the second most important industry. Yukon's tourism motto is "Larger than life" (非同凡响), and its major appeal is its nearly pristine nature.

Whitehorse (怀特霍斯) is the capital and largest city of Yukon, which accounts for almost 3/4 of the territory's population and is the largest city in the three Canadian territories. The second largest is Dawson City which was the capital until 1952.

2. The Northwest Territories

Northwest Territories (N.W.T.) is the second largest of the three territories in Canada with a land area of 1,140,835 square kilometres. It extends from the 60th parallel to the North Pole and includes several large islands located in the Arctic Ocean.

The population is about 41,786 (2016) and more than half of the people are aboriginal. The largest community is Yellowknife, which has been the capital city since 1967 and is known as the Diamond Capital of North America. Most people are living in the Mackenzie River Valley or around Great Slave Lake.

The Northwest Territories' Official Languages Act recognizes eleven official languages with English and French included, which are more than in any other political division in the Americas.

3. Nunavut (努纳武特地区)

The establishment of Nunavut, which means "our land" in Inuktitut (因纽特语), represents a landmark event in the history of Inuit and Canada. On April 1, 1999, Nunavut became the newest federal territory of Canada, encompassing the central and eastern Arctic regions, covering 1,932,255 km^2 of land and 160,935 km^2 of water. This makes it the largest of all Canada's provinces and Territories and the fifth largest administrative division in the world. Originally part of the Northwest Territories, Nunavut was separated officially from the Northwest Territories on April 1, 1999 though the actual boundaries had been established in 1993. Nunavut is both the geographically largest and the least populated of the provinces and territories of Canada. It has a population of 35,944(2016), spread over an area of the size of Western Europe, of whom 85 percent are Inuit.

Winter is close to nine months long in this region, with snow covering the ground for most of the year. Mining, shrimp and scallop (扇贝) fishing, hunting and trapping, arts and crafts production are the key industries. Tourism is also a growing industry.

Iqaluit (伊卡卢伊特) is the territorial capital and the largest community of Nunavut, with a population of 7,740 (2016). It has the distinction of being the smallest Canadian capital in terms of population.

IV Climate

People tend to think that as Canada is a northern country, its winters must be harsh and long. But contrary to popular belief, on the whole Canada is a very sunny land with a distinctive change of seasons. Climatic conditions range from the extreme cold of the Arctic regions to the moderate temperatures of more southerly latitudes. The south-western coast has a relatively mild climate.

Significant Climatic Changes in Canada

Generally speaking, spring begins in mid-March and ends in mid-May. It is regarded as a transitional time in Canada. In many parts of Canada, the first sign of spring is the trickling (流淌) of sap (树液) from thousands of maple-trees. It is in spring that farmers reap their special harvest — maple-syrup (枫树汁) to make delicious sugar products.

Summer is longer than spring, lasting for about four months in places near the U.S-Canadian border, from mid-May to mid-September. Average summer temperatures range from 8°C in the far north to more than 22°C in some parts of the far south. Warm and sunny, it's the golden time for vacationers.

Autumn is brief but spectacular, beginning from mid-September to mid-November. Leaves turned into millions of shades of gold and scarlet against the background of a blue sky.

Winter is the longest season in most of Canada, prolonging from mid-November to mid-March. Average January temperatures range from -35°C in the far north to 3°C in southwestern British Columbia. Canadians will never deny that they have more than their share of ice and snow. It is a golden time for skiing, skating, ice-fishing and tobogganing (滑雪撬).

Climate and Canadian Life

Climate has been a factor in the development of Canada because people have settled where temperatures are warmest and agricultural growing seasons longest. Southern Ontario and southwestern British Columbia have the mildest climates and greatest population densities in Canada. In contrast, the central and northern regions are sparsely populated.

The permafrost (永久冻结带) region in the north poses (形成) great challenges for settlement and development. Yukon, the Northwest Territories, the Nunavut Territory, northern Québec and Labrador, and the far northern areas of Ontario and Manitoba are all affected by this condition.

V Natural Resources

Canada is rich in valuable natural resources that are commercially indispensable to the economy. Most are specific to one region or another; for this reason separate resource-based economies have tended to develop across Canada.

Forestry

Canadian forests cover about one third of the country's land area and abound in commercially valuable stands of timber, especially in British Columbia, Québec, northern Ontario, the northern Prairie Provinces, and the Maritimes.

Mineral resources

Canada's extensive mineral resources provide valuable exports and also supply domestic industries. Five of the country's six major regions contribute to these resources. The Québec portion of the Appalachian Region has the world's largest reserves of asbestos (石棉), along with deposits of copper and zinc.

The Canadian Shield is a rich source of metals such as nickel, copper, gold, uranium (铀), silver, aluminum, and zinc. Minerals from the shield helped fuel the manufacturing development of southern Ontario and Québec.

The Great Plains region is rich in reserves of crude petroleum and natural gas; these are concentrated in the Prairie Provinces, particularly in Alberta. These fuel deposits are responsible for the dynamic energy-producing economy of these provinces.

The western Canadian Cordillera provides copper, lead, zinc, molybdenum (钼), and asbestos; the Canadian Arctic Archipelago (多岛海区) provides zinc and lead. Increasingly important to the mining industry, the Canadian Arctic Archipelago features the world's northernmost base metal mine, the Polaris mine, on Little Cornwallis Island.

Hydroelectric Energy

The river and lake systems of the country combine with topography to make hydroelectric energy one of the permanent natural assets of Canada. Here British Columbia and the shield provinces are particularly well endowed. As with other natural resources, much of the energy is exported.

Wild life

The wildlife of the country is extensive and varied and attracts tourists from around the world. But it is the fish stocks that have the greatest economic value. Saltwater fish in the Pacific and the Atlantic Oceans, as well as freshwater fish in Canada's numerous lakes and rivers, are economically significant and also provide a source of food and revenue for many local communities.

Cougar (美洲狮)   Polar bear (北极熊)   Moose (驼鹿)   Raccoon (浣熊)

B. History

First inhabited for thousands of years by aboriginal peoples, Canada has evolved from a group of European colonies into an officially bilingual, multicultural federation. France sent the first large group of settlers in the 17th century, but Canada came to be dominated by the British until the country peacefully attained full independence in the 20th century. Its history has been affected by its inhabitants, its geography, and its relations with the outside world.

First Peoples

Many indigenous peoples have inhabited the region that is now Canada for thousands of years and have their own diverse histories. Indigenous peoples include First Nations people (Canadian Indians), Inuit (因纽特人) and Métis[①]. Indigenous peoples contributed significantly to the culture and economy of the early European colonies and have played an important role in fostering a unique Canadian cultural identity.

European Contact (985 — 1600)

There are a number of reports of contact made before Columbus between the first peoples and those from other continents. It is said that British, Portuguese and Spanish explorers had visited Canada, but it was the French who first began to explore further inland and set up colonies, beginning in 1534 with French navigator Jacques Cartier (1491 — 1557), who in 1534 first explored and described the Gulf of St. Lawrence and the shores of the Saint Lawrence River, which he named Canada and claimed its shores for the French crown.

Under Samuel de Champlain (1574 — 1635), who was regarded "father of New France" and

---

① 梅蒂斯人：加拿大的土著居民有三类，即原住民族（First Nations），因纽特人（Inuit）和混血民族梅蒂斯人（Métis）。原住民族旧称美洲印第安人；因纽特人旧称爱斯基摩人（Eskimo）。原住民和因纽特人是北美古老的土著居民，但混血民族梅蒂斯人则是欧洲人在加拿大进行殖民活动以来新兴的土著居民。Métis 一词来自法语，原指在加拿大的法国男子与原住民族妇女所生的后代，后泛指所有欧洲人在加拿大与原住民族通婚所生的子女。

"founder of Québec City," the first French settlement was made in 1605 at Port-Royal (today's Annapolis Royal), and in 1608 the heart of New France was established, which later grew to be Québec City. The French claimed Canada as their own and 6,000 settlers arrived, settling along the St. Lawrence and in the Maritimes (region of Eastern Canada).

Britain also had a presence in Newfoundland and with the advent of settlements, claimed the south of Nova Scotia as well as the areas around the Hudson Bay.

The first agricultural settlements in what was to become Canada were located around the French settlement of Port Royal in what is now Nova Scotia. The population of Acadians[①], as this group became known, reached 5,000 by 1713.

New France (1604 — 1763)

Québec City became the capital of New France after Champlain's founding in 1608. The coastal communities were based upon the cod (鳕鱼) fishery; the economy along the St. Lawrence River was based on farming. Encouraging settlement was always difficult, and while some immigration did occur, by 1759 New France only had a population of some 60,000. The economy was primitive and much of the population was involved in little more than simple agriculture. The colonists also engaged in a long running series of wars with the Iroquois.

Britain and France repeatedly went to war in the 17th and 18th centuries, and made their colonial empires into battlefields. Numerous naval battles were fought in the West Indies; the main land battles were fought in and around Canada.

The first areas won by the British were the Maritime Provinces. After Queen Anne's War (1701 — 1714), Nova Scotia was ceded (割让) to the British. This gave Britain control over thousands of French-speaking Acadians. Not trusting these new subjects, the British brought in Protestant settlers from Europe and a new migration of Yankees from New England who transformed Nova Scotia.

Canada was also an important battlefield in the Seven Years' War, during which Great Britain gained control of Québec City after the Battle of the Plains of Abraham in 1759, and Montreal in 1760.

Canada under British Imperial Control (1764 — 1867)

With the end of the Seven Years' War and the signing of the Treaty of Paris on February 10, 1763, France ceded almost all of its territory in North America. Violent conflict continued during the next century, leading Canada into the War of 1812 and a pair of Rebellions in 1837.

In 1838 a new Whig[②] government sent Lord Durham to examine the situation and his *Durham Report* strongly recommended responsible government. A less well received recommendation, however, was the amalgamation (合并) of Upper and Lower Canada in order to forcibly assimilate the French speaking population. The Canadas were merged into a single, quasi (准)-federal colony, the United Province of Canada, with the *Act of Union* (1840).

Once the United States agreed to the 49th parallel north as the border separating it from western British North America, the British government created the Pacific coast colonies of British

---

① 阿卡迪亚人: 17世纪定居于阿卡迪亚的法国殖民者的后裔，其中许多是梅提斯人。该殖民地位于现今加拿大东部的海洋省份(新斯科舍、新不伦瑞克和爱德华王子岛)、魁北克局部以及今美国缅因州至肯尼贝克河部分。

② 英国辉格党: 产生于17世纪末，19世纪中叶演变为英国自由党。该党标榜实行"自由的、开明的原则"，反对君主制，拥护议会制度。1714年以后的半个世纪中，辉格党一直在政治上占优势，连续执政达46年之久。到18世纪末期，辉格党势力逐渐衰退。

Columbia in 1848 and Vancouver Island in 1849. They were eventually united in 1866.

A set of proposals called the Seventy-Two Resolutions were drafted at the 1864 Québec Conference. They laid out the framework for an independent Canada. They were adopted by the majority of the provinces of Canada, and became the basis for the London Conference of 1866.

Dominion of Canada (1867 — 1914)

On July 1, 1867, with the passing of the *British North America Act* by the British Parliament, the Province of Canada (divided into Québec and Ontario), New Brunswick, and Nova Scotia became a federation. The term dominion was chosen to indicate Canada's status as a self-governing colony of the British Empire, the first time it was used in reference to a country.

With the construction of the Canadian Pacific Railway, the new country expanded East, West and North, to assert its authority over a greater territory. Manitoba joined the Dominion in 1870 and British Columbia in 1871. In 1905, Saskatchewan and Alberta were admitted as provinces.

Canada in World Wars and Interwar Years (1914 — 1945)

Canada's participation in the First World War (1914 — 1917) helped to foster a sense of Canadian nationhood. As a result of the war, the Canadian government became more assertive and less obedient to British authority.

Canada is sometimes considered to be the country hardest hit by the interwar Great Depression. The economy fell further than that of any nation other than the United States. The financial crisis of the Great Depression, soured (恶化) by rampant corruption, had led Newfoundlanders to relinquish (放弃) responsible government in 1934 and become a crown colony ruled by a British governor.

Canada's involvement in the Second World War began when Canada declared war on Germany on September 10, 1939, one week after Britain. Canadian forces were involved in the failed defense of Hong Kong, the Dieppe Raid (迪耶普突袭) in August 1942, the Allied invasion of Italy, and the Battle of Normandy.

Prosperity returned to Canada during the Second World War. With continued Liberal governments, national policies increasingly turned to social welfare, including hospital insurance, old-age pensions, and veterans' pensions.

In 1949 Newfoundland and Labrador, until then a British dominion separate from Canada, chose in a hotly contested referendum to become Canada's tenth province.

Industrial growth was matched by population growth. Immigration, mostly from Europe, and the postwar baby boom (a great increase in the birthrate) raised Canada's population by 50 percent, from 12 million to 18 million, between 1946 and 1961.

Canada's foreign policy during the Cold War was closely tied to that of the U.S., demonstrated by membership in NATO, sending combat troops into the Korean War, and establishing a joint air defense system (NORAD) with the U.S.

In the 1960s, a Quiet Revolution took place in Québec. Québécois nationalists demanded independence and tensions rose until violence erupted during the 1970 October Crisis, when Québec nationalists and FLQ[①] members kidnapped British diplomat James Cross and Québec provincial cabinet minister Pierre Laporte, who was later murdered. The October Crisis raised fears in Canada of a militant terrorist faction rising up against the government.

---

① Québec Liberation Front: 魁北克解放前线，激进的魁北克独立组织。

In 1980 and 1995, Canada had two referendums on Québec sovereignty. Although Québec has voted twice against independence, the question has never been settled or gone away. On April 1, 1999, Nunavut was separated officially from the Northwest Territories and is now the newest, largest, and northernmost territory of Canada. While long standing issues like immigration continued to demand attention, new debates over same-sex marriage (made legal in Canada in July, 2005) and international peacekeeping would increasingly take the forefront.

As of 2015, Justin Trudeau (贾斯廷·特鲁多) is the Prime Minister of Canada, leading the Liberal Party in a majority government. Trudeau is the second-youngest Canadian Prime Minister, after Joe Clark. He is the eldest son of Pierre Trudeau, and the first to be related to a previous holder of the post.

Chapter 7
Political System and National Economy

> **章节导读**
>
> 本章主要介绍加拿大的政治体制和经济状况。政体方面主要介绍该国以三权分立为原则的议会制度、司法体制和政府构成。在经济方面列举了该国国民经济的主要产业分布和特点,以及建国至今经济发展的过程和趋势。

I Political System

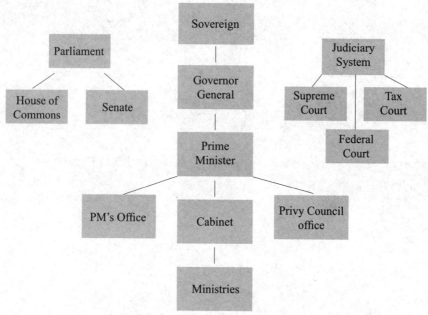

Construction of the Canadian Government

Political System

Canada is an independent federation governed under a parliamentary democracy and constitutional monarchy (君主立宪制). It is a member of Commonwealth (英联邦). The Canadian political system as it is known today was first drafted by the "Fathers of Confederation" at the Québec Conference of 1864. This then became law when the *Constitution Act* was passed in 1867. This act gave the formal executive authority to Queen Victoria (Queen of Great Britain) which made Canada a sovereign democracy. The Canadian political system is therefore loosely based on the British system.

Now, Canada is a Federal state with the Queen still the head of state. Her powers are extremely limited however, as the Parliament passes the laws which the Queen gives the "Royal Assent" as the final step.

Governor General of Canada

The Governor General is appointed by The Queen (on the advice of the Canadian Prime Minister) and carries out all the Royal obligations when the Queen is not in Canada. The length of office is normally five years.

Head of Government

Canada's Head of Government is the Prime Minister who is an elected representative of the people of Canada and head of his political party and has the mandate to govern through policies and programs.

The Houses of Parliament

Located in Canada's capital city, Ottawa, there are 3 main sections to the Canadian Parliament: the Queen as the Head of state; the Senate (appointed on the Prime Minister's recommendations) and the elected House of Commons. The Federal Government has the power to "make laws for the peace, order and good government of Canada" which includes international policies, defense, immigration, criminal Law, customs and border control.

Canadian Parliament Buildings

➢ *The Senate*

The Senate is made up of 105 Senators who are appointed by the Governor General on the recommendation of the Prime Minister. These Senators are men and women from all of the Provinces and from a wide variety of backgrounds. Each Province or Territory has a set number of Senators — 24 each from the Maritimes, Québec and Ontario; 6 each from Alberta, BC, Manitoba and Saskatchewan; 6 from Newfoundland and Labrador; and a further 1 each from the three Territories.

The main role of the Senate is to read over and examine the "Bills" sent from the House of Commons though they can also initiate Bills. This process ensures that no rogue bills will become law, though only rarely do the Senate reject a Bill —— sending it back to the House for amendment. The Bills are subjected to the full legislative process by the Senate and if passed will be given to the Governor General for Royal Assent and thus become Law.

➢ *The House of Commons*

The real power is held by the House of Commons. Here, the members of Parliament (MP's) are elected by the general public during a Federal election — normally every 5 years. The country is split up into 308 constituencies (选区) by population size and whichever candidate has the most votes wins the right to represent that constituency and take their "seat" in the Parliament.

Most candidates represent a particular political party and the party with the most "seats" takes over as the Government. The main parties in Canada are Conservatives Liberals, New Democratic

Party, Bloc Québecois and The Green Party to name the largest.

The leader of the political party that wins the election becomes the Prime Minister of Canada. The Prime Minister effectively runs the country with the support and advice of his Cabinet. The Cabinet is made up of "Ministers" chosen by the Prime Minister to be responsible for certain areas of the Government.

The MP's main duties are debating the laws to be made and, depending on their Party, either supporting or opposing the Government. The opposition is the political party with the second most seats in the House and their main job is to hold the government accountable (负责任的) for their decisions.

The Supreme Court of Canada

The Supreme Court of Canada is the highest court in Canada. Courts administer justice. They decide who is right and who is wrong in cases or disputes brought to them. The Supreme Court makes the final decision over disputes in Canada. Nine justices (judges) are on the Supreme Court of Canada.

Provincial Governments

Governmental powers in Canada are divided between the central or federal government and the provincial and territorial governments. Territories have less autonomy (自治权) from the federal government than provinces have.

The head of the provincial government is the premier (加拿大省份的主要行政官员), who is appointed by the lieutenant governor (副总督) after his or her party wins a general election. The premier's role is similar to that of the prime minister in Ottawa.

The three territories are administered by Ottawa through the Department of Indian Affairs and Northern Development. The chief executives are commissioners, appointed by the federal government and assisted by local councils.

Foreign Affairs

Foreign policy is coordinated by Canada's Department of Foreign Affairs and International Trade. Canada belongs to a variety of major international organizations. One is the Commonwealth of Nations, which developed gradually after World War I as former British colonies gained their independence.

Canada was a charter member (发起人) of the United Nations (UN). Other international groups that Canada has joined are the International Monetary Fund (国际货币基金会); World Bank; World Trade Organization; Organization for Economic Cooperation and Development (1961); Group of Eight; and Asia-Pacific Economic Cooperation organization (1994).

II National Economy

Canada is one of the world's wealthiest nations, and a member of the Organization for Economic Co-operation and Development (OECD,经合组织) and Group of Seven (G7,七国集团). Historically, much of its wealth has been generated through the extraction and processing of natural resources, especially fish, furs, timber, minerals, and farm produce. Now manufacturing and service activities have been added, and Canada now has one of the most complex economies in the world. Canada is also highly integrated into the global economy through trade, with more than a third of its GDP dedicated to exports.

Agriculture

Agriculture is not as important to the Canadian economy as it was in the 19th century, but it continues to be the mainstay (支柱) of several regions and is a significant source of export income. Canadian farms, fisheries and ranches produce a wide variety of crops, livestock, food, feed, fibre, fuel and other goods by the systematic raising of plants and animals which are dependent upon the geography of the province.

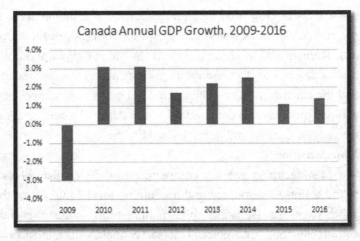

Farms in Canada are about equally divided between crop raising and livestock production. Wheat is the most important single crop, and the Prairie Provinces of Alberta, Manitoba, and Saskatchewan form one of the greatest wheat-growing areas of the world.

Forestry

Forest products contribute significantly to regional and rural economies in Canada. It is estimated that the full range of forestry activities generates roughly 1 in 15 Canadian jobs, with activities concentrated in British Columbia, Québec, and Ontario. Despite heavy harvesting by early settlers, forests, mainly coniferous (松柏科的), still cover 34 percent of the country's land area. Most of the forestland is owned and managed by the provincial and federal governments.

Canadian wood products are among the finest in the world. The famous ones include Canadian softwood lumber and Canadian pulp (纸浆), which is known for strong, light-colored paper products. Canada is the world's largest producer of newsprint (新闻用纸) and exports the vast majority of it. It is also the world's second largest producer of pulp, the third largest producer of sawn lumber, and the world's largest exporter of softwood lumber.

Fisheries

Fisheries and Oceans Canada (DFO) has six administrative regions: Pacific, Central and Arctic, Québec, Maritimes, Gulf, and Newfoundland and Labrador. Canada is one of the world's largest exporters of fish and seafood. Cod (鳕), herring (鲱), crab, lobster, and scallops (扇贝) have been the most important exports from the Atlantic coast, and halibut (大比目鱼) and salmon (鲑) from the Pacific coast. There is also a commercial freshwater fishery in Ontario, focused on Lake Erie. Commercial sport fishing industries have been developed throughout Canada.

Furs

In many ways, the fur industry created Canada in the pre-Confederation period. But by the late 20th century demand for fur had declined, and the income of indigenous (本土的) trappers had suffered severely. Canada's remaining fur farms are mainly concentrated in Ontario, Nova Scotia, Québec, and British Columbia. Trapping is carried on primarily in northern Canada; Ontario, Québec, Alberta, Saskatchewan, and Manitoba are the main producers of wildlife pelts.

Mining

Mining in Canada has a long history of exploration and development. The country is one of the world's leading producers and exporters of minerals such as uranium (铀), zinc, potash (碳酸钾), nickel, elemental sulfur, asbestos, cadmium (镉), platinum, gypsum (石膏), copper, lead, cobalt (钴), titanium (钛), and molybdenum (钼). Much exploration and development activity in Canada is now devoted to diamond mining, especially in the Northwest Territories, the Prairie Provinces, and the Canadian Shield. Oil and natural gas are also important to Canada's mining industry. Oil and gas production is centered mainly in Alberta, where crude oil and natural gas are transported throughout Canada and to the United States.

Manufacturing

Manufacturing is a key component of the Canadian economy, employing about 15 percent of the country's workforce and accounting for 17 percent of the GDP and around 75 percent of goods exported. Canada's chief manufacturing industry is transportation equipment, especially automobiles and auto parts. This sector makes up almost one-quarter of the total value of the country's manufacturing output. In recent decades, the transportation equipment industry has evolved toward a single continental market in North America. Other significant manufacturing sectors include food processing, paper products, chemical products, primary metal processing, petroleum refining (石油加工), electrical and electronic products, metal fabricating, and wood processing. Many of these manufactures rely on Canada's vigorous resource industries.

Energy

As a large country rich in natural resources, Canada's energy industry is one of the biggest in the world. Each year the country produces much more energy than it consumes, making it a significant exporter of this resource, especially to the United States. Canada is the world's second-largest producer of hydroelectricity after China and also the world's sixth-largest producer of electricity generated by nuclear power, producing 97 billion kwh in 2013. In April 2014, Ontario became the first jurisdiction in North America to fully eliminate coal as a source of electricity generation.

Foreign Trade

Canada has just 0.6 percent of the world's population, but accounts for 4 percent of total exports in world trade. Exports have always been important to Canada's economy. In the early colonial period, the leading Canadian items of export were fish and furs. During the 19th century, timber became the staple export item. With the improvement of railway lines early in the 20th century and settlement of the prairies, wheat became the chief item of export. Gradually, manufacturing industries emerged and now produce more than three-quarters of Canada's exports.

Most of Canada's foreign trade is with the United States. A large portion of this trade is made up of motor vehicles and motor vehicle parts. Canada also has significant export trade with other countries, including the United Kingdom, Germany, South Korea, the Netherlands, and China. Canada's leading imports include machinery, transportation equipment, communications and office equipment (especially computers), and other consumer goods.

Currency and Banking

The unit of currency in Canada is the Canadian dollar, which consists of 100 cents (C$1.234 equals US$1, in July, 2021). The Bank of Canada, which was founded in 1935 and is owned by the federal government, has the sole right to issue paper money for circulation.

In everyday commerce, the banks in Canada are generally referred to in two categories: 1) the five large national banks and 2) smaller second tier (等级) banks. The five largest banks in Canada are the Royal Bank of Canada, the Toronto Dominion Bank, the Bank of Montreal, the Bank of Nova Scotia, and the Canadian Imperial Bank of Commerce. The Big Five are not just Canadian banks, but are instead better described as international financial conglomerates (金融机构), each with a large Canadian banking division.

Notable second tier banks include the National Bank of Canada, the Mouvement Desjardins (technically not a bank but an alliance of credit unions), HSBC Bank Canada, and ING Bank of Canada. These second tier organizations are largely Canadian domestic banking organizations. Insurance companies in Canada have also created deposit-taking bank subsidiaries.

Most foreign-owned and major domestic banks in Canada have their head offices in Toronto, and a few are based in Montréal. Trust and mortgage loan companies, provincial savings banks, and credit unions also provide banking services. Securities exchanges operate in Toronto, Montréal, Winnipeg, Calgary, and Vancouver.

Transportation

Since the earliest explorations, water travel has been important to Canada. The St. Lawrence-Great Lakes navigation system extends 3,769 km from the Gulf of St. Lawrence into the center of the continent. The opening of the St. Lawrence Seaway in 1959 contributed greatly to industrial expansion, but the seaway is declining in significance with the growth of inter-modal transport (联运).

Canada does not have a large merchant marine (商船) and the great majority of Canadian overseas trade is carried in ships of other countries. Most ships of Canadian registry (船舶的国籍) operate along the coast, on the St. Lawrence Seaway, or on the Great Lakes. Ships called lake carriers, or "lakers," are built in eastern Canada specifically for the Seaway-Great Lakes traffic.

Rail transportation has been crucial to the formation of Canada but has declined in recent decades, due chiefly to the popularity of motor vehicles. The two major railways are the Canadian National (CN), formerly a federally owned corporation, and the Canadian Pacific Railway (CPR). Their declining revenues led Ottawa to create a combined passenger network, VIA Rail, in 1977. However, revenue from passenger service was not sufficient to cover the costs of the service, and in 1990 half the routes were closed.

Canada has one of the world's best highway systems; good roads are essential to a country of such wide spaces, scattered people, and geographic barriers. The national highway system in Canada carries about a third of all road traffic in the country. The Trans-Canada Highway, completed in 1962, stretches from St. John's, Newfoundland and Labrador, to Victoria, British Columbia.

Canada's largest airline, Air Canada, maintains a broad network of domestic and international routes. Air travel is particularly important in the far north because the widely scattered communities of the region are not connected by road or rail and water transport is limited to the brief summer periods. The busiest airports in Canada are Lester B. Pearson International in Toronto, Vancouver International, Trudeau and Mirabel in Montréal, and Calgary International.

Tourism

Canada boasts a large domestic and foreign tourist industry, the second largest country in the world. Its incredible geographical variety is a significant tourist attraction. Much of the country's tourism is centered in the busiest regions: Toronto, Montreal, Vancouver, Whistler[①], Niagara Falls, Vancouver Island, Canadian Rockies, British Columbia's Okanagan Valley[②], and the national capital region Ottawa. The large cities are known for their culture, diversity, as well as the many national parks and historic sites. Visitors are also drawn to Canadian wilderness areas. There are 17 World Heritage sites in Canada, including one of the oldest, Nahanni National Park in Northwest Territories, and one of the newest, the Red Bay Basque Whaling Station in Newfoundland and Labrador. Of these 17 sites, 8 of them are Cultural Heritages and 9 are Natural Heritages.

---

① 惠斯勒：不列颠哥伦比亚省辖镇之一，距温哥华125公里，是世界知名的冬季滑雪胜地，每年都有百万人为当地举世闻名的高山滑雪和山地自行车场地慕名而来。惠斯勒空气纯净、景色宜人，被很多人视为疗养胜地。
② 欧肯那根谷：位于加拿大不列颠哥伦比亚省中部，是加拿大第二大葡萄酒生产地，最出名的就是世界上最名贵的冰酒。

Chapter 8   Society and Culture

> **章节导读**
>
> 本章主要介绍加拿大的社会文化，涉及加拿大人的生活方式、节假日、教育状况、文学、艺术、体育等主题。作为西方发达国家之一，加拿大拥有优质的教育资源，世界知名的文学、艺术、体育成就。

I Canadian Society

Canadian People

As a nation of immigrants, Canada is usually described as being a "mosaic" (马赛克), where no particular concept of an overarching Canadian identity would be promoted. Some of the ethnic groups in Canada are: English, French, Irish, Scottish, German, Italian, Ukrainian（乌克兰人）, Dutch, Polish, Chinese, South Asian, Jewish, West Indian, Portuguese and Scandinavian. About 45% of all Canadians are of British descent (血统), and about 29% are of French ancestry. French Canadians, most of whom live in Québec, have kept the language and many customs of their ancestors.

Way of Life

The complex regional and cultural composition of Canadian society means that there is no single Canadian way of life, but certain generalizations can be made. Canada enjoys a high standard of living. Most Canadians are well housed, fed, and clothed. Canadians also enjoy an advanced, efficient health care system that is universally available to all citizens and landed immigrants (immigrants who are allowed permanent residence in the country) regardless of their location, income, or social standing. Canadians see this system of socialized medicine as a defining characteristic of their national identity.

The nature of Canadian households has changed considerably over the past quarter-century. With the liberalization of divorce legislation in the late 1960s and changing social attitudes about marriage, the number of single-parent households and common-law unions (事实婚姻) has increased. On July 20, 2005, Canada became the fourth country in the world to legalize same-sex marriage nationwide with the approval of the *Civil Marriage Act*.

Holidays and Important Dates

Such holidays as Christmas, Good Friday (耶稣受难节), and Easter are among the most widely celebrated holidays in Canada. The country's Scottish element is reflected in its enthusiastic celebration on New Year's Day and Halloween, and its American links in the observation of Thanksgiving, Labor Day, Mother's Day, and Father's Day.

National holidays particular to Canada are Canada Day (July 1), commemorating the creation of the Dominion of Canada (加拿大自治领）; and Victoria Day in May, commemorating the

British monarch who played the greatest role in Canadian history.

1. Canada Day (Canada's National Day, 加拿大国庆日)

Canada Day celebrates the events that occurred on July 1, 1867, when the *British North America Act* created the Canadian federal government. On that day, Canada was united as a single country with three provinces: Nova Scotia, New Brunswick and the Province of Canada (which was later divided into Ontario and Québec). Before 1982 Canada Day had been known as Dominion Day, which was officially renamed "Canada Day" by an Act of Parliament on October 27, 1982.

Canada's national celebration is always observed on July 1, unless that date falls on a Sunday, in which case it is observed the following day. Communities all across Canada celebrate with outdoor public events, such as parades, carnivals, festivals, barbecues, air and maritime shows, fireworks and free musical concerts. Many revelers (狂欢者) wear red and white in honor of Canada's national colors. Parliament Hill in Canada's Capital city of Ottawa, Ontario, holds the largest free outdoor celebration concert in Canada.

Prime Minister Justin Trudeau greets the crowd during Canada Day celebrations on Parliament Hill in Ottawa on July 1, 2016.

Canada Day is also considered a Family Day with outings, picnics and celebrations of the birth of the nation. All Canadians are entitled to Canada Day off work — although some people have to work, like Police, Fire and emergency service workers.

2. Victoria Day

Victoria Day is a public holiday celebrated on the last Monday preceding May 25. It is to honor Queen Victoria's birthday. Canada is the only country that commemorates Queen Victoria with an official holiday. The Sovereign's birthday was first observed in Ontario in 1845. After the death of the Queen, an Act was passed by the Parliament of Canada establishing a legal holiday on May 24 in each year (or May 25 if May 24 fell on a Sunday) under the name Victoria Day. In 1952 the celebration was established on the Monday preceding May 25, making it the first long weekend of the summer season.

Several cities hold a parade on the holiday. The most prominent parade takes place in the monarch's namesake city of Victoria, British Columbia.

Rideau Canal Skate-way, with the Chateau Laurier in the background

3. Winterlude — Canada's Winter Celebration (冰雪节)

Winterlude was created in 1979 to celebrate Canada's unique northern climate and culture. It is held in Ottawa-Gatineau[①] each February. The event is one of Ottawa's most important tourist draws, attracting hundreds of thousands of visitors each year. It is more than a festival; it's a celebration of Canada's distinctive northern identity.

Winterlude outdoor activities include public skating along the canal and skating displays, snow carving and ice sculpture competitions, musical concerts at the Winterlude Snowbowl, children's play areas, an "ice lounge," bed race and waiter race, and numerous off-site events. Winterlude is most famous for the Rideau Canal Skateway which is cleared for ice skating displays and musical concerts. It is claimed to be the world's largest and second longest skating rink winding 7.8 kilometers through the heart of the Capital from Dows Lake to the National Arts center.

Other primary sites include Jacques Cartier Park in Gatineau which is turned into a massive snow park with slides and structures, events and activities for children and the snow sculpture competition. Confederation Park, better known as Crystal Garden, is the site for the ice sculpture competition, the ice lounge and musical concert. Dow's Lake has a large skating area and hosts the various bed and waiter races.

II Education

General Introduction

Education in Canada is provided, funded and overseen by federal, provincial, and local governments. There is no national or federal department of education and no integrated (统一的) national system of education. Education is a provincial responsibility and the curriculum is overseen by the province. Each province has a Department/Ministry of Education headed by a minister who is an elected member of the provincial cabinet or, in the case of the Yukon and Northwest Territories, a counselor. Within the provinces under the Ministry of Education, there are district school boards administering the educational programs.

The federal Government is responsible for education in the Yukon and Northwest Territories, Native Indian schools, military stations and military colleges. In addition, it finances vocational training for adults, and provides financial support to the provinces for the operating cost of post-secondary education.

Canada spends about 7% of its GDP on education and offers a multiplicity of top quality education programs for students home and abroad. Since the adoption of section 23 of the Constitution Act, 1982, education in both English and French has been available in most places across Canada.

Education in Canada is generally divided into Elementary (Primary School), followed by Secondary (High School) and Post-Secondary (University, College).

The Canadian education system is a system with much diversity. Most Canadian education systems continue up to grade twelve (age seventeen to eighteen). In Québec, the typical high school term ends after Secondary V/ Grade eleven (age sixteen to seventeen); following this,

---

① 加蒂诺：加拿大城市，位于魁北克省西南部，地处渥太华河和加蒂诺河的汇流处。隔河与加拿大首都渥太华相望。

students who wish to pursue their studies to the university level have to attend CEGEP, which is a two or three year college program taken after high school and before university. (CEGEP is a French acronym [首字母缩拼词], meaning "College of General and Vocational Education".)

The ages for compulsory schooling also vary, but most require attendance in school from age 6 to age 16. In some cases, compulsory schooling starts at 5, and in others it extends to age 18 or graduation from secondary school.

Kindergarten to Grade 12 education is publicly funded and free to all Canadian citizens and permanent residents until the end of secondary school — normally, age 18. In Québec, college level education is also free to Québec residents, but tuition is charged for university education. All other Canadian students pay tuition fees to attend colleges and universities. Canada generally has 190 school days in the year, officially starting from September (after Labor Day, the first Monday in September) to the end of June (usually the last Friday of the month).

Elementary Education (K-12)

Elementary education in most provinces and territories covers the first 6 or 8 years of compulsory schooling. It refers to grades 1 through 6, but may also include grades 7 and 8. Almost 98 per cent of elementary students go on to the secondary level. The elementary school curriculum emphasizes the basic subjects of language, mathematics, social studies, science, health and physical education, and introductory arts; some jurisdictions include second-language learning.

Preschool programs or kindergartens, operated by local school authorities, provide pre-elementary education for 4 — 5 year-olds. Kindergarten programs are offered in elementary schools in all provinces and territories.

Secondary Education

Following elementary or middle school, children proceed to secondary school (also called high school or senior high school) where they continue to grade 12 (grade 11 in Québec). Curriculum programs at the secondary level include both academic and vocational programs. In China we used to have 2 streams in high school, sciences and liberal arts. Canada also has 2 streams in high school: academic and commercial. But university entrance may be gained only from the academic stream.

In the first years, students take mostly compulsory courses, with some options (选修科目). The proportion of options increases in the later years so that students may take specialized courses to prepare for the job market or to meet the differing entrance requirements of postsecondary institutions. Secondary school diplomas are awarded to students who complete the requisite number of compulsory and optional courses. In most cases, vocational and academic programs are offered within the same secondary schools; in others, technical and vocational programs are offered in separate, dedicated (专门的) vocational training centers. For students with an interest in a specific trade, programs varying in length from less than one year to three years are offered, many of them leading to diplomas and certificates. About half of all Canadians have a high school graduation certificate.

Postsecondary Education (Colleges & Universities)

The Association of Universities and Colleges of Canada (AUCC) defines two distinct types of post-secondary institutions in Canada: universities and colleges. In Canada, universities are distinct from colleges. Universities grant university degrees, which include bachelor's degrees, master's degrees, and doctoral degrees; and colleges, similar to community colleges in the United States, provide diplomas (文凭,毕业证书), which are generally awarded for successful completion of two- and three-year college and institute programs. Some colleges are enabled by provincial legislation to provide a limited set of bachelor's degree programs or provide bachelor's degrees through joint programs with universities. This ability is highly restricted and must be renewed yearly.

As of 2016 there are 96 universities in Canada. 1.8 million students are enrolled in university. The oldest university in Canada is Université Laval[①], established in 1663. The largest one is the University of Québec, which is a system of ten provincially-run public universities in Québec, with its headquarters in Québec City. The university has more than 87,000 students, making it the largest university in Canada.

Besides Universities there are thousands of public and private colleges and institutes in Canada. Of these, over 150 are recognized public colleges and institutes. These educational institutions may be called public colleges, specialized institutes, community colleges, institutes of technology, colleges of applied arts and technology, or cégeps. The private colleges are most often called career colleges. Colleges and institutes offer a range of vocation-oriented programs in a wide variety of professional and technical fields, including business, health, applied arts, technology, and social services. Some of the institutions are specialized and provide training in a single field such as fisheries, arts, paramedical technology, and agriculture.

Provincial and territorial governments provide the majority of funding to their public universities, with the remainder of funding coming from the federal government, tuition fees, and research grants. The primary variation between universities in the provinces is the amount of funding they receive. Universities in Québec receive the most funding and have the lowest tuition fees, while universities in Atlantic Canada generally receive the least funding.

Tuition costs at universities averaged $6,191 in 2015 — 2016, with international student fees for an undergraduate program averaging about $14,350 annually. In comparison, undergraduate students in Ontario ($7,868) paid the highest average tuition fees in Canada, followed by students in Saskatchewan ($6,885) and Nova Scotia ($6,817). Education is also funded through the money that governments transfer to individual students through loans, grants, and education tax credits (课税减免). Under the *Constitution Act of 1982*, the federal government is largely responsible for funding higher education opportunities for Aboriginal learners.

Among G7[②] countries, Canada has the highest proportion of post-secondary education graduates and one of the highest percentages of university graduates in the workforce. Between 1999 and 2009, the proportion of adults aged 25 to 64 with post-secondary education in Canada increased from 39% to 50%.

---

① 拉瓦尔大学：一所享誉全球的高等研究型学府，为加拿大最顶尖的十所高校G10联盟和15所研究型大学U15大学联盟成员学校之一，是一所著名公立大学。学校坐落于魁北克省的首府魁北克市，为加拿大第一所大学，也是北美第一所法语授课的高等院校。
② 七国集团：主要工业国家会晤和讨论政策的论坛，成员国包括美国、英国、德国、法国、日本、意大利和加拿大。

University of Toronto   University of British Columbia

Rank	Canada's Top 10 Universities
1	University of Toronto
2	McGill University
3	The University of British Columbia
4	University of Alberta
5	Université de Montréal
6	McMaster University
7	University of Waterloo
8	The University of Western Ontario
9	University of Calgary
10	Queen's University at Kingston

(Source: QS World University Rankings, 2018)

III Arts and Sports

Literature and Important Writers

The field of Canadian literature is large and complex, and includes voices from the various regions and many cultural groups of the country.

Notable Canadian poets, among others, include Irving Layton (1912 — 2006) with his *Waiting for the Messiah* and Dorothy Livesay (1909 — 1996) with her *Archive for Our Times*. Hugh MacLennan, Robertson Davies, Sinclair Ross and Margaret Laurence set new standards for Canadian fiction in the mid-20th century. Children around the world have enjoyed *Anne of Green Gables*, by L. M. Montgomery, a 1908 novel set in rural Prince Edward Island. Other important writers have followed, such as Margaret Atwood, Gabrielle Roy, and Alice Munro, who won the Nobel Prize for Literature in 2013 with her short stories. Many have drawn on their experiences as immigrants or members of minority groups in their fiction: Mordecai Richler (Jewish), Michael Ondaatje (Sri Lankan), and Neil Bissoondath (Caribbean) are just a few examples.

Visual Arts

The earliest works of visual arts in North America were produced by indigenous groups. European colonists introduced their artistic traditions almost as soon as they settled in the land that became Canada.

However, the defining moment for post-Confederation Canadian art, is generally acknowledged to have been the formation of the Group of Seven in Toronto during the 1910s and 1920s. The post-Impressionist images of elemental nature created by these painters have inspired generations of Canadian artists. Other distinctly Canadian schools were the Canadian Group, the Contemporary Art Society, Les Automatistes, and Painters Eleven. The Canadian Group, formed in Toronto in 1933, practiced regionalist painting, which took daily life as its subject matter. The Contemporary Art Society was formed in Montreal in 1940 to produce experimental work based on Parisian models.

There are thousands of artists now at work in Canada, producing paintings, sculptures, and other media of great variety. Among the best-known are Michael Snow, Joyce Wieland, Greg Curnoe, and Bill Reid.

Musicians

Pianist Glenn Gould is probably Canada's most widely recognized classical musician, particularly for his innovative interpretations of Bach. In the 1990s, guitarist Liona Boyd and opera tenor Ben Heppner were among the more visible Canadians on the international stage.

In the past, Canadian popular-music artists looked to the United States as the primary market for their music. However, a thriving Canadian popular-music industry emerged in the 1980s and 1990s; a few particularly well-known Canadian performers are Bryan Adams, Céline Dion, k.d. lang, Shania Twain, and Alanis Morissette.

Sports

Although **lacrosse** (长曲棍球), a sport with Aboriginal origins, is Canada's oldest sport and official summer sport, **ice hockey** (冰球) is its most popular sport. At the professional level, there are six National Hockey League (NHL) teams in Canada, including two of its most venerable, the Montréal Canadiens and the Toronto Maple Leafs.

In Canada, the term football is used to refer to Canadian football and American football collectively, or either sport specifically, depending on the context.

Canadian football is played almost exclusively in Canada. It was originally more closely related to rugby until the Burnside rules brought the game closer to its American counterpart.

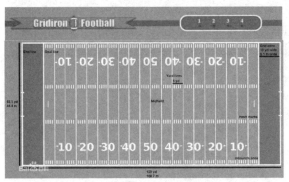

The Burnside rules were a set of rules that transformed North American football from a rugby-style game to the gridiron-style[①] game played in both Canada (Canadian football) and the United States (American football). The rules introduced sweeping changes to the way football was played.

Both the Canadian Football League (CFL), the sport's top professional league, and

---

① 烤盘足球: 美式足球（美式橄榄球）和与其相似的加拿大式足球的球场常被昵称为"烤盘"，因为球场上标示线纵横的样式看起来如同一个可以把食物放在火炉上烧烤的烤盘。也因为这个原因，美式足球和加拿大式足球被统称为"烤盘足球"。因为两者间美式足球更具有代表性，其他英语国家常用"烤盘足球"来专指美式足球。

Football Canada, the governing body for amateur play, trace their roots to 1884 and the founding of the Canadian Rugby Football Union. Currently active teams such as the *Toronto Argonauts* and *Hamilton Tiger-Cats* have similar longevity. The CFL is the most popular and only major professional Canadian football league. Its eight teams, which are located in eight cities, are divided into two divisions of four teams each (East and West). The league's nineteen-week regular season runs from mid-June to early November. Its championship game, the Grey Cup, is the country's single largest sporting event and is watched by nearly one third of Canadian television households. Canadian football is also played at the high school, junior, collegiate, and semi-professional levels.

Baseball has been played in Canada since at least 1838, and a Canadian professional league was established in 1876. The Montréal Expos became Canada's first major league baseball team in 1969. The *Toronto Blue Jays* began play eight years later and became one of the sport's most successful teams, attracting more than 4 million fans in a single season and winning the World Series twice: 1992, which was the first World Championship won by a Canadian team in the history of Major League Baseball, and 1993.

Basketball is the fastest growing sport in Canada, and attracts many young Canadians from all backgrounds. Canada Basketball is a non-profit organization and the governing body for basketball in Canada. This national federation was founded in 1928. The organization is responsible for the selection and training of players who represent the Men's and Women's national teams and then represent Canada in international competition.

Since there is no professional basketball league within Canada, many Canadian men and women playing basketball after university and college choose to play professionally overseas. Some are playing in the NBA (National Basketball Association of the U.S.).

Another sport form worth mentioning is **curling** (冰壶运动), which is a team sport with similarities to bowls and shuffleboard (沙狐球), played by two teams of four players each on a rectangular sheet (冰壶场地) of carefully prepared ice. Teams take turns sliding heavy, polished granite stones down the ice towards the target. The complex nature of stone placement and shot selection has led some to refer to curling as "chess on ice" (冰上博弈). The game of curling is thought to have been invented in late medieval Scotland Today, the game is most firmly established in Canada, having been taken there by Scottish emigrants. The Royal Montreal Curling Club, established in 1807, is still active in North America.

Canada consistently produces Olympic medal winners in a variety of sports, including ice hockey, rowing, track and field, and most notably, ice skating. A large and growing number of ordinary Canadians regularly participate in sporting leagues, fitness classes, and individual exercise.

Understanding the UK & Ireland

A General Survey of the UK

章节导读

本章为英国的开端篇，旨在通过对英国国家基本情况的介绍，使读者对英国有一全面认识，为后续章节的学习奠定基础。

The United Kingdom is the 78th-largest country in the world and the 11th-largest in Europe. It has a population of 65,347,832, according to 2017 estimates. The UK is a founding member of the North Atlantic Treaty Organization (NATO) and the United Nations (UN), where it holds a permanent seat on the Security Council (安理会). It is also one of the world's major nuclear powers.

Let's firstly straighten out a few basic facts about this powerful country.

Brexit (脱欧)

Brexit (short for "British exit") is the popular term for the United Kingdom's withdrawal from the European Union.

The UK joined the European Communities on 1 January 1973, with membership confirmed by a referendum in 1975. In a referendum on 23 June 2016, 51.9% voted in favor of leaving the European Union, and 48.1% voted in favor of remaining a member of the European Union. For the UK to leave the EU it had to invoke Article 50 of the Lisbon Treaty[①] which gives the two sides two years to agree the terms of the split. Theresa May[②] triggered (启动) this process on 29 March, 2017, meaning the UK is scheduled to leave on Friday, 29 March 2019. On January 31, 2020, the UK has officially withdrawn from the EU after 47 years of having been a member state of the EU and its predecessor.

Country Name

In full, the official name of the country is the United Kingdom of Great Britain and Northern

---

① 《里斯本条约》是在原《欧盟宪法条约》的基础上修改而成，又被称为"简化版欧盟宪法条约"。2007年10月，欧盟各国领导人在里斯本就新条约文本达成一致，条约获得欧盟全部27个成员国的批准。《里斯本条约》第50条——退出条款——规定"任何成员国可以根据本身的制宪要求，决定退出联盟"，并制定了实施程序。有退欧意向的成员国需要与欧盟进行为期两年的协商，如果两年谈不拢，只有全部成员国同意才可延长谈判期。这是欧盟以往所有条约中未曾有过的规定，是一种体制性改革。

② 特蕾莎·梅：1956年10月出生，毕业于牛津大学圣休学院。2016年7月13日任英国首相，成为英国历史上第二位女首相。2017年3月28日特蕾莎·梅正式签署"脱欧"信函，29日递交欧盟。2019年6月7日，特蕾莎·梅正式辞去执政党保守党领导人一职。同年7月24日，鲍里斯·约翰逊接任特蕾莎·梅，成为英国新一任首相。

Ireland. It's usually shortened or abbreviated to the United Kingdom or the UK, Great Britain, Britain, or sometimes informally England.

Many foreigners say "England" and "English" when they mean "Britain", or the "UK," and "British." This is very annoying for the 5 million people who live in Scotland, the 3 million in Wales and 1.8 million in Northern Ireland who are certainly not English (about 55 million people live in England). However, the people from Scotland, Wales, Northern Ireland and England are all British. So, what is the difference between the names "Great Britain" and "the United Kingdom," and what about "the British Isles"?

➢ *The United Kingdom*

As abbreviated to the "UK," it is the political name of the country which is made up of England, Scotland, Wales and Northern Ireland. Several islands off the British coast are also part of the United Kingdom; all these islands do recognize the Queen.

➢ *Great Britain*

"Great Britain" is the name of the island which is made up of England, Scotland and Wales and so, strictly speaking, it does not include Northern Ireland.

➢ *The British Isles*

"The British Isles" is the geographical name that refers to all the islands off the north west coast of the European continent: Great Britain, the whole of Ireland, the Channel Islands and the Isle of Man (马恩岛).

The nickname of the country is John Bull (约翰牛). In the 18th century, a Scottish writer John Arbuthnot wrote a book called *The History of John Bull* in which he described the frankness and funniness of a gentleman called John Bull, in order to exemplify the Englishmen. So the nickname spread wide and has become a synonym for Britain. It is a personification of England or the English people as stolidity (不易激动的) and determination. It marks the national character.

Location and Size

The United Kingdom lies off the northwest coast of Europe and is separated from the European continent by the North Sea, the Strait of Dover (多佛尔海峡,在英国东南部和法国北部之间) and the English Channels. The country includes the island of Great Britain, the north-eastern part of the island of Ireland and many smaller islands. Northern Ireland is the only part of the United Kingdom that shares a land border with another sovereign state — the Republic of Ireland.

Component Parts

The United Kingdom is consisted of four parts: England, Scotland, Wales, and Northern Ireland. Each part was once ruled separately. Each has its own culture and its own native language.

England is the largest of the four with an area of 130,000 square kilometers, which takes up nearly 60% of the British Isles. It is the most populous and richest section of the country.

Scotland, with an area of 78,760 square kilometers, occupies the northern part of the British Isles. About two thirds of Scotland is covered by the Highlands. The highest mountain on the island, Ben Nevis, is in the highlands.

Most of **Wales** is mountainous. The area is about 20,700sq kilometers, which takes up less than 9% of the whole island.

Northern Ireland, with an area of 14,147sq kilometers, occupies about one-sixth of the island of Ireland. Before the early 20th century, it was part of Ireland as a whole. In 1920 Northern Ireland became part of the United Kingdom, with a separated parliament and self-government.

Capital

London, the capital of the United Kingdom is located in England. It is the biggest city in Europe and the world's seventh biggest city, with more than 8 million residents. Greater London was created in 1965. It includes the City of London and 32 boroughs. London has great churches like Saint Paul's Cathedral and Westminster Abbey (威斯敏斯特教堂). It has a castle called the Tower of London and a large public square called Trafalgar Square (特拉法尔加广场). There's Big Ben, the famous clock tower at the Houses of Parliament. There's also a famous shopping and entertainment center called Piccadilly Circus (皮卡迪利广场,戏院及娱乐中心,交通交叉口和大众集会的地方). Now London has become the great center of commerce, administration, culture and transportation of Britain, and of the largest international ports in the world.

Language

English is the official language of the United Kingdom and spoken by most of the population. The major languages are English, Gaelic (盖尔语) and Welsh. Now less than a quarter of all Welsh people (765,864 out of 3,063,456) speak Welsh and only 1% speaks only Welsh. Scottish Gaelic and Irish Gaelic are still spoken, although they have suffered more than Welsh from the spread of English. However, all three languages are now officially encouraged and taught in schools.

The United Kingdom is the birthplace of the English language. Today, English is spoken in more parts of the world than any other language. English developed from Anglo-Saxon and is a Germanic language (日尔曼语). However, all the invading peoples, particularly the Norman French, influenced the English language and many words in English are French in origin. Nowadays all Welsh, Scottish and Irish people speak English (even if they speak their own languages as well), but all the countries have their own special accents and dialects, and their people are easily recognizable as soon as they speak. A southern English accent is generally accepted to be the most easily understood, and is the accent usually taught to foreigners.

Currency

The official currency in the UK is the British Pound Sterling. Under this system 100 pence is equal to one pound. The symbol used for pounds is "£" or is sometimes shown as GBP (Great Britain Pound) and the symbol used for pence is "p." Therefore two pound forty pence would be written: £2.40 or GBP 2.40. Twenty pence would be written 20p.

Currently the currency in use is as follows:

Coins: 1 pence, 2 pence, 5 pence, 10 pence, 50 pence, one pound, 2 pounds. Both 1 and 2 pence pieces are bronze; the 5, 10, 20 and 50 pence pieces are silver; and the 1 and 2 pound coins are gold. All coins carry the Queens head on the front.

The notes start at £5, £10, £20, £50, and £100 pounds. You won't often see the larger notes any more to combat loss to counterfeits (伪造品). There are other currencies as well. In Scotland, some of the Channel Islands and elsewhere, they have their own printed/minted coins and notes, they are exchanged at the equivalent of the Pound Sterling. Scottish notes are legal tender (法定货币) in the rest of the UK, but Channel Islands notes and coins are not.

The Europe Union established the euro as its unit of currency, and other EU members made the transition to the euro between 1999 and 2002. However, the British government elected not to do so and instead retained the pound as its currency.

Religion

The main religion in Britain is Christianity as practiced by the Anglican (英国国教的) Church.

Followers of this branch of Christianity are known as Protestants (新教徒) and make up the majority of the population. There are also many Roman Catholics. The Queen is head of the Church of England.

The National flag

England — The cross of St George, a red cross on a white ground dates from the time of Crusades. After James I succeeded to the throne, it was combined with the cross of St. Andrew in 1606.

St George (ca. 275/281 — 23 April 303) was a brave Roman soldier who protested against the Romans' torture of Christians and died for his beliefs. He is the patron saint of England since the 1270's and among the most famous of Christian figures.

Scotland — The cross saltier (X形十字,圣安得鲁十字) of St Andrew, patron saint of Scotland, is a diagonal (斜的) white cross on a dark blue ground (This color was adopted for the general background of the Union Flag). The reason for the white surround the red cross of St George is that it is an heraldic (纹章学的) taboo to place red directly on blue.

Ireland — The cross saltier of St Patrick, patron saint of Ireland, is a diagonal red cross on a white background. This was combined with the previous Union Flag of St George and St Andrew, after the Act of Union of Ireland with England (and Wales) and Scotland on 1 January 1801, to create the Union Flag that has been flown ever since. Saint Patrick was the patron saint and national apostle (传道者) of Ireland who is credited with bringing Christianity to Ireland.

The Queen

The queen has very little power when compared with earlier English kings and queens. Today, an elected prime minister and Parliament hold most government power. But Elizabeth II is popular with her people. You'll find her image on every British stamp, banknote, and coin!

The National Anthem

The National Anthem is "God Save the Queen," which was a patriotic song first publicly performed in London in 1745 and came to be known as the National Anthem at the beginning of the 19th century. The words and tune are anonymous, and may date back to the 17th century. There is no authorized version of the National Anthem as the words are a matter of tradition. The words used today are those sung in 1745, substituting "Queen" for "King" where appropriate. On official occasions, only the first verse is usually sung, as follows:

God Save the Queen	天佑女王
God save our gracious Queen!	上帝保佑我们慈祥的女王！
Long live our noble Queen!	我们高贵的女王万寿无疆！
God save the Queen!	上帝保佑我们的女王！
Send her victorious,	赋予她胜利，
Happy and glorious,	快乐与显赫，
Long to reign over us,	长久君临臣民，
God save the Queen.	上帝保佑女王。

The National Emblem (象征) of the UK

The Sovereign's coat of arms has evolved over many years and reflects the history of the Monarchy and of the country. In the design, the shield shows the various Royal emblems of different parts of the United Kingdom: the three lions of England in the first and fourth quarters, the lion of Scotland in the second and the harp of Ireland in the third. The shield is supported by the English lion and Scottish unicorn and is surmounted (在……顶上覆盖着) by the Royal crown. Below it appears the motto of the Sovereign, Dieu et mon droit ("God and my right"). The mottoes read "In defense" and "No one will attack me with impunity (不受惩罚)."

The National Flower

What are the Symbols of England, Scotland and Wales? Each nation in Britain has its own patron saint and floral emblem:

England — St. George // the Rose
The flower has been adopted as England's emblem since the time of the Wars of the Roses — civil wars (1455—1485) between the royal house of Lancaster (whose emblem was a red rose) and the royal house of York (whose emblem was a white rose).

Scotland — St. Andrew // the Thistle (蓟) and Scottish Bluebell
The Thistle, a prickly-leaved purple flower was first used in the 15th century as a symbol of defense. The Scottish Bluebell is also seen as the flower of Scotland.

Wales — St. David // the Daffodil (水仙花)
Daffodil is traditionally worn on St. David's Day. The vegetable called leek is also considered to be a traditional emblem of Wales.

Northern Ireland — St. Patrick // the Shamrock (三叶草)
Shamrock is a three-leaved plant similar to clover. An Irish tale tells of how Patrick used the three-leafed shamrock to explain the Trinity. His followers adopted the custom of wearing a shamrock on his feast day.

Commonwealth of Nations

The Commonwealth of Nations, generally and simply known as "the Commonwealth," is formerly (1931 — 1949) British Commonwealth of Nations. Nearly all of them former territories of the British Empire. The Commonwealth is now a free association of sovereign states comprising the United Kingdom and 53 members of its former dependencies, such as Canada, Australia, New Zealand, South Africa and India. The countries of the Commonwealth cover more than 29,958,050 sq km, equivalent to 20% of the world's land area, and span all six inhabited continents. These countries have chosen to maintain practical cooperation, and acknowledged the British monarch as their symbolic head. The chief institutions of the organization are the Commonwealth Secretariat, which focuses on intergovernmental aspects and coordinate commonwealth activities.

➢ *History of the Commonwealth*

Historically, the Commonwealth was an evolutionary outgrowth of the British Empire. It was originally created as the British Commonwealth of Nations through the Balfour Declaration at the 1926 Imperial Conference, and formalized by the United Kingdom through the Statute of Westminster in 1931. The rapid growth of nationalism in other parts of the empire from the 1920s produced a long series of grants of independence, beginning with that to India in 1947, and required a redefinition of the Commonwealth. Most of the dependent states granted independence chose Commonwealth membership. The current Commonwealth of Nations was formally constituted by the London Declaration in 1949, which modernized the community and established the member states as "free and equal."

➢ *The Role of the British Government*

Britain has huge overseas investments, both government and private, in the Commonwealth. When Britain joined the European Economic Community (later succeeded by the European Union) in 1973, the trade privileges of member countries began to be reduced. Commonwealth members have trade agreements with the EU. Many of the exports of Commonwealth countries go to other member countries. In 1996, the Commonwealth Africa Investment Fund was established to increase investment in that continent. There are also significant educational links between members, as many British teachers travel overseas and many students from commonwealth members study in Britain. Other cultural links include the Commonwealth Games, a sporting competition held every four years.

The human symbol of this free association is the Head of the Commonwealth, currently Queen Elizabeth II, and the 2018 Commonwealth Heads of Government Meeting appointed Charles, Prince of Wales to be her designated successor, although the position is not technically hereditary. The Queen is the head of state of 16 member states, known as the Commonwealth realms, while 32 other members are republics and 5 others have different monarchs.

➢ *Commonwealth Advantage*

The Commonwealth differs from other international bodies. It has no formal constitution or bylaws. The members have no legal or formal obligation to one another; they are held together by shared traditions, institutions, and experiences as well as by economic self-interest.

With the UK free-visa endorsement, it means that citizens of commonwealth countries do not require visas to enter the United Kingdom. The endorsement covers commonwealth citizens for a period of 6 months, an entitlement to use the British / EEA immigration channel at United Kingdom ports of entry. A Commonwealth Heads of Government Meeting is held every two years.

Free trade is also the granted economic benefit amongst the Commonwealth nations, as to remove barriers of trade between member states. The idea of promoting renewed inter-Commonwealth trade emerged in the late 20th century as a response to the evolution of the global economy. This concept of a multilateral Commonwealth free trade area has especially become popularized in Britain among Eurosceptics and Brexiters who campaigned for withdrawal from the

EU. However, at the 2005 Summit in Malta, the heads of government endorsed Commonwealth members pursuing free trade amongst one another in order to assist the development of poorest members by allowing them duty-free and quota-free access to the markets of developing and developed countries. The heads of government also endorsed looking into ways to strengthen dialogue, networking, and collaboration on trade and economic issues between Commonwealth members.

At the meeting in Singapore in 1971, members adopted a declaration that restated the Commonwealth's voluntary and cooperative nature and committed the organization to promoting international peace, human rights, democracy, fighting racism, opposing colonial domination, and reducing inequities in wealth.

A Collection of Fast Facts of the UK

Full Name	United Kingdom of Great Britain and Northern Ireland
Countries in the UK	England, Scotland, Wales, and Northern Ireland
National Flag	The Union Flag / the Union Jack
Type of Government	Constitutional monarchy
Capital City	London
Highest mountain	Ben Nevis in Scotland, at 1,343m
Longest river	River Severn, 354 km long
Largest lake by area	Lough Neagh, 396 km^2
Major languages	English, Welsh, Irish Gaelic, Scottish Gaelic
Main Religion	Christianity
Major ethnic groups	British, Irish, West Indian, South Asian.
Total population	65,347,832 (Population Estimate as 2017 Census)
Annual population growth rate	0.8% (Population Estimate as 2015 Census)
Top 5 populous cities	London 8,673,713; Birmingham 1,101,360 Leeds 766,399; Glasgow 606,340; Sheffield 563,749
Total area	243,610 km^2
Natural Resources	Coal, petroleum, natural gas, tin, limestone (石灰石), iron ore, salt, clay, chalk, gypsum (石膏), lead, silica (硅石), arable land

Chapter 9
Geography and History of the UK

> **章节导读**
>
> 本章内容分为地理和历史两大部分。地理部分介绍了英国的地理特征、主要山脉、湖泊和河流、气候和自然资源状况以及主要城市。历史部分介绍了英国的国家重要史实和重大历史事件、时代变迁与发展。

A. Geography

I. Geographic Features

The island of Great Britain can be divided into two major natural regions — lowland zone (平原区) and the highland zone (山地区). The zones are divided by an imaginary line running through England from the River Exe on the southwest coast to the mouth of the River Tees on the northeast coast. Historically, most people in Britain have lived in the lowland zone rather than in the harsher highland zone.

The lowland zone which is in the south and east consists mostly of rolling plains and its largest city is Birmingham. It receives less rain and more sunshine than the highland zone and much of the soil is fertile. Most of the lowland region is less than 150m above sea level, and the hills rarely reach more than 300m above sea level. It has been extensively inhabited, farmed, and grazed for thousands of years. Most of Britain's population lives densely into the lowland zone. The metropolis of London and most of Britain's large cities are located there.

The highland zone consists of the broad central upland (高地) known as the Pennines (奔宁山脉), the Lake District, and most of Wales and Scotland. The Pennines are a low-rising mountain range known as the "backbone of England." The highest elevations in the British Isles are in the highland zone. The highland zone is cooler than the lowland zone, and receives more rainfall and less sunlight. In many places farming is impossible. Even where it is feasible, the soil is often thin and stony, with a hard rock formation (岩层) below. Rainwater often cannot escape readily; so many areas tend to be waterlogged (积水的).

England has a total area of more than 130,000 square kilometers, comprising mostly low hills and plains. The capital is London, which has the largest metropolitan area in both the United Kingdom and the European Union.

Scotland has a total area of 78,772 square kilometers. The mainland of Scotland comprises the northern third of the land mass of the island of Great Britain. Its landscape is much affected by glaciations (冰川作用) as the whole of Scotland was covered by ice sheets during the Pleistocene[①] ice ages. From a geological (地质学的) perspective, the country has three main sub-divisions.: the Highlands and Islands, the Central Lowlands and the Southern Uplands. About two-thirds of Scotland is covered by the Highlands. The chief range in the Highlands is the Grampian Mountains[②], which contain Ben Nevis (1,334m), the highest mountain on the Island of Great Britain.

Wales covers an area of 20,779 square kilometers. It is geographically divided into the industrial south, the central plateaus and lakes and the mountainous north. Most of Wales is mountainous, mainly formed by the Cambrian Mountain Range. Its highest peak Snowdon (1,085m) is the second highest mountain in Britain. In Wales, only 12% of the land is arable (可耕作的), 6% is covered with forest, and much of the land is pastureland for sheep and cattle. The most fertile land in Wales is found near the coast and in the interior valleys.

Northern Ireland is in the north-east of the island of Ireland. The central part is composed of plains surrounded by highlands and mountains. On the central plain lies Lough Neagh (内伊湖), the largest freshwater lake both on the island of Ireland and in the British Isles. Northern Ireland is mainly agricultural, with industry concentrated in the two parts of Belfast and Londonderry.

II Rivers, Lakes and Mountains

Rivers

Since Britain has a moist climate with much rainfall, rivers and lakes are numerous. The rivers in Britain have been major sources of communication and travel since ancient times. The Romans reached what is now London by sailing down the Thames. Rivers and a series of canals built to connect some of them were important for transporting goods and raw materials during the Industrial Revolution. Rivers also acted as borders between people and served as boundaries between geographical and administrative areas.

Rivers in central and eastern Britain tend to flow slowly and steadily all year long, and the rivers and streams moving westward down from the Highlands tend to be swift and turbulent. The two longest rivers are the River Severn (338 km) in the southwest of England and the River Thames, which flows through the capital and is the main source of London's water supply. The River Thames is the deepest river in the UK.

Important ports in the UK grew up at the mouth of navigable rivers including Liverpool (The River Mersey), Bristol (The River Severn), Newcastle (The River Tyne) and Glasgow (The River Clyde).

---

① 更新世，亦称洪积世（从2,588,000年前到11,700年前），英国地质学家莱伊尔1839年创用，1846年福布斯又把更新世称为冰川世。地质时代第四纪的早期。

② 格兰扁山脉，苏格兰三大主要山脉之一，横跨苏格兰中部，为苏格兰高地与苏格兰低地间的自然屏障。最高峰本内维斯山海拔1,344千米，为大不列颠群岛的最高点。

Major Rivers in the UK by Length

River	km	Nation
1. River Severn	354	Wales & England
2. River Thames	346	England
3. River Trent	297	England
4. River Great Ouse	230	England
5. River Wye	215	Wales & England
6. River Ure / River Ouse, Yorkshire	208	England
7. River Tay	188	Scotland
8. River Spey	172	Scotland
9. River Clyde	172	Scotland
10. River Nene	161	England
11. River Tweed	155	England & Scotland
12. River Avon, Warwickshire	154	England
13. River Eden, Cumbria	145	England
14. River Dee, Aberdeenshire	140	Scotland
15. River Witham	132	England
16. River Teme	130	Wales/England
17. River Don, Aberdeenshire	129	Scotland
18. River Bann	122	Northern Ireland
19. River Ribble	120	England
20. River Avon, Bristol	120	England
21. River Tyne	118	England
22. River Derwent, Yorkshire	115	England
23. River Aire	114	England
24. River Nith	114	Scotland
25. River Tees	113	England
26. River Medway	113	England
27. River Mersey	113	England
28. River Dee, Wales	112	Wales/England
29. River Don, South Yorkshire	112	England

Lakes

It is estimated that there are 50,000 lakes in the United Kingdom. Many of the UK's most picturesque lakes are found in the Lake District, the Scottish Highlands, the Welsh mountains and Northern Ireland. The UK's largest lake by area is Lough Neagh (內伊湖) in Northern Ireland, and the largest by volume is Loch Ness (尼斯湖) which contains nearly double the amount of water in all the lakes of England and Wales combined. The largest natural lake in England is Lake Windermere located in the Lake District, which is an area of mountains and lakes in northwestern England. It is commonly recognized as the most beautiful part of England, where William Wordsworth and the other Lake Poets were inspired by the perfection of water, trees and heather-covered slopes.

Coastline

For a small country of islands, Britain has a great length of coastline (about 11,450 kilometers) which is highly irregular, with many bays and inlets that provide harbors and shelters for ships and boats. Coastal trade involving the ships sailing along the coast has been carried on since ancient times. The western coast is characterized by cliffs and rocky headlands (向水中突出的陆地). On the more gentle southern and eastern coasts, there are many sand or pebble beaches as well as tall limestone (石灰岩) or chalk (白垩) cliffs, and the most famous of which are the White Cliffs of Dover in the southeast.

Mountains

Ben Nevis (1,343 meters) in western Scotland is the tallest mountain in the United Kingdom. Wales is almost entirely covered by craggy (多峭壁的) mountains and deep, green valleys. The highest peak is the huge mountain called Snowdon (1,085m). Northern Ireland consists of hilly highlands similar to those of Scotland. The highest part of Northern Ireland is the Mourne Mountains in the southeast, with a maximum elevation of 852 m above sea level.

III Climate and Natural Resources

Climate

Britain has a temperate, maritime climate, which is damp and warm all year round. The air temperature is about 10 degree centigrade, varying from around 5℃ in the coldest month (January) to 17℃ in the warmest month (July) on average. Rain or overcast (多云的,阴的) skies can be expected for up to 300 days each year. That's why so much of the countryside is lush and green! Britain has a steady rainfall throughout the whole year. The average annual rainfall is over 1,000mm. There is a water surplus in the north and west, and a water deficit (缺乏) in the south and east.

In no country other than England, can one experience four seasons in the course of a single day. "Other country have a climate; in England we have weather." This comment is from British people to describe the peculiar meteorological conditions (气象条件) of the country.

Natural Resources

Britain is rich in coal, petroleum, and natural gas deposits. The other main natural resources are iron ore, limestone (石灰石), clay, shale (页岩), chalk and tin. Coal and petroleum are the most important. For many years, coal was mined extensively, providing the primary source of energy in Britain. It was also exported. Only small quantities of oil had been found in Britain before big oil fields were discovered under the North Sea, east of the British Isles in 1965. By 1980, the annual output of oil had reached 100 million tons. Britain has become the fifth largest oil exporter in the world.

Forest

With its mild climate, varied soils and long growing season, Britain has a diverse pattern of natural vegetation. Trees grow well and quickly. Originally, most of the country was covered with thick, deciduous forests (落叶林) in which oak trees predominated. For a long time, prehistoric settlers did not have tools strong enough to cut down the heavy oak forests. Over the centuries, the expanding human population cut back the forests, so that today only 11.8 percent of the United Kingdom is forested, roughly 3 million hectares. Efforts have been made in Britain to grow more trees and expand the managed forest areas. Local authorities have the power to protect trees and woodlands. It is an offense to cut down trees without permission, and when the trees protected by the government die, they must be replaced.

Animals

An estimated 30,000 animal species live in Britain, although many have limited distribution and are on the endangered list. Britain has many smaller mammals. The only surviving large mammals are red deer, which live in the Scottish Highlands and in Exmoor in southwestern England, and roe deer (狍), found in the woodlands of Scotland and southern England. Semi wild ponies also inhabit Exmoor and the Shetland Islands (苏格兰东北的设得兰群岛). Many smaller mammals inhabit Britain, including badgers (獾), foxes, red squirrels, and wildcats. The red squirrel is now limited mainly to the Isle of Wight and Scotland.

Britain is home to a large variety of birds. About 200 species are regularly seen in Britain. Bird watching is a popular national pastime. The most common are birds that remain year-round, such as blackbirds, chaffinches (花鸡,一种欧洲鸣禽), sparrows, and starlings (八哥). Other well-known resident birds include crows, kingfishers (鱼狗), robins (知更鸟), wrens (鹪鹩), woodpeckers, and various tits (山雀). Cuckoos, swallows, and swifts (褐雨燕) are the best-known summer visitors.

IV Major Cities

As the first industrialized country in the world, The United Kingdom boasts many cities that have long been known to the world, such as London, Birmingham, Manchester, Edinburgh, Glasgow etc.

London

London is the capital of the United Kingdom. With a history of nearly 2,000 years, it was founded by the ancient Romans soon after they invaded Britain in AD 43. The city has been destroyed several times by invaders and in 1666, the Great Fire of London burned down a large part of the city.

The City of London is located at the center of the metropolitan area and serves as the financial center, where there is a concentration of banks, insurance companies and stock exchanges. The City of London and 12 surrounding boroughs are referred to as Inner London, while the remaining 20 boroughs are the Outer London.

During the 18th and 19th centuries, London was the world's largest city. It sat at the center of a vast and powerful British empire that circled the globe. The city was heavily damaged by German bombing during World War II (1939 — 1945). The damaged areas were rebuilt after the war.

The residents of this sprawling city today are a mix of many races and nationalities. Many Londoners come from former British colonies, such as India, Pakistan, Jamaica, and South Africa. This makes London one of the world's most international cities. Now London has become the great center of commerce, politics, administration, culture and transportation of the United Kingdom, and of the largest international ports in the world. As the biggest manufacturing center, London has such industries as printing, publishing, food processing, chemicals, clothing and electric and mechanical engineering.

To the east of the City of London is the large area called the East End, which is the industrial area and the port of London, With houses for workers, this used to be poorest quarter of London, but nowadays luxuries houses have been built on the waterfront (滨水地区) and some of the richest people live there. To the west are the shops and theatres of the area vaguely known as the West End. The southern part of this area is the City of Westminster①(威斯敏斯特市,伦敦市的一个行政区,英国议会所在地), the political center of the country, where are located the Buckingham Palace, the Palace of Westminster, White Hall, No.10 Downing Street and Hyde Park.

Other Cities

The United Kingdom has other capital cities such as Edinburgh in Scotland, Belfast in Northern Ireland, and Cardiff in Wales.

Major cities of England include:

➢ *Birmingham*

Birmingham in central England is the largest and most populous British city outside London, with a population of 1,101,360 in 2014. The city was a powerhouse of the Industrial Revolution in England, a fact which led to Birmingham being known as "the workshop of the world" or the "city of a thousand trades." Its heavy industry, particularly in such fields as metallurgy (冶金), machinery-building, automobile manufacture and chemicals is important to the nation's economy.

Today, although Birmingham's industrial importance has declined, it has developed into an international commercial centre and an important transport, retail, events and conference hub. As a home to five universities, the city is the largest centre of higher education in the UK outside London. Birmingham has a greater length of canals than Venice in Italy. Originally built to support the city's trade, they are used primarily by pleasure craft (游艇) today. People from Birmingham are known as "Brummies," a term derived from the city's nickname of "Brum."

➢ *Manchester*

Situated in the south-central part of North West England, Manchester is the place where the industrial Revolution started and has long been the center of Britain's textile industry. The other industrial products from Manchester, such as machinery, aircraft, clothing, paper, and chemicals are also important. Today, Manchester is a centre of the arts, media, higher education and commerce with a population of 530,300 as of 2015. It is the "fastest-growing city" economically and the thirdmost visited city in the United Kingdom by foreign visitors. The city is connected with the Sea by a 57-kilometer-long Manchester Ship Canal built in 1894. The city's best known

---

① 威斯敏斯特市位于伦敦市（City of London）的西边、泰晤士河北岸，是伦敦下属33个单一管理区里面，两个被称为"市"的管理区之一。过去所谓的伦敦原本只是指今日伦敦市（City of London）的范围，因此威斯敏斯特地区是伦敦市西方郊外的另外一个市镇，中间隔着一片原野，但在历经长年的发展之后伦敦市与威斯敏斯特地区早已连成一气。伦敦著名的西区（West End）大部分都落在威斯敏斯特市境内，除此之外，整个联合王国的控制中枢也都位于该市范围内。

newspaper, *The Guardian*, is read all over the world. The University of Manchester, established in 1880, is a pride of the city. Manchester is well-known for being a city of sport. Two Premiership (足球超级联赛) football clubs bear the city's name, Manchester United and Manchester City.

➢ *Leeds*

Leeds is a city in West Yorkshire, England, with a population of around 781,700 (2016), making it the third-most populous British city after London and Birmingham. The name Leeds means "people of the fast-flowing river," in reference to the River Aire (艾尔河) that flows through the city. Leeds is the largest centre outside London for financial and business services with more than 30 national and international banks located in the city including the only subsidiary (附属的) office of the Bank of England in the UK. It is also the UK's third largest manufacturing centre with around 1,800 firms and 39,000 employees. Outside London, Leeds has the third busiest railway station and tenth-busiest airport in terms of passenger numbers in England. Leeds has five universities (the University of Leeds; Leeds Beckett University; Leeds Trinity University; and the University of Law; and Leeds Arts University) and has the fourth largest student population in the country.

➢ *Liverpool*

Liverpool is situated in North West England, with an estimated population of 478,580 in 2015. During the 19th century, Liverpool was a major British port, second only to London. The broad estuary of the Mersey River was the main scene of activity. Today, this stretch of the river is used mostly by ferries and recreational craft. The city is home to the oldest Black African community in the country and the oldest Chinese community in Europe. Several areas of the city centre were granted World Heritage Site status by UNESCO in 2004.

Major cities in Scotland include:

➢ *Edinburgh*

Edinburgh is a fine old city and has been recognized as the capital of Scotland since at least the 15th century. The 2016 official population estimates are 464,990 for the city of Edinburgh, making it the Scotland's second most populous city and the seventh most populous in the United Kingdom. Edinburgh's Old Town and New Town together are listed as a UNESCO World Heritage Site. It is now one of the important financial and transportation centers in Britain. The main industries are shipbuilding, chemicals, distilling (蒸馏) and brewing (酿造). It also serves as the hub of communications of Scotland and a center of art and culture. Every year from mid-August to mid-September, Edinburgh welcomes thousands of visitors to its world famous Edinburgh International festival, which was first held in 1947.

➢ *Glasgow*

Glasgow is the largest city in Scotland and third most populous in the United Kingdom with a population of 606,340 in 2016. The city is situated on the River Clyde (克莱德河) in the country's west central lowlands. From the 18th century, it became one of Europe's main hubs of transatlantic trade with the Americans. With the Industrial Revolution, the city and surrounding region grew to become one of the world's pre-eminent centers of engineering and shipbuilding, constructing many innovative and famous vessels. Glasgow was known as the "*Second City of the British Empire*" for much of the Victorian era and Edwardian period. In the late 19th and early 20th centuries, Glasgow grew to a population of over one million, and was the fourth-largest city in Europe, after London, Paris and Berlin.

Today, Glasgow is one of Europe's top twenty financial centers, and is home to many of Scotland's leading businesses. The city has particular strengths in shipbuilding, engineering, food and drink, printing, publishing, chemicals and textiles as well as new growth sectors such as optoelectronics (光电子学), software development and biotechnology. Glasgow forms the western part of the Silicon Glen, which is a nickname for the high tech sector of Scotland. A growing number of Blue chip① financial sector companies have significant operations or headquarters in the city. The city is also famous for the University of Glasgow, which was established in 1451 and is the fourth oldest university in the English-speaking world. A person from Glasgow is known as a Glaswegian, which is also the name of the local dialect.

Major cities in Wales and Northern Ireland are:

➤ *Cardiff* (卡迪夫)

Cardiff, the capital of Wales, is Europe's youngest Capital with a population of 346,100. It is one of the largest coal shipping ports in the world, and a center of iron and steel industry in Britain. Industry has played a major part in Cardiff's development for many centuries, as the main catalyst for its transformation from a small town into a big city.

Cardiff is home to four major institutions of higher education: Cardiff University, Cardiff Metropolitan University, University of South Wales and the Royal Welsh College of Music & Drama. The total number of higher education students in the city is around 43,900.

➤ *Belfast* (贝尔法斯特)

Belfast, the capital of Northern Ireland, has a population of 483,418. It is an important industrial, commercial and cultural center in Northern Ireland. The main industries include ship building, linen, man-made fibers and aircraft manufacture. The majestic City Hall building is a landmark located in Donegall Square in central Belfast. The name *Belfast* translates as "Mouth of the (River) Farset." This term refers to the sand bar that formed where the River Farset met the River Lagan at Donegall Quay and flowed into Belfast Lough (湖), which became the hub around which the city developed. It is the largest urban area in Northern Ireland, and the province of Ulster and the second-largest city in Ireland. Belfast has been the capital of Northern Ireland since its creation in 1920 by the Government of Ireland Act.

B. History

British History Timeline

Celts	Romans	Saxons	Vikings	Normans	Tudors	Victorians	WW II
500 BC	AD 43	450	793	1066	1485	1837	1939+

---

① 蓝筹股：又称绩优股，实力股，通常指那些经营业绩较好，具有稳定且较高的现金股利支付的公司股票。多为长期稳定增长的、大型的、传统工业股及金融股。蓝筹股在市场上受到追捧，因此价格较高。"蓝筹"一词源于西方赌场，在西方赌场中，有三种颜色的筹码、其中蓝色筹码最为值钱。

Thousands of years ago, Great Britain was joined to Europe and was covered with ice. About 15,000 years ago, the weather became warmer. The ice melted and the sea level rose. Great Britain became an island about 8,000 years ago. Little is known about people inhabiting the British Isles in the pre-Celtic period (before 800 BC). Some monuments built by them have been preserved such as Stonehenge, erected some time before 1000 BC or Newgrange monument built around 3200BC.

The Celts

The word Celt comes from the Greek word, Keltoi, meaning barbarians. The first Celtic tribes, the Goidels or Gales (盖尔人) are believed to have come to the British Isles between 800 & 700 BC. Two centuries later, they were followed by the Brythons or ancient Britons after whom the country was called Britain. No-one called the people living in Britain during the Iron Age *Celts* until the eighteenth century. In fact, the Romans called these people Britons, not Celts.

The Celts were a warlike people who tended to have battles that frequently devolved into individual combats; where the victor would cut off the head of the loser and display it on a pole outside his hut. From around 750 BC to 12 BC, the Celts were the most powerful people in central, northern Europe and Northwest Europe. They were dominated by three main Celtic groups:

- the Gauls (高卢人，高卢是西欧一古老地区，基本相当于现代的法国和比利时)
- the Britons (两千年前罗马人入侵时不列颠南部的凯尔特人)
- the Gaels (盖尔人，苏格兰、爱尔兰或马恩岛的说盖尔语的凯尔特人)

The Celts were ancestors of the Scots, the Irish and the Welsh, and their languages are the basis of Welsh and Gaelic. Celtic civilization in Britain was most advanced in the south and southeast. The Celts lived both in villages and in OPPIDA (towns). Celtic society was divided into three main classes: the warrior aristocracy; the Druids (古代盖尔人或不列颠人中的牧师) who were the religious leaders and at the same time teachers; and everyone else. Women were also regarded highly amongst the Celts, which was unusual during ancient times, some even becoming tribal leaders. Celtic Britain was far from united. There was no union among the tribes, and wars were frequent. By the time of Julius Caesar, Celtic peoples have dominated the British islands.

Roman Britain (55BC — 410AD)

British recorded history begins with the Roman invasion. The first Roman invasion was led by Julius Caesar in 55 BC. But Britain was not conquered until some 90 years later, under Emperor Claudius, in 43 AD. For nearly 400 years, Britain was under the Roman occupation.

The Romans brought the Britons into great contact with Roman civilization. One of the greatest achievements of the Roman Empire was its system of roads. They constructed a network of roads between the large towns. Many of them are still in use now because of their remarkable solidity. They also allowed the movement of agricultural products from farm to market. The Roman built many towns, roads, baths, temples, amphitheaters (古罗马的圆形剧场，竞技场) and beautiful villas and buildings. They also brought to Britain the new religion, Christianity, which had thoroughly replaced the old Celtic gods by the close of the 4th century, but Romanization was not successful in other areas. Apart from the villas and fortified settlements, the great mass of the British people did not seem to have become Romanized and people did not adopt the Latin language. Therefore, Latin did not displace Celtic.

The Anglo-Saxon Conquest (446 — 871)

Germanic tribes from northwestern Europe began to raid Roman-occupied Britain in the third century, carrying away grain, cattle, and other valuables. In the mid-5th century, not long after Roman troops were withdrawn from Britain, a new wave of invaders, the three Teutonic tribes (日耳曼人的,条顿人的) — Jutes (朱特人), Saxons, and Anglos, collectively known as the Anglo-Saxons — came to Britain across the North Sea in search of land for settlement.

According to tradition, the first important settlement was made about 449 on Britain's eastern coast by the Jutes, who had fished and farmed in Jutland (日德兰半岛,由丹麦的大陆部分和德国北部组成). Then came the Saxons, users of the short-sword from northern Germany, from the end of the 5th century to the beginning of the 6th century. In the second half of the 6th century, the Anglos, also from northern Germany, arrived. Unlike the Romans who only took 35 years to conquer all of Britain except the (Scottish) Highlands, the Angles, Saxons, and Jutes fought for more than two centuries before they controlled even half of the island. It was a bitter struggle, but the Germanic tribes were thorough in their conquest of Britain. For nearly two centuries, the invaders penetrated the island by way of its inland rivers, ravaging as they advanced. Roman civilization was destroyed; its language, religion, and customs disappeared. Most of the native Britons were killed, enslaved, or driven into Wales and to Brittany (in France).

About 613 the Anglo-Saxon conquest of central Britain was completed. Anglo-Saxon England was divided into a number of small kingdoms. The Jutes occupied the region called Kent, between the Thames River and the Strait of Dover. The Saxons settled to the south and the west of London. Their major kingdoms were Sussex, Essex, and Wessex. The Angles, who gave their name to the country, settled in the eastern coast from the territory of the Saxons northward into the Scottish lowlands. They formed the kingdoms of East Anglia (英吉利,英格兰的中世纪和晚期拉丁语名称), Mercia (麦西亚,英格兰中部的一个盎格鲁-撒克逊王国), and Northumbria (诺森伯兰,北英格兰-盎格鲁-撒克逊王国).

Constant conflicts followed during the four centuries after the conquest of Britain. The Anglo-Saxons warred among themselves, against the Welsh (Britons in Wales), and later against Danish and Norwegian invaders (the Vikings). The more powerful Anglo-Saxon kingdoms absorbed their weaker neighbors. From the seven major kingdoms that developed during the invasions, three dominant states emerged — Northumbria, Mercia, and Wessex.

Anglo-Saxon domination lasted for four centuries, though it did not include Scotland, where the Picts (皮克特人,英国北部的古代民族之一) and the Scots established a separate kingdom. The Anglo-Saxon period can be characterised as a period of transition from a tribal to feudal organisation of society. Although they were barbarians, the Anglo-Saxons were more advanced than the Britons had been before the Roman occupation. They laid the foundations of the English state, divided the country into shires (郡), with shire courts and shire reeves (地方行政官), or sheriffs, responsible for administering law. They devised an effective farming system which was in use to the 18th century. Finally, they created the Witan (盎格鲁-撒克逊时代的议会) to advise the king, the basis of the Council which still exists today.

They brought to Britain their own Teutonic religion, which was dominant over Christianity until the end of the 6th century, when in 597 Saint Augustine, sent by Pope Gregory I, arrived in Kent to convert the people of the British Isles to Christianity. By the end of the seventh century, missionaries had converted all of England and monasteries (修道院) were established and became centers of learning. Christianity played an important role in civilizing the Anglo-Saxons.

Viking and Danish Invasions (793 — 1066)

From the 8th century the Anglo-Saxons had to face Scandinavian invaders — the Danes and the Norsemen (meaning "people from the North"), sometimes referred to as Vikings — who came across the North Sea, just as the Anglo-Saxons had done 400 years earlier, and occupied parts of Britain.

Vikings were great travelers and sailed in their long boats all over Europe and the Atlantic Ocean, where they traded, raided, and often settled. They were also farmers, fishermen, trappers and traders. Viking craftsmen made beautiful objects out of wood, metal and bone; Viking women were skilful weavers, producing fine, warm textiles. The reason for most Vikings to sail overseas was simply searching for better land for their farms. At home their land was not very good for farming. Norway was very hilly, Sweden was covered in forests, and Denmark had a lot of sandy land.

The Scandinavian invasions continued till the 11th century, when they were defeated at sea by Alfred the Great (849 — 899), king of Wessex and the founder of the British navy. The Vikings settled peacefully in an area of Britain which became known as Danelaw (施行丹麦法的英国地区) and eventually the Vikings were assimilated.

Alfred the Great was noted for resisting the Danes and uniting the various English kingdoms under one rule. He is also the father of the British Navy and a promoter of learning and legal system as well as a skillful military leader and administrator. Alfred is the only English king to be labeled "the Great."

The Norman Conquest (1066)

The Norman conquest of England began in 1066. In January 1066, King Edward, the last Saxon king, died childless. He had promised to leave the English throne to his cousin William, but he chose Harold, his wife's brother as king. So William led his army to invade the Kingdom of England. In October 1066, during the important battle of Hastings, William of Normandy's army of some 12,000 horses and 20,000 foot soldiers defeated King Harold Godwinson's 25,000 Saxons on Senlac Hill near Hastings. King Harold was killed. He is one of only two Kings of England to have died in battle (the other being Richard III). On Christmas Day, William was crowned king of England. This resulted in Norman control of England, which was firmly established during the next few years.

The Norman Conquest of 1066 was an important event in English history. It brought about many consequences. William confiscated (没收) almost all the land and gave it to his Norman followers. He replaced the weak Saxon rule with a strong Norman government. So the feudal system was completely established in England. Relations with the Continent were opened, and civilization and commerce were extended. Norman-French culture, language, manners, and architecture were introduced. The church was brought into closer connection with Rome, and the church courts were separated from the civil courts. The Norman Conquest also had important consequences for the rest of the British Isles, paving the way for further Norman invasions in Wales and Ireland, and the extensive penetration of the aristocracy of Scotland by Norman and other French-speaking families.

The Plantagenet (金雀花王朝, 1154 — 1485) and Tudors (都德王朝, 1485 — 1603)

From 1154 to 1547 much of English history was shaped by the shifting alliances of the Plantagenet and Tudor kings. Royal succession was by no means assured during this period of conflict and disease—nearly half the population was killed by the Black Death in 1348 — 1349. International relations were dominated by struggle with France, including the Hundred Years War (1337 — 1453). In domestic politics, Wales was subjugated (被征服) by 1288, and Scottish independence was recognized in 1314, when English forces were defeated by Robert Bruce at the Battle of Bannockburn.

The Wars of the Roses (battles between the House of Lancaster, symbolized by the red rose, and that of York, symbolized by the white) in the period from 1455 to 1485 illustrated that those who could obtain the greatest military power from a majority of rival barons were able to claim the throne. Henry Tudor, descendant of Duke of Lancaster won victory of the Wars of the Roses in 1485 and put the country under the rule of the Tudors. It weakened the great medieval nobility and promoted the development of English society. It also allowed the Tudor monarch to establish a powerful central government. The Tudor Period (1485 — 1603) was a turning point in English history. England became one of the leading powers. The two famous rulers of the House of Tudor were **Henry VIII** (28 June 1491 — 1428 January 1547) and **Elizabeth I** (7 September 1533 — 1524 March 1603).

Britain's most famous king was **Henry VIII** (1509 — 1547), remembered not only for his six wives (two of whom he had beheaded), but also for bringing about the Reformation. He established the Church of England as the national church of the country, and made himself the supreme head of the Church of England. As a result of the Reformation, England became a Protestant country, rather than a Catholic one.

Henry VIII's reform stressed the power of the monarch and certainly strengthened Henry's position; Parliament had never done such a long and important piece of work before, its importance grew as a result. Henry also took advantage of a growing resentment for the excessive wealth and privilege of the Church; thus he was able to seize enough monastic lands and property to finance his rule. He created the Royal Navy, which became the basis of future British sea power.

Henry's quarrel with the Church was centered on the Pope's refusal to annul (废除) his marriage with Catherine of Aragon (阿拉贡,西班牙东北部的前王国), who could not give him a male heir to the throne.

Portrait of Henry VIII

The Elizabethan Age (1558 — 1603)

Under **Elizabeth I**, daughter of Henry VIII and Anne Boleyn, England entered a Golden Age. Among the events of the Elizabethan Age were the defeat of the Spanish Armada (西班牙无敌舰队) in 1588, Sir Walter Raleigh's discovery of tobacco in Virginia, and Sir Francis Drake's circumnavigation of the world. The Elizabethan age saw the flourishing of English poetry, music and literature and produced the world's greatest playwright William Shakespeare. It was also the end of the period when England was a separate realm before its royal union with Scotland.

Queen Elizabeth I

The Elizabethan Age is viewed so highly because of the contrasts with the periods before and after. It was a brief period of largely internal peace between the English Reformation and the battles between Protestants and Catholics and the battles between Parliament and the Monarchy that engulfed the seventeenth century. The Protestant/Catholic divide was settled, for a time, by the Elizabethan Religious Settlement, and Parliament was not yet strong enough to challenge royal absolutism. England was also well-off compared to the other nations of Europe and the century's long conflict between France and England was largely suspended for most of Elizabeth's reign.

The Stuarts (斯图亚特王朝, 1603 — 1714)

The **Stuart period** of British history usually refers to the period between 1603 and 1714. After the death of Elizabeth, the "Virgin Queen" who left no male heir, the throne was occupied by James VI of Scotland. James inaugurated the Stuart dynasty as James I and ruled the kingdom of England, Scotland, and Ireland for 22 years, from 1603 to 1625, often using the title King of Great Britain, until his death at the age of 58. The period ended with Queen Anne and the accession of George I from the House of Hanover.

Conflict between the Crown and Parliament characterized the Stuart period. James I would have preferred to have no Parliament at all, since he was a firm believer in the Divine Right of Kings, which was the belief that kings received their power from God and thus could not be deposed (废黜).

His Successor Charles I dissolved Parliament and introduced a period of absolute rule which lasted eleven years. The result of the conflict was **Civil War** (1642 — 1649), also called the Puritan Revolution. The Civil War ended with the Parliamentary victory. Charles I was condemned to death and his son, Charles II was exiled. The English Civil War overthrew feudal system in England and led to the replacement of English monarchy first with the Commonwealth of England (1649 — 1653), and then with a Protectorate (1653 — 1659, 护国公政体), under **Oliver Cromwell's** personal rule. He was an English military and political leader best known for his involvement in making England into a republican Commonwealth and for his later role as Lord Protector of England, Scotland, and Ireland from 1653 until his death in 1658. It also shook the foundation of the feudal rule in Europe. Under the rule of Oliver Cromwell, a period of republicanism followed, but after Cromwell's death in 1658, the monarchy was restored and prospered under Charles II, the late King's son who was asked to return from his exile in France as the king. This was called **the Restoration**.

The Glorious Revolution of 1688

In 1685 Charles II died and was succeeded by his brother James II, who was a Catholic king in a country that was thoroughly Protestant and wanted nothing to do with the Pope in Rome. James wanted to change the State religion of England back to Catholicism. He is best known for his belief in absolute monarchy and his attempts to create religious liberty for his subjects. Both of these went against the wishes of the English Parliament and of most of his subjects. So the English politicians rejected James II, and appealed to a Protestant king, the Dutch Stadtholder William of

Orange (荷兰执政奥兰治亲王威廉), to invade and take the English throne.

William landed in England in 1688 and the takeover was relatively smooth, with no bloodshed, nor any execution of the king. This was known as the "Glorious Revolution." It was indeed a revolution and paved the way for Parliament's dominance over the Crown. James was then replaced not by his Catholic son, James Francis Edward, but by his Protestant daughter Mary II and his son-in-law William III, who became joint rulers in 1689. Authority was simplified when Mary's death in 1694 left William the sole monarch.

The overthrow of James II in 1688 was the second time in the 17th century that a Stuart king had lost his crown. However, unlike Charles I, his father, James II did not lose his head as well.

James II made one serious attempt to recover his crowns when he landed in Ireland in 1689, but, after the defeat of the Jacobite (英王詹姆斯二世的拥护者，1688年后斯图尔特王朝的拥护者) forces by the Williamite forces at the Battle of the Boyne in the summer of 1690, James returned to France. He lived out the rest of his life under the protection of his cousin and ally, King Louis XIV.

The Glorious Revolution of 1688 is the greatest landmark in the history of England. This revolution is so called because it achieved its objective without any bloodshed. The struggle between the King and the Parliament ended in victory for the people (i.e. the representative of the people — the parliament). It marks the end of absolutism, never since has the monarch held absolute power, and the beginning of modern English parliamentary democracy. The Bill of Rights as a result, was drawn up by the parliament to lay on limits on the powers of the monarch, and in the meanwhile, to set out basic civil rights on the constitutional level. The Bill of Rights therefore has become one of the most important documents in the political history of Britain. For Catholics, however, it was disastrous both socially and politically. Catholics were denied the right to vote and sit in the Westminster Parliament for over 100 years afterwards. They were also denied commissions in the army and the monarch was forbidden to be Catholic or marry a Catholic, thus ensuring the Protestant succession.

Georgian Era (1714 — 1830) and Victorian Age (1837 — 1901)

England and Scotland were united in 1707 by the Act of Union. The **House of Hanover** succeeded the House of Stuart as monarchs of Great Britain and Ireland in 1714 and held that office until the death of Victoria in 1901. George I of Hanover was the first British monarch of the House of Hanover and Queen Victoria was the last. The dynasty provided six British monarchs:

- George I (r.1714 — 1727)
- George II (r.1727 — 1760)
- George III (r.1760 — 1820)
- George IV (r.1820 — 1830)
- William IV (r.1830 — 1837)
- Victoria (r.1837 — 1901).

The Georgian era includes the reigns of the kings George I, George II, George III and George IV, i.e. covering the period from 1714 to 1830. Sometimes the reign of William IV (1830 to 1837) is also included.

During George I's reign the powers of the monarchy diminished and Britain began a transition to the modern system of cabinet government led by a prime minister. Towards the end of his reign, the actual power was held by Sir Robert Walpole, Great Britain's first actual prime minister. George died in 1727 on a trip to his native Hanover, where he was buried.

The Victorian Age comprised the second half of the 19th century and is generally agreed to stretch through the reign of Queen Victoria from June 1837 until her death on the 22nd of January 1901. It was preceded by the Georgian era and succeeded by the Edwardian period.

Queen Victoria was the only child of Edward Duke of Kent, the granddaughter of George III and was a descendant of most major European royal houses. At age eighteen Victoria ascended the English throne in June, 1837, following the death of her uncle King William IV. In 1840 she married her first cousin Albert. She arranged marriages for her children and grandchildren across the continent, tying Europe together; this earned her the nickname "the grandmother of Europe."

The Victorian Age was a period in which Britain became the strongest world power: along with the greatest financial and commercial power, the sea power and the colonial power were greatly developed with the profits gained from the overseas British Empire, as well as from industrial improvements at home which allowed an educated middle class to develop. It was a tremendously exciting era when many artistic styles, literary schools, as well as social, political and religious movements flourished. It was a time of prosperity, broad imperial expansion, and great political reforms.

The Victorian Age was also a time of tremendous scientific progress and ideas. The Industrial Revolution had already occurred, but it was during this period that the full effects of industrialization made themselves felt, leading to the mass consumer society of the 20th century. This is also the period when the railway network developed all over the country.

During the early part of the era, the House of Commons was headed by the two parties, the Whigs and the Tories. From the late 1850s onwards, the Whigs became the Liberals; the Tories became the Conservatives. These parties were led by many prominent statesmen.

An 1883 painting of Queen Victoria (1819 — 1901). Behind the queen is a portrait of her deceased (已故的) consort, Prince Albert. The box beside her is labeled "First Lord of the Treasury."

Without a doubt, The Victorian Age was an extraordinarily complex age, which has sometimes been called the Second English Renaissance. It is, however, also the beginning of Modern Times.

Queen Victoria's nearly 64-year reign (1837 — 1901) used to be the longest in British history, until that of the present monarch (Queen Elizabeth II) who exceeded that length on the throne in 2017. Queen Victoria was succeeded by her eldest son, the Prince of Wales, who reigned as King Edward VII. Today it is her great-great granddaughter that rules the United Kingdom, and Elizabeth's consort, Philip, is Victoria's great-great grandson.

The Industrial Revolution (1760 — 1850)

The **Industrial Revolution** refers to the mechanization of industry and the consequent changes in social and economic organization in Britain in the late 18th and early 19th centuries. It started with the mechanization of the textile industries, the development of iron-making techniques and the increased use of refined coal. The onset of the Industrial Revolution marked a major turning point in human history; it forever transformed the way people live and work in most parts of the world.

Before the Industrial Revolution, most people lived by farming. There was little industry. Any manufacturing was done in homes or in small workshops close to home. People used craft skills, such as weaving or woodworking, to produce goods for their families or to sell in towns. The Industrial Revolution took production into big factories. People moved from the countryside into industrial cities. New roads, canals, railroads, and steamships were built to carry factory-made goods and the raw materials. The British government was eager to increase the country's income from trade, and it encouraged industry. Business people also hoped to make more money. They saw opportunities to profit from new inventions and new ways of making goods.

The invention of the steam engine was an important step in the Industrial Revolution. The first batch of big factories in Britain grew up around the textile industry. Huge factories were also built near sources of iron, coal, and water. Three regions of Britain — northern England, central England, and central Scotland — became industrial zones and workers moved to big new industrial cities such as Birmingham, Manchester, Newcastle on Tyne, and Glasgow as more and more factories opened there.

From the 18th century, new agricultural machines began to replace more and more of the traditional farming implements that had been used for centuries. By about 1800, the new inventions and work techniques in Britain spread to Europe and North America. A second phase of the Industrial Revolution began about 1850. Inventors discovered new processes, such as better ways to make steel.

There were several reasons for Britain becoming the first country to industrialize: First, Britain had a favorable geographical location to participate in European and world trade; it was a country in which the main towns were never too far from seaports, or from rivers, which could distribute their products. Second, Britain had political stability and a peaceful society. Third, Britain had a good foundation in economy. Fourth, Britain had many rivers, which were useful not only for transport but also for water and steam power. Britain also had useful mineral resources. The last reason was that British engineers had skilled craftsmen.

Typical inventions during the Industrial Revolution include:
- John Kay's flying shuttle in 1733;
- James Hargreaves' Spinning Jenny in 1766;
- Richard Arkwright's water frame in 1769;
- Edmund Cartwright's power looms in 1784;
- James Watt's steam engine in 1765.

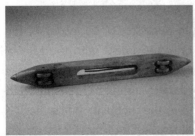

John Kay's flying shuttle   James Hargreaves' Spinning Jenny   James Watt's steam engine

Britain in the Twentieth Century

Queen Elizabeth II

The 20th century is a period of the decline of Britain as a world power, a period of crises of the two world wars, from which Britain emerged as a victor, but greatly weakened. Britain firstly suffered from the loss of manpower and considerable disruption of the economy and society during World War I from 1914 to 1918. Later in 1929, the shock waves from the New York Stock Market Crash sent Britain into depression and left millions of people out of work. In World War II the country was also severely damaged with its cities being devastated by bombing and blitz, and with even worse damages on its economy. It is then followed by the disintegration (瓦解) of Britain's colonial empire and the effort to adjust Britain to the new situation by joining the other developed capitalist countries of Western Europe in EEC (European Economic Community, 欧洲经济共同体). On 23 June, 2016, however, following the national referendum on the UK's membership on the EU, in which 51.9% of votes cast were in favor of leaving the European Union (EU), Britain has withdrew from the EU, which is widely known as "Brexit," a portmanteau of "British" and "Exit."

In 1952 Princess Elizabeth was crowned Queen Elizabeth II. As Britain entered the 1960s, new universities were built and a reinvigorated culture emerged. While its heavy industry struggled, Britain led the world in fashion and pop music. Inflation and unemployment soared in the 1970s and endless strikes resulted from labor unrest.

In 1973 Britain joined the European Community, but there seemed to be few obvious economic benefits. Margaret Thatcher came to power in 1979 and went on to win two more elections. By 1990 her popularity was so diminished that her party replaced her with John Major, who won the 1992 election. But a reinvigorated Labor Party under Tony Blair won in 1997. The economy remained weak, and Britain continued to distrust the European Community. Nationalism continued to simmer (酝酿;骚动) in Scotland and Wales, and conflict continued in Northern Ireland. Especially with the recent movement in Scotland, a Scottish Parliament was re-established following the 1997 referendum, in the form of a developed unicameral legislature with its 129 members. The Scottish Parliament has its authority over many areas of domestic policy. In the 2011 Scottish Parliament general election, the Scottish National Party (SNP), which supports Scottish independence, won an overall majority and legislated for an independence referendum on 18 September 2014. The result, however, rejected independence with a majority of 55% to 45% on an 85% voter turnout.

David Cameron became Prime Minister from May 2010 to June 2016, as leader of the Conservative Party since 2005 and also the head of a coalition government with the Liberal Democrats. In July 2016, Theresa May was elected by the ruling conservative party in the wake of the Brexit referendum. Although May promised a bill to incorporate existing EU laws into UK domestic laws, the terms of withdrawal are still under negotiation at the moment. While the UK remains a full member of the EU, the UK government has invoked Article 50 of the Treaty on EU (the formal procedure for withdrawing) at the end of March 2017.

Chapter 10
Political System and Economy of the UK

章节导读

本章为英国的政治经济篇。政治体系部分介绍了英国的政府结构、议会和选举政策、内阁和枢密院，以及司法体系。经济部分旨在使读者对英国经济产业、金融体系、交通和旅游情况有一较为全面的了解。

A. Political System

Government of the United Kingdom

Form of Government	Constitutional Monarchy
Head of state	Monarch
Head of government	Prime minister
Legislature	Bicameral legislature: House of Commons, 650 members House of Lords, 805 members (687 life peers, 92 hereditary peers and 26 bishops as Lord Spiritual)
Voting qualifications	Universal at age 18
Constitution	Unwritten; partly statutes, partly common law and practice
Highest court	House of Lords High Court of Justiciary (the supreme criminal court of Scotland)

Parliamentary Democracy

The UK is a parliamentary democracy with a constitutional Monarch as Head of State with limited powers. The principle behind British democracy is that the people elect Members of Parliament (MPs) to the House of Commons in London at a general election, held no more than five years apart. Most MPs belong to a political party, and the party with the largest number of MPs in the House of Commons forms the government. Britain's democratic government is based on a constitution composed of various historical documents, laws, and formal customs adopted over the years.

Constitution

The British constitution regulates how the country is governed and ensures that the government acts at all times within the rule of law and that the government serves the people, and not that the people serve the government.

In Britain, monarch was gradually replaced by a limited, representative government based on **unwritten constitution**. The constitution is said to be "unwritten" because it is taken partly from various written documents and partly from unwritten customs and laws. These legal rules and laws are contained in documents such as Magna Carta 1215 (自由大宪章), The Petition of Rights 1628 (权利请愿书), Habeus Corpus Act 1679 (人身保护法), the Bill of Rights 1689 (权利法案), the Act of Settlement 1701 (王位继承法), the Act of Union 1707 (联合法案) and the Act of Union 1800. The two main features of the British Constitution are the Rule of Law and the Supremacy of Parliament.

The most important part of the English constitution is **the Magna Charta, or Great Charter**, sealed by King John in 1215. This document limited the king's power in several ways. Chiefly, it took away his right to collect taxes without the noble's consent. A few years later John's successor, Edward I, called the first meeting of Parliament, England's legislative body.

The Constitutional Monarchy

Queen Elizabeth II and Prince Philip at the official coronation (加冕礼, 1953)

The politics of the United Kingdom of Great Britain and Northern Ireland takes place in the framework of a constitutional monarchy, in which the Monarch is head of state and the Prime Minister of the United Kingdom is the head of government.

Constitutional monarchy (君主立宪制) means that the power of the monarch is limited by the country's constitution, the legal authority is given to Parliament and the executive authority to the government. The Sovereign reigns, but does not rule ("临朝而不理政" "统而不治"). The country is governed in the name of the Sovereign by His or Her Majesty's Government who is responsible to the Parliament.

Executive power is exercised by the UK government, the devolved governments of Scotland and Wales, and the Executive of Northern Ireland. Legislative power is vested in both the government and the two chambers of Parliament, the House of Commons and the House of Lords, as well as in the Scottish parliament and Welsh and Northern Ireland assemblies. The judiciary is independent of the executive and the legislature, though several senior judges are still members of the House of Lords.

The British monarchy has been a hereditary position since the 9th century. Primogeniture (长子继承权) has been the rule of succession, and when there are no sons, the eldest daughter ascends the throne. This was the case when Elizabeth II succeeded to the throne in February 1952 upon the death of her father, George VI. Her husband, Prince Philip, has the title of Prince Consort, but no rank or privileges. The current heir to the throne is Elizabeth II's eldest son, Charles, Prince of Wales. According to the Act of Settlement of 1701, only Protestants are eligible to succeed to the throne. A regent (摄政王) may be appointed to rule for the sovereign if he or she is underage (未成年的).

As the official head of state, the monarch formally summons and dismisses Parliament and the ministers of the Cabinet. The monarch also serves as head of the judiciary, commander in chief of the armed forces, and Supreme Governor of the Church of England and the Church of Scotland. In reality, the government carries out the duties associated with these functions. Theoretically, the monarch appoints all judges, military officers, diplomats, and archbishops, as well as other church officers. The monarch also bestows honors and awards, such as knighthoods and peerages. In reality, all of these appointments are made upon the advice of the prime minister. The prime minister declares war and peace and concludes treaties with foreign states in the name of the crown. The monarch serves as the ceremonial head of the Commonwealth of Nations and is the ceremonial head of state for 16 Commonwealth countries.

The real work of the monarchy consists largely of signing papers. The monarch has the right to be consulted on all aspects of national life and review all important government documents. The monarch may also meet with the Privy Council, a now largely ceremonial body made up of Cabinet members that serves in an advisory capacity to the monarch. Since Britain is a democracy, the monarchy could potentially be abolished if a majority of the population decides to do so. In the early 21st century the monarchy generally remained popular. Tourism related to the royal family brings a substantial amount of money into the country.

The Parliament

England has been called "the mother of parliaments," as its democratic institutions having set the standards for many democracies throughout the world. The Parliament of the United Kingdom of Great Britain and Northern Ireland is the supreme legislative body in the United Kingdom and British oversea territories. The parliament is bicameral (两院制的), with an upper house, the House of Lords, and a lower house, the House of Commons. The Queen is the third component of the legislature. The House of Commons is far more influential than the House of Lords.

The House of Lords includes two different types of members: the Lords Spiritual (the senior bishops of the Church of England) and the Lords Temporal (members of the Peerage) whose members are not elected by the population at large, but are appointed by the Sovereign on advice of the Prime Minister. The House of Commons is a democratically elected chamber with elections to it held at least every 5 years.

Parliamentary sessions are held each year and begin in October or November. The two Houses of Parliament meet in separate chambers at the Houses of Parliament in London, officially called the *Palace of Westminster*. The Parliament of the United Kingdom legislates for the entire nation and includes representatives from England, Scotland, Wales, and Northern Ireland. By constitutional convention, all government ministers, including the Prime Minister, are members of the House of Commons or, less often, the House of Lords. Parliament is elected roughly every five years and is dissolved by the crown on the advice of the prime minister, who then calls a general election.

➢ *The House of Lords*

The House of Lords was previously a largely hereditary aristocratic chamber, with 574 life peers (爵位不能世袭的终身贵族), 92 hereditary peers, and 26 bishops.

The House of Lords today is more a place of discussion and debate than one of power, and it normally passes legislation already approved by the House of Commons. Its members are not elected. The House of Lords comprises the lords temporal, the lords spiritual, and the law lords. The House of Lords was stripped of most of its power in 1911, and now its main function is to revise legislation. The powers of the House of Lords are limited because most Britons believe that in a modern democracy a nonelected house should only act as a forum for opinion, one that is comparatively free from party politics and pressures.

➢ *The House of Commons*

The Countries of the United Kingdom are divided into parliamentary constituencies of broadly equal population. Each constituency elects a Member of Parliament (MP) to the House of Commons at General Elections and, if required, at by-elections (known in the United States as a special election). MPs in the House of Commons may remain MPs until Parliament is dissolved, which must occur within 5 years of the last general election, as stated in the Parliament Act 1911.

Over the history of the House of Commons, the number of Members of Parliament (MPs) has varied for different reasons; for instance, the increases in recent years are resulted from the rapid growth in the population. There are currently 650 MPs, corresponding to approximately one for every 100,169 people.

In modern times, all Prime Ministers and Leaders of the Opposition have been drawn from the Commons, not the Lords. The House of Commons is the source of real political power in the United Kingdom. Its members are democratically elected by citizens over the age of 18. Certain groups are denied the right to vote, including members of the House of Lords, and those convicted of corrupt or illegal election practices in the previous five years.

General Election

A session of Parliament lasts for five years unless the Prime minister dissolves Parliament. At the end of the five-year term or before, a general election has to take place so new members of parliament can be elected by the people. The election is called by the Prime Minister.

The General Election in the UK resembles the election for a Congressman or Senator in the U.S. However, unlike the U.S., the voters can only vote for an MP to represent them in the House of Commons, they do not choose the Prime Minister (PM). He/she is voted for within their party. The Lords are appointed or inherited. The last General Election was in 2015, when conservative won 330 seats and became the leading party and therefore the Government.

Who Can Become an MP?

People are nominated as candidates to become MPs. Any one over the age of 21 can be a candidate. When an MP gets the most votes for his constituency, he gains a seat. This means he has a place in Parliament. An individual can only be a member of either of these two Houses, and members of the House of Lords are legally barred from voting in elections for members of the House of Commons.

The Government

Her Majesty's Government Coat of Arms

Her Majesty's Government is the government of the United Kingdom. It is answerable to the House of Commons. However, neither the Prime Minister nor members of the Government are elected by the House of Commons. Instead, the Queen requests the person most likely to command the support of a majority in the House, normally the leader of the largest party in the House of Commons, to form a government. The Prime Minister and most members of the Cabinet are, by convention, members of the House of Commons.

Under the Constitution of the United Kingdom, executive authority notionally lies with the monarch but is exercised in practice by her ministers. Her Majesty's Government is the collective name for these ministers, and it is effectively an executive authority for the UK.

The Prime Minister

The Prime Minister is the Head of Her Majesty's Government. He or she is the leader of the party that holds most seats in the House of Commons. The Prime Minister and Cabinet (consisting of all the most senior government department heads) are collectively accountable for their policies and actions to the Sovereign, to Parliament, to their political party, and ultimately to the electorate.

The monarch goes through the ceremony of appointing a prime minister.

The prime minister presides over the Cabinet and selects the other Cabinet members, who join him or her to form the government. Acting through the Cabinet and in the name of the monarch, the prime minister exercises all of the theoretical powers of the crown including making appointments. Every week, the Prime Minister appears before the House of Commons and must answer the questions put to him or her by the members of Parliament.

The Prime Minister is based at 10 Downing Street, which along with most government departments, is located in Westminster. The Prime Minister also has a house in the country called Chequers (英国首相乡间别墅) near Ellesborough in Buckinghamshire, England, which was given to the nation as a country retreat for the serving Prime Minister by the Chequers Estate Act 1917. It is used as the Prime Minister's non-London residence.

Number 10 Downing Street in London

The Cabinet

The Cabinet is the collective decision-making body of Her Majesty's Government, composed of the Prime Minister and 21 or 22 Cabinet Ministers, the most senior ministers of the government.

The most important ministers are called Secretaries of State. The Secretaries of State are in charge of a Government Department (a ministry). Each minister is responsible for his department. The prime minister serves as the first lord of the treasury and as the minister for the civil service.

In addition to the various secretaries of state, the Cabinet includes the ministers who hold traditional offices — such as the Lord President of the Council (枢密院大臣), the Paymaster General (主计大臣), and the Lord Privy Seal (掌玺大臣) — and Ministers without Portfolio (不管部部长或大臣), who do not have specific responsibilities but are assigned to specific tasks as needed. The Lord Chancellor (上议院的大法官) holds a unique position.

The Prime Minister has the power to move members of the Cabinet from post to post, or to dismiss individuals from the Cabinet. Former Cabinet ministers may retain their positions as members of Parliament.

The Cabinet meets on a regular basis, usually weekly, on a Tuesday morning to discuss the most important issues of government policy, and to make decisions. The Prime Minister normally has a weekly audience with the Queen thereafter.

Two key doctrines of Cabinet government are collective responsibility and ministerial responsibility. Collective responsibility means that the Cabinet acts unanimously, even when Cabinet ministers do not all agree upon a subject. If an important decision is unacceptable to a particular Cabinet member, it is expected that he or she will resign to signify dissent. Ministerial responsibility means that ministers are responsible for the work of their departments and answer to Parliament for the activities of their departments.

Shadow Cabinet

The Shadow Cabinet is a senior group of opposition spokespeople in the Westminster system of government. They are under the leadership of the Leader of the Opposition, form an alternative cabinet to that of the government, and whose members *shadow* or mark each individual member of the government. Members of a shadow cabinet are often but not always appointed to a Cabinet post if and when their party gets into government. It is the Shadow Cabinet's responsibility to pass criticism on the current government and its respective legislation, as well as offering alternative policies.

The Privy Council (枢密院)

The Privy Council is a large, and generally ceremonial, body of more than 450 members that developed out of the royal council that existed in the Middle Ages. By the 18th century, the Privy Council had taken over all the powers of the royal council. The Privy Council comprises all current and former Cabinet members, as well as important public figures in Britain and the Commonwealth. The council advises the monarch and arranges for the formal handling of documents. It has a large number of committees, each with a specific task, such as dealing with outlying islands, universities, or legal matters. The most important committee is the Judicial Committee of the Privy Council, which is the highest court of appeal for certain nations in the Commonwealth, for church-related appeals, and for disciplinary committees of some professions.

The Judiciary

Britain has a long judicial history. Its legal system has been emulated (仿效) throughout the world and many of its key principles and rights are part of the U.S. law. The principles which derived from British law include: the right to trial by jury; the right to due process of law; freedom from unlawful imprisonment, called the writ of habeas corpus (人身保护权令状); the trial system of prosecution and defense; and the presumption that a person is innocent until proven guilty.

The judicial system has its roots in the Anglo-Saxon period, when the monarch established local courts to provide justice for all subjects. The British legal system relies on common law (习惯法), which is based on custom and on decisions in previous legal cases, called precedents. Common law originated in the 12th century, growing out of the rules and traditions that ordinary people had worked out over time. Through the centuries common law evolved as it incorporated legal decisions made in specific cases, and it remains the basis of British law except when superseded (代替) by legislation. Unlike the United States, Britain does not have a Supreme Court that reviews legislation to determine its constitutionality; that responsibility falls to Parliament.

Britain has several layers of courts and two kinds of legal proceedings, criminal and civil. Criminal law is concerned with acts punishable by the state, such as murder. Civil law involves disputes between private parties, either individuals, organizations or companies. The final court of appeal for both civil and criminal cases is the House of Lords, where appeals are heard by the law lords.

The Main Political Parties

The UK has a multi-party system and since the 1920s, the two largest political parties have been the *Conservative Party* and the *Labour Party*. Although coalition and minority governments have been an occasional feature of parliamentary politics, the first-past-the-post (得票最多者当选) electoral system used for general elections tends to maintain the dominance of these two parties; however, each has relied upon a third party in the past century to deliver a working majority (使执

政党得以继续执政所需的议会中的多数) in Parliament.

The *Liberal Democrats* is the third largest party in the British parliament. Besides the three major political parties, the UK also has various minor ones, some of whom have seats in parliament.

The leader of the political party with the most MPs in the House of Commons is asked by the Queen to become the Prime Minister and to form a government that will manage the country.

B. National Economy

An Overview

The United Kingdom is a highly developed country and one of the seven major Western economic powers, whose economy is the second largest in Europe after Germany and the fifth-largest in the world (2015) measured by nominal Gross Domestic Product (GDP). British economy is based on the Anglo-Saxon model, focusing on the principles of liberalization, the free market, and low taxation and regulation.

Economic Sectors

The British were the first in the world to enter the Industrial Revolution, and, like most industrializing countries at the time, it initially concentrated on heavy industries such as ship-building, coal mining, steel production, and textiles. The empire created an overseas market for British products, allowing the United Kingdom to dominate international trade in the 19th century. However, as other nations industrialized and the surplus labor from agriculture began to dry up, the United Kingdom started to lose its economic advantage. As a result, heavy industry declined throughout the 20th century. The British service sector, however, has grown substantially, and it made up about 78.4% of GDP in 2014 and employed almost four-fifths of the workforce. The service industries include finance, retailing, wholesaling, tourism, business services, transport, insurance, investment, advertising, public relations, market research, education, administration, and government and professional service.

New Industries

New industries include microprocessors and computers, biotechnology, new materials and other high-tech industries. There are three areas in Britain which have seen some high-tech industrial growth: (1) the area between London and South Wales, (2) the Cambridge area of East Anglia and (3) the area between Glasgow and Edinburgh in Scotland. The third area is the most spectacular of the three and is now often referred to as the "Silicon Glen" (硅谷).

The Government's Role in the Economy

Like many modern developed countries, the United Kingdom has a mixed economy. This means that some sectors of the economy are operated by the government and some are operated by private businesses. Since World War II (1939 — 1945), Britain has worked to balance the mix of private and public enterprises in order to maximize the country's economy and ensure the economic well-being of its citizens. The public component consists of the welfare system, which includes socialized medicine, known as the National Health Service, plus government controls over business, banking, and the money supply. The welfare system provides support from before birth to the grave. The government also seeks to encourage competition in the economy and to increase productivity by sponsoring and subsidizing (补助) training and educational programs.

Economy of the United Kingdom

GDP (PPP)	$2,849 trillion (2016) (5th)
GDP growth	2.0% (2016)
Inflation (CPI)	1.6% (2016)
Labor force	31.75 million (includes unemployed) (2016)
Main industries	Machine tools, industrial equipment, scientific equipment, shipbuilding, aircraft, motor vehicles and parts, electronic machinery, computers, processed metals, chemical products, coal mining, oil production, paper, food processing, textiles, clothing and other consumer goods.
Exports	$460 billion (2015) (9th)
Main export partners	USA 14.6%, Germany 10.1%, Switzerland 7%, China 6%, France 5.9%, Netherlands 5.8%, Ireland 5.5% (Main Export Partners Estimate as 2015 Census)
Imports	$625 billion (2015) (6th)
Main import partners	Germany 14.8%, China 9.8%, USA 9.2%, Netherlands 7.5%, France 5.8%, Belgium 5%

Agriculture

Britain's land surface is minimal compared to many other nations, and by European standards, its agriculture sector is small in terms of employment and contribution to the GDP. But British agriculture is very intensive and highly productive. Only a few farmers employ full-time farm workers. In Northern Ireland, all are self-reliant rural farmers without land rental. The British government has adopted the European Union's Common Agricultural Policy on subsidies for agriculture.

➢ *Livestock Farming*

Many of Britain's full-time farms are devoted to livestock farming — raising cattle for dairy products or beef, or raising sheep for wool and meat. The treatment of farm animals became a growing concern in Britain in the late 20th century. Factory farming of chickens produced protests, as did the practice of raising calves in confined spaces. Concerns over animal welfare have led some British citizens to become vegetarians.

Grave concern arose in the 1980s over cattle infected with bovine spongiform encephalopathy (BSE), popularly known as mad cow disease. Human beings who eat infected beef may develop Creutzfeldt-Jakob disease (CJD). BSE was first discovered in Britain in 1986, and consumer's confidence in British beef declined. In 1996, the European Union banned Britain from exporting any beef or beef by-products. After taking considerable action by the government to halt the spread of the disease, the EU lifted the ban in 1999.

Livestock farmers in Britain faced another crisis in 2001, when several cases of foot-and-mouth disease were detected in a British slaughterhouse. This highly infectious viral disease, which rarely infects humans, can quickly cripple cattle, sheep, pigs, and other animals with cloven hooves. As the outbreak spread across the British countryside, the British government ordered the slaughter of more than 1 million animals to eliminate the virus.

➢ *Crop Farming*

Most crop farming in Britain takes place in eastern and central south England and in eastern

Scotland. The leading crops in the early 2000s were wheat, sugar beets, potatoes, barley, and rapeseed (油菜籽). As the concern has grown about the use of fertilizers, pesticides, and biologically engineered seeds and their effect on the environment, some farmers have turned to organic farming, with support from the government.

Forestry

Britain was once covered with thick forests. The kind of forests in the UK is called temperate forests. Temperate forests usually comprised of deciduous (落叶的) forests and coniferous (松柏科的) forests. But in some places, there is another type of forest called broad-leaved (阔叶的) evergreen forest. Over the centuries the expanding human population steadily deforested nearly the entire country, felling trees for fuel and building materials. Despite the fact that trees could grow quickly in the cool, moist climate of the United Kingdom, only remnants of the great oak forests remained at the end of the 20th century.

Fishing

At one time, the fishing industry not only provided a cheap source of protein for Britons, but it was also the training ground for the Royal Navy. Today, fishing is a far less vital economic activity. Fish and fish products are both imported into and exported from Britain. In recent decades, over-fishing and conservation restrictions imposed by the European Union have caused a decline in the deep-sea industry.

Mining

Mining has been enormously important in British economic history, for example, in ancient times, traders from the Mediterranean shipped tin from the mines of Cornwall; salt mining dates from prehistoric times. But today these tin mines are exhausted, and the last tin mine in Britain closed in 1998. Britain's abundant coal resources were very important during the Industrial Revolution. Today, coal has become less important to the British economy and supplies an ever-smaller proportion of Britain's total energy need.

Raw materials for construction form the bulk of mineral production, including limestone (石灰石), dolomite (白云石), sand, gravel (沙砾), sandstone, common clay, and shale (页岩). Some coal is still mined, but petroleum and natural gas are far more important.

Manufacturing

Manufacturing accounted for about 15 percent of the gross domestic product (GDP) and total employment in manufacturing is 2.7 million in 2016.

The history of manufacturing in Britain is unique because Britain was the birthplace of the Industrial Revolution, during which new methods of manufacturing products were developed. Instead of being made by hand, many products were made by machine. Production moved from small craft shops to factories. Textiles, shipbuilding, iron, and steel emerged as important industries, and coal remained the most important industrial fuel. The Industrial Revolution dramatically raised the overall standard of living.

In the last half of the 20th century, the structure of British industry changed substantially. The coal mining and cotton textile industries declined sharply. As coal production declined, oil production replaced it as a major industry. As of 2010, the UK has around 3.1 billion barrels of proven crude oil reserves, the largest of any EU member state. Motor vehicle production became a significant part of the industrial base but was subject to severe foreign competition. As incomes increased, consumer demand rose for durable goods such as cars and kitchen appliances.

British industrial production also expanded into the equipment for communication, including fiber optics (光学), computers, computer-controlled machine tools, and robots. Growing industries in recent decades include paper products and publishing; chemicals and pharmaceuticals (制药的); rubber and plastics; and electronic and optical equipment.

Banking and Financial Services

Britain is one of the world's leading financial centers. Historically, the financial services industry has been based in the City of London in an area called the Square Mile (伦敦金融区). The City is a small part of the Greater London metropolitan area that surrounds it. The City concentrates on more than 500 banks and financial institutions. The London Stock Exchange, the London International Financial Futures and Options Exchange (伦敦国际金融期货和期权交易所), the London Metal Exchange, the Bank of England, and the Lloyd's of London insurance market are all based in the City. It also has the largest concentration of foreign bank branches in the world.

Leeds, Manchester, Cardiff, Liverpool, Edinburgh, and Glasgow have developed as financial centers in recent decades. However, commentators suggested that some banks will relocate out of the UK due to the result of "Brexit" referendum.

Banking System

Financial system is formed of the central bank, commercial banks and other financial institutions. The banking system also includes insurance companies, trust and investment banks, savings banks, the Stock Exchange. There are three types of banks: High Street Banks, Building Societies and Direct Bank.

High Street Banks are the main banks, such as Royal Bank of Scotland, HSBC, NatWest, Citibank, and Barclays.

Building Societies such as Woolich, Abbey National, and Halifax were created for those who wanted to save in order to buy a house, and they offer pretty much the same services as the other banks.

Direct Banks such as Co-op (Smile.co.uk) and First Direct don't have branches, but you can bank at First Direct at the Post Office and Co-op bank at their grocery outlets. There are telephone banks which have grown in popularity over the last few years.

The Bank of England, chartered in 1694 and nationalized in 1946, is the central bank of the United Kingdom and the model on which most modern central banks have been based. It is the second oldest central bank in operation today, and the world's 8th oldest bank. Standing at the centre of the UK's financial system, the Bank is committed to promoting and maintaining monetary and financial stability as its contribution to a healthy economy. In 1998, it became an independent public organization, wholly owned by the Treasury Solicitor on behalf of the government, with independence in setting monetary policy. Of the eight banks authorized to issue banknotes in the UK, only the Bank of England can issue banknotes in England and Wales, where its notes are legal tender (法定货币). Bank of England notes are not legal tender in Scotland and Northern Ireland, but are accepted there along with the respective countries' national banknotes.

Transportation

Britain has historically been an innovator and a world leader in many forms of transportation, from shipping, rail systems to aviation.

➢ *Shipping*

Britain is an island, so shipping has always been important in its history. The irregular coastlines provide many natural harbors. 3,200 km of canals and navigable rivers have been conductive to shipping. As early as the 16th century Britain defeated Spain, its greatest rival at sea. In the 17th and 18th centuries, France was defeated, then Germany in the early 20th century. Prior to World War II, Britain had the largest merchant fleet in the world. It continued to be the world's leading country in shipping until World War II. While the Germany submarine attacks sank many British vessels, the tremendous output of the American shipbuilding industry made the United States the world leader. Today, most British passenger shipping involves ferry trips to the continent of Europe or to Ireland. Oil tankers and dry bulk (散装) cargo make up the majority of oceanic shipping.

British ports were nationalized in the late 1940s, and in recent years most have moved into the private sector or are governed by independent trusts[①]. The most important port in the United Kingdom is London; other important commercial ports are at Forth in Scotland, Grimsby and Birmingham in eastern England, Liverpool in western England, and Southampton and Dover in southern England.

➢ *Railways*

The Victorian era was known as the Railway Age. The world's first public railway was the Stockton and Darlington, which opened in 1825. In 1955, a modernization program began to replace steam trains with diesel and electric ones. The last steam locomotive was withdrawn in 1968.

A railway tunnel beneath the English Channel was completed in 1993, connecting England and the European continent. Trains carry both passengers and freight through the tunnel. Motorists can drive their cars on and off the train. The trip through the tunnel takes about 35 minutes.

The Eurostar, a high-speed passenger train that connects England with continental Europe, leaves from Waterloo Station in London.

The majority of the railway lines in Great Britain is owned and operated by the railway infrastructure company Network Rail, with a 16,116 kilometers throughout England, Wales and Scotland, and a further 803 kilometers in Northern Ireland Railways. The government is to spend £30 billion on a new high-speed railway line, which is expected to be operational by 2026.

➢ *The London Underground*

The London Underground, also known by its nickname the "Tube," is a metro system that serves Greater London and the home counties of Buckinghamshire, Essex and Hertfordshire. Its first section opened in 1863, making it the oldest underground metro system in the world — although in fact, approximately 55% of the current network is above the ground, as it generally runs on the surface in outlying suburbs. The system comprises eleven lines, serving 270

---

① 托拉斯，生产同类商品或在生产上有密切联系的垄断企业，为了获取高额利润而从生产到销售全面合作组成的垄断联合。

stations with more than 500 trains running during peak periods. The eleven lines collectively handle approximately 4.8 million passengers a day. In 2016 — 2017, they carried 1.379 billion passengers, making it the world's 11th busiest metro system.

In Glasgow, Liverpool, Tyne and Wear, Manchester, and Sheffield, there are also urban rail systems.

➢ Air Travel

British Airways is one of the world's leading airlines, flying to all six continents and serving over 160 destinations. The number of passengers and the volume are the second-largest in the UK behind "easy jet[①]."

Along with other industries, Britain's airlines were nationalized after World War II and then were privatized in the late 1980s. It was formed in 1974 by combining the two state-run airlines. Together with Air France, British Airways in 1976 introduced the first supersonic passenger service, using the Concorde[②] aircraft. Concorde service was discontinued in 2003. Britain has numerous independent airlines as well. London's main airports, Heathrow (希思罗机场) and Gatwick (盖特威克机场), are among the world's busiest centers for international travel. There are nearly 150 other licensed civil airfields in Britain.

➢ Roads

In Britain, about 90 percent of all passenger travel is by road, and primarily by private car rather than public transportation. In the UK, vehicles are expected to drive on the left and keep to the left lane on multi-lane carriageways except when overtaking (超车). The growth in cars was paralleled by rising public concern about the environmental effects of increased traffic and especially about air pollution. The Transport Act of 2000 gave local authorities the power to charge drivers for use of the roads in an effort to reduce congestion. In 2003 London motorists began to pay for the privilege of driving into the center of the city.

Tourism

Tourism is an essential part of Britain's income. It has brought tremendous economic benefits to the country. Visitors to Britain come from all over the world. They were attracted by Britain's heritage and arts, historic buildings, monuments, museums, and galleries. With over 36 million tourists arriving in 2014, the United Kingdom is ranked as the eighth major tourist destination in the world.

London has become the second most visited city in the world. It is crowded with tourists throughout the year. Among the sites regularly visited by millions are the Tower of London, the Houses of Parliament, Buckingham Palace, and Westminster Abbey. At night, visitors enjoy the hundreds of theaters and pubs in London. Great cathedrals from the Middle Ages still dominate the skylines of many English cities. In Scotland, historic Edinburgh Castle looms over the capital. In Wales, the remains of Tintern Abbey and the small but beautiful Saint David's Cathedral are outstanding. There are a lot of stately (堂皇的) homes in Britain. Among the more famous is

---

① 易捷航空公司：成立于1995年，是英国一家提倡不提供不必要服务的廉价航空公司，因其低价、简洁的服务而受到英国大众的欢迎。
② 协和式飞机：一种由法国宇航和英国飞机公司联合研制的中程超音速客机，为世界上少数曾投入商业使用的超音速客机。

Blenheim Palace①, the home of the Churchill family. Hampton Court Palace, located outside of London, was one of the homes of Henry VIII. The Palace of the Holyrood House in Scotland served as the residence of the monarchs of Scotland since the 16th century.

Among other worthwhile places to visit are Oxford and Cambridge, both are university towns with many ancient buildings, and the Tudor home in which William Shakespeare was born.

---

① 布伦海姆宫：亦称丘吉尔庄园，是欧洲最大的宫殿之一，被誉为英国最美丽的风景，距离英国牛津仅仅有8英里，占地2100英亩，已被联合国列为世界文化遗产。由约翰·范布勒爵士和尼古拉斯·霍克斯莫尔于1705—1722年设计。这座庄园是安妮女王为了表彰和嘉奖温斯顿·丘吉尔的祖上马尔伯勒公爵一世赢得了1704年"布伦海姆之战"的伟大胜利而赐予的。1874年11月30日丘吉尔诞生在这里，晚年又与妻子一起回到布伦海姆宫来安享晚年。

Chapter 11 Society and Culture of the UK

> **章节导读**
> 本章内容分为四部分，分别介绍了英国人及其生活方式、节假日和文化习俗、教育体系以及英国文学。

I British People and Their Ways of Life

General Characters & Manners of the People

It is very difficult to generalize about the British. The characteristics of the people living in different regions and of different social classes vary enormously. However, the following are regards as general qualities of the British, especially the upper and upper-middle classes in the south of England.

➢ *Exclusiveness*

"I am British, you stay away from me. I am exclusive. I am quite happy to be myself. I do not need you. Leave me alone." This is the best-known quality of the British people, particularly of the English people. That is because of the special geographical location and the distinct development of its history. King James Bible, Shakespeare's plays, the British Parliament as early as 1215 and the Industrial Revolution account for the shaping of their general character.

➢ *Conservativeness*

Generally speaking, the British tend to be reserved. They have to wait a long time before they are prepared to try something new; they do not accept change although they are told to, for example, the use of fireplaces in the large cities such as London, Liverpool, Manchester and Birmingham.

➢ *Politeness*

Language — Most British people use the words "please" and "thank you" all the time, particularly when asking for or after receiving help from someone.

Punctuality — British people expect punctuality especially in the work place or place of study. This means that if a lecture begins at 2pm, you must be present in the lecture room at or before 2pm.

Day to day etiquette — British people will normally queue in shops or whilst waiting for buses, buying tickets and so on. You should expect to do the same.

— Most people in the UK have mobile phones. It is considered impolite to use a mobile phone in certain formal situations such as in lectures and meetings.

— When you are invited to dinner, ten minutes late is excellent. When at table, it is polite to sit straight, to keep your elbows off the table and never to talk with your mouth full of food; you can learn from the others, ask what to do if you are not sure and keep the conversation going.

— It is customary to leave a 10% tip when eating in restaurants for good service (but not in fast food restaurants such as McDonalds).

➤ Love of Privacy

The following words best describe British people's attitude towards privacy.

"My home is my castle. The wind can come in, but the Kings and Queens and human beings can never come in without my permission."

➤ Stiff Upper Lip

The British do not show their feelings very much. They always keep a stiff upper lip, to exercise great self-restraint in the expression of emotion, especially in the face of adversity.

➤ Sense of Humor

The humor is self-deprecating (自贬的), that is, laughing at oneself. British people enjoy making fun of their own customs, class system and even their government.

Ways of Life

Knowing the customs of a country is, in effect, a guide to understanding the soul of that country and its people. Britain is the birthplace of Newton, Darwin, Shakespeare and the Beatles, home of the world's largest foreign exchange market and the world's richest football club — Manchester United, the inventor of the hovercraft (气垫船), and JK Rowling, the author of the Harry Potter books. From Scotland to Cornwall, Britain is full of customs and traditions. A lot of them have very long histories. Funny or strange, they're all interesting and are all part of the British way of life. Throughout this section, you will have the chance to discover the customs and traditions of Great Britain.

➤ Marriage and Family Life

The family structure in Britain is changing. The once typical British family headed by two parents has undergone substantial changes during the twentieth century. In particular, there has been a rise in the number of single-person households. Fifty years ago, this would have been socially unacceptable in Britain. In the past, people got married and stayed married. Divorce was very difficult, expensive and took a long time. Today, people's views on marriage are changing. Many couples, mostly in their twenties or thirties, live together without getting married. Only about 60% of these couples eventually get married. In the past, people married before they had children, but now about 40% of children in Britain are born to unmarried parents. In 2000, around a quarter of unmarried people between the ages of 16 and 59 were cohabiting (同居) in Great Britain. Before 1960 this was very unusual, but in 2001, around 23 percent of births in the UK were to cohabiting couples.

In 2004, civil partnerships for homosexual couples were introduced, and since 2014, same-sex marriage has been legal in England, Wales and Scotland.

Marriage is legal at age 16, but usually takes place when people are in their mid to late 20s, and many women do not want to have children immediately. They prefer to concentrate on their jobs and put off having a baby until late thirties. The number of single-parent families is increasing. This is mainly due to more marriages ending in divorce, but some women are also choosing to have children as lone parents without being married.

➤ Housing

Most people in England live in urban areas. More people are buying their own homes than in the past. About two thirds of the people either own, or are in the process of buying, their own homes. Most of others live in houses or flats that they rent from private landlord, the local council, or housing association. For purchasing their property, most people make the payment with a special loan called a mortgage (抵押贷款), which they must repay, with interest, over a long period of time, usually within 25 years.

Most houses in England are made of stone or brick from the local area where the houses are built. The colors of the stones and bricks vary across the country. England has many types of accommodation. In large cities, people often live in apartments, which are called *flats*. In most towns, there are streets of houses joined together in long rows. They are called *terraced houses* (联排). The main types of houses in England are:

- Detached (a house not joined to another house) (独栋)
- Semi-detached (two houses joined together)
- Terrace (several houses joined together)
- Flats (apartments)

➢ *Eating*

Britain has a diverse population, given its large number of immigrants, food is therefore diversified accordingly. British food has traditionally been based on beef, lamb, pork, chicken and fish, and generally served with potatoes and one other vegetable. The most common and typical foods eaten in Britain include sandwich, fish and chips, pies like the Cornish pasty, trifle and roasts dinners. Some of the main dishes have strange names like Bubble & Squeak and Toad-in-the-Hole (面拖烤香肠、裹面粉、牛奶、鸡蛋糊后油煎的肉或肠).

The staple foods of Britain are meat, fish, potatoes, flour, butter and eggs. Many of the dishes are based on these foods. Some of the most traditional foods are described in below:

Fish and chips are a classic, traditional national food of England, consisting of fried battered fish and hot potato chips. It is a common take-away food, originally served in a wrapping of old newspapers. But this practice has now largely ceased, with plain paper, cardboard, or plastic being used instead.

Yorkshire pudding[①] is a traditional and popular British dish, originating from the North-east of England, made from flour, eggs and milk, baked in the oven and usually moistened with gravy (肉汁).

Toad-in-the-Hole is similar to Yorkshire pudding but with sausages cooked in a mixture of eggs, milk and flour.

Lancashire Hotpot is a stew originating from Lancashire in the North West of England. It consists of lamb or mutton and onion, topped with sliced potatoes and baked in the oven in a heavy pot on a low heat.

Bubble & Squeak (土豆卷心菜炒肉)

Bubble & squeak (sometimes just called bubble) is a traditional English dish made with the shallow-fried leftover vegetables from a roast dinner. The chief ingredients are potato and cabbage, but carrots, peas, brussels sprouts, and other vegetables can be added. It is traditionally served with cold meat from the Sunday roast, and pickles. Traditionally, the meat was added to the bubble and squeak itself, although nowadays, it is more commonly made without meat. The

---

① 约克郡布丁：口感类似软面包，味道略咸，呈咖啡杯的形状，中间凹陷绵软，外围则香脆。由于约克郡布丁易于吸收肉汁，因此与烤牛肉一起食用,是英国人周日晚餐的重要组成部分。"烤牛肉加约克郡布丁"被称为英国的国菜。

cold chopped vegetables (and cold chopped meat if used) are fried in a pan together with mashed potato until the mixture is well-cooked and brown on the sides.

Nowadays, many traditional foods such as beef and potatoes have given way to poultry and pasta dishes. Fast food has also become more available, and hamburger restaurants now rival the traditional fish-and-chip shops in popularity. Numerous Chinese and Indian restaurants and pizza houses provide take-away service, and many pubs (public houses) serve anything from snacks to full meals as well as alcoholic beverages.

   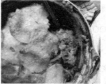

Fish & chips   Yorkshire pudding   Toad-in-the-Hole   Lancashire Hotpot   Bubble & Squeak

The English people generally eat three meals a day. A traditional English breakfast consists of any or all of the following: bacon, sausages, grilled or fried tomatoes, mushrooms, eggs, or toast. Kippers (smoked herring) or black pudding[①] (blood pudding) may also appear on the menu. However, fewer people now eat a cooked breakfast on a regular basis, preferring various combinations of cereal, toast, juice or fruit, and tea or coffee.

The midday meal is usually referred to as lunch and the evening meal as dinner or, when it is less formal, as supper. Working-class people tend to call the midday meal dinner and the meal they have in the early evening — "tea." The tradition of afternoon tea, when tea, biscuits, and cakes are enjoyed at about 4:00 p.m., has declined. Similarly, many people no longer have more than a light lunch or snack in the middle of the day.

> *Socializing*

The Brithis often say "Pleased to meet you" when meeting for the first time. People usually shake hands when first introduced or when greeting and parting in business and other formal situations. Otherwise, many English people will simply say "Hello" or "Hi" when they see each other. Among friends, women are often kissed (by men and women) lightly on one cheek. The use of first names is widespread; titles such as "Mr." and "Mrs." are being used less frequently, even when children address adults.

It is customary to respect people's privacy by telephoning before visiting. When invited to a meal by friends, guests often bring a bottle of wine or another small gift.

Pubs continue to be one of the main places for people to get together in the evenings. Older people often meet their friends in the morning, to chat over coffee or tea and a scone (烤饼). Relaxing at home, however, is still more popular.

Sports and Recreation

Sports play an important part in the life of the British and are popular leisure activities. A great number of major sports originated in the United Kingdom, including: Football (soccer), squash (壁球), golf, boxing, rugby, cricket, snooker (斯诺克台球), billiards (台球), badminton and curling (冰壶).

---

① 黑香肠,血肠：用猪血、乳脂以及谷粒制成 。

Cricket — The traditional summer sport is cricket. It is England's national sport and often is played on village greens on Sundays from April to August.

Football (soccer) — Winter-time national sports are football (soccer) and Rugby Union. Football is undoubtedly the most popular sport in England and has been played for hundreds of years. Some of England's football teams are world famous, the most famous being Manchester United, Arsenal and Liverpool. In the English Football League, there are 92 professional clubs. These are semi-professional, so most players have other full-time jobs. Hundreds of thousands of people also play football in parks and playgrounds just for fun. The highlight of the English football year is the FA (Football Association) Cup Final in each May.

Rugby — Rugby originated from Rugby school in Warwickshire (沃里克郡). It is similar to football but played with an oval ball. Players can carry the ball and tackle each other. The best rugby teams compete in the Super League final each September. For many years, Rugby was only played by the rich upper classes, but now it is popular all over the country.

Tennis — Modern lawn tennis was first played in England. The world's most famous tennis tournament is Wimbledon (温布尔登). It started at a small club in south London in the nineteenth century. It begins on the nearest Monday to June 22, at a time, when English often have the finest weather. Millions of people watch the Championships on live TV. It is traditional for visitors to eat strawberries and cream whilst they watch the tennis.

Horse-racing — One of the most popular spectator sports is horse-racing. People can place bets (赌注) on the races at legal off-track (赛场外) betting shops. Ascot, a small town in the south of England, becomes the centre of horse-racing world for one week in June. It's called Royal Ascot because the Queen always goes to Ascot. She has a lot of racehorses and likes to watch racing.

Foxhunting — Traditionally Boxing Day[①] is a day for fox hunting. The huntsmen and huntswomen ride horses. They use dogs too. The dogs (fox hounds) follow the smell of the fox. Then the huntsmen and huntswomen follow the hounds. Before a Boxing Day hunt, the huntsmen and huntswomen drink hot wine. But the tradition of the December 26th is changing. Now, some people want to stop Boxing Day hunts (and other hunts too). They don't like fox hunting. For them, this is not a sport — it is cruelty.

Rowing — In the nineteenth century, students at Oxford and Cambridge were huge fans of rowing. In 1829, the two schools agreed to hold a race against each other for the first time on the Thames River. The Oxford boat won and a tradition was born. Today, the University Boat Race is held every spring in either late March or early April.

With the exception of U.S. citizens, the British watch more television than anyone else in the world and claim that one reason for this is the high quality of British programming. Videos are also popular, but many people equally enjoy watching films at the cinema. All types of music and theater are well supported. The country is also rich in art galleries and museums.

---

① 节礼日：为每年的12月26日，圣诞节次日或是圣诞节后的第一个星期日，是在英国和英联邦部分地区庆祝的节日，一些欧洲国家也将其定为节日。这一日传统上要向服务行业工人赠送圣诞节礼物。这些礼物通常被称为"圣诞节礼盒"（Christmas Boxes），所以英语中把这一节目称为"Boxing Day"。

II Holidays and Special Days

Britain has relatively few public holidays compared with other European countries. They are usually described as Bank Holidays, because they are days when banks are officially closed. Many holidays and festivals in Britain are centuries old, some involving months of careful planning and preparations, others requiring simply a worrying desire to make a complete and utter fool of oneself.

What are public holidays?

Generally, public holidays include bank holidays, holidays by Royal Proclamation and "common law holidays." Banks are not allowed to operate on bank holidays. When public holidays in the Christmas and New Year period fall on Saturdays and Sundays, alternative week days are declared public holidays.

What is a bank holiday?

A bank holiday is a colloquial term for a public holiday in the United Kingdom, some Commonwealth countries, and the Republic of Ireland. The term comes from the time when banks were shut and so no trading could take place.

Bank Holidays Act 1871 designated four holidays in England, Wales and Ireland (then the entire UK), and five in Scotland, but today, the term is colloquially used for Good Friday and Christmas Day.

Bank Holidays Act 1871	
England, Wales and Ireland	**Scotland**
	New Year's Day
Easter Monday	Good Friday 耶稣受难日（复活节前的星期五）
Whit Monday 圣灵降临节	First Monday in May
First Monday in August	First Monday in August
Boxing Day/St Stephen's Day	Christmas Day

There are currently 8 permanent bank and public holidays in England, Wales and Scotland, and 10 in Northern Ireland. These include Christmas Day and Good Friday, which in England, Wales and Northern Ireland are common law holidays (they are not specified by law as bank holidays but have become customary holidays because of common observance). If a bank holiday is on a weekend, a "substitute" weekday becomes a bank holiday, normally the following Monday.

Traditionally many businesses close on Bank Holidays to enable the workers to have a holiday. This time is often spent with the family on mini breaks and outings.

Does the UK have a National Day?

National Days are not celebrated in the same extent, as National Days are in a number of other countries. Only St Patrick's Day in Northern Ireland (and the republic of Ireland) and St Andrew's Day in Scotland (from 2007) are taken as the official holidays. All the other national days are normal working days. Each part of the United Kingdom has its own Saint's Day:

Brief Introduction to National Days

➢ *St David's Day (1 March)*

St David's Day is the national day of Wales celebrated in Wales on 1 March, in honor of St David, the patron saint of Wales. He was a Celtic monk, abbot (修道士) and bishop, who lived

in the sixth century. He spread the word of Christianity across Wales. The most famous story about Saint David tells how he was preaching to a huge crowd and the ground is said to have risen up, so that he was standing on a hill and everyone had a better chance of hearing him.

St David's Day is commemorated by the wearing of daffodils or leeks. Both plants are traditionally regarded as national emblems. On St David's Day, some children in Wales dress in their national costume, which consists of a tall black hat, white frilled cap and long dress. The national flag of Wales, depicting a fiery red dragon against a green and white background, is also flown.

➢ *St Patrick's Day (17 March)*

St Patrick's Day is the national day of Northern Ireland and Republic of Ireland. Saint Patrick is the patron saint of Ireland. He is credited with bringing Christianity to Ireland. Born in Britain, he was carried off by pirates and spent six years in slavery before escaping and training as a missionary. The most famous story about Saint Patrick is his driving the snakes from Ireland. The stories of Saint Patrick and the snakes are likely  a metaphor for his bringing Christianity to Ireland and driving out the pagan (异教的) religions (serpents were a common symbol in many of these religions). Saint Patrick's Day has come to be associated with everything Irish: anything green and gold, shamrocks and luck. Most importantly, St Patrick's Day is a traditional day for spiritual renewal and offering prayers for missionaries worldwide.

➢ *St George's Day (23 April)*

St George's Day is the national day of England. According to a story dating back to the 6th century, St George rescued a maiden by slaying a fearsome fire-breathing dragon. The Saint's name was shouted as a battle cry by English knights who fought beneath the red-cross banner of St George during the Hundred Years War (1338 — 1453). Some people wear a red rose on St George's Day.

➢ *St Andrew's Day (30 November)*

St Andrew's Day is the national day of Scotland. He was one of Christ's twelve apostles (门徒). Some of his bones are said to have been brought to what is now St Andrews① in Fife during the 4th century. Since medieval times, the X-shaped saltire (X形十字) cross upon which St Andrew was supposedly crucified (在十字架上钉死), has been the Scottish national symbol.

---

① 圣安德鲁斯：坐落在英国苏格兰东海岸法夫行政区，是苏格兰历史上最著名的城镇之一，也是中世纪时苏格兰王国的宗教首都。圣安德鲁斯有苏格兰最古老的大学。作为高尔夫球的发源地，圣安德鲁斯名扬天下，历史悠久。圣安德鲁斯的名字来源于圣徒安德鲁，他是耶稣的12使徒之一，相传他在帕特雷殉教时被钉在X形十字架上。

Brief Introduction to Some Holidays and Celebrations

➤ *Guy Fawkes or Bonfire Night (5 Nov.)* (盖伊·福克斯之夜/篝火之夜)

"Guy Fawkes Night," also known as "Bonfire Night" or "Fireworks Night" by some, marks the date November 5, 1605, when Guy Fawkes and his fellow conspirators attempted to kill King James I and the Members of Parliament, and to blow up the Houses of Parliament. On the very night that the Gunpowder Plot was foiled, bonfires were set alight in London to celebrate the safety of the King, and ever since then, the day has been celebrated with fireworks and bonfires. In 1606, Parliament agreed to make 5th November a day of public thanksgiving. However, it is not a public holiday.

Preparations for Bonfire Night celebrations include making a dummy of Guy Fawkes, which is called "the Guy." Some children even keep up an old tradition of walking in the streets, carrying "the Guy" they have just made, and beg passersby for "a penny for the Guy." The kids use the money to buy fireworks for the evening festivities. On the night itself, Guy is placed on top of the bonfire, which is then set alight; and fireworks displays fill the sky. But this practice has died out in recent years. The fear of strangers, the fact that children are not allowed to buy fireworks and the negative association with begging, have all put an end to it. Many people still hold bonfire parties and BBQs and invite their friends to gather around the fire with them. However, because of the rising number of accidents that occur every year, many communities hold professionally organized public displays. Some of the venues for these public bonfires are in parks, fields, and on hills.

Bonfire Night is not only celebrated in Britain. The tradition crossed the oceans and established itself in the British colonies during the centuries. It was actively celebrated in New England as "Pope Day" as late as the 18th century. Today, November 5th bonfires still light up in far out places like New Zealand and Newfoundland in Canada.

➤ *Remembrance Day (11 Nov. or the preceding Sunday)*

The Cenotaph on Whitehall, London

Remembrance Day (sometimes known informally as Poppy Day[1]) is a Memorial Day observed in Commonwealth of Nations member states since the end of the First World War, when people remembered the members of their armed forces who had died in the line of duty. The day is also marked by war remembrances in many non-Commonwealth countries. It is observed on 11 November in most countries to recall the end of hostilities of World War I on that date in 1918. The common British, Canadian, South African, and ANZAC (澳

---

[1] 英联邦各国在阵亡将士纪念日这一天佩戴红罂粟花，这里的红罂粟在植物性质上是虞美人的两个变种，与鸦片罂粟不是同一种植物。红色的罂粟花最初生长在西欧大陆，但在19世纪的拿破仑战争中，战士的鲜血染红了整片土地，红色的罂粟花开满田野。于是，在士兵间流传着这样的说法：罂粟花鲜红的花瓣是长眠地下的战友的鲜血染成的。英联邦国家选择将红罂粟定为国殇纪念花，成为包含战争之中牺牲的所有阵亡将士的象征。

新军团) tradition includes a one- or two-minute silence at the eleventh hour of the eleventh day of the eleventh month (11:00 am, 11 November), as that marks the time (in the United Kingdom) when the armistice (停战协议) became effective. In the United Kingdom, the main observance is Remembrance Sunday, held on the Sunday nearest to 11 November. Typically, poppy wreaths are laid by representatives of the Crown, the armed forces, and local civic leaders, as well as by local organizations. The main national commemoration is held at Whitehall, in Central London.

➢ *Christmas (25 Dec.)*

In Britain, less emphasis is placed on Christmas Eve than in other countries, and much more is made of Christmas Day and Boxing Day. Carol singing, midnight church services and going out to the pub are some of the activities that many families enjoy.

Night time on Christmas Eve is a very exciting time for young children. It is the time when Santa or Father Christmas comes. They hang up their stockings and go to sleep. Santa and his elves (小精灵) make all the toys for Christmas in his home in Greenland. On Christmas Eve, he piles all of the toys onto his sleigh and rides across the sky with his 9 reindeers. In the morning, when the children wake up, they open their stocking presents. Traditionally on Christmas Eve, mince pies and sherry (or milk) are left out for Santa, and nowadays, carrots are left for his reindeers. Most children are in bed before midnight waiting for Santa to visit.

The Queen's Message

One Christmas ritual, not drawn from an ancient tradition, is the British monarch's broadcast on Christmas day. The tradition began in 1932 when King George V read a special speech written by Rudyard Kipling. The broadcast was an enormous success. It began, "I speak now from my home and from my heart, to you all…" Queen Elizabeth II continues the tradition to this day. Every year, she broadcasts her message on Christmas Day, and it is heard by millions of people all over the world. In England, most people watch or listen to it whilst digesting their Christmas Dinner!

Images of Christmas

Many Christmas traditions, including the Christmas card, originated in the UK. Yule logs (圣诞节原木形大蛋糕), plum pudding, mince pies, fruitcakes, wassailing, the Christmas goose, mistletoe, holly and carol singing, are all firmly rooted in British soil.

Christmas Carols

Christmas carols have their roots in medieval England, when minstrels (中世纪的吟游歌手) traveled from castle to castle. Today, they would be called carollers. In addition, poor people in England would go wassailing (挨户唱歌报圣诞佳音), they would bring their mugs to the door of rich houses, hoping for a share of the wassail (酒宴) bowl. The drink in the bowl was called lambswool. It was a brew of hot ale with sugar, eggs, spices and roast apples floating in it.

Today, carolers generally collect money for charity. The "Round Table" in England often sends a big sleigh with a Christmas tree, and people sing and play carols around the cities and towns of England. In Wales, each village may have several choirs which rehearse well in advance of the holidays and then go caroling and collecting money for charity.

Christmas Trees

Christmas trees are an integral part of the Christmas decorations in most British households. It is a tradition borrowed from Germany, where it is said that German Martin Luther was the first person to decorate a tree with candles and to bring it indoors to show his children what stars looked like at night in the forest. It didn't become popular in Britain until the nineteenth century, when Queen Victoria's husband Prince Albert introduced the custom from Germany.

Nowadays in the UK, you will find a variety of trees, from real trees with roots that can be replanted after the festivities, to felled (砍伐的) trees that get recycled, to plastic imitations that get unpacked every year. No one seems to be able to agree which is the most environmentally friendly option. The tree will be decorated with lights, tinsel (光片), baubles (装饰球), chocolate figures and coins, and the obligatory angel/fairy on the top.

Christmas Dinner

In the past some very strange things were eaten around Christmas. At lavish Christmas feasts in the Middle Ages, swans and peacocks were sometimes served. The flesh was painted with saffron (番红花粉) dissolved in melted butter and the birds were served as being wrapped in their own skin and feathers, which had been removed and set aside prior to roasting.

Around Victorian times, another traditional Christmas feast was roasted goose or roasted turkey. The week before Christmas, London meat markets were crammed with geese and turkeys, many imported from Germany and France, although some were raised in Norfolk, and taken to market in London. The birds were walked from Norfolk to the markets in London. To protect their feet, the turkeys were dressed in boots made of sacking (帆布) or leather, and geese had their feet protected with a covering of tar (沥青).

parsnips

Nowadays, if you sit down with a typical British family on Christmas day, the starter is probably going to be prawns (对虾) or smoked salmon (三文鱼). The main course is more than likely to be turkey, often free-range (散养的), and the bigger the better. Although goose has been making a bit of a comeback (再度流行起来), and for the vegetarian in the family a nut roast (干果蔬菜片), this is normally served with potatoes (roasted, boiled, mashed, or maybe all three), vegetables, roasted parsnips①, and stuffing with gravy and bread sauce. This is usually followed by Christmas pudding; a rich fruit pudding served with brandy sauce or brandy butter.

The Wishbone

Chickens and turkeys contain a y-shaped bone known as the furcular (锁骨), but more commonly it is referred to as the wishbone② (如愿骨). Traditionally, this is removed from the carcass (骨架) of the roasted bird, and dried out. It is then given to two people (usually children), who have to hook their little finger round an end each and pull it apart until it breaks, whilst making a wish. The person who gets the "bigger half" of the wishbone will have his or her wish "come true." Of course, in the great tradition of making wishes, you mustn't tell anyone what you have wished for, or it won't come true.

---

① 欧洲防风：又名欧洲萝卜、芹菜萝卜。其叶子像芹菜；根部颜色像白萝卜，但是形状和味道像胡萝卜。欧洲防风与防风是同科非同属，只是防风的药理作用比较强，而欧洲防风却当作蔬菜。欧美国家有食用欧洲防风的传统习惯，在古希腊和古罗马时代已有栽培。欧洲防风含钾丰富。

② 如愿骨：一种非常古老的占卜方法，可追溯到古罗马时期。如果两个人都有秘密的愿望，可以找一块鸡的锁骨，两个人在心里默念自己的愿望，拿住骨头的两端用力拉，直到V字型的骨头断开，拿到较长骨头那个人的愿望就会实现。luck break成了圣诞大餐的重头戏。

Pantomime (英国在圣诞节期间上演的童话剧)

Pantomime or "panto" is traditionally performed at Christmas, with family audiences consisting mainly of children and parents. British pantomime is now a popular form of theatre, incorporating song, dance, buffoonery (滑稽), slapstick (闹剧), in-jokes (圈子里的笑话), audience participation, and mild sexual innuendo (暗示). There are a number of traditional story-lines (故事情节), and there is also a fairly well-defined set of performance conventions. Throughout the United Kingdom, many theatres in cities and provincial towns continue to have an annual pantomime, and it is very popular with Amateur Dramatics societies. The Pantomime season lasts from around December to February. You should be able to see pantomime productions in many village halls and similar venues across the country.

➢ *Boxing Day*

In England, Wales, parts of Canada, and in some other countries of the Commonwealth of Nations, Boxing Day is a popular term applied to December 26, the day following Christmas Day. This word comes from the custom which started in the Middle Ages around 800 years ago: churches would open their "alms (救济品) boxe" (boxes in which people had placed gifts of money) and distribute the contents to poor people in the neighborhood on the day after Christmas. Traditionally on that day, the gentry would give presents, generally of money, to servants, tradespeople, and others of humble life. These presents came to be known as Christmas boxes. The tradition continues today — small gifts are often given to delivery workers, such as postal staff and children who deliver newspapers. Boxing Day is now simply a leisure day and a very busy day in the sporting calendar. It is a legal bank holiday, banks and most offices, but not shops, close for all of the Christmas-to-New-Year period.

III Education

Education is an important part of British life, because a highly developed nation depends upon educated professionals and a skilled workforce. The literacy rate in Britain is one of the highest in the world at over 99 percent. Children are required by law to receive education until they are 16 years old. Education is compulsory, but school is not, children are not required to attend school. They could be educated at home.

Primary & Secondary Education

Education is free for all children from 5 to 18. Children's education in England is normally divided into two separate stages. They begin with primary education at the age of 5 (at age 4 in Northern Ireland), and this usually lasts until they are 11. They study English, arithmetic, science, religious education, history, geography, music, art and crafts, physical education, and information technology. At the age of 11, they move on to regular high schools, known as secondary schools, where they stay until they reach 16, 17 or 18 years of age.

➢ *Types of Schools in Britain*

For primary and secondary education, there are two main categories of school: local authority maintained schools (State Schools) and independent schools (Private/Public Schools).

State schools are maintained by local government and offer pupils free education up to the age of 18. State schools are funded from taxes and most are organized by Local Authorities (LA).

Independent schools or private schools are called *public schools*, a term that means just the opposite in the United States. *Public schools* in the United States are called *state schools* in Britain. Public schools are private institutions that charge attendance fees, parents pay for their children's education.

Private schools that take pupils from the age of 7 to the age of 11, 12, or 13 are called preparatory schools; and private schools that take older pupils from the age of 11, 12, or 13 to 18 or 19 are often referred to as public schools. Only 7 percent of British students attend private school. Independent schools are free from government control. Now, there are about 2,500 independent schools in the whole country.

The most famous schools in Britain are private boarding schools, such as Eton College (which is a private secondary school in Berkshire County in southern England. The preparatory school was founded by King Henry VI in 1440. A statue of Henry VI stands in the courtyard of the college), Harrow School, Rugby School, and Winchester School. These famous private schools, founded during the Middle Ages, are theoretically open to the public, but in reality are attended by those who can afford the fees. Many of Britain's politicians and entrepreneurs have attended these private schools, as these schools usually cater to the wealthy and influential. But they also offer some scholarships to gifted poorer children. Local authorities and the central authority also provide assistance to some families who are unable to pay the fees. Only a small percentage of the population can attend these ancient and highly prestigious schools. A variety of other schools are also private, including kindergartens, day schools, and newer boarding schools.

➢ *Curriculum and the School Year*

England and Wales have a national curriculum of core courses for students 5 to 16 years old, and all government-run schools, state schools follow the same National Curriculum. The schools are inspected by the Office for Standards in Education. National tests at the ages of 7, 11, and 14 assess students' progress. Schools must provide religious education and daily collective worship for all pupils, although parents can withdraw their children from these options.

The school year is 39 weeks' long and is divided into six terms and the term *form* is used to designate grade;
- September to October
- October to December
- January to February
- February to March
- April to May
- June to July

The main school holidays are: Christmas (2 weeks), Spring (2 weeks) and Summer (6 weeks) holidays.

➢ *Tests*

An examination, known as the "Eleven-plus" test, is given to all children after they have finished primary education at age 11 to test the children's knowledge in English and arithmetic. Those who do well will go on to grammar schools.

Grammar schools are selective, which offer academically oriented general education. Grammar schools are university preparatory schools. In 1960s and 1970s, Comprehensive schools were established; almost all of the former grammar schools have been absorbed into the comprehensive schools. Comprehensive schools, on the other hand, are non-selective, and they do not select pupils on grounds of ability. They take children of all abilities and provide a wide range of secondary education. Secondary modern schools provide vocational education rather than preparation for university entrance.

At the age of 16, prior to leaving secondary school, students take an examination called the GCSE (General Certificate of Secondary Education). All students are tested in Mathematics, English literature, English composition, Chemistry, Biology, Physics, History or the Classics, one modern language or an Ancient language, and one other subject, such as Arts, Business, or Technology.

After completing the GCSE, some students (about a third) leave school usually taking lower-level jobs in the work-force, others go onto technical college, whilst others continue at high school for two more years and take a further set of standardized exams, known as A levels, in three or four subjects. These exams determine whether a student is eligible for university.

Higher Education

➤ Introduction

Higher education refers to a level of education that is provided by universities, vocational universities, community colleges, liberal arts colleges, institutes of technology and other collegiate level institutions, such as vocational schools, trade schools and career colleges that award academic degrees or professional certifications.

British higher education sector, over the last few decades, has been growing at an unprecedented pace. Now, there are over 180 higher education institutions, including universities, university sector colleges and teacher-training colleges.

The percentage of young people entering universities in Britain is far lower than in the United States, where more than half attend. In Britain, there is more emphasis on segregating pupils at the lower levels on the basis of ability. There has been an even greater increase in students benefiting from higher education, from 621,000 in the 1970s to almost 2.3 million in 2016.

➤ Types of Universities

Britain has about 90 universities, which may be classified into 6 main categories:
- Ancient universities — the seven universities founded between the 12th and 16th centuries;
- The University of London, The University of Wales and Durham University (杜伦大学) — which were chartered in the 19th century;
- Red Brick universities — the six large civic universities chartered at the turn of the 20th century before World War I;
- Plate glass (平板玻璃) universities — the universities chartered in the 1960s;
- The Open University — Britain's "open to all" distance learning university (est. 1968);
- New Universities — the post-1992 universities formed from polytechnics or colleges of Higher Education.

The foremost ancient universities are the University of Oxford and the University of Cambridge, both founded in the Middle Ages.

The University of Oxford, located in the city of Oxford, is the oldest surviving university in the English-speaking world and is regarded as one of the world's leading academic institutions. It is a federation of 35 colleges, each with its own structure and activities. Although the exact date of foundation remains unclear, there is evidence of teaching there as far back as the 11th century. The University grew rapidly from 1167 when Henry II banned English students from attending the

University of Paris. It consistently ranks in the world's top 10. Buildings in Oxford demonstrate an example of every British architectural period since the arrival of the Saxons, including the iconic, mid-18th century Radcliffe Camera.

The University of Cambridge, located in the City of Cambridge, is the second oldest university in the English-speaking world and the fourth oldest in Europe. The university grew out of an association of scholars in the city of Cambridge that was formed in 1209 by the scholars leaving Oxford after a dispute with townsfolk there. Academically, Cambridge is consistently ranked in the world's top five universities and as a premier leading university in Europe by numerous media and academic rankings. Cambridge's alumni include 97 Nobel Laureates as of 2017 while Oxford has 66.

The term *Oxbridge* is used to refer to both universities as a single entity (实体), much as Americans would use the term *Ivy League* in reference to the group of prestigious East Coast universities. As a historic part of British society, the two universities also have a long history of rivalry with each other.

Scotland has equivalent ancient institutions at Edinburgh, Glasgow, and St. Andrews.

"Red Brick" refers to six particular British universities founded in the major industrial cities of England, all of which achieved university status before World War I and were initially established as civic science and/or engineering colleges. They are *University of Manchester, University of Birmingham, University of Liverpool, University of Leeds, University of Sheffield* and *University of Bristol*. Officially, the six institutions are members of the Russell Group (which receives two-thirds of all research grants funding in the United Kingdom).

Aston Webb Building, University of Birmingham

The large number of ultramodern (超现代化的) universities that sprouted up in the last half of the 20th century are often called cement block and plate-glass universities (P-universities). The term "plate-glass" reflects their modern architectural design, which often contains wide expanses of plate glass in steel or concrete frames. This contrasts with the "red brick universities" and the older "ancient universities." "Plate-glass" did not catch on (流行) in the same way as "Red Brick," and it is unusual to hear the 1960s foundations described in this way today.

The phrase "New University" formerly appeared as a synonym for the Plate-glass institutions. Today, the term specifically relates to any of the former polytechnics, Central Institutions or colleges of higher education that were given the status of universities by John Major's government in 1992 — as well as the colleges that have been granted university status since then. These institutions may also be described as post-1992 universities or modern universities.

For those who miss the opportunity for higher education at the age of 18, they can obtain it through the Open University, founded in 1971, which offers extension courses taught through correspondence, television and radio programs, and videocassettes. It also sponsors local study centers and residential summer schools. The purpose of the Open University is to reach people who may not ordinarily be qualified for university.

London has its own great schools. University of London was founded in 1836 as an examining and degree-giving body. Teaching functions were not added until 1898. It comprised at first University College (which had been founded in 1826 as the University of London) and King's College (founded 1829 by adherents of the Church of England). Now it has 19 self-governing colleges, including the Royal Holloway, Goldsmiths, the Royal Academy of Music, King's College, and the London School of Economics. Also, part of the University of London system is the School of Advanced Study, which includes some 10 institutes. With 161,270 internal students and 52,000 international students (2014 / 2015), University of London is among the oldest and largest universities in the UK. In 1878, it became the first university in the UK to admit women. Its Senate House, built in Bloomsbury on the former Duke of Bedford's estate, was completed in 1937 to hold the university's central administration offices.

➢ **Sources of University Income**

All British universities are partially funded by central government grants, except Buckingham University, which is the only private university in the whole country. Government funding is provided mainly through the four funding councils in England, Wales, Scotland, and Northern Ireland. The rest comes variously from various other channels. Tuition fees, donations (捐款), company contributions are all important sources of university income. Britain's universities are legally independent and enjoy complete academic freedom. The administrative of a university alone is responsible for the university's maintenance and development.

➢ **Types of University Degree**

An undergraduate degree normally takes three years to complete. Types of undergraduate degree include:

- BSc (Bachelor of Science) — a science degree
- BA (Bachelor of Arts) — an arts degree
- BEng (Bachelor of Engineering) — an engineering degree
- Undergraduate Master's degree (e.g. MEng) — an enhanced four year undergraduate degree including extra subjects studied at a deeper level

Students who receive good grades in their undergraduate degrees may choose to take a Master's degree, which takes a minimum of one year to complete. Types of Master's degree include:

- MSc (Master of Science)
- MA (Master of Arts)
- MEd (Master of Education)
- LLM (Master of Law)
- MBA (Master of Business Administration)

If you would like to continue to study for a PhD, you will have to conduct a minimum of four years' research after the award of your MSc. In some subject areas, a student may transfer from BSc / BA / BEng to PhD so that they follow a five-year research program for PhD without first obtaining a Master's degree.

Top 10 Universities in the UK
(According to Good University Guide, Times Online, 2016)

1	剑桥大学	Cambridge University
2	牛津大学	Oxford University
3	帝国理工学院	Imperial College of Science, Technology & Medicine
4	圣安德鲁大学	University of St. Andrews
5	杜伦大学	Durham University
6	华威大学	University of Warwick
7	埃克塞特大学	University of Exeter
8	萨默里大学	University of Surrey
9	伦敦经济政治学院	London School of Economics & Politics Science (LSE)
10	伦敦大学学院	University College London (UCL)

IV British Literature

In the course of more than 1,500 years' history, British literature, along with the development of the society, has been always the reliable witness and the romantic interpreter of changes of society. Its contributions to the diversity of world literature and to the development of human civilization cannot be over-emphasized. Today, famous English poets, playwrights, and novelists are quoted, translated, and loved throughout the world. So a glimpse of literature will definitely help deepen the understanding of the British society and culture. This brief pilgrimage to British literature will follow the following outline:

- Old and Medieval English Literature
- Literature in the Renaissance
- Literature in the seventeenth century
- Literature in the eighteenth century
- Romanticism in England
- The Victorian Age
- Literature in the Twentieth century

Old and Medieval British Literature (5th century A.D. — 1485)

English descends from the language spoken by the north Germanic tribes, known as Angles, Saxons and Jutes, who settled in England from the 5th century A.D. onwards. They had no writing until they learned the Latin alphabet from Roman missionaries. Old English literature is mostly chronicle and poetry. Of the earliest heroic poetry, the most important poem now preserved is *Beowulf*, the first long poem in English (altogether 3,183 lines), which is considered the national epic of the English people. In the poem, the unknown poet expresses a hope that the evil should be punished, and the righteous will be rewarded. King Alfred's *The Anglo-Saxon Chronicles* (编年史) (Alfred lived during 849 — 899) is another famous work in Old English.

Middle English literature is a combination of French and Anglo-Saxon elements. Literature that the Normans brought to England with their conquest of England in 1066 is remarkable for its bright, romantic tales of love and adventure, while Anglo-Saxon literature is somber and serious. These features can be easily seen in Romance (传奇文学), the most prevailing kind of literature in medieval England. Geoffrey Chaucer was the first great name in English literature as well as the greatest English writer of the Middle Ages.

Literature in the Renaissance (late 15th century — early 17th century)

The Europe-wide Renaissance, having its origin in north Italy in the 14th century, revived the study of Roman and Greek classics and marked the beginning of bourgeois revolution and liberation of human mind. Scholars and educators claimed themselves as Humanists and began to emphasize the capacities of the human mind and the achievements of human culture, in contrast to the medieval emphasis on God and the contempt for things of this world. The English Renaissance also encouraged the Reformation of the Church, eventually leading to the separation from Roman Catholicism and the establishment of Church of England, i.e. Protestantism.

The movement set England on the road of fast developing in terms of politics, economy and culture. During this period, England enjoyed stability and prosperity and at the end of it, England became the strong power of the world and the ruler of the seas. This social circumstance undoubtedly stimulated the prosperity of literature. In fact, English literature in the Renaissance Period is usually regarded as the highlight in the history of English literature. Major literary genres, such as drama, poetry and prose, developed into their delicate maturity. Thomas Moore, Edmund Spenser, Christopher Marlowe, William Shakespeare and Francis Bacon are the outstanding figures of the English Renaissance.

Literature of the 17th Century

The seventeenth century is an eventful one: the English Revolution (1642), the founding of the English Commonwealth (1649), the Restoration (1660), the Glorious Revolution (1688) and King William's signing *The Bill of Rights* (1689). Henceforth, England has become a country of constitutional monarch.

With these social upheavals, literature of the era was undoubtedly of characteristic of the English bourgeois revolution, and meanwhile of pro-king, such as the Cavalier poets (骑士派诗人), who put their main interest in depicting the court life, or of mystery and fantasy, such as the Metaphysical poets (玄学派诗人). John Milton and John Bunyan were two greatest writers of revolutionary enthusiasm, while John Donne was representative of the Metaphysical poets and Ben Johnson (1572 — 1637) of the Cavalier poets. Another figure we should not forget to mention is John Dryden (1631 — 1700), who is regarded as the most important poet, playwright and literary critic of the Restoration period.

Literature of the 18th Century

Socially, the 18th century saw the firm establishment of capitalism in England, the compromise between the aristocracy and the bourgeoisie in their joint rule over the people, the development of the industrial revolution, the rise of England as a big industrial and colonial capitalist power. Intellectually, the eighteenth-century England is also known as the Age of Enlightenment or the Age of Reason. The Enlightenment was a progressive intellectual movement throughout Western Europe in the 18th century, and it celebrated reason (rationality), equality, science and human beings' ability to perfect themselves and their society. These chief political, social and intellectual events that took place in England in the 18th century formed the important background for the development of the literature of this period.

Under these conditions, the popular press flourished, producing a succession of newspapers and literary periodicals in the manner of the two famous magazines, *Tatler* and *Spectator*, edited by Richard Steele (1672 — 1729) and Joseph Addison (1672 — 1719). Owing to the flourishing of popular press, proses had a rapid development, and novels flourished accordingly in this century. Swift, Defoe, Richardson, Fielding are among the major novelists of the time. In their novels, characters were no longer kings and nobles, but the common people and satire was much used in writing. In terms of poetry, Alexander Pope (1688 — 1744), the representative of the neo-classicism (新古典主义), most popular poetic form of the time advertising reason and regularity, gained the highest exclamation for his mastery of heroic couplets (英雄双行体), poetic lines of iambic pentameter with the same rhyme at the end of every two lines. Richard Brinsley Sheridan (1751 — 1816) was the best dramatist of the era, known for *The School for Scandal*.

Literature of the Romantic Age (1798 — 1832)

The American Revolution (1776) and the French Revolution (1789) ignited the rapid spread of national liberation movements and democratic movements across the European countries, and England was no exception. Under this political and social influences, a new literary movement called romanticism came to Europe and then to England. It was characterized by a strong protest against the bondage of neo-classicism, which emphasized reason, order and "elegant wit." Instead, romanticism gave primary concern to passion, emotion, imagination, inspiration and natural beauty. This movement appeared on the literary arena of England from the publication of *Lyrical Ballads* by Wordsworth and Samuel Coleridge (1772 — 1834, known for his *The Rime of the Ancient Mariner* and *Kubla Khan*) in 1798 to the death of Sir Walter Scott in 1832.

The Romantic Age is an age of poetry, during which a batch of first class English poets were produced, such as William Blake (1757 — 1827, famous for his *Songs of Innocence* and *Songs of Experience*), Burns, Wordsworth, Coleridge, Byron, Shelley and Keats. In terms of achievements of novels, Jane Austin offered us her charming descriptions of everyday life in her enduring works; and the greatest historical novelist Scott (1771 — 1832) impressed us with his masterpiece — *Ivanhoe*, which combines a romantic atmosphere with a realistic depiction of historical background and common people's life. The works of the essayist Lamb represented the romantic proses of the period.

Literature in Victorian Age (1832 — 1901)

During Queen Victoria's long reign (1837 — 1901), England grew from an agricultural country into an industrialized one, and became the workshop of the world as well as its financial and political center. British people, while enjoying the continued prosperity brought by the industrialization, were also plagued by evils of the existing institutions — the government, the law, the church, the education and penal systems, with their injustice, cruelty, hypocrisy and corruption. Romantic poetry of the previous times were found weak in reflecting the new reality and naturally gave way to a new literary trend — Critical Realism, which devoted to exposing and criticizing all the social evils. Novel was the dominant genre of the age and flourished with a galaxy of brilliant novelists, female novelist in particular, appeared on the literature scene. Dickens, Thackeray and female writers Charlotte Bronte (1816 — 1855, noted for her masterpiece *Jane Eyre*, the first important governess novel), Emily Bronte, Anne Bronte (although not as famous as her two elder sisters), Elizabeth Gaskell (1810 — 1865, also referred to as Mrs. Gaskell, known for her biography *Her Life of Charlotte Bronte*) and George Eliot were most important critical novelists of the time.

Along with critical realism, there were novelists of other literary schools. The decadence and hypocrisy of Victorian life is best reflected in the works of Oscar Wilde (1854 — 1900), who advocates the theory of "art of art's sake." The pessimism of the last few decades in the 19th century is seen in Thomas Hardy.

Poetry, though not as glorious as in the Romantic Age in general, still produced some influential poets such as Poet Laureate Alfred Tennyson (1809 — 1892), Robert Browning (1812 — 1889, now remembered for his employment of dramatic monologue in poetry) and his wife Elizabeth Barrett Browning (1806 — 1861, also referred to as Mrs. Browning).

The social contradictions were also reflected in the prose of the time. The important prose-writers who criticized the evil, of the capitalist society, were Thomas Carlyle (1795 — 1881), John Ruskin (1819 — 1900) and Matthew Arnold (1822 — 1888, also a poet).

Literature in the 20th Literature

By the end of the Victorian Age, the glamour of the British Empire was beginning to fade due to the awakening of people in British colonies and their struggling for national independence. The two world wars and internal problems caused Britain to lose its worldwide supremacy as well as losses of numerous lives and people's bitter sufferings, physically and mentally. The dire social situation set an unprecedented background for the development of literature. Thus, besides the tradition of critical realism, of which Galsworthy and Bernard Shaw were most eminent practitioners, new literary schools or movements succeeded one after another, experimenting with new literary techniques.

Roughly speaking, the development of English literature in the twentieth century can be divided into two stages, that is, literature between the two World Wars, and literature after World War II. There are three main trends of literature worthy of our attention. They are *Modernism*, *The Angry Young Men*, and *The Theatre of the Absurd*[①].

Modernism is a rather vague term which is used to apply to the works of a group of poets, novelists, painters, and musicians between 1910 and the early years after the World War II. The term includes various trends or schools, such as imagism, expressionism, stream of consciousness and symbolism. It means a departure from the conventional criteria or established values of the Victorian age. Alienation (陌生化) and loneliness are the basic themes of modernism. The modern poets and writers find in symbol as a means to express their inexpressible selves. Joseph Conrad, Virginia Woolf, James Joyce (see Irish literature) and D. H. Lawrence are the most brilliant novelists under this category, while T. S Eliot, William Butler Yeats (see Irish literature) and Wystan Hugh Auden (1907 — 1973) are the most talented poets who set the tone for modern poetry.

During the 1950's, there appeared a group of young writers who were fiercely critical of the established order. They were called "Angry Young Men," a term taken from John Osborne's play *Look Back in Anger*, which first appeared in 1956. Most of them came from working class families and lower middle families. They wrote about the ugliness and sordidness of life and exposed the hypocrisy of the genteel (上流社会的) class. Their works were written in ordinary, sometimes dirty language. The writers belonging to this group are Kingsley Amis, author of *Lucky*

---

① 荒诞派戏剧：第二次世界大战以后西方戏剧界最有影响的流派之一。20世纪50年代兴起于法国，尔后迅速风靡于欧美其他国家。荒诞派因1962年由英国著名戏剧理论家马丁·艾思林写的《荒诞派戏剧》而得名。其特征是荒诞抽象的主题、支离破碎的舞台形象、奇特怪异的道具功能，使戏剧的直观艺术特点发挥到极致。

Jim (1954), John Wain, author of *Hurry on Down* (1953), John Braine, author of *Room at the Top* (1957) and Alan Sillitoe, author of *Saturday Night and Sunday Morning* (1958).

The Theatre of the Absurd is a term applied to a group of dramatists who were active in the 1950's. The absurdity of human conditions is the main theme of the plays of the school of the theatre of the absurd. In the plays, the dramatists express that life has no pattern of meaning or ultimate significance and that no activity is more or less valuable than another. Samuel Beckett is the representative of the school.

In the late of the 20th century, William Golding, Iris Murdoch, John Fowles, V.S. Naipaul and Doris Lessing are major figures of literature. A new trend in the contemporary literature is the rising of the popular novels, which can be justified by the fact that, J.K. Rowling's *Harry Potter* books sold millions of copies worldwide and dominated bestseller lists at the end of the 1990s and in the early 2000s.

Chapter 12
Understanding the Republic of Ireland

> **章节导读**
>
> 　　本章主要介绍爱尔兰共和国，包括四节内容。第一节主要介绍爱尔兰的首都、主要城市、语言、宗教、国旗、国徽、国歌等基本情况。通过学习本节的内容，读者可对爱尔兰有初步了解。第二节主要介绍爱尔兰的地理特征和历史概况：地理部分介绍爱尔兰的主要河流、湖泊和山脉、气候状况、自然资源以及动植物种类；历史部分主要介绍爱尔兰原始定居者和盖尔人的历史、维京人和诺曼人入侵的历史、宗教信仰和阶级冲突、历史上著名的大饥荒事件以及爱尔兰获得独立的历程。第三节主要介绍爱尔兰的政治制度和经济状况。政治部分主要介绍政府、宪法、国家元首、立法、司法和国家政党；经济部分主要介绍爱尔兰的货币和银行业，并对农业、林业、渔业和旅游业进行了概述。第四节主要介绍爱尔兰的社会和文化特征，包括爱尔兰的民族构成，婚姻和家庭风俗、饮食习惯、住房、社交、体育、节假日、教育和文学贡献等内容。

I A General Survey

　　The island of Ireland is divided into two separate political entities: the independent Republic of Ireland and Northern Ireland, a constituent (构成部分) of the United Kingdom. Dublin is the capital and largest city of the former, Belfast of the latter. The **Republic of Ireland** is a unitary (单一的),

parliamentary republic state in north-western Europe which occupies about five-sixths of the island of Ireland and shares its only land border with Northern Ireland. It is otherwise surrounded by the Atlantic Ocean, with the Celtic Sea to the south, Saint George's Channel to the south-east, and the Irish Sea to the east. The country has historically been divided into four provinces: Connacht (康诺特省), Leinster (伦斯特省), Munster (芒斯特省) and Ulster (阿尔斯特省). The provinces of Ireland serve no administrative or political purposes, but function as historical and cultural entities. The area of the Republic of Ireland is 70,270 sq km, occupying almost 85% of the total land-mass of the island of Ireland. Ireland means "western land" and its vivid green landscapes have earned it the title *Emerald Isle* (绿宝石岛).

The Capital and Major Cities

Dublin has been Ireland's capital city since medieval times. It is the largest city of the Republic of Ireland, and also the largest city on the island of Ireland. Located near the midpoint of Ireland's east coast, at the mouth of the River Liffey, it is the country's principal port and commercial and industrial center. Dublin City is the entire area administered by Dublin City Council. However, when most people talk about *Dublin*, they also refer to the contiguous (邻近的) suburban areas. This area is sometimes known as "Urban Dublin" or the "Dublin Metropolitan Area." A person from Dublin is known as a *Dubliner* or a *Dub*. The urban area population of Dublin City Council was 1,345,402 and the population of the Greater Dublin Area was 1,904,806 in 2016.

Spire of Dublin, one of Dublin's newest monuments and landmarks

Cork[①] is the country's second largest city and major port. Other major cities and towns include Galway, Kildare and Limerick.

Languages

Although the Constitution describes Irish as the "national language," English is the dominant language. English is the main language used in Ireland (spoken with an Irish accent). The traditional Gaelic language is spoken as a community language only in some rural areas mainly in the west and south of the country, which is known as the Gaeltacht (爱尔兰境内的爱尔兰语地区). Road signs are usually bilingual except in Gaeltacht regions. English is overwhelmingly dominant in almost all social, economic and cultural contexts. Most print media and public notice are written in English only.

Polish is the most widely spoken language in Ireland after English and Irish as a result of immigration. Some other European languages like Czech (捷克语), Hungarian (匈牙利语) and Slovak (斯洛伐克语) and Baltic languages — Lithuanian (立陶宛语) and Latvian (拉脱维亚语) are also spoken on a daily basis. Other languages spoken in Ireland include Shelta spoken by Irish Travellers, and a dialect of Scots is spoken by some Ulster Scots people in Donegal. Most secondary school students choose to learn one or two foreign languages.

---

① 科克：爱尔兰的第二大城市，中国上海市的友好城市。它位于爱尔兰南部海岸的一个繁忙的海港。人口约20多万，是南部的商业、文化、经济和政治中心，同时还是众多现代化先锋企业的总部所在地和世界微电子和制药工业的国际化基地。科克有着爱尔兰最大的深水港、爱尔兰国立科克大学，获得了2005年欧洲文化之都的称号。科克是一座历史古城，其"中世纪城市"的风貌被完好地保存下来。

Religions

Religious freedom is constitutionally provided for in Ireland. Christianity is the predominant religion, with the Roman Catholic Church as the largest church. The major religions of Ireland are Roman Catholic and Protestant. In 2011, 84.2% of the population identified themselves as Roman Catholic, 4.6% as Protestant or of another Christian religion, 1.1% as Muslim, and 6.2% as having no religion. Ireland, as the proverb goes, is the "Land of Saints and Scholars." The Republic of Ireland has one of the highest rates of regular and weekly church attendance in the Western World.

Protestant groups include the Church of Ireland (Anglican) and the Presbyterian (长老会的) and Methodist (卫理公会教派的) denominations (教派). The remainders claim no religious beliefs, or belong to the small communities of believers such as Muslims, Jews, Jehovah's Witnesses (耶和华见证会), and Orthodox (东正教). Ireland's constitution guarantees freedom of worship.

National Flag

The Republic of Ireland's flag is made of three equal-sized rectangles of orange, white, and green. The flag is twice as wide as it is tall. The green side is by the flagpole. It was first used in 1848. The green color on the flag represents the native people of Ireland (most are Roman Catholics). The orange color represents the British supporters of William of Orange who settled in Northern Ireland in the 17th century (most of whom are Protestants). The white in the center of the flag represents peace between these two groups of people.

National Emblems

Ireland is the only country in the world with a musical instrument as a national symbol. The mythical lore (传说) of Celtic harps makes them a very special emblem of Ireland's pride. In the 16th century King Henry VIII of England made the harp the official symbol of colonial Ireland by putting it on Ireland's currency and it became a recognized symbol of Ireland. According to the legend, the shamrock (三叶草) was used by St Patrick, the patron saint of Ireland, in the fifth century to demonstrate the meaning of the Trinity (三位一体) when converting the Celts to Christianity. To this day it remains one of Ireland's most famous national emblems.

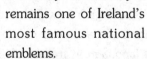

National Anthem

"The Soldier's Song" was written in 1907 by Peadar Kearney, but was not widely known until it was sung both at the General Post Office during the Easter Rising (起义) in 1916 and later at various camps where republicans were interned (拘留). Soon after, it was adopted as the national anthem, replacing "God Save Ireland." The first edition of the song was published in 1916.

Basic Facts about Ireland

Location	West Europe
Capital	Dublin
Area	84,421 sq km
National Day	17 March
Population	4,757,976 (2016 census)
Largest Cities	Dublin, Cork, Galway
Official Languages	English, Irish
Major Religions	Roman Catholic and Protestant
Total Life Expectancy	81 years (2012)
Tota Literacy Rate	99 percent (2014)
Form of Government	Parliamentary, Representative Democratic Republic
Head of State	President of Ireland
Head of government	The Taoiseach (Prime minister)
Legislature	Bicameral (两院制的) legislature
Voting Qualification	Universal at age 18
Gross Domestic Product (GDP, in US $)	307.917 Billion (2016 IMF Statistics)
Unemployment Rate	9.4 percent (2015)
Monetary Unit	1 Euro = 100 eurocent

II Geography and History

A. Geography

Introduction

The Republic of Ireland is in north-western Europe occupying a land area of 70,283 km². Its greatest length, from Malin Head[①] in the north to Mizen Head[②] in the south, is 486 km and its greatest width from east to west is approximately 275 km. The capital and largest city is Dublin, which is located on the eastern part of the island, and whose metropolitan area is home to around a third of the country's 4.75 million inhabitants. The terrain of Ireland is mostly level to rolling interior plain surrounded by rugged hills, low mountains and sea cliffs on west coast. The Emerald Isle is famous for its picturesque landscape with many beautiful lakes, hills and castles. The country boasts semi-tropical bays warmed by the Gulf Stream, quiet sandy beaches, and rocky cliffs that comprise 3500 miles of coastline.

---

① 马林黑德，马林角：位于爱尔兰的最北端，拥有美丽的自然风景，周围是崎岖的海岸线和原始的天然海滩。
② 米曾角：位于爱尔兰斯卡尔地区，是一处独特的半角地区，爱尔兰的最南端。海角通过吊桥与海岸相连，此处有闻名全国的灯塔。

Mizen Head

Rivers, Lakes and Mountains

➢ *River Shannon* (香农河)

The River Shannon is the longest river in Ireland. It is rising from the source Shannon Pot (a small pool on the slopes of Cuilcagh Mountain) in northwestern County Cavan and flowing in a southerly direction to enter the Atlantic Ocean via the 102.1 km long Shannon Estuary. Limerick city[①] stands at the point where the river water meets the sea water of the estuary. Along its course the river runs through or between 11 of Ireland's counties and drains an area of 16,865 km^2, one fifth of the area of Ireland.

According to legend, the Shannon is named after Sionnan, who was the granddaughter of Manannán mac Lir, the god of the sea. She came to this spot to eat the forbidden fruit of the Tree of Knowledge, which was planted by the druids (德鲁伊特,古代凯尔特人的祭司). As she began to eat it, the waters of the pool sprang up and overwhelmed her. She was drawn down into the pool and its water began to flow over the land, forming the River Shannon.

The Shannon has acted as a formidable barrier to move from East to West while providing a marine highway from North to South. It has been an important waterway since ancient times and is now the backbone of a vast network of inland waterways, joined to the Erne via the newly restored Shannon-Erne link. It has influenced the military, social and economic history of Ireland since the beginning of time.

Apart from the Shannon, inland navigation largely depends on the remnants of a canal system built in the 18th and 19th centuries.

➢ *Lough Corrib* (科里布湖)

Ireland is a country of many lakes, known as loughs. **Lough Corrib** is the largest lake in the Republic of Ireland and second largest on the island of Ireland covering 176 km² (after Lough Neagh). It is divided into two parts: a smaller shallower basin to the south and a larger deeper basin to the north. These two parts are connected by a narrow channel. The River Corrib or Galway river connects the lake to the sea at Galway.

Lough Corrib was designated a Ramsar[②] site on 16 June 1996. It has also been designated a

---

① 利默里克市：爱尔兰第三大城市，西海岸最大城市，位于香农河口，滨大西洋深入内陆的香农湾。2014年成为爱尔兰第一文化城市。利默里克在爱尔兰语中是"荒芜的沼泽"的意思，指的是城外的河滩。

② 拉姆萨尔：1971年2月，在伊朗的拉姆萨尔召开了"湿地及水禽保护国际会议"，会上通过了《国际重要湿地特别是水禽栖息地公约》，简称《拉姆萨尔公约》。该公约于1975年12月21日生效，规定每3年召开一次缔约国会议，审议各国湿地现状和保护活动的有关报告和预算。目前世界有100多个国家成为该公约的缔约国，全世界登记湿地总数为648个，总面积4,343万平方千米。

Special Area of Conservation.

In early 2007, large numbers of Cryptosporidium (隐孢子虫,可致体内感染的水中寄生虫) were detected in water from the lake, leading to contamination of the public water supply in Galway city and an outbreak of cryptosporidiosis[①]. The water taken from Lough Corrib was likely contaminated by migration of animal and human faeces (排泄物).

➢ Mountains

Among the principal mountain ranges are the **Wicklow Mountains** (威克洛山脉) in the east, just south of Dublin, rising to more than 915m above sea level. In the far southwest stand another mountain range, **Macgillycuddy's Reeks** (麦吉利卡迪山). Stretching slightly over 19 km, they include the highest mountain in Ireland, Carrauntoohil (卡朗图厄尔山峰) at 1,041 m, the two other 1,000m peaks existing in Ireland, Beenkeragh at 1,010 m, and Caher at 1,001 m, and over 100 other peaks of over 600 m.

Climate

Ireland's mild climate is a reflection of the fact that its shores are bathed by the relatively warm ocean waters of the North Atlantic Drift. Extremely high or low temperatures are virtually unknown. The average winter temperature ranges from 4°C to 7°C, approximately 14°C higher than that of most other places in the same latitude. The average summer temperature ranges from 15°C to 17°C, or about 4 Celsius degrees lower than that of most other places in the same latitudes. Rainfall is heaviest on the westward facing slopes of the hills. The east is much drier. The sunniest part of the country is the southeast. The outstanding feature of the Irish weather is its changeability.

Natural Resources

Ireland's most valuable natural resource is its lowland soils. These soils support rich grasslands, which flourish across much of Ireland and provide extensive pasture for grazing animals. The soils also support a variety of cereals and root crops. Ireland has some natural mineral resources including deposits of zinc (锌), lead, gypsum (石膏), and alumina (氧化铝). Some natural gas deposits are found off the southern and western coasts. Peat (泥煤,草炭) from heaths (石南丛生的荒野) and bogs (沼泽) has long served as an important fuel source for homes and industry, and it is also used to improve soils for cultivation.

Cutting Peat

Peat is the first stage in the transformation of vegetation into coal. For 400 years, people have cut, dried, and burned it for heating and cooking.

Animals and Plants

Ireland's animal life does not differ markedly from that of England or France. Over many centuries of human settlement almost all of Ireland's natural woodlands were cleared, and indigenous animals such as bear, wolf, wildcat, beaver, wild cattle, and the giant Irish deer gradually disappeared.

---

① 隐孢子虫病：由隐孢子虫引起的以腹泻为主要临床特点的人兽共患性肠道原虫病。避免水源污染、饮用开水是最重要的预防措施。

Connemara Pony

Great Auk

However, the hardy and versatile Connemara pony, Ireland's only native pony breed, has been used by Irish farmers since prehistoric times. The great auk (大海燕) was exterminated (灭绝) in the 19th century. Small rodents (啮齿动物, 如鼠或狸) living in forested areas and fields remain numerous across Ireland, as do numerous species of shore and field birds, including many types of gull. Birds of prey (猛禽) are rare. Ireland has no snakes; in fact, the only reptile found in Ireland is a species of lizard. Sedges (莎草, 苔), rushes, ferns (蕨类植物) and grasses provide the dominant plant cover.

B. History

An estimated 70 million people world-wide can claim Irish heritage. From before the arrival of Saint Patrick to the present day Ireland has had a history that could never be called quiet.

First Settlement

The first settlement of Ireland took place sometime around 6000 BC by hunters and fishers along the island's eastern coast, but we know very little about them apart from the fact that they built some fairly impressive monuments like Newgrange (爱尔兰中部古代巨石群组格莱奇古墓,与Stonehenge〈巨石阵〉齐名) and Knowth Passage Tombs and that they fashioned beautiful items from gold and silver.

Newgrange is one of the most important archaeological sites of Ireland and the most important Corridor-Grave in the world.

The Gaels

The Gaels (盖尔人：苏格兰、爱尔兰或马恩岛说盖尔语的凯尔特人), the Celtic-speaking people from Western Europe, found their way to the island sometime between about 600 BC and 150 BC and subdued the previous inhabitants. They introduced many things that persist to this day, including their language, their games, their music, and a typically Irish attitude towards life. It appears that they were seen from the outside as a scary group of people, because the Romans gave them a wide berth (远避), despite their partial occupation of Britain during the 1st century AD.

St Patrick casts out the snakes from Ireland

About the time of Christ the island was organized into five kingdoms, the traditional "Five Fifths of Ireland." By 400 AD seven independent kingdoms had evolved. The kings of these kingdoms often allied their armies to raid neighboring Roman Britain and the Continent. On one of these raids a lad of 16 was captured, returned to Ireland and sold into slavery. During this enslavement a boy turned to religion and some six years later at the age of 22 escaped. The young man studied theology in the Roman church and in 432 AD returned to Ireland, and began a lifelong quest of converting the Irish to Christianity. This was none other than Ireland's patron (守护神) Saint Patrick.

Christianity

Ireland is Christianized by St Patrick in 432 AD. Christianity became the dominant religion of the entire island. In the wake of Christianity there was a flourishing of culture and learning connected with the churches and the monasteries. This early Christian culture helped to account for the power of Catholicism in Ireland to this very day.

The Vikings

The Vikings from Nordic (北欧的) countries first attacked Ireland in 795. They looted (抢劫) monasteries (修道院) and took women and children as slaves. However, the Vikings were not only raiders. They were also traders and craftsmen, and were the first to introduce the concept of money to the island. In the later 9th century they turned from raiding to conquest and founded Ireland's first towns, Dublin, Wexford, Cork and Limerick. They also gave Ireland its name, a combination of the Gaelic word *Eire* and the Viking word *land*. Eventually the Vikings settled down on the island, many became farmers and intermarried with the Irish and accepted Christianity.

The Normans

In 1168 the English invaded the island. These warriors were armed to the teeth and gave themselves the rather unimpressive name "Normans." From then on to about 1400, many Norman moved to Ireland from England and settled in the eastern areas, particularly around Dublin. They built imposing castles and constructed a few roads. Some became assimilated but strife (冲突) persisted between the native Irish and the colonists. This is the beginning of the Anglo-Irish conflict, which was to shape Irish history in the following centuries up until today. In 1367 a law was enacted to keep the two populations separate.

Religion and Class Conflicts

In 1495 Henry VII extended English law over the entirety of Ireland, and assumed supremacy over the existing Irish parliament. When Henry VIII became king of England, England broke with the Catholic Church in 1536. He forced Ireland to break with the Catholic church too, and confiscated (没收) the land that the church possessed. The Irish, however, resisted. At this point the Catholic religion had been the religion in Ireland for a thousand years, and it constituted part of the national identity of the Irish. The Irish Catholic population was persecuted and the Protestant British oppressors took complete control. In 1541 Henry VIII became king of Ireland.

Queen Elizabeth continued the fight against the Irish Catholics, who kept resisting. There was particularly strong resistance in Ulster[①]. It was crushed by the English in 1607, and the Catholic leaders had to flee. The English crown confiscated their land, distributed it among 10,000 poor Protestants from Scotland, who were sent to Ulster to colonize the area. The original Irish population was forced off the land.

---

① 阿尔斯特：原为爱尔兰一地区，在詹姆士一世统治时大部分被并入英国，今为北爱尔兰及爱尔兰共和国所分割。

This is the starting point of the conflict between Catholics and Protestants in the North. These Scots were Calvinists, i.e. a form of Protestants. They quickly became economically and politically dominant, whereas the original population formed an underclass of laborers and tenant farmers (佃农) etc. As Calvinists the Scots were hard working and very productive in trade and industry, Ulster developed differently from the rest of Ireland, which is largely agricultural.

English national politics continue to influence the situation in Ireland. In 1685 — 1688 James II became King of England. James was a Catholic, the Protestants in England were not satisfied with him and he was dethroned by William of Orange, who ruled as joint monarch over England and Ireland with his wife Mary II, a daughter of James II until her death on 1694, and then ruled as sole monarch. James fled to Ireland, where the Irish population supported him. William of Orange and his troops pursued him and they fought a battle, the Battle of the Boyne 1690, a key event in Irish history, where the forces of William defeated the forces of the Catholic King, James.

William and Mary

Penal Times and Rebellion

The first years of the 18th Century saw an attempt to rid Ireland of Catholicism, by implementing laws that restricted Catholic practice while making it extremely advantageous to become a Protestant. For example, they instituted the so-called Penal (刑事的) Laws 1691 — 1793. According to these laws the Catholic majority in Ireland cannot: enter military service, hold public office, practice law, produce or print books, newspapers etc., own land, be ministers, be schoolmasters, pass on land to their children without dividing it, and thus impoverishing (使贫穷) their descendants.

Throughout the 18th century this system of oppression was in effect. The Irish population was reduced to paupers (贫民), having to support themselves as tenant farmers, exploited by the British landlords, many of whom did not even live in Ireland but in Britain, and resources were drained from Ireland to Britain. In part this colonial exploitation helped finance the industrial revolution in England.

It wasn't until the end of the century that Irish people, both Protestants and Catholics this time, started to look for greater freedoms from England. What unite them were the liberal ideas of freedom, equality and brotherhood. These Irishmen saw clearly that their country could not develop economically and socially unless the colonial exploitation was brought to an end.

In 1798 they rose in arms against the British. The rising was crushed by the British army and the leaders were hanged in public. The most famous of the leaders was Wolf Tone (a Protestant), who is considered as a national hero in Ireland to this very day.

The Potato Famine

On 1 Jan 1801, the United Kingdom of Great Britain and Ireland came into existence. Not surprisingly, the union in Ireland was highly unpopular and relations continued to deteriorate (恶化) between the Catholic and Protestant populations. In the 1830s, a movement began to repeal the union. When the potato crops of the 1840s failed, a devastating famine resulted. The English government was so slow to react to the crisis that by the time the famine was over, an estimated one million people had died, and a further one million had left Ireland, arriving in the U.S. and Britain, penniless and desperate. The Irish potato famine created a legacy of emigration from Ireland that did not stop until the late 20th Century. By 1960, the population of Ireland had dwindled to 4.3 million from an 1841 population of over 8 million.

Partial Independence

Following the famine, strong, highly organized Irish political movements were born. Demand for national self-government came to the fore. The Catholics gradually gained parliamentary power and "home rule" (地方自治), a separate Irish parliament within the Union, gained popularity. Using their leverage (影响) in the British parliament, a home rule bill was enacted in 1914, but not put in effect until the end of World War I.

In the twentieth century, Ireland's situation has remained unsettled. In 1920, the British government passed *the Government of Ireland Act*. By it there would be two parliaments in Ireland, one in the north and one in the south. However, both parliaments would be subordinate to the British parliament.

Famine Memorial in Dublin

In 1921 a treaty between southern Ireland and Britain established the Irish Free State (爱尔兰自由邦), a self-governing dominion within the British Commonwealth of Nations. This allowed the Northern Ireland Parliament to take the six northern counties out of the dominion. In the Free State it led quickly to a vicious civil war between both sides; those who agreed with the Treaty, and those who disagreed, but ultimately the treaty stood. The Irish Civil War accounted for 3,000 deaths on both sides. Most of today's political parties of the Irish Republic originate from this deeply divisive (造成不和的) political split.

The Republic of Ireland since the Split

In 1937 southern Ireland drafted and adopted a new constitution, which made an elected president head of state. Furthermore, the name "Irish Free State" was replaced with either Eire or Ireland. It remained formally within the British Commonwealth. Then in 1948 Ireland was made a republic and the last ties with Britain were cut.

After having been denied membership due to its neutral stance during the Second World War and not supporting the Allied cause, Ireland finally became a member of the United Nations in December 1955. Interest towards membership of the European Economic Community (EEC) developed in Ireland during the 1950s, with consideration also given to membership of the European Free Trade Area. In 1972, a referendum was held to confirm Ireland's entry to the European Economic Community, and it finally joined in 1973. Over the past few years it has integrated further into the European Union.

III Political System and National Economy

A. Political System

Politics of the Republic of Ireland take place in a framework of a parliamentary representative democratic republic. The Uachtar á n (President) is the head of state. The Taoiseach (Prime Minister) is the head of government and of a multi-party system. Executive power is exercised by the government. Legislative power is vested in both the government and the Oireachtas (爱尔兰国家议会,由总统和两院组成), the bicameral national parliament. The Judiciary is independent of the executive and the legislature. While there are a number of important political parties in the state, the political landscape is dominated by two opposed and competing Parties: Fianna Fáil[①] and Fine Gael[②].

Constitution

The state operates under the Constitution of Ireland, adopted in 1937. The constitution falls within the liberal democratic tradition. It defines the organs of government and guarantees certain fundamental rights. The constitution may only be amended by referendum (全民公决). Important constitutional referendums have concerned issues such as abortion, the status of the Catholic Church, divorce and the European Union.

Head of State

The head of state is the President of Ireland. In keeping with the state's parliamentary system of government the President exercises largely a ceremonial role but does possess certain reserve powers. The presidency is open to all Irish citizens who are at least 35. The President is elected to a seven-year term of office; no candidate may serve more than two terms. In carrying out certain of their constitutional functions, the President is aided by the Council of State. There is no Vice-President in Ireland. If for any reason the President is unable to carry out his/her functions, or if the Office of President is vacant, the duties of the President are carried out by the Presidential Commission.

Executive

Executive authority is exercised by a cabinet known simply as the Government. Article 28 of the Constitution states that the Government may consist of no less than seven and no more than fifteen members, namely the prime minister, the deputy prime minister and up to thirteen other ministers. The prime minister is appointed by the President after being nominated by the lower house of parliament. The remaining ministers are nominated by the prime minister and appointed by the President.

Legislature

The parliament of the Republic of Ireland is the Oireachtas which consists of the President and two houses: Dáil Éireann (众议院) and Seanad Éireann (also known as the Senate). The Dáil is by far the dominant House of the legislature. The President may not veto (否决) bills passed by the Oireachtas, but may refer them to the Irish Supreme Court for a ruling on whether to comply with the constitution.

Dáil Éireann: Members of the Dáil are directly elected at least once in every five years from mulit-seat constituencies[③]. Membership of the house is open to all Irish and UK citizens who are at least 21 and permanently resident in Ireland. The electorate (选民全体) consists of all Irish and UK

---

① 爱尔兰共和党：成立于1926年，党员约10万。议会第三大党。历史上该党19次单独组阁或联合阁，并在79年中有61年执政。2011年大选惨败。传统上较保守，对内主张减税，增加就业机会，对外主张实行中立政策，支持欧盟一体化建设。2011年1月大选前，领袖为迈克尔·马丁（Michael Martin）。

② 爱尔兰统一党：爱尔兰共和国议会第一大党，也是爱尔兰2011年大选后的执政党，成立于1933年，党员约3.5万人。代表富裕农民、中产阶级和工商业资本家集团利益，系中右翼政党。对内主张削减公共开支，降低税率和私有化；对外主张经济开放，参与欧洲一体化建设。领袖为恩达·肯尼（Enda Kenny）。

③ 多议席选区：议会有固定席位数，众议院的议席是按照选区划分的。

citizens resident in Ireland over the age of 18. Members of the Dáil are known as Teachta Dála or TDs.

Seanad Éireann: The Senate is a largely advisory body. It consists of sixty members called Senators. An election for the Seanad must take place no later than 90 days after a general election for the members of the Dáil.

Judiciary

The Republic of Ireland is a common law[①] jurisdiction. The judiciary consists of the Supreme Court, the High Court and many lower courts established by law. Judges are appointed by the President after being nominated by the Government and can be removed from office only for misbehavior or incapacity, and then only by resolution of both houses of the Oireachtas.

The final court of appeal is the Supreme Court, which consists of the Chief Justice and seven other justices. The Supreme Court has the power of judicial review[②] and may declare to be invalid both laws and acts of the state which are repugnant (不一致的) to the constitution.

B. National Economy

An Overview

Since the 1980s the Irish economy has transformed from being predominantly agricultural to a modern knowledge economy focused on high technology industries and services. The country relies heavily on Foreign Direct Investment. Due to a highly educated workforce and a low corporation tax rate, it has attracted many multinational corporations such as Intel, Microsoft and Google. Ireland is ranked as the ninth most economically free economy in the world, according to the Index of Economic Freedom. In terms of GDP per capita (人均国内生产总值), Ireland is one of the wealthiest countries in the Organization for Economic Co-operation and Development (OECD, 经济合作与发展组织) and European Union (EU). One of the keys to this economic growth was a low corporation tax, currently at 12.5% standard rate.

Agriculture, once the most important sector, is now dwarfed by industry. Although exports remain the primary engine for the Republic's robust (强劲的) growth, the economy experienced unprecedented economic growth fuelled by a dramatic rise in consumer spending and recovery in both construction and business investment from 1995 to 2007, which became known as the Celtic Tiger period. A 2005 study by *The Economist* found Ireland to have the best quality of life in the world.

During 2007 the pace of growth slowed and led to the burst of a major property bubble. The dramatic drop in property prices highlighted (凸显) the over-exposure (过度敞开) of the economy to construction and contributed to the Irish banking crisis. Ireland officially entered a recession in 2008. With the help of a strong growth in exports, the country officially exited (离开) recession in 2010. Following three years of contraction, the economy grew by 0.7% in 2011 and 0.9% in 2012. In March

---

① 习惯法，不成文法：来源和发展于英国的法律系统，以法院决议为基础，根据在这些决议中隐含的学说以及习惯和用法，而不是基于编纂的书面法律。

② 司法审查，亦称"违宪审查"：是西方国家通过司法程序来审查、裁决立法和行政机关是否违宪的一种基本制度。其理论依据是：宪法至上，法律和法令从形式到内容都不得同宪法条文相抵触；司法机关对宪法有最后解释权，议会、政府的法律、法令如果违反宪法，司法机关可以裁决该项法律、法令违宪而无效。

2016 the unemployment rate was reported by the Central Statistics Office (Ireland) to be 8.6%, down from a peak unemployment rate of 15.1% in February 2012. In 2013, Ireland was named the "best country for business" by *Forbes*.

Currency and Banking

Bank of Ireland

On New Year's Day 2002, Ireland, like the other 11 members of the Eurozone, started using Euro notes and Euro coins[①] for cash transactions. Within a few months, the old coins and banknotes in Punts[②] have been withdrawn. As a participant in the single currency, Ireland must follow economic policies established by the European Central Bank (ECB) which is located in Frankfurt, Germany. On January 1, 1999, control over Irish monetary policy was transferred from the Central Bank of Ireland to the ECB. After the transfer, the Central Bank of Ireland joined the national banks of the other EU countries that adopted the Euro as part of the European System of Central Banks (ESCB).

All Irish euro coins bear the same design on their obverse (正面) national side: a Celtic harp based on the Trinity College Harp; the coins' design also features the 12 stars of the EU, the year of issue and the Irish name for Ireland, "Éire," in a traditional Gaelic script.

(Regarding the euro, some confusion regarding the obverse and reverse of the euro coins exists. Officially, as agreed by the informal Economic and Finance Ministers Council of Verona in April 1996, the distinctive national side for the circulation coins is the obverse and the common European side, which includes the coin value, is the reverse.)

Left: Obverse national side of the Irish one euro coin
Right: Common (or European) side of a €1 coin

Agriculture, Forestry, and Fishing

About 17 percent of the total area of Ireland is cultivated, and much of the rest is devoted to pasture. Raising livestock is the chief agricultural activity, and meat products are among the most important agricultural exports. The trade in live animals, notably horses, and dairy products is also important. The principal field crops are wheat, barley, oats, and potatoes. The most fertile farmlands are found in the east and southeast.

Before the arrival of the first settlers in Ireland about 9,000 years ago, the land was largely covered by forests. The growth of blanket bog[③] and the extensive clearing of woodland to facilitate farming are believed to be the main causes of deforestation during the following centuries. Today, about 12% of Ireland is forested, of which a significant majority is composed of mainly non-native coniferous plantations (针叶林) for commercial use. Ideal soil conditions, high rainfall and a mild

---

① 欧元硬币：欧盟成员国于1997年共同决定，发行八种面额的欧元硬币。欧元硬币一面是统一的，称之为common side；而另一面则是由各个国家自行设计，称之为national side。爱尔兰的欧元硬币图案为民族的象征竖琴，以及爱尔兰语国名"Éire"和欧洲12星，代表着十二个创始国。
② 爱尔兰镑：爱尔兰共和国使用欧元前的货币单位。
③ 覆被沼泽：是一种特殊类型的贫营养泥炭沼泽，主要分布于英国、爱尔兰和挪威西海岸、加拿大纽芬兰等地，是在降水量丰沛的海洋气候条件下形成的。

climate give Ireland the highest growth rates for forests in Europe.

The fishing industry expanded in the late 20th century. However, the waters around Ireland and much of Europe have been heavily overfished, and annual fish catches are now subject to quotas (限额) established by the EU. Ireland's catch in 2001 was 417,244 metric tons. Fish farming, both in freshwater and saltwater environments, is becoming more important as natural catches drop.

Tourism

The Irish government actively promotes the tourism industry, which has grown increasingly important to the economy. Dublin, in particular, has become an important tourist destination, in part because of the rapid growth of low-cost air services linking the city to the United Kingdom and mainland Europe. However, the most popular destination for tourists is the rugged west coast, where numerous peninsulas and bluff (陡峭的) cliffs provide a dramatic contrast to the rain-hazed (雨雾笼罩的) loughs of the interior. Many visitors choose to explore the countryside on foot. Horseback riding, cycling, golfing, and boating along Ireland's rivers and loughs are also popular tourist activities.

IV Society and Culture

People of Ireland

Ireland's population is predominantly of Celtic origin, but ancient tribes had inhabited Ireland for thousands of years when Celtic peoples settled the island in the 4th century BC. Over the centuries Ireland absorbed significant numbers of Vikings, Normans and English. More recently, Ireland's membership in the European Union (EU) has  increased the number of citizens of other European countries living in Ireland, and small communities of ethnic Chinese and Indian people also have been established.

Since 1996 Ireland has received small numbers of refugees and asylum (政治避难) seekers from Eastern Europe, Africa and Asia. Ireland also has a small indigenous minority known as Travelers. The number of Travelers is approximately 25,000. They move and camp across the Irish countryside in small groups in enclaves (少数民族聚集地) within cities.

Ireland's economic growth in recent decades has reversed (彻底改变) a long trend of emigration, which initially was to escape the famine and later to seek employment and better lives. In the 1990s immigration began to exceed emigration. In 2002 Ireland's population grew at an annual rate of 1.15 percent, one of the highest rates in Western Europe.

Customs of Ireland

➤ *Marriage and Family*

People usually marry in their early to mid-20s. Most weddings are performed in a church, but a minority is also performed in a registry office. After marriage, many people in rural areas stay close to their family's home and visit frequently. Many couples, particularly in the cities, live together before or instead of marriage.

Typically, the bonds between siblings (兄弟,姐妹) in an Irish family are especially strong. In rural areas, extended families often live near one another, and family members who have moved to Dublin or overseas in search of work often return for Christmas and other family celebrations or funerals. Traditionally, women have not worked outside the home except to help on the family farm, but in Dublin and other cities the majority of women now have jobs. Salary levels for women still lag behind those of men, but gender discrimination is illegal. The Irish have elected two consecutive (连续的) women presidents since 1991.

> *Cuisine*

Irish smoked salmon

Tea Brack

As an agricultural country, Ireland produces many fresh vegetables. Fresh dairy products, breads, and seafood are also widely available. Potatoes, once eaten at every meal, are still regularly served, but the Irish have embraced (接受) other foods such as pasta and rice. Apples, oranges, and pears have long been integral (必备的) to the Irish diet, but are now joined by a wider variety of fruit that have become available since Ireland joined the European Union. Oysters and other shellfish are popular, and smoked salmon is considered an Irish specialty, as are Irish stew and Irish lamb. Irish breads include soda bread and brack (果子面包), a rich, dark loaf containing dried fruit and traditionally served at Halloween.

The Irish generally eat three meals a day. The traditional cooked breakfast consists of any or all of the following: bacon, sausages, grilled or fried tomatoes, mushrooms, eggs, white and black pudding and toast or bread fried in fat or oil. However, fewer people now eat such a morning meal, preferring a lighter breakfast. In recent years, the Irish, particularly those in urban areas, have become much more adventurous in their diet, and now eat a wide variety of European and ethnic food. Pubs (public houses) and cafés serve both snacks and full meals.

The midday meal is usually referred to as lunch and the evening meal as dinner or, when it is less formal, as supper. But some rural people call the midday meal dinner and the early-evening meal tea. Many people, particularly in Dublin, no longer eat more than a light meal or snack in the middle of the day. Those who have an early-evening meal sometimes have another snack — sandwiches, cakes, or biscuits — at around 9 p.m.

Tea and coffee are popular drinks in the home, and Dublin is rapidly developing a café culture. Pubs can be found in nearly every Irish town, where people gather to talk with friends, relax, listen to music, and have a drink. Beer is much beloved in Ireland, especially the dark stout (烈性啤酒) varieties. Renowned local stouts include Guinness[1], Beamish, and Murphy's. Irish whiskey is also a popular alcoholic beverage.

---

[1] 吉尼斯/健力士黑啤酒：1759年，一个名叫阿瑟·吉尼斯的人在爱尔兰都柏林市建立啤酒厂，生产一种泡沫丰富、口味醇厚、色暗如黑的啤酒，这就是吉尼斯黑啤酒。到1833年，它已经发展为爱尔兰最大的一家酿酒厂。时下，吉尼斯黑啤酒在50多个国家酿造生产，销往150多个国家，每年销量约9亿多升。St James's Gate Brewery啤酒厂是都柏林最著名的标志性景点之一，这里有一个圆形的酒吧，可以用360度的视角来欣赏城市的景色。吉尼斯世界记录正是吉尼斯啤酒公司的一个成功创意，其目的是提升吉尼斯品牌的知名度。

➢ Housing

In cities and towns, most Irish people live in houses, although apartments are growing in popularity as urban densities increase. In the countryside, traditional farmhouses constructed of stone or dried peat and covered with thatched roofs have been largely replaced by modern dwellings. Today, most homes are made from concrete, brick, or mortared (砂浆砌合的) stone and have tile roofs (瓦屋顶). In rural areas peat is still cut and dried for use as fuel for cooking and heating.

a 19th-century stone cottage in the west of Ireland

➢ Socializing

The traditional Irish greeting *Céad míle fáilte* literally means "A hundred thousand welcomes." However, the Irish greet one another with common English phrases such as "Hello" and "How are you?" or more casual greetings such as "How's it going?" The most typical Irish greeting is *Dia dhuit*, which means "God be with you." Goodbye is expressed with *Slán* (roughly "Go safely") or the warmer *Slán agus beannacht* ("Go safely, and blessings be with you"). Greetings are generally accompanied by a firm handshake, although in cities and among younger people it is not unusual for women to be kissed on the cheek when greeting. The use of first names is now widespread.

Unless one knows someone well, it is usual to telephone before visiting. Rural people are more likely than urban dwellers to drop in on friends unannounced, as was common practice in the past. People like to meet for conversation in pubs, which are important centers of social life. Visiting in the home takes place during holidays, especially between Christmas and New Year's Day, which is also the time when young people living abroad usually come home to visit. Parties are also popular during holidays.

Sports Sports

The Irish are sports-oriented, and most weekends include some sporting activities for the family or the individual. Popular sports include the two national pastimes: Gaelic football and hurling (爱尔兰式曲棍球), both strictly amateur sports. The women's version of hurling is called *camogie*. The All-Ireland semifinals and finals, sponsored by the Gaelic Athletic Association (GAA), are highlights of the hurling and Gaelic football seasons.

Soccer, rugby, sailing, cycling, golf, and horse and greyhound (快速汽船) racing are also favorite activities. Soccer has become a particularly popular spectator sport in the 1990s, reflecting the enthusiasm surrounding the national team's successes during the first half of the decade. Rugby internationals played at Dublin's Lansdowne Road stadium are considered high points of the sporting year.

Enthusiasts of horse racing flock to the Galway Races in the summer and early fall. Fishing is also a common recreational activity, featuring mainly trout and salmon fishing.

Holidays and Special Days

Public holidays are observed in the Republic of Ireland on:
- New Year's Day, 1 January
- St Patrick's Day, 17 March
- Easter Monday, moveable

- Labor Day/May Day, the first Monday in May
- June Bank Holiday, the first Monday in June
- August Bank Holiday, the first Monday in August
- October Bank Holiday (sometimes called the Halloween holiday), the last Monday in October
- Christmas Day, 25 December
- St Stephen's Day, 26 December

The most recent public holiday to be added was May Day (Labor Day). This holiday, taken as the first Monday in May, was introduced in 1994. Recently, senior politicians have been considering the addition of one or two extra public holidays in order to bring the number of such holidays in Ireland closer to the European average.

St Patrick riding on a snake in St Patrick's Day parade

Saint Patrick's Day (March 17), which honors the patron saint of Ireland, is the most important national holiday and is marked by parades, shamrock decorations, Irish songs and jigs (吉格舞) and sometimes the wearing of green (the national color) to represent the lushness of Ireland — The Emerald Isle. Today St Patrick's Day is celebrated by the Irish as well as many Americans, Canadians and English people.

St Patrick brought Christianity to Ireland. Legend has it that resourceful Saint Patrick used the shamrock, a 3 leaf clover, as a diagram to explain the Holy Trinity to his uneducated congregation (会众). He founded 365 churches, baptized over 120,000 people and consecrated (使就圣职) 450 bishops. According to some Irish writings, St Patrick died on March 17, 461 AD. The anniversary of his death is celebrated as St Patrick's Day.

Education

The Republic of Ireland's education system is quite similar to that of most other western countries. There are three distinct levels of education: primary, secondary and higher (often known as third-level or tertiary) education. In recent years further education has grown immensely. The education systems are largely under the direction of the Government via the Minister for Education and Skills. Recognized primary and secondary schools must adhere to the curriculum established by the relevant authorities. Education is compulsory between the ages of six and fifteen years or until students have completed three years of second level education and including one sitting of the Junior Certificate examination,

In 1973 the requirement to pass the Irish language test in order to receive a second-level certificate was dropped although a student attending a school which receives public money must be taught the language. English is the primary medium of instruction at all levels, except in schools in which Irish is the working language and which are increasingly popular. Universities also offer degree programmes in diverse disciplines, taught mostly through English, with a few in Irish. Some universities also offer some courses partly through other languages such as French, German or Spanish.

There are approximately 3,300 primary schools in Ireland. The vast majority (92%) are under the patronage of the Catholic Church. Schools run by religious organizations, but receiving public money and recognition, cannot discriminate against pupils based upon religion or lack thereof.

Most students enter secondary school aged 12 — 13 and complete their Leaving Certificate Examination aged 17 — 19. Those intending to pursue higher education normally take this examination, with access to third-level courses generally depending on results obtained from the best six subjects taken, on a competitive basis. Ireland's secondary students rank above average in terms of academic performance in both the OECD (The Organization for Economic Co-operation and Development) and EU, having reading literacy, mathematical literacy and scientific literacy test scores better than average. Ireland has the second best reading literacy for teenagers in the EU, after Finland.

Third-level education awards (毕业证书等的授予) are conferred by at least 38 Higher Education Institutions — this includes the constituent or linked colleges of seven universities, plus other designated institutions of the Higher Education and Training Awards Council. The seven establishments of higher education in the Republic of Ireland are ranked amongst the top 500 universities worldwide by the Times Higher Education Supplement. They are: University College Cork — National University of Ireland, Cork (UCC,爱尔兰国立考克大学), University College Dublin — National University of Ireland, Dublin (UCD,爱尔兰国立都柏林大学), National University of Ireland, Galway (UCG,爱尔兰国立高威大学), National University of Ireland, Maynooth (UCM,爱尔兰国立梅努斯大学), University of Dublin, Trinity College Dublin (TCD,爱尔兰圣三一学院), University of Limerick (爱尔兰利默瑞克大学), Dublin City University (爱尔兰都柏林城市大学).

Entry into third-level is generally very high in Ireland, and among young adults (those aged 25 to 34), 41.6% of them have attained third-level degrees — the second highest level in the EU after Cyprus, and substantially ahead of the average of 29.1%.

Ireland has 0.747 of the World's top 500 Universities per capita, which ranks the country in 8th place in the world. In addition, 37 percent of Ireland population has a university or college degree, which is among the highest percentages in the world.

Education in Ireland is free at all levels, including college (university), but only for students applying from the EU. There are charges to cover student services and examinations.

➤ *University of Dublin, Trinity College*

University education in Ireland began with the founding of the University of Dublin, or Trinity College, in 1592 when Queen Elizabeth I issued a charter for Trinity College as "the mother of a university", thereby making it Ireland's oldest operating university. It was modelled after the collegiate universities of Oxford and of Cambridge, but unlike these only one college was established; as such, the designations "Trinity College" and "University of Dublin" are usually synonymous for practical purposes. It is one of the seven ancient universities of Britain and Ireland, as well as Ireland's oldest surviving university.

Trinity College is widely considered to be the most prestigious university in Ireland, and amongst the most elite in Europe. This is principally due to its extensive history, its highly competitive admissions procedure, its reputation for social elitism (精英主义) as well as its unique relationship with both the University of Oxford and the University of Cambridge. A graduate of Oxford, Cambridge, or Dublin can be conferred with the equivalent degree at either of the other two universities without further examination. Futhermore, Trinity College is the only non-Oxbridge institution to be a "sister" to a college at the University of Oxford and the University of Cambridge. Sistership exists between Trinity College and St John's College, Cambridge and also with Oriel College, Oxford (牛津大学奥里尔学院).

A panorama taken from Parliament Square, Trinity College Dublin. The row of buildings is framed by the Public Theatre on the left and the Chapel on the right. In the middle lies Regent House with its archway leading to the Front Gate.

Ireland earned a reputation as an education and cultural center in the early Middle Ages. From the 6th to the 8th century, when Western Europe was largely illiterate, nearly 1,000 Irish missionaries traveled to England and to continental Europe to teach Christianity. Irish missionaries founded monasteries (修道院) that achieved extensive cultural influence, which is especially well known for its contributions to education and literature. Classical studies flowered in ancient Ireland. Distinctive also at the time were the bardic (吟游诗人的) schools of writers and other intellectuals who traveled from town to town, teaching their arts to students. The bardic schools, an important part of Irish education, were suppressed in the 16th century by Henry VIII, king of England.

Literature

For a comparatively small country, Ireland has made a disproportionate contribution to world literature in all its branches. Irish Literature encompasses (包括) the Irish and English languages. The island's most widely-known literary works are undoubtedly in English. Particularly famous examples of such works are those of James Joyce, Oscar Wilde, and Ireland's four winners of the Nobel Prize for Literature: William Butler Yeats, George Bernard Shaw, Samuel Beckett and Seamus Heaney. Three of these were born in Dublin (Heaney being the exception, who has lived in Dublin but was born in County Londonderry), making it the birthplace of more Nobel literary laureates than any other city in the world.

George Bernard Shaw is an Irish-born British playwright. A founder of the Fabian Society, he wrote plays of iconoclastic (打破旧习的) social criticism, including *Arms and the Man* (1894), *Pygmalion* (1913), and *Saint Joan* (1923). He won the 1925 Nobel Prize for literature.

William Butler Yeats is the Irish writer who is considered among the greatest poets of the 20th century. A founder of the Irish National Theatre Company at the Abbey Theatre, Dublin, he wrote many short plays, including: *The Countess Cathleen* (1892). His poetry, published in collections such as *The Winding Stair* (1929), ranges from early love lyrics to the complex symbolist works of his later years. He won the 1923 Nobel Prize for literature.

The novels and short stories of James Joyce are distinguished by their keen psychological insight and use of literary innovations, most notably the stream of consciousness technique. The stories in *Dubliners*, his only collection of short fiction, are generally regarded as models of the genre. His works include *Ulysses* (1922) and *Finnegans Wake* (1939).

In 1937 Irish-born writer Samuel Beckett settled in Paris and began writing in French. Although it was not his native language, French enabled Beckett to create some of his most enduring literary achievements. In perhaps his most famous work, *Waiting for Godot* (1953), Beckett explored the human need for hope and companionship. Beckett used sparse dialogue, clipped conversations, and an absence of plot to symbolize the inconsistencies of language and emotions. He died on December

22, 1989, in Paris, where he had lived for many years.

Seamus Heaney won the Nobel Prize in literature in 1995. Born in rural Northern Ireland, he left his native land to avoid political and religious violence, but his poetry remained centered on the people and places he encountered during his early years in the countryside. Although his poetry appears simple in its language and flow, its structure and references are often complex.

Ireland's oldest literary traditions are found in the Irish language. Indeed, Irish has the third oldest literature in Europe (after Greek and Latin) and the most significant body of written literature of any Celtic language. Furthermore, the historic influence of Irish language traditions, such as a strong oral tradition of legends and poetry, has helped make much English literature in Ireland quite distinctive from that in other countries.

From the older tradition, many Irish writers in English inherited a sense of wonder in the face of nature, a narrative style that tends towards the deliberately exaggerated or absurd and a keen sense of the power of satire. In addition, the interplay between the two languages has resulted in an English dialect, Hiberno-English that lends a distinctive syntax and music to the literature written in it.

Understanding Australia and New Zealand

A General Survey of Australia

> **章节导读**
> 本章以澳大利亚的地理位置、国家标志、人口和语言等基本情况为开篇,之后分别介绍了它的地理特征、动植物、气候、行政区划以及主要城市。

I A General Survey

Australia is an island that is also a continent. It consists of two land masses: the mainland and Tasmania. In land area it is the sixth largest country and the smallest continent. Its area is 7.69 million square kilometers, about the size of the mainland states of the United States, excluding Alaska, and approximately 24 times the size of the British Isles.

Location

Australia lies southeast of Asia between the Indian and Pacific oceans. The name "Australia" comes from the Latin *australis* meaning "of the south." For its location in the southern hemisphere, Australia is often called "the land down under" in the West.

Capital

Canberra, specifically built as a capital city, is located in the Australian Capital Territory (A.C.T.) which is totally enclosed by the state of New South Wales. The A.C.T. is approximately 2,400 square kilometers in area with urban Canberra sitting in the north eastern quarter of the territory. The city is roughly half way between the two largest cities Melbourne and Sydney.

National Flag

The Australian flag is dark blue with the Union Jack (the flag of the United Kingdom) in the upper corner of the hoist, which symbolizes Australia's historical links with Britain and its present-day membership of the British Commonwealth. Underneath is a large white seven-pointed star, known as the Commonwealth Star. Six of its points represent the six original states and the seventh represents the territories. On the right side of the flag are five white stars in the shape of the Southern Cross[①], the bright star groups in the southern skies at night, which represents Australia's location in the Southern Hemisphere. British flags had been the official flag of Australia for years when the Commonwealth was formed in 1901. The design of the present Australian flag was selected after an official competition and was approved by King Edward VII in February 1903.

National Anthem

"Advance Australia Fair" is the official national anthem of Australia. Created by the Scottish-born composer, Peter Dodds McCormick, the song was first performed in 1878, but did not gain its status as the official anthem until 1984. Until then, the song was sung in Australia as a patriotic song. In order for the song to become the anthem, it had to face a vote between the Royal anthem "God Save the Queen", the "unofficial anthem" "Waltzing Matilda" and "Song of Australia." "Advance Australia Fair" received 43.29% of the vote, defeating the three alternatives. "Waltzing Matilda" (28.28%), "Song of Australia" (9.65%), and the existing national anthem "God Save the Queen" (18.78%).

The lyrics officially adopted in 1984 are as follows:

Verse 1	第一段
Australians all let us rejoice,	全体澳大利亚人，让我们快乐吧！
For we are young and free;	因为我们年轻而自由；
We've golden soil and wealth for toil;	我们有金色的土地和劳动可以创造的财富；
Our home is girt by sea;	我们的国土为海洋所环绕；
Our land abounds in nature's gifts	我们的土地富于自然的恩赐，
Of beauty rich and rare;	美丽、富饶而稀有；
In history's page, let every stage	让历史的每一个时期
Advance Australia Fair.	推动美丽的澳大利亚前进。
In joyful strains then let us sing,	让我们快乐地歌唱，
Advance Australia Fair.	前进，美丽的澳大利亚。
Verse 2	**第二段**
Beneath our radiant Southern Cross	在南十字星座灿烂的星光下，
We'll toil with hearts and hands;	我们用自己的心灵和双手辛勤劳作，
To make this Commonwealth of ours	为了将我们的联邦
Renowned of all the lands;	建设得举世闻名；
For those who've come across the seas	对那些远涉重洋到来的人们
We've boundless plains to share;	我们有无尽的土地来分享；
With courage let us all combine	鼓起勇气，让我们一起
To Advance Australia Fair.	推动美丽的澳大利亚前进。
In joyful strains then let us sing,	让我们快乐地歌唱，
Advance Australia Fair.	前进，美丽的澳大利亚。

The wordless orchestral version of "Advance Australia Fair" that is now regularly played for Australian victories at international sporting medal ceremonies, and at the openings of major domestic sporting, cultural and community events, is by Tommy Tycho, an immigrant from

---

① 南十字星座:南半球肉眼可见的星座中最显眼的一个，因此在英国殖民时代早期，南十字星座就被殖民者用来代表澳大利亚。它的位置在正南方。北方的水手，依靠北斗星及北极星来判断正北方向；而在南半球，则靠南十字星座来判断正南方向。南十字星座是澳洲最家喻户晓的星座，被认为是澳洲版的圣诞之星，指引着东方三贤士前往耶稣诞生地伯利恒（Bethlehem）。

Hungary.
Coat of Arms

The Commonwealth coat of arms is the official emblem of Australia. It was granted by King George V in 1912. The central focus of the coat of arms is a shield, on which are the badges representing the six States. The six badges are enclosed by an ermine (fur) border, symbolizing the federation of the States into the Commonwealth. The shield is held by a red kangaroo on the left and an emu[①] on the right, two animals native to Australia. They stand on ornamental rests (支架). As neither animal can move backward easily, they symbolize progress and a nation advancing forward. The crest (顶部) consists of a Commonwealth star, symbolic of national unity, on a gold and blue wreath. In the background of the coat of arms are sprays (小树枝,花簇) of golden wattle (金合欢), with a scroll at the base bearing the word "Australia."

Floral Emblem

Golden wattle is the national flower of Australia. The floral emblem grows naturally in New South Wales, Australian Capital Territory, Victoria and South Australia. It reasonably tolerates frost and drought, and grows widely in temperate regions. Today wattle symbolizes hope, opportunities and the natural wealth of Australia. September 1 is National Wattle Day in Australia, an occasion to inspire national sentiment (感情).

Green and gold, resembling those of golden wattle, are the national colors of Australia. They are popular and widely accepted in sporting events. Almost all Australian national teams wear these two colors.

Population

The population of Australia amounted to 23.94 million in 2015, most living in coastal cities and towns. The center of Australia is sparsely populated. Its vast openness means it has the lowest population density in the world.

Australians come from a rich variety of cultural, ethnic, linguistic and religious backgrounds. While Aboriginal people are the original inhabitants of the land, immigrants from about 200 countries also call Australia home. Until the 1970s the majority of immigrants came from Europe. These days Australia receives many more immigrants from Asia. In June 2015, 28.2% of the population were born overseas.

Languages

With hundreds of aboriginal languages and dialects spoken by indigenous people, English is the predominant and official language of Australia. As a variety of English, Australian English has an accent similar to dialects of the southeast of England. Its grammar and spelling are largely the same as those of British English.

---

① 鸸鹋：澳大利亚的国鸟，国徽上的"守护神兽"之一；为世界上第二大的鸟类，仅次于非洲鸵鸟，因此也被称作"澳洲鸵鸟"。仅分布于澳大利亚，体型较大，最高可达2米，但体重轻盈，极擅奔跑，百米冲刺最高速度可达每小时50km，但身体两侧的翅膀却因经年累月的陆地行走而渐渐退化，失去了飞行能力。

Australians use many words that they consider unique to Australian English. A frequently quoted example is *outback* (内地), meaning a remote, sparsely-populated area. Some words of aboriginal languages have found their way to Australian English, mainly names for plants, animals and places. Immigrants bring into Australia their native tongues. The most common foreign languages spoken at home are Chinese, Italian, and Greek.

Religions

Australia has no state religion. Freedom of worship is guaranteed by the constitution. In the 2011 Census, Christians represented 61% of the population. Non-Christians accounted for about 8% of the population. About 31% of the population stated they had no religion or did not state their religion.

Currency

The unit of currency is the Australian dollar which is divided into 100 cents. The notes are A$5, A$10, A$20, A$50, and A$100. Coins are 5c, 10c, 20c, 50c, A$1 and A$2.

II Geography

Australia is one of the oldest continents; the effects of over 250 million years of erosion have turned it into a flat, low lying and stable land mass. It has a wide variety of landforms. Much of the flat inland is desert. The highest peak is Mt Kosciuszko, in New South Wales, which is 2,228 meters above sea level.

While Australia is often thought of as a dry thinly populated land, this is only true of the inland (or outback) areas. The eastern coast is more heavily populated. The huge interior is hot and dry with vast expanses of sandy desert or stone plains giving way to shrub savannah or mallee (澳大利亚南部产小桉树) scrub. The main mountains are along the eastern coast, known as the Great Dividing Range[①], which has an average altitude of less than 910 meters above sea level. In coastal regions the environments range from tropical rain forest in the north, to pastoral lands and forest in the east and the southeast, to alpine (高山的) country in the Snowy Mountains and central Tasmania.

Australia's deserts are as vast as the Sahara, the snowfields are huge and picturesque. The surfing beaches are among the best in the world. Australia is the only continent without current volcanic activity — the last eruption took place 1400 years ago at Mount Gambier.

Topography(地形学)

Australia is the flattest and lowest land mass with the average elevation of about 330 meters. It can be divided into three major topographic regions: the Eastern Highlands, the Central Lowlands and the Western Plateau.

---

① 大分水岭：澳大利亚东部新南威尔士州以北山脉和高原的总称。位于新南威尔士州以北与海岸线大致平行，绵延约3000千米，宽约160千米～320千米。最高峰科修斯科山海拔2228米，是全国的最高点。在此以西发源的河流注入卡奔塔利亚湾和印度洋，以东发源的河流注入太平洋的珊瑚海和塔斯曼海，大分水岭就由此而得名。

➢ Eastern Highlands

In the east the Great Dividing Range, or Eastern Highlands, separates the east coast from the vast interior plains. This mountainous region comprises of a series of plateaus and mountain ranges dotted with gorges, canyons, valleys and plains. The Range averages about 1,200 meters in height and runs more than 3,500 kilometers along the eastern coast from Cape York in the north to Western Victoria in the south. Tasmania is also a part of this massive range. The range is the source of mountains in Australia and also the main watershed (分水岭) in eastern Australia, dividing streams and rivers which flow directly into the Pacific Ocean on the eastern coast of Australia from those which flow westerly through the interior plains.

➢ Great Western Plateau

The enormous western half of Australia comprises the Great Western Plateau, which is a vast desert and semi-desert region that covers almost 66% of the land area and consists of ancient rocks similar to those of Africa. The Western Plateau has an average elevation of 305 meters. Located on the plateau are the country's four major deserts — the Gibson, Great Sandy, Great Victoria and Simpson. The region is generally flat, broken by various mountain ranges.

➢ Central Lowlands

The vast, rolling plains between the Eastern Highland and the Western Plateau comprise the Central Lowlands. This narrow region contains, from north to south, the Carpentaria Basin, the Lake Eyre Basin and the Murray-Darling Basin. The region has the richest pastoral and agricultural land in Australia but its west-central part is a barren, sandy desert.

Beneath the Central Lowlands is the Great Artesian Basin (大自流盆地), the largest artesian basin in the world. It underlies approximately one-fifth of the entire continent and functions as a life line through the interior of eastern Australia. The basin provides underground freshwater for drinking, irrigation, cattle raising and industry.

Long Coastlines

As the world's largest island bordering two oceans, Australia has a coastline of 25,760 kilometers. Such a long beach is broken up by dramatic cliffs, headlands, inlets, rivers and waterways.

Plants and Animals

➢ Plants

For nearly 50 million years the continent drifted alone over the ocean, separated from the rest of the world. This long-term isolation allowed the plants and animals on the continent to evolve independently into new species. Many amazing animals and flora occur only on this landmass and cannot be found anywhere else. Australia accommodates about 20,000 to 25,000 different native plants. Most of them are well adapted to the challenging environments of drought, fire, soil infertility (贫瘠) and other harsh conditions. Eucalyptus (桉属植物) and acacia (金合欢) are the two dominant kinds in tree flora.

➢ Animals

The continent's long isolation from other land masses allowed native animal species in Australia to evolve into large populations.

Marsupials (有袋动物) are mammals carrying their newborn babies in a pouch (育儿袋) near their belly until the infants are old enough to survive on their own. The best known marsupials of Australia are kangaroos and koalas. The duck-billed platypus (鸭嘴兽) and echidnas

(针鼹鼠) are among the oldest and possibly strangest looking mammals. They are found only in Australasia and are the only mammals to lay eggs. Australia is home to nearly 800 bird species. The most impressive is the emu, the world's second largest bird after the ostrich (鸵鸟).

Climate

Australia is a flat landmass without high mountain ranges and is surrounded by mostly warm oceans. The Tropic of Capricorn (南回归线) runs through the northern part of the country. Such geological features help prevent extremes of cold temperatures. Australia is the driest of all the inhabited continents. Over 80 percent of the continent has an annual rainfall of less than 600 millimeters; the arid deserts, less than 250 millimeters. In most years, large portions of the continent are subject to droughts. Long periods of dry, hot weather, high winds and natural vegetation that burns easily make Australia particularly vulnerable to bushfires.

Female grey kangaroo with joey (baby) in pouch

Despite regional variations, the climate of Australia is broadly divided into three zones: tropical climate in the North, arid climate in the Inland, and temperate climate in the South.

There are four distinct seasons. Because of its location in the Southern Hemisphere, seasons in Australia are opposite to those in the Northern Hemisphere.

III States, Territories & Large Cities

Australia has six states and two territories.

Australian Capital Territory & Canberra

The Australian Capital Territory (ACT) bounds the national capital of Canberra and is the center of government. It is located approximately 290 kilometers south of Sydney, and is home to a number of important national institutions, including Parliament House, the Australian War Memorial and the National Gallery of Australia.

Canberra is unusual among Australian cities as an entirely purpose-built, planned city. The site, previously a New South Wales rural area, was selected for the location of the nation's capital in 1908 as a compromise between rivals Sydney and Melbourne, the two largest cities and sits in between the two. Construction began in 1913 and the federal government moved to Canberra on 9 May, 1927. Canberra houses many breathtaking landmarks and heritage buildings, such as Parliament House, new and old, the High Court of Australia and federal government departments.

New South Wales & Sydney

New South Wales (NSW), known as the Premier State, is Australia's oldest and most populous state. It was originally settled as a penal colony on the shores of Port Jackson where the bustling capital city of Sydney now stands. New South Wales is home to popular attractions including the Blue Mountains and the Hunter Valley wine region.

Sydney is the country's oldest and largest city founded in 1788 as the first European colony in Australia. Despite its beginning as a convict (罪犯) settlement, Sydney has grown into the economic powerhouse of the nation. The Australian Stock Exchange and the Reserve Bank of

Australia are located there, as are the headquarters of many banks and Australia's top companies. Sydney is also a major international tourist destination, renowned for its idyllic (恬静宜人的) beaches, great walks and twin landmarks: the Sydney Opera House and the Harbor Bridge.

Sydney, the state capital of New South Wales, is the country's oldest and largest city and is notable for its beaches.

Northern Territory & Darwin

At the top end of Australia lies the Northern Territory (NT), which is a land of contrasts, ranging from fertile wetlands at the "Top End" to the arid and desert-like landscapes of the "Red Center." The Northern Territory is home to the famous Uluru (Ayers Rock)[1], Kata Tjuta (the Olgas)[2] and Kakadu National Park.

Uluru

Kata Tjuta

Darwin, on the northern coast, is the state capital. The city is notable among the capital cities for its history of major disasters. During WWII, Darwin was bombed 64 times by Japanese aircraft. It was the only locality in Australia to have come under substantial air attack. Darwin is also regularly subjected to heavy thunderstorms of its tropical climate. The city was almost completely destroyed by cyclone (飓风) Tracy in 1974. It was extensively rebuilt. Modern Darwin is a prosperous, cosmopolitan city, a booming tourist destination and an important military base for northern Australia. It serves both as the front door to Australia's northern region and as Australia's gateway to Asia.

Queensland & Brisbane

Queensland (QLD), nicknamed the Sunshine State, is Australia's second-largest state (in size) and is home to the world's most extensive subtropical rainforest, the beautiful Queensland Islands — including the World Heritage-listed Fraser Island[3], and the world famous natural wonder of the Great Barrier Reef (大堡礁), which is the world's largest coral reef system composed of over 2,900 individual reefs and 900 islands stretching for over 2,300 kilometers over an area of approximately 344,400 square kilometers.

---

① 乌鲁鲁巨石（艾尔斯岩）：位于澳大利亚中北部的Alice Springs西南方向约340公里处。艾尔斯岩高348米，长3,000米，基围周长约8.5公里，占地面积约1,200公顷，是世界上最大的独块巨岩，俗称为"人类地球上的肚脐""世界七大奇景"之一。艾尔斯岩的色彩随时间、云彩的变化呈现出棕色、黄色或紫色。1873年一位名叫威廉·克里斯蒂·高斯的测量员横跨这片荒漠，发现了这块与天等高的山。高斯来自南澳洲，故以当时南澳州总理亨利·艾尔斯的名字命名这座石山。如今这里已辟为国家公园，每年有数十万人从世界各地慕名前来观赏。

② 卡塔·丘达石岩（奥尔加山）：位于澳大利亚中部的乌鲁鲁-卡塔·丘达国家公园内，乌鲁鲁（艾尔斯岩）西方约32千米处，但比艾尔斯岩高出200米。此处有36个形状和颜色皆美丽独特的红色风化砂岩圆顶，其中最高的是奥尔加山。它从旷野垂直隆起550米，差不多有两个法国巴黎埃菲尔铁塔的高度。

③ 弗雷泽岛：又译芬瑟岛，绵延于澳大利亚昆士兰州东南海岸，长122千米，面积1620平方千米，是世界上最大的沙岛。由大河带来的泥沙沉积而形成，岛上有著名的亚热带雨林。1992年被联合国教科文组织列入《世界自然遗产名录》。

Brisbane, the state's capital, was founded as a penal (刑事的) colony in 1824. In 1859 it was declared the capital of Queensland. Today Brisbane is Australia's third largest city, a busy port, the hub of rail lines and highways, and the business and cultural center of Queensland. It enjoys more winter sunshine and warmth than most Australian cities and is perfect for outdoor activities and water sports.

South Australia & Adelaide (阿德莱德)

South Australia (SA) sits in the southern central part of the country, and covers some of the most arid parts of the continent. Known as the Festival State, South Australia (SA) hosts over 500 festivals every year.

The state's capital is Adelaide, which is noted throughout Australia for its well-planned city streets and civic parks and gardens. Hosting festivals for everything from arts, wine and food to roses, car races and horse trials, the city has well established itself as the festival capital of Australia.

Tasmania (塔斯马尼亚州) **& Hobart** (霍巴特)

Tasmania (TAS), the smallest state in Australia, is separated from the mainland Australia by Bass Strait. The island, often called the holiday isle, attracts both Australians and overseas visitors with its unspoiled wilderness landscapes.

The capital, Hobart, was founded in 1804 as a penal colony and is Australia's second oldest capital city after Sydney. It is small but full of 19th century buildings. Sandstone warehouses from the port's whaling days and houses of Georgian and Victorian eras have been remarkably well preserved. One-fifth of Tasmania is covered by national parks and wilderness — abundant in driving routes and walking trails — and it is one of the world's most mountainous islands.

Victoria & Melbourne

Victoria (VIC), the garden state, is the smallest of the mainland states in size but is home to the country's second most populated city, Melbourne. Often referred to as the nation's cultural capital, Melbourne is famed for its graffiti laneways, fashion-forward boutiques (精品店) and booming café scene. Victorians' enthusiasm for sport is also legendary and this is where Australian Rules football began. The only thing more sacred than the football is Melbournians love of coffee, and there you'll find some of Australia's best flat whites[1], cappuccinos and piccolo lattes (小杯拿铁).

Melbourne was declared a city by Queen Victoria in 1847.When gold was discovered in the area during the 1850s (which sparked the Victorian gold rush), Melbourne was transformed into one of the largest and wealthiest cities in the World by the 1880s. Upon the federation of Australia in 1901, it served as the national capital and the seat of government for the newly-established Commonwealth of Australia until 1927 — while the planned national capital of Canberra was being constructed.

---

[1] 小白咖啡：起源于澳洲和新西兰的一个奶咖品类，它和其他牛奶咖啡最大的不同在于它的奶泡较薄，几乎不超过5毫米。制作技法上是要比其他奶咖品类稍难。Flat White进入中国后在星巴克被叫做"馥芮白"，在COSTA称为"醇艺白"，而在麦当劳旗下的McCafé则为"特浓奶香"。很多人亲切的称呼它为"小白"。

Western Australia & Perth (珀斯)

Western Australia (WA), the state of excitement, is the largest and most sparsely populated state. It offers an amazing variety of environments from the lush green forests in the south to the dry barren land in the north, from desert in the east to 13,000 kilometers of pristine coastline on the west.

The state's capital is Perth; the fourth most populous city in Australia and famed for its uncrowded beaches, parklands and fresh seafood. Off the coast of Esperance, in the state's south, is Middle Island, which is home to the extraordinary pink-colored Lake Hillier (希勒湖).

Australia also administers Ashmore and Cartier Islands, Christmas Island, the Cocos (or Keeling) Islands, the Coral Sea Islands, Heard and McDonald Islands, Norfolk Island and the Australian Antarctic Territory (covering 42 per cent of the Antarctic continent) as external territories.

Chapter 13
History, Politics and Economy of Australia

章节导读

本章分为三部分,分别介绍了澳大利亚主要的历史发展阶段、基本政治框架和政治制度以及各个行业的经济状况。

I History

The continent of Australia has been inhabited for over 40,000 years by Indigenous Australians. After some visits by fishermen from the north and by European explorers and merchants starting in the 17th century, the eastern half of the continent was claimed by the British in 1770 and officially settled as the penal colony of New South Wales on 26 January 1788. As the population grew and new areas were explored, another five largely self-governing Crown Colonies were successively established over the course of the 19th century.

On 1 January 1901, the six colonies federated and the Commonwealth of Australia was formed. Since federation, Australia has maintained a stable liberal democratic political system and remained a Commonwealth Realm. The current population of around 24 million is concentrated mainly in the large coastal cities of Sydney, Melbourne, Brisbane, Perth, and Adelaide.

Prehistory

The first human habitation of Australia is estimated to have occurred between 42,000 and 48,000 years ago. The first Australians were the ancestors of the current Indigenous Australians; they arrived via land bridges and short sea-crossings from present-day Southeast Asia.

European Colonization

The first definite sighting of Australia was in 1606 by the Dutch navigator Willem Janszoon. This date may be taken as a convenient starting point for the written history of Australia. Between 1606 and 1770, an estimated 54 European ships from a range of nations made contact with Australia. However, no attempts to establish settlements were made.

In 1770, Englishman Lieutenant (海军上尉) James Cook sailed along and mapped the Australian east coast, which he named New South Wales and claimed for Britain. Very quickly Britain extended its claim to cover the whole of Australia.

The expedition's discoveries provided impetus (推动力) for the establishment of a penal colony there following the loss of the American colonies that had previously filled that role. The British then turned to Australia as a place to deport criminals. On May 13, 1787, the 11 ships of the First Fleet set sail from Portsmouth, England to Botany Bay in New South Wales under the command of Governor Arthur Philip. The party actually landed a short distance away at Sydney Cove, where the penal settlement was established on Jan. 26, 1788. The date is now celebrated as Australia Day and those convicts (罪犯) and marines (水手) on board are acknowledged as the Founders of Australia. The settlement was named Sydney after Britain's home secretary, Lord Sydney, who was responsible for the colony. Phillip became the first governor of the colony and encouraged exploration of the neighborhood.

Convicts worked as assigned laborers after their arrival in the colony. Unfortunately, few of them had farming or trade experience, nor did they understand the new environment. As a result, their initial attempts at farming failed. Through the 1790s the whole settlement faced perpetual food shortages.

John Macarthur and the wool industry featured on the front of the A$2 note

Some relief arrived with the 2nd fleet in 1790. It also brought to Sydney two men who were to play important roles in the colony's future. One was William Wentworth, who became a leader of the movement to abolish convict transportation and establish representative government. The other was John Macarthur, one of the founders of the Australian wool industry, which laid the foundations of Australia's future prosperity.

Expansion of Colonization

Throughout the 19th century, Australia underwent the major processes that laid the foundation for its present society. The most prominent ones were the establishment of new colonies along the coasts and the opening up of the interior for sheep and cattle raising. European resettlement of the continent proceeded gradually from the eastern coast toward the center.

Gold Rush

In 1851, Edward Hargraves (1816 — 1891), an immigrant from England, found gold near Bathurst in New South Wales. Word quickly spread. Within a week there were hundreds of people digging there for gold. Shortly afterwards gold was discovered in even greater abundance in the newly formed Victoria. Later significant deposits were uncovered in other states except South Australia. From 1851 to 1861, Australia exported more than 124 million pounds worth of gold alone. By the turn of the century it had become the world's largest producer of gold.

There is no doubt that the gold rushes had a profound impact on the development of Australia's economic, political and social systems. Since 1851 many adventurers were attracted to Australia from all over the globe. The total population of Australia increased from 430,000 in 1851 to 1.7 million in 1871. Within a few years new arrivals outnumbered the convicts transported in the previous 70 years. They began to demand trial by jury, representative government, a free press and the other symbols of liberty and democracy.

Among all the foreign gold diggers, the biggest fraction was Chinese. The Chinese immigrants referred to the Australian gold fields as "*Xin Jin Shan.*" The Californian gold rush was in decline by the 1850s and had become known as "*Jiu Jin Shan.*" Motivated by racism and by the fear of fiercer competition, miners and colonists launched campaigns to oust (驱逐) the Chinese from the goldfields. In 1856 Victoria restricted the entry of Chinese. Eventually, the exclusion of all but European settlers gave the colonies a "White Australia" policy.

The gold rushes were followed by rapid economic expansion. The goldfield towns grew quickly and sparked a huge boost in business investment and stimulated the market for local produce. The thriving economy also spurred the development of state infrastructure. The 1850s witnessed the construction of the first railway and the operation of the first telegraphs.

Federation

Before 1900, there was no actual country called Australia. The six colonies on the continent, having individually gained responsible government between 1855 and 1890, managed most of their own affairs like six separate countries while remaining part of the British Empire. The Colonial Office in London retained control of some matters, notably foreign affairs, defense and international shipping. On 1 January 1901, federation of the colonies was achieved after a decade of planning, consultation and voting, and the Commonwealth (联邦) of Australia was born, as a Dominion of the British Empire. The Australian Capital Territory (A.C.T.) was formed from New South Wales in 1911 to provide a location for the proposed new federal capital of Canberra (Melbourne was the capital from 1901 to 1927). The Northern Territory was transferred from the control of the South Australian government to the Commonwealth in 1911.

Australia in Two World Wars

The First World War began when Britain and Germany went to war in August 1914. As part of the British Empire, Australia sent some 330,000 soldiers (out of a population of only about 4,500,000) overseas during the war. Troops were sent to take possession of German New Guinea and some other islands and many more to fight at Gallipoli, on the Turkish coast, in France and in the Middle East. Both Australian victories and losses on World War I battlefields contributed significantly to Australia's national identity.

In 1939 Australia entered World War II again as an ally of Britain. In 1940 — 1941, Australian forces played prominent roles in campaigns against Germany and Italy in Europe, the Mediterranean and North Africa, as well as against Japan in southeast Asia and other parts of the Pacific. At the peak of its war effort in 1943, Australia's armed forces numbered about 633,400 — from a population of 7,300,000.

After Singapore fell in February, 1942, Japanese aircraft bombed towns in northwest Australia and Japanese midget (小型的) submarines attacked Sydney harbor. With many of its troops fighting in North Africa, Australia was suddenly faced with the threat of Japanese invasion. With Britain preoccupied with her own fight for survival, Australia turned to the United States as a new ally and protector.

1940s Australian troops

Postwar Australia

The years after the war brought increased economic activity and industrial expansion. The need for more farmers and industrial workers led to highly successful attempts to attract European immigrants. Since the 1970s and the abolition of the White Australia Policy, immigration from Asia and other parts of the world was also encouraged. As a result, Australia's demography (统计学), culture and image of itself were radically transformed.

The final constitutional ties between Australia and the United Kingdom ended in 1986 with the passing of the Australia Act 1986, ending any British role in the Australian States, and ending judicial appeals (上诉) to the UK Privy Council (枢密院). Australian voters rejected a move to become a republic in 1999 by a 55% majority. In its postwar foreign policy, Australia allied itself closely with the United States and participated in Asian affairs.

II Political System

The Commonwealth of Australia is a constitutional monarchy with a federal parliamentary system of government — "Constitutional" because the powers and procedures of the Commonwealth Government are defined by a written constitution, and "Monarchy" because Australia's Head of State is the monarch of the United Kingdom.

Constitution

The Constitution of Australia, which came into force on 1 January 1901, is based on British parliamentary traditions and includes elements of the United States system. It establishes the Commonwealth government, defining its structure, powers, procedures and the rights and obligations of the states in relation to the Commonwealth.

Other pieces of legislation that have constitutional significance for Australia are the *Statute of Westminster 1931* and the *Australia Act 1986*. Together, these Acts had the effect of severing all constitutional links between Australia and the United Kingdom. Therefore, even though the Constitution was originally given legal force by an Act of the United Kingdom parliament, the Australian Constitution can be amended only by Australian people through a national referendum (公民投票) in which all adults on the electoral roll must participate. Any constitutional changes must be approved by a double majority — a national majority of electors as well as a majority of electors in a majority of the states and territories (at least four of the six). The double majority provision makes alterations to the Constitution difficult, and since Federation in 1901 only eight out of 44 proposals to amend the Constitution have been approved.

Separation of Powers

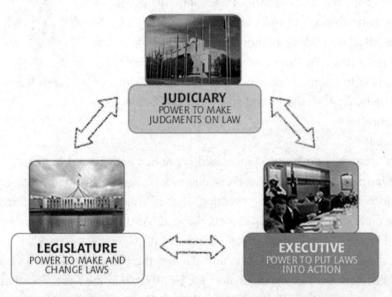

The diagram illustrates the principle of the separation of powers.

Separation of powers refers to a model in which political powers and responsibilities are distributed among several, often three, branches: the legislature (立法的), the executive (行政的) and the judiciary (司法的). It is believed that separation of powers protects democracy and prevents tyranny. Under the Australian Constitution, the three arms of federal government are:
- Legislature: The Commonwealth Parliament
- Executive: The Queen, whose executive power is exercisable by the Governor-General, the Prime Minister, Ministers and their Departments
- Judiciary: The High Court of Australia and subsidiary Federal courts

Each arm of federal government has separate and distinctive powers and areas of responsibility.

➢ Executive

Queen of Australia

As a member of the Commonwealth of Realms, Australia recognizes the British monarch as sovereign. Thus, Queen Elizabeth II has been the reigning monarch of Australia since February 6, 1952. She is officially called *Queen of Australia* when in Australia or performing duties on behalf of Australia abroad.

Republicanism

Republicanism has always been there in the Australian background. It is a movement to change Australia's status as a constitutional monarchy to a republic. Republicans believe that their head of state should be an Australian citizen instead of the British monarch. In the 1990s the issue was bought to the forefront of national debate by the Australian Labor Party which first made republicanism its official policy. In 1999, Australians were asked to vote in a referendum to determine whether their nation would become a republic. The referendum was defeated and Australia decided to remain a constitutional monarchy. In recent years the prevailing mood towards the monarchy suggested by most polls is one of indifference or apathy (冷漠).

Governor-General (总督)

In Australia, the Queen is constitutionally represented by the Governor-General at the federal level and by the Governors at the state level. The Governor-General is appointed by the Queen on the recommendation of the Australian Prime Minister. The Governor-General usually holds office for five years. The role of the Governor-General is primarily symbolic and cultural. In practice, the Prime Minister and the cabinet are in control of government departments and run the business of government.

Prime Minister & Cabinet

The Prime Minister is:
- the most senior minister in the Australian Parliament,
- the key spokesperson for Australia,
- the leader of the government,
- the head of Cabinet.

In practice, the executive power is possessed by the Prime Minister and the Cabinet. But neither of the two is mentioned in the Australian Constitution. Their roles and functions derive constitutionally from their membership of the Federal Executive Council (联邦行政咨询委员会) and from convention.

The office of Prime Minister is in practice the most powerful political office in the

Commonwealth. The Prime Minister is head of government for Australia and holds office on commission (任命) from the Governor-General. Except in rare circumstances, the Prime Minister is always the leader of the political party which has the most seats in the House of Representatives.

The Cabinet, a council of senior Ministers presided over by the Prime Minister, is responsible for managing the policy directions and business of the government. Major policy and legislative proposals are decided by the Cabinet. The Prime Minister selects Ministers for Cabinet positions. These Ministers meet at least once a week to discuss vital issues without the Governor-General. Since the Australian Constitution does not recognize the Cabinet as a legal entity (实体), its decisions have no legal force. Decisions made by the Cabinet should be ratified by the Federal Executive Council, a body composed of the Governor-General and Ministers. The Executive Council makes no real decisions, serving mainly to give formal approval to decisions of the Cabinet.

➢ *Legislature*

<u>Bicameral Parliament (两院制议会)</u>

Federal legislative power in Australia is vested in a bicameral parliament, consisting of the Queen represented by the Governor-General, a Senate and a House of Representatives. The essence of a parliamentary democracy is that citizens elect representatives to make laws on their behalf.

The Senate consists of 76 members (12 from each state and 2 from each territory). Senators are popularly elected under a form of proportional representation; senators from states are elected to six-year terms and senators from territories are elected to three-year terms. According to the Australian constitution, the House should have about twice as many members as the Senate. The number of members from each state is proportional to its population, but must be at least five. From 2001 to the present the House has 150 members, all of whom are directly elected to three-year terms. Members of the House of Representatives reflect the interests of their electorates when they make speeches. They also assist people in their electorate to solve problems about such things as pensions, migration and taxation.

The two Houses have equal powers, except that there are restrictions on the power of the Senate to introduce or directly amend some kinds of financial legislation. The role of Members and Senators is to:

• set up parliamentary committees to examine government bills;

• investigate how the government spends money in the budget by participating in estimates committees, which are held twice a year;

• question the government each day in Question Time in both the House of Representatives and the Senate.

<u>Functions of Parliament</u>

Parliament has three main functions: legislation, scrutiny (examining the government), and formation of government.

The most important function of Parliament is to make new laws and change or improve old ones. Laws and major policy decisions are made in the House of Representatives and reviewed in the Senate. A bill becomes a law only after it has been passed in identical form by both Houses of the Parliament and has been approved by the Governor-General.

The government or executive implements the laws and other decisions of the Parliament. However, the Parliament likes to check or scrutinize what the government does, especially how the government spends money. The opposition plays an important part in the scrutiny activities of Parliament.

Another function of the Parliament is to provide the members of the Executive Government from its membership. After a general election the political party with the support of a majority of members in the House of Representatives becomes the governing party and its leader becomes the Prime Minister. The Prime Minister and his / her Cabinet are responsible to Parliament, and through it, to the people.

➢ *Judiciary (司法系统)*

Law

The law of Australia consists of statute law and common law. Although Parliament can override (撤消,推翻) common law by passing legislation, this does not mean that Parliament is dominant over judges and the courts. The strict insulation of judicial power is a fundamental principle of the Constitution of Australia. The independence of the courts and judges, and their separation from the legislative and executive branches of government, is regarded as of great importance.

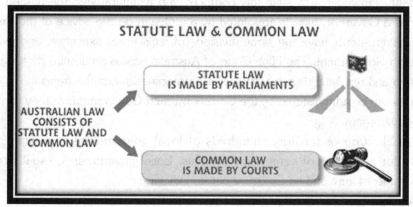

Courts

The Constitution establishes the High Court of Australia and empowers the Commonwealth Parliament to create other federal courts including the Federal Court of Australia, the Family Court of Australia and the Federal Magistrates Court of Australia.

The High Court of Australia, the highest in the Australian court hierarchy, consists of a chief justice and six other justices, each of whom is formally appointed by the Governor-General. The functions of the High Court are to interpret and apply the law of Australia, to decide disputes involving acts of the federal parliament and to hear appeals from Federal, State and Territory courts. The Court is the final court of appeal for the whole Australia.

Three Levels of Government

The Federal, State and Local governments make up the 3 levels of government in Australia. Each level has different responsibilities.

The Federal Government passes laws affecting the whole nation. Its legislative power is limited to a few key areas, including coinage, taxation, banking, insurance, defense, foreign affairs, postal and telecommunications services, trade and immigration.

Although the six states federated to form the Commonwealth Government, they still have their own constitutions and retain the legislative power over matters not controlled by the

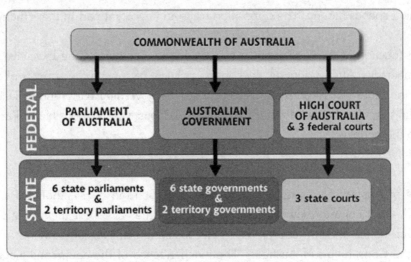

Australian Federation

Commonwealth. However, if a state law conflicts with a federal law, the federal law prevails. Each State has a Governor, who is appointed by the Queen on the advice of the Premier of that State. State governments have the same divisions of legislature, executive, and judiciary as the Commonwealth Government. The High Court of Australia acts as an umpire (仲裁人), interpreting the constitution and resolving disputes between Commonwealth and the states.

Territories can be administered by the Commonwealth Government, or they can be granted a right of self-government.

Within each state or territory, hundreds of local governments are established to take responsibility for a number of community services. Local governments, usually referred to as councils, have a legislature and an executive but no judiciary.

Major Parties

Three political parties dominate Australian politics.

- **The Liberal Party of Australia (LP)** is a party of the center-right which broadly represents business, the suburban middle classes and many rural people.
- **The National Party of Australia (NP)** is a conservative party which represents rural interests. In practice, the Liberal and National parties have frequently combined in coalition (联合) governments and opposition, at both the federal and state levels.
- **The Australian Labor Party (ALP)** is a social democratic party founded by the trade union movement and broadly represents the urban working class, although it increasingly has a base of middle class support.

III National Economy

Australia has a prosperous, Western-style market economy. Its annual GDP has been growing by an average of 3.3 percent since 1990, well above the rate of world growth and ahead of other developed economies. GDP in 2016 reached A$64,660 billion. The stable economic growth is coupled with low inflation. Inflation rate in 2016 was 1 percent.

Agriculture
➢ *Crops*

Agriculture in Australia is a major industry and employs only 3.6 percent of the total workforce. The country is self-sufficient in almost all foodstuffs and is a major exporter of wool, meat, dairy products, and wheat. 80% of all agricultural production is exported. Although only 6.4 percent of Australia's total land area is arable (适于耕种的), this acreage is of great economic importance. In Australia, farm sizes range from relatively small part-time farms to operations of more than 5,000 hectares. In general, farming is characterized by large scale, highly mechanized and efficient operations.

➢ *Horticulture (园艺)*

Horticulture is one of Australia's largest industries, and produces a wide variety of fruit, vegetables, nuts, nursery products and cut flowers. Major horticultural sectors include grapes, macadamias (澳洲坚果), garden plants, potatoes, tomatoes, citrus (柑橘类) fruits, apples, bananas and chestnuts (板栗). Australia is one of the few countries that produce licit (合法的) opium (鸦片) for medicinal purposes. This industry, centered in Tasmania, is subject to strict controls.

➢ *Livestock*

The arid and semiarid regions provide the most extensive type of soils through the Australia continent. These soils, with the recurrent (周期性发生的) droughts, are more suitable for light livestock grazing than for farming.

➢ *Sheep Industry*

Wool has been a staple (主要产品) of the Australian economy since the colonial period, and it was important to the development of agriculture as the country's largest industry. Australia remains the world's largest wool producer and exporter. Historically, up to 90% of Australian wool was exported. Lamb has become an increasingly important product as the sheep industry has moved its focus from wool production to the production of prime lamb. Live export of cattle and sheep from Australia to Asia and the Middle East is a large part of Australian meat export.

New South Wales is famous for sheep farming and wool producing.

➢ *Beef Industry*

Australia is one of the world's leading producers of cattle and beef. Dairy products are Australia's fourth most valuable agricultural export. Dairying is now mainly concentrated in Victoria and Tasmania.

Mining

The mining industry has been an important factor in the social and economic growth of Australia. The gold discoveries of the 1850s were responsible for the first big wave of free immigration and for the settlement of some inland areas. The mining sector has expanded significantly since the 1970s, with major discoveries of iron ore, petroleum, coal, and natural gas. Today, Australia is self-sufficient in most minerals of economic significance, and in several cases is among the world's leading producers. The minerals industry in general is the country's largest export earner.

Australia is the world's largest producer of both gem or near-gem diamonds and industrial-grade diamonds. About three-fourths of the nation's output is mined in Western Australia.

About 96 percent of Australia's iron-ore production also takes place in Western Australia.

Almost all of the iron ore is exported to Japan; Australia is now Japan's major supplier.

Coal is the country's top export earner and coal mining is heavily concentrated in New South Wales and Queensland.

Manufacturing

Principal branches of the Australian manufacturing sector by value of production are metals and metal products, food products, transportation equipment, machinery, chemicals and chemical products, textiles and clothing, wood and paper products, and printing, publishing, and recording media. Despite Australia's wealth of mineral resources, mineral processing is limited. Manufacturing facilities are concentrated in New South Wales (especially in Sydney and Newcastle), Victoria (primarily in the Melbourne metropolitan area), and secondarily in the state capitals and main provincial centers.

Tourism

As one of Australia's most important industries, tourism grew rapidly in the late 20th century, and it now represents one of the most dynamic sectors in the Australian economy. International tourism received a major boost from the highly successful Summer Olympic Games hosted in Sydney in 2000.

The strong growth in domestic tourism has tapped the expanding range of attractions in each state and territory — amusement and theme parks, zoos, art galleries and museums, certain mines and factories, national parks, historic sites, and wineries. Some of the most popular attractions are Queensland's spectacular Great Barrier Reef, the Northern Territory's Kakadu National Park, and the famous beach resorts in the Brisbane, Cairns, and Sydney regions.

Banking & Finance

➤ *Banking System*

The first Australian bank was established in Sydney in 1817. The current banking system includes:

- the Reserve Bank of Australia, which is Australia's central bank with responsibility for regulating monetary policy including the official interest rate,
- Big Four banks: the Commonwealth Bank of Australia, the Australia and New Zealand Banking Group, the Westpac Banking Corporation, and the National Australia Bank,
- a variety of credit unions, credit cooperatives, and building societies (建屋互助会) operating partly as banks, finance companies and money-market corporations, as well as some foreign banks.

➤ *Currency*

Australia used pounds, shillings and pence until 1966, when it adopted the decimal system with the Australian dollar divided into 100 cents. The basic unit Australian dollar is often abbreviated to $, A$ or $A, $AU or AU$.

Australia's notes are printed on plastic polymer (聚合体), a technology pioneered in Australia. These notes are more counterfeit-proof (防伪的), durable and cleaner than traditional paper money.

Brightly colored Australian notes, printed by Note Printing Australia, come in A$100, A$50, A$20, A$10 and A$5. Australian coins are produced by the Royal Australian Mint. There are A$2, A$1, 50 cent, 20 cent, 10 cent, and 5 cent units.

Chapter 14　Culture and Society of Australia

> **章节导读**
> 本章分为五部分，分别介绍了澳大利亚的多元文化特色、教育体制、以及文学、体育和主要节日。

I　Culture

Multiculturalism is Australia's main social policy. At times people think of Australians as Anglo-Australians. However, a large number of people from a wide variety of cultural, linguistic, and religious backgrounds are also Australians. Generally speaking, Australian culture belongs to Western culture. It has inherited English and European cultural tradition and contains aboriginal, Asian and American culture. Consequently, a multi-culture and multination cultural system came out.

Aboriginal Culture

Australia is the land on which the Aborigines lived and developed generation by generation. Therefore its culture has been consequentially influenced by Aboriginal culture. The Aborigines made a great contribution to Australian culture. For example, the origin of many Australian place's names is closely related with its society, economy, geography and history. The word *kangaroo* came from Aboriginal language, later "Kangaroo land" became the nickname of Australia.

Culture of English and European Tradition

Since 1788, the primary basis of Australian culture until the mid-20th century has been Anglo-Celtic, although distinctive Australian features had been evolving from the environment and Indigenous culture.

Australia follows the English pattern. In politics, Australia is a member of Commonwealth of Nation. In language, English is its parent language. In culture, Australia inherited lots of tradition of Britain. Therefore, Australia is sentimentally attached to its mother land, Britain. This complex can be seen from its national song "Advance Australia Fair." Some of the lines are as follows: *Britannia then shall surely know; beyond wide ocean's rolls; her sons in fair Australia's land; still keep a British soul*. Due to the traditional relations, in the Australian minds, Australia is still a British inalienable part of empire. In an Australian heart, old land, old country, old home are all synonyms (同义字) of Britain.

Asian Culture

Australian mainstream culture, in the key of English and European culture, has melted lots of Asian factors. In Australian towns, restaurants and shops run by Chinese, Vietnamese, Japanese and Koreans can be easily found. Chinese people have made great contributions to Australian culture. In Australian English, there are many words with Chinese characteristics: Fan-tan[①], a gambling game; *Yum cha* (饮茶); and *Dim-sim* (点心); like a Pakapoo (pigeon) ticket[②], a slang, meaning something that is indecipherable or confusing.

American Culture

Over the past 50 years, Australian culture has been strongly influenced by American popular culture (particularly television and cinema). After World War I, American jazz, dancing and popular music were introduced to Australia and became predominant. Afterwards a lot of choreographic (舞蹈艺术的) and jazz music was widely accepted and became more and more popular as an anthem for the youth generation fighting for personal freedom. From the 1920s, a number of Hollywood films gushed into Australia. During World War II Australia was a popular holiday place for American soldiers.

With the coming of modern American culture, American English, as the carrier of its culture was introduced into Australia. Some phrases reflect the admiration towards Americans. Australians who imitated the manners or speech of American soldiers on holiday are called *Woolloomooloo Yanks*; Women who like to accompany American soldiers are named *Yank-happy*, the word widge refers to women who behave wildly and like wearing American fashionable dresses. In the 1950s, some common American expressions were used by Australians too, such as *hi, so long, sure, wow, guy, see you*, etc. Even the name of Australian currency was changed to dollar and cent from pound and penny.

Plenty of immigrants from all over the world not only changed Australians' eating custom and living pattern, but also enriched their thought and culture. They brought their civilizations to the Australian continent, and molded colorful Australian culture.

II Education

An Overview

Education in Australia follows the three-tier (等级) model which includes primary education, followed by secondary education and tertiary education (高等教育). The school year varies between states and institutions, but generally runs from late January until mid-December. Most States and Territories operate on a four-term per year system, with a short holiday between terms and a long summer holiday in December and January. Universities normally operate over two semesters and the academic year begins in mid to late February and ends in November.

Primary & Secondary Education

Schooling in Australia is compulsory for all children between 5 and 15 years of age (16 in Tasmania). It starts with a preparatory year followed by primary and secondary school.

Primary schools provide basic education for children up to 12 or 13 years of age, after which they transfer to a secondary school. Of Australian students attending primary and secondary schools, about two-thirds are enrolled in Government schools, with the other third in independent

---

① 番摊：中国古老的作庄赌博游戏。
② 白鸽票：彩票的俗称，源自19世纪后半叶来自广东的华人在澳大利亚使用的一种彩票，澳大利亚人看不懂，便称之为"难懂的东西"。

schools, mainly Roman Catholic schools. Both government and independent schools are required to follow the same curriculum (课程) frameworks.

Two options are open to students when they complete three or four years of high school. They may choose to receive further education at a technical or agricultural college or other training institutions. Students who choose to continue at the high school level undertake two more years of study before taking an examination coordinated by the state for the purpose of university entrance. Due to limited space, not every student can expect to obtain a university place. Entrance numbers are primarily based on the number of students for whom the Commonwealth authorities are able to provide financial support.

Tertiary Education

There are two types of tertiary education programs: those offered by institutions and industry in the vocational education and training (VET) sector, and those offered by universities and other higher education providers.

Vocational education and training provides students with the skills required in a modern economy and delivers (提供) competency-based training that is practical and career-oriented.

The Australian higher education system comprises:
- 39 universities, of which 37 are public institutions and 2 are private;
- a number of other specialist institutions that provide approved courses at the higher education level.

Degrees in Australia can take from three to six years to complete and are divided into two distinct tracks: the ordinary degree and the honors degree. The ordinary degree varies in length by field and university. Arts subjects are typically completed in three years, sciences in four years, and medicine in five years. An honors degree is required for a student to advance to the master's level. After completion of the ordinary degree the university invites a student to complete the honors degree. The honors degree takes an additional year to complete and involves mainly independent study leading to a research dissertation.

Diversity and autonomy (自主权) are central features of Australian universities. Each university has the freedom to specify its own mission and purpose, modes of teaching and research, constitution of the student body and the range and content of educational programs. The majority of students live at home and attend university in their home states. In all universities, students have substantial control of the student unions, councils and athletic clubs. Compulsory fees that support these activities are collected from students by the universities.

QS World University Rankings® 2016 — 2017

University		Rank
Australian National University	澳大利亚国立大学	22
University of Melbourne	墨尔本大学	42
University of Sydney	悉尼大学	46
University of New South Wales	新南威尔士大学	49
University of Queensland	昆士兰大学	51
Monash University	莫纳什大学	65
University of Western Australia	西澳大学	102
University of Adelaide	阿德莱德大学	125
University of Technology Sydney	悉尼科技大学	173

Australian National University (ANU)
ANU is a public research university founded on August 1,1948 and located in Canberra. It is often ranked as a leading university in Australia on a number of measures.

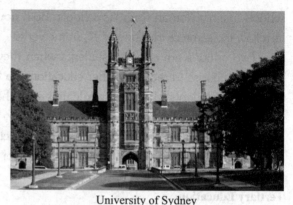

University of Sydney
Founded in 1850, it is the oldest and one of the largest universities in Australia with over 47,000 students, including nearly 9,000 international students from more than 80 different countries.

III Literature

Australian literature in English began soon after the settlement of the country by Europeans and reflected a range of influences, from English literary traditions to the storytelling of Indigenous Australians and the European settlers and convicts (罪犯) who arrived in Australia in the late 18th century. It has developed certain well-defined qualities: a love of the vast, empty land with its unique plants and animals, a compelling (非常强烈的) sense of the worth of the common people, and freedom from the bondage of European traditions. Today's writing also reflects the cultural diversity of contemporary Australian society.

Australian writers have produced a diverse range of internationally acclaimed (称赞) novels, drama, poetry and non-fiction. Their works have increasingly been recognized through international literary awards. Many prominent authors have sought inspiration in English and European literature, and these cultural relationships remain strong.

The oral storytelling of Indigenous Australians, convicts and settlers contributed to the development of distinctive Australian writing styles. Early authors explored themes of Indigenous and settler identity, alienation, exile and relationship to place.

Australia's vast, dry landscape itself became a character in early Australian works of literature. Dislocated from their countries of origin in the early days of Australia's settlement, many writers struggled with notions of what it meant to be Australian. Strong sentiments of egalitarianism (平等主义) — a wish to be free of the old society of class and privilege — were born and surfaced in Australian literature from that time.

Some early stories were of the "ripping yarn" (非同寻常的历险故事) variety, typified in *Robbery under Arms* (1882), a bushranger (丛林逃犯, 绿林好汉) novel by Thomas Alexander Browne, published under his pseudonym Rolf Boldrewood. Most of Boldrewood's novels were romances and his lead characters English gentlemen, but his outback settings introduced the Australian environment to many readers. Likewise, the poetry of

Adam Lindsay Gordon (1833—1870)

English settler Adam Lindsay Gordon[①] (1833 — 1870) helped foster understanding of Australian identity. Gordon's *Bush Ballads* and *Galloping Rhymes* became so popular in England that he was commemorated in the Poets' Corner of Westminster Abbey (the only Australian to be so recognized). Moral debate about the treatment of convicts underpinned (构成……的基础) Marcus Clarke's melancholy masterpiece, *For the Term of His Natural Life*[②] (1874). It is possibly the most famous 19th century Australian novel and is still published today.

The New Nationalism

The second half of the 19th century saw rapid social evolution, great cultural enthusiasm and new-found nationalism in Australia. Universities, libraries and museums were established, and journals such as the *Bulletin,* the *Republican, Australian Town and Country,* the *Sydney Worker* and *Truth* published the short stories of aspiring authors.

Among them was Henry Lawson (1867 — 1922), whose first collection of stories appeared in 1894, followed by *While the Billy Boils* in 1896, generally considered his best prose collection. Born in a tent on the goldfields in New South Wales in 1867 and raised in rural poverty and city squalor (恶劣条件), Lawson wrote with compassion about the lives and struggles of Australian pioneers — the men and women of the bush. Lawson helped define an Australian character based on mateship (同伴之谊) and perseverance in the face of adversity.

Joseph Furphy (1843 — 1912), an outstanding writer of Australian fiction before World War I, was also inspired by the country's new-found nationalism. His masterpiece novel *Such Is Life* (1903), a fictional account of the lives of rural Australians in the late 1800s, shifted Australian fiction away from the colonial romance genre and earned him the reputation of "Father of the Australian novel."

A Shift in Mood

Until the Depression in 1929, most novels were optimistic about the "lucky country", past and present. However, in the late 1930s the literary mood shifted and darker world views were explored. An important writer in the early 20th century was Miles Franklin, whose feminism set her apart in a time of conservatism. Her most famous novel is *My Brilliant Career* (1901), which was made into an acclaimed film in 1979. Franklin died in 1954 and her will provided for the establishment of an annual literary award. Today The Miles Franklin Award, the first and most prestigious literary award in Australia, celebrates Australian character and creativity and is awarded for the novel of the year that has the highest literary merit and presents Australian life in any of its phases. The Award this year is worth A$ 6,000.

Indigenous Writers

The first written Indigenous works were translations of traditional myths and legends originally told in song and oral narrative. Aboriginal writing in English is a relatively new phenomenon,

---

① 亚当·林赛·戈登（1833—1870）：采用澳大利亚民谣形式创作的澳大利亚早期诗人，也是一位带有传奇色彩的英国骑士。他的诗大多以古代或英国的人和事件为题材，但具有鲜明的地方色彩。尤长于风景抒情诗和骑士诗。在创作手法上，极力效仿英国诗人拜伦，他的创作风格曾引起人们对新兴澳大利亚诗歌的注意。1870年6月24日，在诗集《丛林歌与奔马谣》出版的第2天，开枪自杀身亡。其塑像列入伦敦诗人角，题为"澳大利亚诗人"。

② 《无期徒刑》：是一部关于英国澳大利亚流放犯的经典长篇小说，作者是澳大利亚殖民时期重要作家马库斯·克拉克。该作品问世以来在国际上引起了广泛的关注。在《无期徒刑》中克拉克无情地抨击了英国流放制度的罪恶，为殖民时期英国流放犯的清白做了坚定的辩护。作者通过主人翁鲁弗斯的遭遇揭示了流放制度对人们心灵的摧残，再现了澳大利亚早期英国流放犯生活的真实境遇，具有深刻的社会现实意义。

starting with David Unaipon (1872 — 1967), who made a significant contribution to literature and science and to the advancement of Aboriginal people. Unaipon's book *Native Legends* (1929) was the first to be published by an Aboriginal writer. This was followed by *Myths and Legends of the Australian Aborigines* (1930). In 1989, the University of Queensland Press established the David Unaipon Award, which recognizes and provides publishing opportunities for new Indigenous writers.

David Unaipon (1872—1967), preacher, author and inventor

Other well-known Indigenous authors include the playwright Jack Davis, the writer Mudrooroo and the poet Oodgeroo Noonuccal, whose *We Are Going* (1964) was the first book of published poetry by an Aboriginal Australian. Sally Morgan's *My Place* (1987) was considered a breakthrough memoir (文集) that brought Indigenous stories to wider notice. Since the 1960s, there has been a marked increase in publications by Indigenous writers, including poetry, fiction, drama, biography and autobiography, and political and sociological writing. In 2007, Indigenous writer and land rights activist Alexis Wright won the Miles Franklin Award for her novel *Carpentaria*.

Post-World War II Literature

The demand for popular fiction continued to grow in the second half of the 20th century. Prominent authors included Nevil Shute (1899 — 1960), an Englishman who settled in Australia and wrote novels including *A Town Like Alice* (1950), and Morris West (1916 — 1919), who wrote 29 novels, including *The Shoes of the Fisherman* (1963). Colin Thiele wrote around 100 works, including novels set in rural Australia such as *Sun on the Stubble* (1961), *Storm Boy* (1963) and *Blue Fin* (1969).

At this time, many writers sought to examine the relationship between people and the environment. For some, this included promoting reconciliation with Indigenous Australians and developing a greater appreciation of their relationship with the land.

In 1973, Patrick White (1912 — 1990) a novelist, short story writer, and playwright, became the first Australian to win the Nobel Prize for Literature. He published twelve novels, two short-story collections, eight plays, and works of non-fiction. Since Patrick White, Australia has produced a steady stream of outstanding novelists. Many have set their characters and narratives in Australia, although some have also achieved success with stories based in Asia, Europe and North America.

To most of the world, the best known Australian novel may be *The Thorn Birds* (《荆棘鸟》, 1977), written by Colleen Margaretta McCullough (1937 — 2015). Another famous contemporary writer worth mentioning is John Maxwell Coetzee (1940 —), the winner of 2003 Nobel Prize in Literature, who moved to Australia from South Africa in 2002 and became an Australian citizen in 2006.

Australian Literary Awards

Patrick White (1912—1990)

There are more than 30 literary awards in Australia, including major government-funded prizes and specialist competitions. The most well-known include the annual Miles Franklin Literary Award[①] and the Australian Vogel Literary Award.

The Miles Franklin Award was bequeathed (遗赠) by the will of Australian novelist Miles Franklin for "a published novel or play portraying Australian life in any of its phases." The Vogel Award is Australia's richest award for an unpublished manuscript and has helped launch the careers of some of Australia's most successful writers. The Barbara Jefferies Award, instituted in 2007, honors Australian novels that depict women in a positive light.

Four state governments — New South Wales, Queensland, Victoria and Western Australia — also fund annual literary prizes and the Australian Government has announced a Prime Minister's Literary Prize for fiction and non-fiction books.

> **Quick Facts of Prize Winners**
> - Australian authors have won many international awards, including the Nobel Prize for Literature (Patrick White, 1973), the Man Booker Prize (Thomas Keneally, 1982; Peter Carey, 1988 and 2001; DBC Pierre, 2003) and the Pulitzer Prize for Fiction (Geraldine Brooks, 2006).
> - Adam Lindsay Gordon is the only Australian with a bust in Poets' Corner in Westminster Abbey.
> - Three Australians have received the Queen's Gold Medal for Poetry: Michael Thwaites in 1940, Judith Wright in 1991, and Les Murray in 1998.

IV Sports

Australia is a sports-mad nation. Sport plays an important part in Australian culture. Many Australians over the age of 15 regularly participate in organized sporting activities.

At an international level, Australia is a strong competitor in cricket, hockey, netball, rugby league (联盟式橄榄球), rugby union (联合式橄榄球), and performs well in cycling, rowing and swimming. Nationally, other popular sports include Australian rules football, horse racing, football (soccer) and motor racing. Australia also boasts a particularly rich tennis tradition. Melbourne hosts the annual Australian Open, one of the four Grand Slam tennis tournaments.

Australia is one of the only three countries that have competed at every summer Olympic Games of the modern era, winning its first two medals in 1896, five years before it existed as a country. Australia hosted the 1956 Summer Olympics in Melbourne and the 2000 Summer Olympics in Sydney, and has ranked among the top five medal-takers since 2000. Australia has also participated in every Commonwealth Games. It hosted the 1938, 1962, 1982 and 2006 Commonwealth Games. Other major international events held regularly in Australia include annual international cricket matches and the Formula One Australian Grand Prix (一级方程式大奖赛).

---

① 迈尔斯·弗兰克林文学奖：在澳大利亚二十余种文学奖中，该奖项是澳大利亚最负盛名的文学奖项。这个奖项的创始人是已故著名澳洲民族主义女作家，《我的璀璨生涯》(*My Brilliant Career*)作者迈尔斯·弗兰克林（1879—1954），其在1948年即立遗嘱将财产设立为奖项，每年颁发奖金给优秀、杰出的描写澳洲风土人情的文学作家。自1957年第一届迈尔斯·弗兰克林文学奖颁布以来，该奖已经历了52年50届（1973、1983、1988年未颁奖），共有38位作家获奖。截止到2008年，奖金已由最初的500镑累积到42,000澳元，澳大利亚作家视此文学奖为最高荣誉。

V Holidays and Special Days

Name	Date
New Year's Day	1 January
Australia Day	26 January
Good Friday	Easter
Easter Saturday	the Saturday following Good Friday
Easter Monday	the Monday following Good Friday
ANZAC Day	25 April
Queen's Birthday	the 2nd Monday in June
Christmas	25 December
Boxing Day	26 December or 27 December

Australia Day

Australia Day is celebrated as Australia's official National Day on the 26 January, commemorating the arrival of the First Fleet at Sydney Cove on January 26, 1788 and the founding of the first permanent European settlement in Australia. Australia Day is the biggest day of celebration in the country and is observed as a public holiday in all states and territories. The formal celebrations begin on the eve of Australia Day and continue all through the next day. The ceremony is marked by flag hoisting, community awards presentation (Each year as people around the nation celebrate what makes the country great, there are some very special Aussies being recognized for their great work. These awards are known as the Australian of the Year Awards) and citizenship ceremonies along with local events, breakfasts, and merrymaking. Parades and fireworks are also a common feature in the national day celebrations of Australia. The most popular site of concerts, festivities and lightshows is the lawns of Parliament House in Canberra, the Capital city of Australia.

Easter

Australia is the land of people from a number of cultures. For this reason, Australia has a different style of celebrating the Easter festivity. There are certain things that are specific to Australia. To say for example, in major part of Northern hemisphere, the Easter bunny (rabbit) is considered to be one of the most important symbols of Easter. But in Australia, rabbits, or bunnies, are seen as pests, which have cost Australian farmers a lot of money and damaged many landscapes. Owing to this, the Aussie people have found another alternative Easter symbol, namely Bilby. The Bilby is a small mammal with large ears that is native to Australia. For some people, it is now the Easter Bilby that brings chocolate and decorated eggs to children on an Easter Sunday morning. Chocolate models of the Easter Bilby are sold to raise money to help preserve the Bilby population.

ANZAC (澳新军团) Day

ANZAC stands for Australian and New Zealand Army Corps. It commemorates the landing of Australian and New Zealand troops at Gallipoli on 25 April 1915. The date, 25 April, was officially named ANZAC Day in 1916. The spirit of ANZAC recognizes the qualities of courage, mateship (同伴之谊) and sacrifice which were demonstrated at the Gallipoli landing. ANZAC Day is a time to remember the deaths and sufferings in war, the courage of fighting men and women, and the ever-present hope for the peoples of the world to live together in harmony and lasting peace.

Commemorative (纪念的) services are held at dawn on 25 April, the time of the original landing, across the nation, usually at war memorials. This was initiated by returned soldiers after the First World War in the 1920s as a common form of remembrance. The first official dawn service was held at the Sydney Cenotaph (纪念碑) in 1927, which was also the first year that all states recognized a public holiday on the day. Initially dawn services were only attended by veterans who followed the ritual of "standing to" before two minutes of silence was observed, broken by the sound of a lone piper playing the "Last Post." Later in the day, there were marches in all the major cities and many smaller towns for families and other well-wishers.

Queen's Birthday

The Queen's Birthday celebrates the birthday of Queen Elizabeth II who is not only Queen of the United Kingdom but also Queen of Australia. The day has been observed since 1788, when Governor Arthur Phillip declared a holiday to mark the birthday of King George III. Until 1936 it was held on the actual birthday of the Monarch, but after the death of King George V it was decided to be celebrated on the second Monday of June except in the state of Western Australia where the Queen's Birthday holiday is celebrated in late September or early October. Neither date marks the real birthday of the sovereign. The holiday also marks the start of the Australian ski season, though it is quite common that there is no skiable snow until later in the month.

Christmas

For the majority of Australians, Christmas down under has all the glitter, tinsel and razzmatazz (活力) of a Christmas in New York, London, Paris or Vancouver. The major difference is one of WEATHER. Whereas the northern hemisphere is in the middle of winter, Australians are baking in summer heat. It is not unusual to have Christmas Day well into the mid 30°C. The heat of early summer in Australia has an impact on the way that Australians celebrate Christmas and on which northern hemisphere Christmas traditions are followed.

Some uniquely Australian Christmas carols have become popular and are included alongside the more traditional carols sung at carol services and at Christmas church services: John Wheeler's "The Three Drovers" is perhaps the best known of these. Many light-hearted Australian Christmas songs have become an essential part of the Australian Christmas experience. These include Rolf Harris's "Six White Boomers" (large Kangaroos), Colin Buchanan's "Aussie Jingle Bells" and the "Australian Twelve Days of Christmas."

Instead of the usual image of a reindeer drawing Santa's sleigh, many Australians cherish the image of six white boomers, hopping the sleigh across the sky.

Christmas time is holiday time in Australia, with many Aussies taking Christmas / New Year's holidays to bake themselves in the sun and to enjoy the great Australian outdoors.

The Christmas break is also an opportunity for sports fans to enjoy two major sporting events: the Boxing Day Test and the Sydney to Hobart (霍巴特，塔斯马尼亚州府) Yacht Race. The 26 December is the opening day of the Boxing Day Test between the Australian Cricket Team and an international touring side at the Melbourne Cricket Ground. This has been well attended since the first match in 1950, and watched by many others on television. In Sydney one of the world's most prestigious ocean races, the Sydney to Hobart Yacht Race, starts on Boxing Day from Sydney Harbor.

Chapter 15　Understanding New Zealand

章节导读

本章内容分为四部分,分别介绍了新西兰的概况、地理和历史、政治制度和国家经济发展状况,以及社会和文化特征。

I　A General Survey

New Zealand, a small island country located in the South Pacific Ocean and a close neighbor to Australia, has a landscape renowned for its varieties, and in particular, its scenic snow-capped mountains and rolling green pastures. The culture of New Zealand is a synthesis (综合体) of home-grown and imported cultures. Modern New Zealand society is a fusion of Polynesian① (波利尼西亚的), Asian and European cultures. New Zealanders are recognized globally for their progressive humanitarian stance, liberal politics and world-leading social welfare, and enjoy a high quality of life. Before we scrutinize the details of this nation, let's have a glimpse of some basics about it.

---

① 波利尼西亚人:大洋洲东部波利尼西亚群岛的民族群体的总称,有10多个支系,90多万人,新西兰的原住民毛利人也是波利尼西亚人。

A Collection of Fast Facts of New Zealand

Basic Facts	
Capital	Wellington
Area	268,680 sq km
People	
Population	4,692,700 (2016 estimate)
Population growth rate	2.1 percent (2016 estimate)
Population density	16.7 persons per sq km (2014 estimate)
Largest cities, with population	
Auckland	1,614,400 (2016 estimate)
Wellington	207,900 (2016 estimate)
Christchurch	374,900 (2016 estimate)
Hamilton	161,200 (2016 estimate)
Dunedin	127,000 (2016 estimate)
Ethnic groups	
European	67.6 percent
Maori	14.6 percent
Pacific Islander	6.9 percent
Asian	9.2 percent
Languages	
English (official), Maori 毛利语 (official), Polynesian languages	
Religious affiliations	
Protestant	24 percent
Anglican	21 percent
Roman Catholic	13 percent
Buddhist	1 percent
Nonreligious	13 percent
Other (including Jewish and Hindu)	28 percent
Health and Education	
Total Life Expectancy	80.7 years (2015 estimate)
Female	84.4 years (2015 estimate)
Male	77 years (2015 estimate)
Government	
Form of Government	Parliamentary democracy
Head of State	Governor-general, representing the British monarch
Head of government	Prime minister
Legislature	Unicameral legislature
	House of Representatives: 120 members
Constitution	
No written constitution; political system closely modeled on that of the United Kingdom.	
Highest Court	Court of Appeal
Monetary Unit	
1 New Zealand dollar ($NZ), consisting of 100 cents	

Capital City — Wellington

Whatever else it may be, Wellington is, first of all, the capital of New Zealand and the geographical, cultural, commercial, cosmopolitan center of the country. In population, it is New Zealand's second largest city. Being the nation's capital and the seat of its government, Wellington has transformed itself via its café, fashion, restaurant, nightlife and artistic culture into a New Zealand's hot urban destination in the past few years.

Ethnic Groups

New Zealanders of European descent, who are often known by the Maori name as Pakeha [(新西兰)白种人], comprise about 68 percent of the population. They are usually described as the largest ethnic group, but in fact they are ethnically mixed.

Pacific Islanders and East Asians account for about 7 percent and 9 percent of the population respectively. Maori, the native inhabitants of New Zealand, are the largest non-European group. They are a people of Polynesian origin who, in 2014, constitute some 14.6 percent of New Zealand's population. More than 95 percent of Maori live on New Zealand's North Island. Many Maori live in the East Cape area, where they form the majority of the population. Others live in the large cities of New Zealand, such as Auckland and Wellington.

Official Languages

English and Maori are the official languages of New Zealand. Maori became an official language in 1987. New Zealand English is close to Australian English in pronunciation, but has several subtle differences. Some of these differences show New Zealand English has more affinity (相似) with the English of southern England than Australian English does. Several of the differences also show the influence of Maori speech. The New Zealand accent also has some Scottish and Irish influences from the large number of settlers. Maori is only used in New Zealand and nowhere else in the world. In the *Treaty of Waitangi* in 1840, Queen Victoria promised the Maori that their language would be protected. In the present, the Maori language is commonly used in the media and at school. In April 2006, New Zealand became the first country to declare sign language as an official language, alongside Maori and English.

Religions

The majority of New Zealanders are Christian. Anglicans traditionally have formed the largest single denomination. The next largest Christian groups are Presbyterians and Roman Catholics. Religious practice is stronger among Maori and Pacific Islanders than among Pakeha. The Maori Christian churches, the Ringatu Church (founded in 1867) and the Ratana Church of New Zealand (1918) have relatively small but consistently active membership.

Flag of New Zealand

The New Zealand flag is the symbol of the realm government and people of New Zealand. It is a defaced blue ensign (国旗) with the Union Flag in the canton, and four red stars with white borders to the right. The stars represent the constellation of Crux, the Southern Cross, as seen from New Zealand. The flag proportion is 1:2 and the colors are red, blue and white. Proportion and colors are identical to the Union Flag.

Six flags other than the New Zealand Flag are flown for official purposes in New Zealand. They are The Queen's Personal Flag for New Zealand, Governor-General's Flag, New Zealand Red Ensign (英国商船旗), New Zealand White Ensign (皇家海军旗), Royal NZ Air Force Ensign,

and New Zealand Civil Air Ensign.

New Zealand National Anthems

New Zealand holds a rare position in the world in that it has two national anthems of equal standing — "God Defend New Zealand" and "God Save The Queen." Both of these anthems have origins which have been inspired by the fire of patriotism yet were written under different situations.

Coat of Arms

The first quarter of the shield depicts four stars as representative of the Southern Cross, three ships symbolizing the importance of New Zealand's sea trade; in the second quarter is a fleece representing the farming industry. The wheat sheaf in the third quarter represents the agricultural industry, whilst the crossed hammers in the fourth quarter represent the mining industry. The supporters on either side of the shield consist of a Maori Chieftain (首领) holding a taiaha (a Maori war weapon) and a European woman holding the New Zealand Ensign (国旗). Surmounting the Arms is the St. Edward's Crown which was used in the Coronation (加冕礼) ceremony of Her Majesty Queen Elizabeth II. The crown symbolizes the fact that Her Majesty is Queen of New Zealand under the *New Zealand Royal Titles Act 1953*.

Kiwiana (Objects and symbols regarded as national icons)

"Kiwiana" is the term used to describe items relating to New Zealand's unique culture and history. Some notable items of Kiwiana people will probably encounter on their trip to New Zealand are listed below.

➤ *National Bird: Kiwi Bird (奇异鸟,鹬鸵)*

The Kiwi bird is the country's indigenous flightless bird. It occurs only in New Zealand and is a New Zealand Kiwiana icon — New Zealanders even take their nickname from the little critter.

➤ *National Flower*

New Zealand's impressive ponga, or tree fern (桫椤), can grow to a towering height of 15 meters. With more than 150 fern species growing in New Zealand, the plant has become a national symbol.

➤ *Kiwifruit*

Originally known as Chinese gooseberries, kiwifruits were first introduced to the country by early settlers. Since then they have become synonymous with New Zealand, and are a major export earner.

➤ *Sheep*

Being the back bone of the New Zealand economy for over a century, sheep were first introduced by English settlers in the 19th century. Merino sheep (美利奴绵羊), prized for their fine wool, cloak Alps' foothills.

II Geography and History

A. Geography

Land and Resources
➢ *Land*

The total land area of New Zealand is 268,680 sq km, about the same size as Japan or the British Isles. The North and South islands make up almost the entire area of the country.

The North Island, 113,729 sq km in area, is one of the two main islands of New Zealand, the other being the South Island. Approximately 76% (3,148,400) of New Zealand's population lives in the North Island. Several important cities are in the North Island, notably New Zealand's largest city, Auckland, and Wellington. Snow-capped Mount Ruapehu is one of the world's most active volcanoes and the largest active volcano in New Zealand. It is the highest point in the North Island.

The South Island is the larger of the two major islands of New Zealand with an area of 154,951 square km. The South Island is often called the Mainland (somewhat humorously) because it existed first according to Maori legend and is larger than the North Island. The South Island only has a resident population of 991,100, about a quarter of New Zealand's four million inhabitants.

➢ *Natural Resources*

Land is one of the country's most valuable resources. More than half of the land area is either cropland or pastureland. Most of the arable land is found on the east coasts of both islands, in particular the Canterbury Plains. Pastures for livestock grazing dominate in north-central and western North Island and southern South Island.

About 31 percent of the land area is forested. The country has 6.4 million hectares of old-growth forest, much of which is designated for preservation. In addition, some forests are plantations of imported species such as the radiata pine (辐射松). New Zealand's rivers and lakes are an important natural resources as the source of hydroelectricity. Mineral resources are limited, with some reserves of coal, gold, iron ore, and limestone. Significant stocks of natural gas and less plentiful reserves of oil are located both offshore and in the western region of the North Island.

Climate

New Zealand is located in the Southern Temperate Zone, south of the tropics. It has a mild climate with four seasons. The warmest months of summer are January and February and the coldest months of winter are June and July. Inland areas have cooler winters and warmer summers than coastal areas, where the moderating influence of the ocean creates a more temperate climate.

B. History

The first inhabitants of New Zealand, the Maori, are thought to have arrived over 1,000 years ago, traveling on canoes from a South Pacific homeland. Maori named the land Aotearoa ("Land of the Long White Cloud") and developed a very successful society.

The first European to sight New Zealand was Abel Tasman, a Dutch navigator who saw the

South Island's West Coast in 1642. Although he never set foot on New Zealand soil, he annexed it for Holland under the name "Staten Landt" —— later changed to New Zealand by Dutch mapmakers.

In 1769, Briton Captain James Cook was searching for a southern continent when his cabin boy sighted land near Gisborne (吉斯伯恩,新西兰北岛东岸港市). Cook circumnavigated (环航) and mapped the country. He established friendly relations with some Maori. European migration began soon after and by 1839 there were an estimated 2,000 Europeans in New Zealand.

On February 6, 1840, representatives of Britain and Maori chiefs signed the *Treaty of Waitangi* at Waitangi in the Bay of Islands, establishing British law in New Zealand while guaranteeing Maori authority over their land and culture, and granting the Maori British citizenship. Although there are continuing debates about the proper interpretation of the Treaty, it is considered New Zealand's founding document. After the signing of the Treaty, the number of British migrants increased enormously. A gold rush during the 1860s attracted even more migrants from around the world, yet Britain remained the "homeland" for most settlers and the majority of New Zealand's infrastructure was built on British models. Independence from Britain was formally proclaimed in 1947 and since that time New Zealand has increasingly developed its own unique culture: a mix of those that have settled the country throughout the centuries.

From the beginning, the country has been in the forefront in instituting social welfare legislation. New Zealand was the world's first country to give women the right to vote (1893). It adopted old-age pensions (1898), a national child welfare program (1907), social security for the elderly, widows, and orphans, along with family benefit payments, minimum wages, a 40-hour workweek and unemployment and health insurance (1938), and socialized medicine (1941). In recent years, New Zealand has introduced extremely liberal social policies. In June 2003, parliament legalized prostitution and in Dec. 2004, same-sex unions were recognized.

III Political System and National Economy

Political System

The politics of New Zealand takes place in a framework of a parliamentary representative democratic monarchy. The basic system is closely patterned on that of the Westminster System, although a number of significant modifications have been made. New Zealand's head of state is the Queen of New Zealand, currently Elizabeth II, but actual government is conducted by a Prime Minister and Cabinet drawn from an elected Parliament.

The New Zealand monarchy has been distinct from the British monarchy since the *New Zealand Royal Titles Act of 1953*, and all Elizabeth II's official business in New Zealand is conducted in the name of the Queen of New Zealand, not the Queen of the United Kingdom. In practice, the functions of the monarchy are conducted by a Governor General, appointed by the monarch on the advice of the Prime Minister. New Zealand was the first country in the world in which all the highest offices were occupied by women between March 2005 and August 2006: the Sovereign Queen Elizabeth II of New Zealand, Governor-General Dame Silvia Cartwright, Prime Minister Helen Clark, Speaker of the New Zealand House of Representatives Margaret Wilson and

Chief Justice Dame Sian Elias.

National Economy
➢ Economy & Industry

New Zealand has a mixed economy, dominated by an export-focused agricultural sector, together with significant manufacturing and service sectors. The economy is strongly trade-oriented with food and beverages representing a large proportion of exports. New Zealand has developed a world-wide reputation for top quality produce from meat (New Zealand lamb is particularly renowned) to dairy products, seafood, fruit and vegetables, and boutique wines. Service industries, including tourism, consultancy and education, are also extremely significant to the New Zealand economy.

➢ Currency and Banking

The New Zealand dollar (currency code NZD) is the currency of New Zealand. It is normally abbreviated with the dollar sign $, or alternatively NZ$ to distinguish it from other dollar-denominated currencies. It is often informally known as the "Kiwi (dollar)" and is divided into 100 cents.

Banking New Zealand Style

The Reserve Bank of New Zealand (founded in 1934) has the sole power of issue. It acts as a wholesale distributor to the trading banks and manages the design and manufacturing of the currency. It also withdraws damaged or unusable notes and coins to manage the quality of currency in circulation.

IV Society and Culture

Culture

New Zealand has a unique cultural identity, quite unlike anywhere else in the world. Decidedly multi-cultural, modern New Zealand society is a fusion of Polynesian, Asian and European cultures.

The earliest cultural tradition in New Zealand was that of the Maori, who developed a rich and diverse Polynesian culture in geographic isolation from the other cultures of Polynesia. European settlers brought with them their own traditions, which eventually dominated the country's cultural life. Since the 1950s the cultural fabric of New Zealand has become increasingly diverse with the immigration of peoples from the Pacific Islands and Asia.

➢ Pakeha Culture

Cultural activity among people of European descent, who are known as Pakeha in New Zealand, has long been strong, but until recently tended to follow British models. Cultural output was high in both quality and quantity. However, it was complicated by strong links with Britain because London was, in many respects, the cultural capital of New Zealand. The most acclaimed

New Zealand artists produced their famous works as expatriates (移居国外的人) in England. Artists and writers who stayed in New Zealand tended to feel alienated from, and unappreciated by, overseas European society. Even expatriate artists, however, explored their New Zealand roots. In the second half of the 20th century, Pakeha culture developed in its own right, producing many notable writers and artists whose works draw on the New Zealand experience.

> ## Maori Culture

Maori Haka Dance

In most ancient Maori communities, men hunted and plowed, while women weeded, wove, and cooked. Group activities included food gathering, food cultivation and warfare. Individuals specialized in different arts: poetry, oratory, tattooing (文身) and the carving of wood, bone and stone. Nowadays, traditional Maori culture is expressed in song, dance, oratory, woodcarving, weaving, and architecture. Maori artists also bring Maori perspectives to canvas painting, fiction and poetry writing and other art forms. The modern Maori have made a concerted effort to preserve their culture. In the 1980s they initiated a revival of their language and other traditions. By that time many Maori had assimilated into the predominant European culture. The majority of Maori had become urban dwellers, and younger Maori did not know the Maori language. Today Maori culture thrives in both traditional and reinvented traditions.

Customs

> ## Marriage and Family

Weddings are often followed by a sit-down meal and dancing. Among those of European origin, families tend to be small, and most own their homes. Many young adults leave for several years to travel and work in other countries (often the United Kingdom). This time abroad is commonly referred to as Overseas Experience, or OE.

Among the Maori, the extended family remains important, and several generations may live in the same house. Also important to the Maori is the community center, called the *marae*, a Maori community facility which consists of a carved meeting house, a dining hall and cooking area as well as the marae atea (sacred space in front of the meeting house). The marae is a symbol of tribal identity. It is a meeting place where people can discuss and debate various issues, and in which Maori customs are given ultimate expression. On the marae, official functions such as celebrations, weddings, christenings, tribal reunion and funerals take place.

> ## Eating

Traditional British-style big breakfasts and hearty meals of meat and potatoes have gradually given way to a more diverse and health-conscious diet. New Zealanders have long eaten beef, pork, mutton and fish, and are now eating more poultry.

Fruit is plentiful, as are dairy products. New Zealand produces fine wines, and beer is a popular beverage. Popular takeout foods at lunchtime include meat pies, sandwiches and filled bread rolls. Chinese food, pizza, hamburgers and fried chicken are all available for a takeout dinner in addition to the more traditional fish and chips and lamb roast. In the main cities, restaurants serve a wide range of cuisine, including Thai, Malaysian, Chinese, Indian, Greek and Mexican food.

New Zealanders generally eat three meals a day, and many still enjoy the British traditions of a morning cup of tea and afternoon tea at about 3 or 4 p.m. The main meal is usually in the evening between 6 and 7 p.m. although it is more likely to be around 8 PM when dining out.

➢ *Socializing*

New Zealanders usually shake hands when meeting someone (in formal circumstances, a man normally waits for a woman to offer her hand first), and first names are commonly used after an initial introduction. Informal greetings include the New Zealand version of "Good day," pronounced *Gidday*, or a simple "Hello" or "Hi." The Maori may greet each other with a hug or the traditional *hongi* — pressing noses together with eyes closed and making a low "mm-mm" sound. The Maori greeting *Kia Ora*, which is a wish for good health, is now becoming far more widely used among the population in general (and in the tourism industry in particular). "Kia Ora" may be answered with the same.

New Zealanders frequently entertain in the home, and *barbies* (barbecues) are especially popular on summer weekends. There are few formal codes of etiquette, and social relations are generally casual. New Zealanders have a reputation for genuine hospitality toward visitors, and often invite people into their homes soon after making their acquaintance.

➢ *Recreation*

New Zealanders are keen sport participants and fans. Many will get up in the middle of the night to watch a broadcast of their team playing abroad. Rugby Union football is traditionally the favorite national sport. The All Blacks are New Zealand's national rugby union team. Rugby League football, soccer, hockey, cricket, softball, netball (a form of basketball), water sports and track and field are also popular. Women participate actively in all these sports except professional rugby. New Zealanders take part in a variety of international sporting events, such as rugby, soccer, cricket, tennis and sailing competitions. Popular leisure activities include beach swimming, fishing, skiing and hiking. Other recreational activities include home improvements, gardening, watching television and socializing at home or in a pub. New Zealanders may also spend weekends in their holiday homes or seaside cabins—known as bachs in the North Island and cribs in the South Island.

Holidays and Special Days

The official public holidays of New Zealand include New Year (the first two working days in January are public holidays), Waitangi Day (6 February), Easter (Good Friday through Easter Monday), Anzac Day (25 April), Queen Elizabeth II's Birthday (observed the first Monday in June), Labor Day (the fourth Monday in October), Christmas Day (25 December) and Boxing Day (26 December).

➢ *Waitangi Day*

Waitangi Day marks the occasion in 1840 when the United Kingdom signed the *Treaty of Waitangi* with the indigenous Maori. Under this treaty, New Zealand became a British colony. The Maori ceded (放弃) sovereignty to the British in return for legal protection as British subjects. The

Maori were guaranteed possession of their land, but with the limitation that they could sell only to the monarchy.

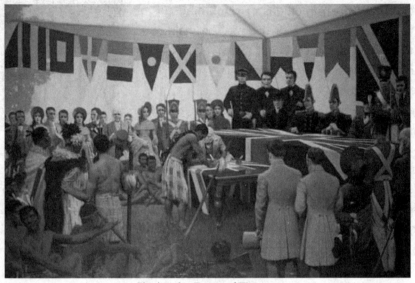

Signing the *Treaty of Waitangi*

Maori leader Tāmati Wāka Nene is shown signing the treaty in front of British officials and witnesses. Other Maori signatories are assembled on the left.

➢ *Anzac Day (奥新军团日)*

Anzac is an acronym (首字母缩略词) for Australia and New Zealand Army Corps. Along with Australia, New Zealand remembers its war dead every year on Anzac Day (25 April). It marks the anniversary of the 1915 landing on Gallipoli (加里波利), Turkey, of the Australian and New Zealand Army Corps (ANZAC). The landing was part of the ill-advised campaign, during the First World War, to capture the Dardanelles (达达尼尔海峡) and force Turkey, which was an ally of Germany, into submission. Thousands of Australian and New Zealand troops were killed before the campaign was abandoned.

A Australian
N & New
Z Zealand
A Army
C Corps

Anzac Day is a day to remember the courage of the soldiers in this battle and the courage and sacrifice of all men and women who have served their country in times of war. A parade is held in many cities and towns on Anzac Day.

➢ *Boxing Day*

Boxing Day derives from an old British tradition of giving small boxed gifts to service workers and trades-people on the day after Christmas. It is now a day for visiting and relaxing. In addition to these holidays, each province has an Anniversary Day commemorating its founding.

Education

Education in New Zealand is nominally free for all primary, intermediate and secondary schooling. However, most schools also ask for a "voluntary donation" from parents, informally known as "school fees" or a "parental contribution".

➤ Primary and Secondary Education

Education in New Zealand is compulsory for all children aged 5 through 16. Disabled students with special educational needs can stay until the end of the year when they are 21. Students spend eight years in primary school, often transferring to specialized intermediate schools for the final two years. Secondary schooling generally takes five years, and it remains tuition-free for students under the age of 20. Most students attend public secular schools; only a minority attends private or church-affiliated schools.

➤ Higher Education

The system of higher education in New Zealand includes eight universities. The largest two are the University of Auckland (founded in 1882), at Auckland, and Massey University (1926), with campuses at Auckland, Palmerston North and Wellington. Other institutions of higher education are the University of Waikato (1964), at Hamilton; the Victoria University of Wellington (1899), the University of Canterbury (1873), at Christchurch; the University of Otago (1869), at Dunedin; Lincoln University (1990, formerly Lincoln Agricultural College), near Christchurch and the Auckland University of Technology (2000, formerly the Auckland Institute of Technology). Several colleges provide teacher training, and polytechnic institutions offer degree programs, diplomas and certificates in various technical and professional trades.

Literature

The modern literary canon of New Zealand was founded by Katherine Mansfield, one of the 20th-century's greatest short-story writers. Mansfield launched her writing career in England, but the influence of her New Zealand upbringing pervades her work.

Female writers have long predominated in New Zealand fiction writing, especially the novel. Janet Frame, Keri Hulme, Margaret Mahy, Margaret Sutherland, Fiona Kidman and Sylvia Ashton-Warner are just a few of New Zealand's many acclaimed female writers.

Important male writers include Maurice Shadbolt, Maurice Gee, Witi Ihimaera, Vincent O'Sullivan and Owen Marshall. Along with Hulme and Ihimaera, contemporary Maori writers include Patricia Grace and Alan Duff. Maori-authored works such as Grace's *Mutuwhenua* (1978) address difficult questions of biculturalism and the survival of the Maori community and culture.

James K. Baxter, author of *Beyond the Palisade* (1944) and other poetry collections, is widely regarded as New Zealand's preeminent poet. Maori poet Hone Tuwhare published the first major Maori poems in English, drawing on his Maori oral tradition and urban working-class life. His direct, lyrical verse and command of the vernacular are evident in his collections *No Ordinary Sun* (1964) and *Sapwood and Milk* (1973).

The oral literary tradition is a vital part of Maori society. Traditional Maori literature consists of history, tales, poems and legends, all of which have been preserved through the generations by oral recitation. The Polynesian ancestors of the Maori established tribal kin groups in defined territories, following Polynesian custom. Each group produced a complex oral tradition concerning all aspects of its life. Some traditions were exclusive to the Maori tribe that composed them; others came to be known and used universally. The strikingly poetic language of the compositions aided their memorization and recitation. The main types of composition are *whakapapa* (genealogy), *karakia* (incantations), *korero* (narratives), *whakatauki* (sayings) and *waiata* (sung poetry).

英语国家概况（第二版）

尊敬的老师：

您好！

为了方便您更好地使用本教材，获得最佳教学效果，我们特向使用该书作为教材的教师赠送本教材配套参考资料。如有需要，请完整填写"教师联系表"并加盖所在单位系（院）公章，免费向出版社索取。

北京大学出版社

教 师 联 系 表

教材名称	英语国家概况（第二版）		
姓名：	性别：	职务：	职称：
E-mail：	联系电话：	邮政编码：	
供职学校：	所在院系：		（章）
学校地址：			
教学科目与年级：	班级人数：		
通信地址：			

填写完毕后，请将此表邮寄给我们，我们将为您免费寄送本教材配套资料，谢谢！

北京市海淀区成府路 205 号
北京大学出版社外语编辑部　李　颖
邮政编码：100871
电子邮箱：evalee1770@sina.com

邮 购 部 电 话：010-62534449
市场营销部电话：010-62750672
外语编辑部电话：010-62754382